COMMUNITY-BASED DISASTER RISK REDUCTION

The Kanji character [*Kizuna*] means bonding, the essence of CBDRR

COMMUNITY, ENVIRONMENT AND DISASTER RISK
MANAGEMENT   VOLUME 10

COMMUNITY-BASED DISASTER RISK REDUCTION

EDITED BY

RAJIB SHAW

Graduate School of Global Environmental Studies,
Kyoto University, Kyoto, Japan

United Kingdom – North America – Japan
India – Malaysia – China

Emerald Group Publishing Limited
Howard House, Wagon Lane, Bingley BD16 1WA, UK

First edition 2012

Copyright © 2012 Emerald Group Publishing Limited

Reprints and permission service
Contact: booksandseries@emeraldinsight.com

British Library Cataloguing in Publication Data
A catalogue record for this book is available from the British Library

ISBN: 978-0-85724-867-1
ISSN: 2040-7262 (Series)

ISOQAR certified
Management Systems,
awarded to Emerald for
adherence to Quality
and Environmental
standards ISO 9001:2008
and 14001:2004,
respectively

Certificate Number 1985
ISO 9001
ISO 14001

INVESTOR IN PEOPLE

CONTENTS

PART II: ASIAN EXPERIENCES

PART III: CENTRAL AMERICAN EXPERIENCES

PART IV: AFRICAN EXPERIENCES

PART V: THE WAY AHEAD

LIST OF CONTRIBUTORS

Gaby Breton	Center for International Studies and Cooperation (CECI), Montreal, Canada
Heather Campbell	Catholic Relief Services (CRS), Timor-Leste
Christo Coetzee	African Centre for Disaster Studies, Northwest University, Potchefstroom, South Africa
Glenn Fernandez	International Environment and Disaster Management Laboratory, Graduate School of Global Environmental Studies, Kyoto University, Kyoto, Japan
Alberto dos Reis Freitas	Catholic Relief Services (CRS), Timor-Leste
U Ko Ko Gyi	Myanmar Engineering Society, Yangon, Myanmar
Umma Habiba	International Environment and Disaster Management Laboratory, Graduate School of Global Environmental Studies, Kyoto University, Kyoto, Japan
Tsuneki Hori	International Environment and Disaster Management Laboratory, Graduate School of Global Environmental Studies, Kyoto University, Kyoto, Japan
Mikio Ishiwatari	Japan International Cooperation Agency, Tokyo, Japan
Takako Izumi	MERCY Malaysia, Kuala Lumpur, Malaysia

Jonas Joerin   International Environment and Disaster
                             Management Laboratory, Graduate School
                             of Global Environmental Studies, Kyoto
                             University, Kyoto, Japan

Aki Kogachi   International Environment and Disaster
                             Management Laboratory, Graduate School
                             of Global Environmental Studies, Kyoto
                             University, Kyoto, Japan

Ramasamy   Department of Applied Geology,
Krishnamurthy   University of Madras, Chennai, India

Fuad Mallick   Postgraduate Programs in Disaster
                             Management, BRAC University, Dhaka,
                             Bangladesh

U Than Myint   Myanmar Engineering Society, Yangon,
                             Myanmar

Yuki Matsuoka   United Nations International Strategy for
                             Disaster Reduction, Hyogo, Japan

Jessica Mercer   OXFAM Australia, Timor Leste

Farah Mulyasari   International Environment and Disaster
                             Management Laboratory, Graduate School
                             of Global Environmental Studies, Kyoto
                             University, Kyoto, Japan

Yuko Nakagawa   SEEDS Asia, Kobe, Japan

Huy Nguyen   International Environment and Disaster
                             Management Laboratory, Graduate School
                             of Global Environmental Studies, Kyoto
                             University, Kyoto, Japan

Dewald van Niekerk   African Centre for Disaster Studies,
                             Northwest University, Potchefstroom,
                             South Africa

Sunil Parashar   International Environment and Disaster
                             Management Laboratory, Graduate School
                             of Global Environmental Studies, Kyoto
                             University, Kyoto, Japan

Joy Jacqueline Pereira   Southeast Asia Disaster Prevention
                           Research Institute (SEADPRI-UKM),
                           Institute for Environment and
                           Development (LESTARI), Universiti
                           Kebangsaan Malaysia (UKM), Malaysia

Rajib Shaw   International Environment and Disaster
                           Management Laboratory, Graduate School
                           of Global Environmental Studies, Kyoto
                           University, Kyoto, Japan

Mitsuko Shikada   SEEDS Asia, Kobe, Japan

Yukiko Takeuchi   International Environment and Disaster
                           Management Laboratory, Graduate School
                           of Global Environmental Studies, Kyoto
                           University, Kyoto, Japan

Tong Thi My Thi   International Environment and Disaster
                           Management Laboratory, Graduate School
                           of Global Environmental Studies, Kyoto
                           University, Kyoto, Japan

Phong Tran   Faculty of Economics and Development
                           Studies, College of Economics, Hue
                           University, Hue, Vietnam

Noralene Uy   International Environment and Disaster
                           Management Laboratory, Graduate School
                           of Global Environmental Studies, Kyoto
                           University, Kyoto, Japan

ABOUT THE EDITOR

Rajib Shaw
Graduate School of Global Environmental Studies, Kyoto University,
Kyoto, Japan

Rajib Shaw is Associate Professor in the Graduate School of Global Environmental Studies of Kyoto University, Japan. He works closely with the local communities, NGOs, governments, and international organization, including the United Nations, especially in the Asian countries. He is currently the chair of the United Nations Asia Regional Task Force for Urban Risk Reduction. His research interests are: community-based disaster risk management, climate change adaptation, urban risk management, and disaster and environmental education.

BRIEF INTRODUCTION OF THE SERIES

COMMUNITY, ENVIRONMENT AND DISASTER
RISK MANAGEMENT

This series connects academic research to field practice, strengthening the links between the environment, disaster, and community. The series is developed on field evidences and community practices, and thus provides specific guides to professionals, which are grounded in rigorous academic analysis. The has a specific focus on community-based disaster risk management, urban environmental management, human security, water community, risk communication, climate change adaptation, climate disaster resilience, and community-based practices.

BRIEF INTRODUCTION OF
THE VOLUME

Community-Based Disaster Risk Reduction
Communities are at the core of disaster risk reduction, and community-based approaches are getting increasing focus in national disaster risk reduction plans. In the case of past disasters, communities were always the first responders, and took leading roles in the postdisaster recovery. The roles of communities in predisaster preparedness are also very important. Community-based disaster risk reduction (CBDRR) has been a popular term for the past several years, and there are numerous tools, guidelines, and handbooks published by different organizations. However, there are limited numbers of books on this subject, which would be useful for education and research. This book is the first comprehensive book on CBDRR, citing field examples and research results.

PREFACE

Communities are at the core of the risk reduction initiatives, since it is related to their lives and properties. There are different ways of putting the term, community-based, community-centered, community-owned, etc. Needless to say, risk reduction initiatives started at the community level. Even before the existence of the states, the communities were the managers and solution providers. They used to take care of themselves individually or collectively. At that time, it was not called "community-based," since it was the only option available. After the establishment of the state, the government took control of disaster risk reduction and failed in several cases. Thus, over the past 30–40 years, the concept of community-based or community-centered has emerged once again, and is now gaining momentum.

Community-based disaster risk reduction (CBDRR), as termed in the book, is a joint endeavor of different stakeholders at different levels. While nongovernmental organizations (NGOs) have taken a leading role in lobbying for CBDRR, the change in the trend is more toward government-based CBDRR. This is a new trend, and needs to be recognized in the current governance context. The other issue is the increasing need for the academic orientation of CBDRR. CBDRR is recognized as a process, and research and education in disaster risk reduction need to recognize this process. This is also a new trend, and is considered very important in contributing to future professional development of the subject.

Each country, each community, has its own character, and this needs to be recognized when discussing CBDRR. This book covers examples from Asia, Africa, and Central America, and each case has its own way of implementing CBDRR. This book focuses mainly on two issues: the roles of different stakeholders, and the specific characters of the regions. This book is a modest attempt on this topic. Needless to say, it does not cover each and every aspect of CBDRR. There is still lots to do, and lots to study. I hope that this book will be a good trigger for future research in the subject. I will be delighted if readers consider the book useful.

Rajib Shaw
Editor

PART I
OVERVIEW

CHAPTER 1

OVERVIEW OF COMMUNITY-BASED DISASTER RISK REDUCTION

Rajib Shaw

INTRODUCTION

Definition of community varies based on its perspective. Many people describe community in different ways. McMillan & Chavis (1986) described community as "a feeling that members have of belonging, a feeling that members matter to one another and to the group, and a shared faith that members' needs will be met through their commitment to be together." This definition is preferred in the current context because of its general nature. Community includes not only the people living in a certain location, but also the local government, local business sectors, local academic bodies, and nongovernment organizations (NGOs) (Shaw, 2006a).

As more research on development has been conducted in various fields in recent years, the approach to disaster risk reduction is becoming more and more community-based (Blaikie, Cannon, Davis, & Wisner, 1994; Quarantelli, 1989; Mileti, 2001), and much more effort has been put into incorporating disaster management aspects into the holistic development of communities (Shaw & Okazaki, 2003; Twigg & Bhatt, 1998). Almost two decades ago, Maskrey (1989) had rightly pointed out that disaster management should not be treated as one single issue, but should be

Community-Based Disaster Risk Reduction
Community, Environment and Disaster Risk Management, Volume 10, 3–17
Copyright © 2012 by Emerald Group Publishing Limited
All rights of reproduction in any form reserved
ISSN: 2040-7262/doi:10.1108/S2040-7262(2012)0000010007

incorporated into the socioeconomic activities of local people. The rationale for community involvement or community-based activities is now well rehearsed (Twigg, 1999). Because community-based activities (and community-based organizations) are deeply rooted in the society and culture of an area, they enable people to express their real needs and priorities, allowing problems to be defined correctly and responsive measures to be designed and implemented. Twigg (1999) also argues that existence of community-based organizations allows people to respond to emergencies rapidly, efficiently, and fairly, and therefore available community resources (even if scarce) will be used economically. Maskrey (1989) pointed out that "top-down" programs in which communities are not involved tend not to reach those worst affected by disaster, and may even make them more vulnerable.

Most disaster management systems are designed using command and control management structures, one that is top-down and with logistics-centered responses. It can be highly bureaucratic and frequently operates under explicit or implicit political constraints that impinge on the effective delivery of emergency services. Due to this, engagements of the community under this scheme were characterized by the following: (a) lack of participation that results to failures in meeting the appropriate and vital humanitarian needs, (b) unnecessary increase in requirement for external resources, and (c) general dissatisfaction over performance despite the use of exceptional management measures. Recognizing these limitations, the community-based disaster management (CBDM) approach promotes a bottom-up approach, working in harmony with the top-down approach, to address challenges and difficulties. To be effective, local communities must be supported to analyze their hazardous conditions, their vulnerabilities and capacities as they see them.

It is common knowledge that people at the community level have more to lose because they are the ones directly hit by disasters, whether it is a major or a minor one. They are the first ones to become vulnerable to the effects of such hazardous events. The community therefore has a lot to lose if people do not address their own vulnerability. On the other hand, they have the most to gain if they can reduce the impact of disasters on their community. The concept of putting the communities at the forefront gave rise to the idea of CBDM. At the heart of the CBDM is the principle of participation. Through the CBDM, the people's capacity to respond to emergencies is increased by providing them more access and control over resources and basic social services. Using a community-based approach to manage disasters certainly has its advantages.

Community-based disaster-related activities are termed differently over time. Over more than 100 years ago, before the existence of most of the states, people or communities were taking care of themselves through collective actions during the disasters. After the formation of state, government-based disaster risk reduction program started, which failed to serve the needs of the people and communities. For the past 20–30 years, we have been again talking on the need of community-based disaster risk reduction (CBDRR). Thus, community-based approach is not new. Rather, we are going back to the old and traditional approaches of risk reduction. CBDM had been a popular term in later 1980s and 1990s, which gradually evolved to community-based disaster risk management (CBDRM), and then to CBDRR. CBDRM and CBDRR are often used with similar meaning, with enhanced focus on "risk"; however, there still exists a thin line of distinction. While CBDRR focuses more on predisaster activities for risk reduction by the communities, CBDRM focuses a broader perspective of risk-reduction-related activities by communities, both during, before, and after the disaster.

Emphasis or need of CBDRR is found to be similar in both developing and developed countries, as argued by Shaw and Goda (2004). In Japan, in many rural mountain communities, shifting the damage risk of one community makes other communities vulnerable. In a river basin system, upstream community should be strongly linked to the downstream community, and communication regarding community-level interventions should be well coordinated. In a recent intervention, Shaw and Takeuchi (2011) pointed out that local institutions play important roles in mobilizing and organizing communities in the small and medium cities in Japan.

PARTICIPATION OF COMMUNITIES

CBDRR strengthens social cohesion and cooperation within the community and society. It builds confidence among individuals, households, and communities for any undertaking including disaster preparedness and mitigation. Through CBDRR it is hoped that communities would be strengthened to enable them undertake any programs of development including disaster preparedness and mitigation.

A "culture of coping with crisis" and "culture of disaster risk reduction" exist in all communities, and thus any risk assessment process should involve participation of people and incorporate their perception of vulnerability and capacity. Community and supporting agencies share common motivation and ownership for the initiation and sustainability of community-based disaster management. Genuine people's participation within capacity-building objectives, with specific focus on important vulnerable groups like women, elderly, and children, is found to be important in both cases of Bangladesh and Vietnam. Involvement of the Mother's Club in Bangladesh, and Veteran Association, Women Association in Vietnam, and training and awareness raising of school children can be part of these activities (Shaw, 2006a). For training and capacity building, wider stakeholder involvement and participation, effective networking, and knowledge capitalization were essential to make the training effective into actions. Legislation and incorporation of community-based disaster management in development planning and budgeting is extremely crucial and serves the major pillar of policy integration.

With the analysis from CBDRR in two countries (Bangladesh and Vietnam), Shaw (2006a) concluded that following are a few general statements that are applicable to different contexts of community activities: (1) local institutions (both formal and informal) play a critical role in sustaining the community initiatives, (2) integration of community initiatives in the government policies and practices is important to upscale the efforts, (3) local change agents play crucial roles in grassroot implementation, and (4) synergy of grassroot efforts with the development policy is regarded as the measure of the success of project implementation.

INDIGENOUS AND LOCAL KNOWLEDGE

Any local population would have local knowledge regarding vulnerabilities and capacities. They are repositories of traditional coping mechanisms suited for their specific environment that they have developed from previous experiences in dealing with disasters. Due to exposure and proximity to hazardous conditions, a local population responds first even before assistance from aid-givers arrives at times of crisis. By using what is available locally, a timely response is possible. Timeliness in emergency response is critical because this determines how many lives would be saved or how many properties can be prevented from being damaged (Shaw, Sharma, & Takeuchi, 2009).

Indigenous knowledge research aims to facilitate the targeting of development resources more effectively on the poor. The compatibility of local ideas with scientific ones is a central issue. It is absolutely necessary to facilitate communication between scientists and local people, on the assumption, fundamental to development interventions, that science may have something to offer them in tackling their problems. Furthermore, it is possible that if scientific and indigenous knowledge are comparable, and if scientists are able to access local knowledge, this might enhance new development of research practices. Sillitoe, Barr, and Alam (2004) have given a great example of mapping indigenous and scientific soil knowledge for effective floodplain management in Bangladesh. Combining scientific names as well as local names of the soil types, and their productivity, the study showed the unique way of resource utilization by using maps. However, studies showed a number of interesting challenges of incorporating indigenous knowledge into the development processes (Sillitoe & Bicker, 2004).

While exploring indigenous and traditional knowledge, we came across different terminologies: indigenous knowledge (IK), traditional knowledge (TK), local knowledge, community-based knowledge, indigenous knowledge systems and practices (IKSP), indigenous technical knowledge (ITK), and traditional and local knowledge system. Each of these terms has its specific meaning and application. Thus, there is a variation of traditional, indigenous, local, and community-based on one side, and knowledge, wisdom, and technology on the other. Shaw et al. (2009) has described traditional knowledge as a cumulative body of knowledge, know-how, practices, and representations maintained and developed by peoples with extended histories of interaction with the natural environment, while indigenous is attached to place and indigenous people. ITK is more framed on a technological perspective, like the use of fertilizers, use of certain plants like *Neem* to protect from insects, use of poultry excreta in vegetable gardens as nitrates, etc. IK is more framed on a cultural perspective, like the folk song for awareness raising (Bangladesh) and water-puppet show to tell a flood story (Vietnam).

Shaw et al. (2009) discussed the IK and its implications in CBDRR. The IK itself can be considered as the nutrition guide, which provides general information on traditional wisdom, generated over the years; however, it does not talk about the application. In contrast, TIK can be considered as the cook-book for traditional knowledge and wisdom. A very interesting evolution of TIK can be observed from the 1950 to the 1980s (Shaw, 2007). While we have seen the strong development of modern technology in recent years, the mid-1980s saw the start of an emphasis to incorporate traditional knowledge as an integral part of the development framework. IK began to be increasingly used in designing development projects, with specific focus on community interventions.

One of the major issues of IK is that, in many cases, it evolved as part of the survival process of the people and communities (Shaw & Takeuchi, 2007). Thus, IK is very much characterized by a multidisciplinary nature and is based on food security, human and animal health, education, natural resource management, and various other community-based activities. The other issue of IK is its dynamic evolution. IK is the result of a continuous process of experimentation, innovation, and adaptation. It has the capacity to blend with knowledge based on science and technology and should therefore be considered complementary to scientific and technological efforts to solve problems in social and economic development. The third point of IK is the challenge of documentation. In most cases IK is orally transmitted and thus, the challenges of its implementation are not properly documented. The fourth important challenge is the classification of IK. IK can be classified based on geographical, thematic, and organizational contexts, and in many cases there are overlaps. It is important to recognize that due to climatic changes and other social changes, communities have practiced or adopted new forms of indigenous knowledge based on the principles in the changing environment. TIK is intended to recognize the change, and use the traditional knowledge and wisdom in the evolving context of CBDRR.

HUMAN SECURITY AND COMMUNITY PARTICIPATION

The relationship between human security and the environment is most pronounced in areas of human dependence on access to natural resources (Shaw, 2006b). Environmental resources are critical part of the livelihoods of many people. When these resources are threatened because of environmental changes, people's human security is also threatened, and people move from the rural areas to the marginal lands, which leads to a decline in the household income. This relationship is captured in the promotion of sustainable development. Two other fields – environmental security and sustainable development – emerged and grew roughly during the same period as human security and human development. Although the environmental security focuses more on nature, increasing complexities in the subject have urged for a holistic view and synergy between natural and built environment.

Disaster management has a direct connotation to human security. Many of the natural disasters like flood and drought are directly related to the environmental degradation and climate change. These events affect the poor the most by affecting their lives, properties, and livelihoods. Therefore, by creating disaster-resilient communities, it is possible to enhance human security. The governments and other stakeholders are increasingly becoming aware of the relationship between ecological stability and human security. Civil society has mobilized strongly to promote sustainable development and increase awareness of its importance. The emphasis of the governments, however, is more on improved environmental management. There has been little concrete action at local level to ensure the participation of affected communities. Although some countries have taken pro-community measures to enhance environmental sustainability, thereby reducing the impacts of disasters, there is still a long way to go in the direction of synergy of community-based natural resource management and disaster risk management.

The concept of vulnerability is the key and a common concept for human security and environment and disaster management. Human security focuses on analyzing who is vulnerable, how does action by local people in particular place and condition affect vulnerability, and what actions could be taken to reduce or mitigate vulnerability. Linking human security paradigm (Khagram, Clarke, & Radd, 2003) with sustainable science framework and vulnerability analysis framework entails placing particular emphasis on human conditions. It highlights the linkage between vulnerability and change in human and environmental conditions and interactions of hazards and exposures at different levels of place, region, and world. This is closely linked to the sustainable livelihood framework (Moser & Norton, 2001), where reliance and vulnerability are seen as counterparts of one another, and people's resilience depends largely on assets and entitlements that individuals, households, and communities can mobilize and thus manage to face hardships. Therefore, higher the resilience, higher the human security and livelihood security, and lesser would be the vulnerability.

Simply speaking, enhancing human security for environment and disaster management is like enhancing people's choices, and increasing their resilience to cope with the adverse impacts of the events. A good correlation is found in Vaux and Lund (2003), where the impacts of 2000 drought and 2001 earthquake of Gujarat, India, are described with specific focus on the livelihood security of rural women. To cope with the natural disaster impacts, the key focus area was to improve livelihood options. These livelihood options were enhanced through institutional development and asset creation, and were aimed at enhancing human security. Small-scale community-based institutions have helped in sustaining the efforts in longer terms (Shaw, 2006b).

SUSTAINABILITY AND UPSCALING ISSUES

Community involvement often faces the problem of sustainability over a longer period of time (Shaw & Okazaki, 2003). Government, nongovernment, and international organizations implement various programs before and after the disasters. Many of them are very successful during the project period; however, some of them gradually diminish as the years pass. There are many reasons for gradual decrease of people's involvement in a project. The most common elements are partnership, participation, empowerment, and ownership of the local communities. Unless the disaster management efforts are sustainable at individual and community level, it is difficult to reduce the losses and tragedy. While people should own the problems, consequences, and challenges of any mitigation and/or preparedness initiative, it is necessary to see people's involvement in a broader perspective, which is related to policy and strategy.

It has been a common notion that grassroot initiatives are the responsibilities of the NGOs. They have been the leading actors in this field for several years, and have made significant contributions. However, many of the NGO's activities face the problem of sustainability over a longer period of time, especially once the NGO withdrew from the field. Many of the NGO programs are poorly designed and so they are unable to either attract continuing support or transfer project ownership to communities. Continuation of community activities over a longer period of time needs a policy environment at local level, as well as local institutions to continue the activities. Thus, even though the initiatives are started with the NGO interventions, it is important to link them to the local government activities, and incorporate them into policies to ensure its sustainability and replication of innovative efforts to other parts of the disaster-prone areas. The major challenges of the CBDRR are: (1) sustainability of the efforts at the community level and (2) incorporation of the CBDRR issues at the policy level. To be effective and to create sustainable impact, the application of the CBDRR must go beyond the initiative of communities, NGOs, and a handful of local governments. As part of an advocacy for more responsive and effective governance, national and state governments should look at integrating CBDRR in their policy and implementing procedures (Shaw & Okazaki, 2003).

Shaw and Okazaki (2003) observed that for a CBDRR to be successful, implementers should be adept in identifying and mobilizing as many stakeholders as necessary. With case studies from six countries (Bangladesh, Cambodia, India, Indonesia, Nepal, and Philippines), it is observed that in some cases, relationships among stakeholders are formal and legislated (e.g., in Philippines and India), but some cases also show that informal relationships do not hinder partnership arrangements at the community level. Most of the projects promote tangible accumulation of physical and economic assets to reduce vulnerability. These are in the form of:

— Village contingency fund, and availability of credit for income-generating activities;

- Micro-solutions, small- and medium-scale infrastructure project that reduces impact of hazards;
- Equipment and materials such as for latrines, water supply, warning – communication, and rescue and evacuation facilities.

Some studies focus on providing intangible "assets" such as technology in disaster resistant construction, and access to information centers (Shaw & Okazaki, 2003). Most have attempted to integrate these projects into regular development planning and budgeting to ensure sustainability. This is done through legislation and incorporating vulnerability assessment and reduction into regular development project. Based on the experiences of the case studies from the above-mentioned six countries, following is a list of the factors that enhance the sustainability of CBDRR:

1. Promote and strengthen a "culture of coping with crisis";
2. Enhance people's perception on vulnerability;
3. Recognize motivation of community initiative;
4. Increase community participation and empowerment through institutionalization;
5. Focus on need-based training approaches;
6. Involve diverse stakeholders based on the needs and objectives in both formal and/or informal ways;
7. Promote tangible and intangible accumulation of physical, technological, and economic assets as the project outputs;
8. Promote the integration of community initiatives into regular development planning and budgeting to ensure sustainability.

The other issue of CBDRR is the upscaling of the initiative. There have been too many good practices; however, most of the good practices have remained confined to their local communities only. Their potential in influencing attempts to reduce vulnerability in other parts of the world is enormous. While an innovative approach is found to be effective in one village, one district, the challenge is how to disseminate the best practices widely.

STAKEHOLDER PARTICIPATION

It is also very important to note that there appears to be an emerging trend on the "users" of the CBDRR approach (Shaw, 2009). The starting point for sustainability in CBDRR lies on our understanding of the importance of the indigenous coping mechanisms of communities. The role of stakeholders is to strengthen coping capabilities rather than falling into a trap of replacing them by imposing external culture. If we do this, community ownership is not promoted which leaves a question mark on attaining sustainability. On the other hand, we also must realize that individual households and communities are generally unaware of the hazards they face, underestimate those they knew of, and overestimate their ability to cope with crisis. They also tend not to put much trust in disaster reduction strategies, and rely heavily upon emergency assistance when the need arises. This is why NGOs are getting increasingly involved in disaster reduction focused primarily on public awareness and advocacy programs. They particularly seek to encourage the desired shift in emphasis from emergency assistance and disaster response to the more engaged roles of local community participation in planning, vulnerability assessment, and risk management practices. On the other hand, recognizing that disasters happen at the local level, local governments are the primary actors in promoting the adoption of local disaster action plans. Oftentimes, these are developed as a response from a recent catastrophic event as the general public and community demand for better preparedness and emergency response at the local level.

Shaw (2009) has concluded that the key point in the role of local actors is partnership and collaboration. Each group has its own resources, knowledge base, and information. Sharing of information is extremely important. A proper information management system is required to utilize the right information at the right time at the right place. Collaboration and partnership plays the key role here. As understood from the earlier discussion, no single organization or agency can perform all the roles in the disaster reduction system. Policy makers, local disaster managers, community organizers, trainers, and academic institutions have important roles in their respective premises. Local media can play a useful role in information dissemination. In many places, it is seen that community radio is an effective tool in engaging local communities in decision-making.

ABOUT THE BOOK

This book is an attempt to highlight the different issues of CBDRR. The book has 20 chapters, which are divided into five parts. Part 1 is the overview of CBDRR, and consists of five chapters. Part 2 consists of Asian examples of CBDRR, and has eight chapters. Part 3 consists of Central

American experiences, and has three chapters. Part 4 consists of African examples, and has three chapters. Finally, Part 5 consists of one chapter, and focuses on future perspectives of CBDRR.

Chapter 1 summarizes some of the issues related to CBDRR. The chapter focuses on community participation, human security, indigenous and local knowledge, stakeholder participation, upscaling, and sustainability issues. It is important to recognize the importance of the concept of human security in CBDRR.

Chapter 2 examines the histories of community-based organizations for DRR in Japan of Suibo, flood fighting in Japanese; Syubo, fire fighting; Jisyubo, self-help DRR; and NGOs. These organizations are playing crucial roles in rescue and relief activities in the Great East Japan earthquakes in 2011. Also, it reviews an approach of Japan International Cooperation Agency (JICA), which defines communities as main actors in disaster risk reduction, and government agencies and other organizations concerned as supporting actors to the communities.

Chapter 3 focuses on (1) review of the case studies of CBDRR by Asian NGOs; (2) observe the role of NGOs in CBDRR projects in Malaysia, Cambodia, and India; (3) address the issues and challenges that Asian NGOs are facing in the process of CBDRR implementation; and (4) discuss the way-forward and innovative way for the future CBDRR. Each case study has a different focus in the program, and it showcases the variety of CBDRR programs and different role of NGOs in CBDRR.

In Chapter 4, roles of the universities in CBDRR projects are described, followed by evolution of university network and its education research agenda in the Asia Pacific region. University is usually not considered as a prominent player in the CBDRR; however, the chapter emphasizes the linkages between the academic research and community-based field practices.

Chapter 5 emphasizes that a company may have operations in any parts of the world, they have roots to the communities that they belong to, that is through their employees and their families, and they are the ones who provide stable performance and thus bring profit to the company. This basic hypothesis is the core of this chapter. The chapter is intended to show some key responsibilities in the corporate sectors, starting from the top-level decision makers, mid-level managers, and employees.

Chapter 6 shows that in Bangladesh CBDRR is increasingly being recognized by NGOs, governmental agencies, and international organizations, and is emerging as a key response to adapt with these natural disasters. This chapter explores major disasters in Bangladesh and their impact. Then the focus shifts to how community evolves innovative approaches to deal with these disaster risks and how CBDRR approach can be institutionalized and finally concluding remarks.

Chapter 7 focuses on community-based approaches in urban India. Disasters are common in Indian cities; communities have created and utilized their own coping mechanism to deal with such situation and strengthen their resilience by adopting methods to adjust to the risk situation. For example, during Mumbai Floods 2005, slum communities showed their resilience by adapting to the risk situation. With the support of social organization, they were able to adopt ways to cope well with the risk situation. The chapter shows some of the innovative examples of community-based urban risk reduction.

Chapter 8 describes the example of the participation of different civil society organizations (CSOs) for CBDRR in Indonesia as the lessons learned; how to capitalize the CSOs for effective CBDRR; as well as exploring the issues on how to mobilize those CSOs for CBDRR in tailoring the needs and enhancement for the future.

Chapter 9 analyzes the concept and level of partnership between a community and a local government (Kobe city) through theoretical aspects described in a partnership framework. The developed partnership framework is applied to evaluate a potential partnership between communities, called disaster prevention welfare communities "BOKOMIS"), and the local government of Kobe City.

Chapter 10 describes a unique postdisaster reconstruction effort in Myanmar, after the Nargis cyclone of 2008. Community-based and school-based education is done through developing mobile knowledge resource center (using truck and ship), and reaching the most unreachable parts of the country. The process of involvement of the local government, school students, teachers, and parents is considered to be a sustainable approach in CBDRR in the country.

Chapter 11 describes the Philippines experiences. Even before the concept became a generally accepted approach by the international community at the end of the 1990s, Philippine grassroots organizations had already pioneered the development and implementation of CBDRM activities. With the passage of a new disaster management law in 2010, the government has officially adopted CBDRM as a model to engage communities in DRR undertaking, with the hope that heightened involvement would translate to communities being more responsive and self-managing when emergencies do arise. This chapter outlines the recent trend and achievements in CBDRM activities.

Chapter 12 describes the development of CBDRR in Vietnam, and discusses the status of existing CBDRR activities and case studies in Thanh Hoa, Thua Thien Hue, and Quang Nam Province. From that, the authors try to point out the shortcomings of CBDRR projects and propose the potential measures that can be applied to upscale the implementation of CBDRR in Vietnam.

Chapter 13 reports on CBDRR approaches undertaken by Catholic Relief Services (CRS) in partnership with local communities, NGOs, and government authorities in Timor-Leste. This is in order to identify how CBDRR processes are contributing to the overall goals of the NDRMP at the local level.

Chapter 14 provides the overview of the progress of CBDRM in Central America. The chapter includes literature review, project data (or project profile) collection and its statistical analysis, and conducted interviews. The chapter provides the briefs of the profile of the CBDRM in the Central American region, followed by identification of the results, outcomes, and lessons. It discusses the effective and sustainable CBDRM initiative, and finally concludes with implications for further researches.

Chapter 15 synthesizes the findings from *"The Program of Risk Reduction in the Reconstruction Process of the Communities' Habitat Project"* sponsored by the United Nations Development Programme (UNDP), and executed by the Center for International Studies and Cooperation (CECI) in Guatemala. The chapter describes participatory, responsive community-based approach to the needs of victims in disasters, which has resulted in best practices in the intervention following important catastrophes.

Chapter 16 describes the experiences of the project titled "Strengthening Local Structures and Early Warning Systems (Reforzamientos de Estructuras Locales y Sistemas de Alerta Temprana: RELSAT)," which was implemented in Cartago, Costa Rica during 1999–2001. The chapter also reviews the status of the community early warning system (CEWS) operation 10 years after RELSAT implementation and identifies factors affecting the maintenance of CEWS. The chapter briefly concludes with implications for project designers or planners at the national and local government, NGOs, and donor agencies toward sustainable community-based disaster risk preparedness.

Chapter 17 provides the reader with insight into the current application of CBDRR projects in a number of African countries. Various cultures and ethnic affiliations on the continent have diverse views on "disasters" and the reasons for their occurrence. It therefore stands to reason that the application of CBDRR would also vary significantly.

Chapter 18 describes community-based climate change adaptation experiences of Burkina Faso, and its relation to CBDRR. With the profile of the country and its socioeconomic conditions, the chapter describes the community-based adaptation practices and its implications in community-coping mechanism in the changing conditions.

Chapter 19 presents issues that underline risk reduction strategies for a drought situation within a social protection framework in Malawi. With the scope of the Malawi Social Action Fund (MASAF), the chapter outlines the approaches related to the community-based drought risk reduction in Malawi, and suggests recommendations for its future improvements.

Finally, Chapter 20 summarizes the key observations from the case studies, and suggests future directions for CBDRR. The chapter also analyzes regional experiences and stakeholder participation to draw key lessons for future CBDRR activities.

ACKNOWLEDGMENTS

This chapter is an output of several years of research on CBDRR in different countries. The experiences and support over years are highly acknowledged.

REFERENCES

Blaikie, P., Cannon, T., Davis, I., & Wisner, B. (1994). *At risk: Natural hazards, people's vulnerability, and disaster.* London: Routledge.

Khagram, S., Clarke, W. C., & Radd, S. F. (2003). From the environment and human security to sustainable security and development. In L. Chen, S. Fukuda-Parr & E. Seidensticker (Eds.), *Human insecurity in a global world* (pp. 108–135). Massachusetts, USA: Harvard University Press.

Maskrey, A. (1989). *Disaster mitigation: A community-based approach.* Oxford: Oxfam.

McMillan, D. W., & Chavis, D. W. (1986). Sense of community: A definition and theory. *Journal of Community Psychology, 14,* 6–23.

Mileti, D. S. (2001). *Disasters by design.* Washington, DC: Joseph Henry Press.

Moser, C., & Norton, A. (2001). *To claim our rights: Livelihood security, human rights and sustainable development* (79 pp.). London: Overseas Development Institute (ODI).

Quarantelli, E. L. (1989). Conceptualizing disasters from a sociological perspective. *International Journal of Mass Emergencies and Disasters, 7,* 243–251.

Shaw, R. (2006a). Critical issues of community based flood mitigation: Examples from Bangladesh and Vietnam. *Journal of Science and Culture, Special Issue on Flood Disaster Risk Reduction in Asia, 72*(1–2), 62–71.

Shaw, R. (2006b). Community based climate change adaptation in Vietnam: Inter-linkage of environment, disaster and human security. In S. Sonak (Ed.), *Multiple dimension of global environmental changes* (pp. 521–547). New Delhi, India: TERI publication.

Shaw, R. (2007). Essentials of indigenous knowledge: An overview. DRH Idea Workshop in Delhi, 19–20 February 2007.

Shaw, R. (2009). Role of local actors in community based disaster risk reduction. Perspectives in disaster management, METU, ISDR, WBI, 123–145.

Shaw, R., & Goda, K. (2004). From disaster to sustainable civil society: The Kobe experience. *Disaster, 28*(19), 16–40.

Shaw, R., & Okazaki, K. (2003). *Sustainability in grass-roots initiatives: Focus on community based disaster management* (99 pp). Kobe, Japan: UNCRD Publication.

Shaw, R., Sharma, A., & Takeuchi, Y. (2009). *Indigenous knowledge and disaster risk reduction: From practice to policy* (490 pp.). New York, USA: NOVA Publication.

Shaw, R., & Takeuchi, Y. (2007): Indigenous knowledge and technology for disaster reduction. *Asia Pacific Tech Monitor*, Special Volume (November/December), 20–26.

Shaw, R., & Takeuchi, Y. (2011). Role of local institutions in climate related disasters in small and medium sized cities of Japan. *Asian Journal of Environment and Disaster Management, 3*(2), 137–150.

Sillitoe, P., Barr, J., & Alam, M. (2004). Sandy-clay or clayey-sand? Mapping indigenous and scientific soil knowledge on the Bangladesh floodplains. In A. Bicker, P. Sillitoe & J. Pottier (Eds.), *Development and local knowledge* (pp. 174–201). Oxon, UK: Routledge.

Sillitoe, P., & Bicker, A. (2004). Hunting for theory, gathering ideology. In A. Bicker, P. Sillitoe & J. Pottier (Eds.), *Development and local knowledge* (pp. 1–18). Oxon, UK: Routledge.

Twigg, J. (1999). The age of accountability? Future community involvement in disaster reduction. *Australian Journal of Emergency Management, 14*(4), 51–58.

Twigg, J., & Bhatt, M. (1998). *Understanding vulnerability: South Asian perspectives*. London: ITDG.

Vaux, T., & Lund, F. (2003). Humans security of working women: Response to crisis. In L. Chen, S. Fukuda-Parr & E. Seidensticker (Eds.), *Human insecurity in a global world* (pp. 137–161). Massachusetts, USA: Harvard University Press.

CHAPTER 2

GOVERNMENT ROLES IN COMMUNITY-BASED DISASTER RISK REDUCTION

Mikio Ishiwatari

INTRODUCTION

The community plays a crucial role in disaster risk reduction (DRR). The Hyogo Declaration adopted at the World Conference on Disaster Reduction held in Kobe in 2005 stresses that strengthening community-level capacities to reduce disaster risk at the local level is especially needed (UN International Strategy for Disaster Reduction [UNISDR], 2005). Following the Great East Japan Earthquake on March 11, 2011 in Japan, community-based organizations (CBOs) have conducted various activities, such as searching and rescuing victims, closing gates, monitoring tsunamis, assisting evacuation, firefighting, and operating evacuation shelters at the risk of their staff's lives, while local governments lost their staff and facilities in the functions of disaster management. Some 250 volunteer members of firefighting CBOs were dead or are still missing.

The CBOs have been managing disasters in Japan for centuries. These organizations are Suibo-dan in Japanese for flood fighting, Syobo-dan for firefighting, and Jisyubo for mitigating earthquake disasters. Government roles in community-based disaster risk reduction (CBDRR) have changed

Community-Based Disaster Risk Reduction
Community, Environment and Disaster Risk Management, Volume 10, 19–33
Copyright © 2012 by Emerald Group Publishing Limited
All rights of reproduction in any form reserved
ISSN: 2040-7262/doi:10.1108/S2040-7262(2012)0000010008

with changes in society. Useful lessons for development assistance can be learned from these changes.

Japan International Cooperation Agency (JICA) has shifted assistant approaches in disaster management from structure measures to integrating one of structures, nonstructures, and community-based activities. Since JICA is a bilateral agency, its assistance targets government agencies in developing countries. While JICA has increased assistance in CBDRR, methods for supporting the government agencies in CBDRR remain nonestablished. This chapter examines the history of CBOs and government roles in CBDRR in Japan. Also, the paper reviews JICA's projects of CBDRR in Nepal and Kenya. It examines how the agency utilized Japanese experiences for these projects. It further aims to propose methods of development assistance for CBDRR.

CBO AND GOVERNMENT IN DRR

It is important to involve various stakeholders such as government agencies, nongovernmental organizations (NGOs), and research institutions in DRR. Among these, local governments are expected to sustainably support communities' efforts of disaster management (Hada et al., 2009; Shaw & Okazaki, 2004). Motoyoshi argues that the governments and communities should cooperate to reflect their efforts in local DRR plans to protect the communities (Motoyoshi, 2006).

Various practices of local governments' support to communities have been reported. Subsidy provided by a local government strengthens the efforts of NGOs and CBOs for earthquake disaster management in Aichi Prefecture (Kawabata & Fukuwa, 2009). Disaster-response drills raise the awareness of communities for managing earthquake disasters, and enhance the capacity of local governments to collect damage information in the fields (Hisada, Murakami, & Zama, 2008).

Some issues have been found. Interactive risk communication among communities, governments, and specialists should be established to encourage the communities to take self-help actions (Katada & Kanai, 2010; Yamada, 2008). There is a perception gap between local governments and communities in their roles. The communities expect local governments, Suibo-dan in Japanese for flood fighting, and Syobo-dan for firefighting to play greater roles in evacuation and rescue activities than their actual capacities (Katada, Kodama, Kanai, Iwasaki, & Teshima, 2004). For rehabilitation following the Hanshin-Awaji Great (Kobe) Earthquake in

1995, the governments were forceful in decision-making, and people were too dependent on the governments (Shaw & Goda, 2004).

Kawata stressed before the Great East Japan Earthquake that local governments must explain the contents of the hazard maps for communities (Kawata, 2010). Sole hazard maps produced by the local governments do not encourage the communities to be evacuated. Only 3.8% of people were evacuated when tsunami warnings were issued at the Chili Earthquake in February 2010.

Kamee reports that people at less than 20% of sites suffering from sediment disasters were evacuated before disasters occurred in Japan in 2007 (Kamee, 2010). Local governments should take the opportunity of identifying risk areas to promote early warning and evacuation systems, and disaster management drills at normal times.

In developing countries, where governments have limited capacity to protect their citizens, the communities have to rely on their own knowledge and coping mechanisms to mitigate disaster damages. In developed countries, communities heavily rely on the governments to support and protect the communities, since traditional community systems have been abandoned for more individual lifestyles and forms of association (Twigg, 1999). These recent studies have mainly focused on relationships between communities and local governments, but have not covered changes in the relationship.

HISTORY OF CBOS IN DRR IN JAPAN

Three major types of CBOs in disaster management have been functioning in Japan for centuries. These are Suibo-dan for flood fighting, Syobo-dan for firefighting, and Jisyubo for mitigating earthquake disasters. Suibo-dan and Syobo-dan have a membership of some 900,000 in total, or about 7 percent of total population in Japan. Jisyubo has some several-decade-long history (Table 1).

Compared with other countries, the Japanese have comparatively higher participation in volunteer organizations of these CBOs that have embedded relationships with the government. Each specific act stipulates the activities and roles of these CBOs, and each authority of the national government is supervising and supporting these CBOs. On the other hand, the Japanese have lower participation in nonembedded organizations, such as volunteers and NGOs, than other countries. This is because the Japanese think that the

Table 1. CBOs in Japan.

Organization	Targeted Disaster	Act	Supervising Government Organizations	Period of Formation	Number of Staff or Organization
Suibo-dan	Flood	Flood Fighting Act	Ministry of Land, Infrastructure, and Transport	17th century	Staff: 900,000 (duplicated between two organizations)
Syobo-dan	Fire	Fire Defense Organization Act	Fire and Disaster Management Authority (FDMA)	18th century	
Jisyubo	Earthquake	Basic Act on Disaster Reduction	Cabinet Office FDMA	1970s	Organization: 140,000
NPO	All	Act to Promote Specified Non-profit Activities	Cabinet Office	After Kobe earthquake in 1995	Organization: Over 2,000

government should be responsible for dealing with social problems (Haddad, 2006).

The transition of these organizations in Japan indicates that various external factors, such as centralization or decentralization of government, modernization of state and society, and urbanization have affected government roles in CBDM (Fig. 1).

Suibo: Flood Fighting

Suibo is community-based activities of flood fighting in Japan, such as reinforcing river banks and assisting people's evacuation during floods, and has played a crucial role in flood disaster management in the history of Japan (Japan Water Forum [JWF], 2007). It is the communities' wisdom that inevitably emerged to survive flood disasters (Kida, Miyamura, & Takahashi, 1992). Each community has invented various countermeasures through its on-site fighting activities against floods. Indigenous knowledge has been transferred in the field from generation to generation (Matsuki, 2010). The Japanese government stresses that the flood control structures promoted by the government agencies and Suibo conducted by communities work together to mitigate flood damages like "a pair of wheels on one axle

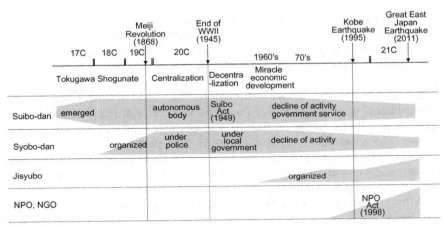

Fig. 1. History of Japanese CBOs in Disaster Management.

of vehicles." Currently 1,808 Suibo-dan are functioning with roughly 890,000 members in total (River Bureau & MLIT).

The government roles in supporting CBOs have been changing for the last two centuries because of various drastically changing situations, such as the Meiji revolution for starting modernization, democratization following the Second World War, and miracle economic development in the 1960s. During the Edo Era from the 17th to 19th centuries, wastelands or marshland were newly reclaimed as paddy fields on a large scale throughout the country. The communities had to protect their own lands and developed properties from floods with self-help or community-assistance efforts. The Tokugawa Shogunate (Bakufu), a feudal regime of Japan, was able to protect only castles or city areas by structures because of limited technologies and budget. The members of Suibo-dan were skilful at flood fighting, and were familiar with the characteristics of floods and the behavior of the inundation in their river basins (Takahashi, 2004). Suibo activities have not generally changed until today. The members of Suibo-dan are still engaged in patrolling river banks at normal and disaster times, piling stocks of materials, issuing early warning by using temple bells and conch shell horns, and mobilizing volunteers for reinforcing banks during floods (Kazama, 1985). The Tokugawa Shogunate and feudal domains repeatedly issued ordinances to raise awareness of farmers in Suibo. Otherwise, communities might lose their motivation when floods did not occur for some years (Kazama, 1988).

The Japanese government of a modern state, which overthrew the Tokugawa Shogunate at the Meiji Revolution in the 1860s, started to manage Suibo-dan in line with centralization of governing mechanisms. The government intended to systematically organize Suibo-dan to mitigate flood damages, and to increase agricultural production (Uchida, 1994). A new law authorized Suibo-dan as an autonomous body under supervision by the governments in 1890. The river law stipulated in 1896 that the prefectural governors assigned by the central government have primary responsibility for Suibo. The government order stipulates in 1915 that Suibo-dan has to store Suibo materials at warehouses, to install river-level gauges for monitoring floods, and to conduct Suibo drills. Some 1.3 million members were engaged in Suibo at roughly 4,000 organizations in 1939 (Watanabe, 1939).

After the Second World War, serious floods causing over 1,000 deaths occurred almost every year. To mitigate these damages, the Suibo Law was enacted in 1949 (Inoue & Morita, 1980). Also, this new law aims to reorganize a Suibo system to address drastic social changes of communities caused by an agrarian reform led by General Headquarters, the Supreme Commander for the Allied Powers (Sumi, 2006).

For the past few decades, the functions of self-help or community assistance for Suibo have been lessened. The capacities of Suibo-dan are decreasing. River banks were broken at a flood disaster in Nigata Prefecture in 2004 at areas where Suibo was not sufficiently conducted (Okuma, 2010). Miyamura stresses that Suibo-dan is extinguishing, and that the government agencies are supporting Suibo-dan with great difficulty (Miyamura, 2000). The government agencies are annually holding flood-fighting drills to keep a technology level of Suibo-dan at regional, and municipality levels throughout the country. Also, minister for land, infrastructure, and transport annually honors several members of Suibo-dan for their distinguished services to encourage their efforts.

There are several reasons for this decline in Suibo. Since damages caused by floods have decreased because of constructing flood-control structures of river banks and dams, Suibo-dan has not utilized its technology in the field, leading to loss of their knowledge. Modernization and urbanization weakened the traditional structures of communities. The relationships between community members have declined, because migrated residents do not participate in community events such as traditional community festivals (Haruyama & Tujimura, 2009). The new body of laws for Suibo accelerated the breakdown of Suibo-dan and Suibo (Miyamuara, 1985). Suibo-dan changed to governmental organizations from CBOs in the context of institution and finance. Currently, local governments finance activities conducted by Suibo-dan, and the central government subsidizes expenses for materials and facilities. The governmental agencies provide Suibo-dan with disaster information by communication systems. Ordinary people recognize Suibo as a service provided by the government (JICA, 2003). Kikuchi argues that the government has strengthened its control over Suibo-dan, weakening the community's capacities of Suibo during economic growth and modernization from the 1950s (Kikuchi, 2004).

Suibo-dan is currently facing the following issues (Cabinet Office 2010; Ogawa, 2009; Okuma, 1988; River Bureau & MLIT):

- The number of Suibo-dan members has decreased by 30 percent for the last 40 years because the members are aging and changing their life styles. Some 70 percent members are office workers who are difficult to engage in Suibo in the daytime.
- Public awareness of Suibo is decreasing.
- While inundation in urban areas by localized torrential rains becomes serious because of urbanization, Subo-dan's countermeasures against the urban inundation are not well established.

Ministry of Land, Infrastructure, and Transport and Tourism (MLIT) (2009) started the following new activities to enhance Suibo:

- Establishment of a collaborative mechanism with NGOs, which are actively involved in disaster management after the Great Hanshin-Awaji (Kobe) Earthquake in 1995.
- Dispatch of experts to local governments for transferring Suibo technologies from 2007.

Syobo: Fire Fighting

Syobo-dan is a nonstanding organization for firefighting in Japan. The members of Syobo-dan have other main jobs, and voluntarily participate in Syobo activities. Syobo-dan took the field at over 220,000 events with over 3 million members in total in 2009. Syobo-dan has the following advantages (Committee on Strengthening Syobo-dan, 2010):

- Real relevance for the needs of community: The members live in their community and are well acquainted with situation in the community.
- Large-scale mobilization: The total number of the members is some six times of professional staff of firefighting agencies. Syobo-dan is expected

to play a crucial role during enormous disasters, such as the Kobe Earthquake in 1995.
- Ready to response: The members are trained at normal times.

While Syobo-dan has roots in community, it was developed by a government initiative. The Tokugawa Shogunate organized firefighting CBOs in Edo, the former Tokyo, in the 18th century. The Japanese government reorganized Syobo-dan under police agencies in 1927. After the Second World War, Syobo-dan was separated from the police agencies, and was transferred to local governments in line with a democratization policy of General Headquarters of the Supreme Commander for the Allied Powers.

Syobo-dan faces same problem of Suibo-dan of decreasing and aging members (Fire and Disaster Management Agency [FDMA], 2010). The total number of members has constantly decreased from 1.3 million in 1965 to 880,000 in 2010. The national government is promoting recruiting campaigns, awarding private companies supportive to Shobo-dan, and encouraging female members. Also, the national government provides local governments with grants for facilities.

Jisyubo: Earthquake Disaster Management

Jisyubo is CBO for managing disasters, in particular earthquakes. Basic Act on Disaster Control Measures stipulates that Jisyubo is voluntarily organized in the spirit of neighbors' collaboration. Jishubo activities are guided and mobilized with a soft touch by local governments rather than being truly self-motivated (Bajek, Matsuda, & Okada, 2008). Some 140,000 Jisyubo were established at 74 percent of municipalities in 2010 in Japan (FDMA, 2010). Comparing with Suibo and Syobo, Jisyubo has a shorter history. The government started to encourage communities to organize Jisyubo in the 1970s. The Kobe Earthquake in 1995 reminded the importance of Jisyubo, since over 80 percent of victims buried under collapsed buildings were rescued by neighbors.

While the cover ratio of Jisyubo has increased, some established Jisyubo face difficulties to sustain activities. At flood disasters in Gifu Prefecture, 2002, Jisyubo did not effectively function, since it became inactive during recent years (Shibata, 2003). Jisyubo faces the following issues (FDMA, 2007):

- Some members of Jisyubo cannot engage in activities during day time because of their own daily works, and are aging.

– Community members lack awareness of the importance of the activities.
– It is difficult to find out community leaders.
– Members can utilize limited spaces, facilities, and information.
– The activities become stereotyped, and difficult to continue.

Kuroda pointes out the following issues for local governments, which promote to organize Jisyubo (Kuroda, 1998).

– limited human resources for support to communities;
– institutional weakness in compensation for death, injury, or accidents;
– limited measures for capacity development of Jisyubo.

NGO

NGOs and nonprofit organizations (NPOs) in disaster management substantially started activities at the Great Hanshin-Awaji (Kobe) Earthquake in 1995 in Japan. This year of 1995 is called as "the first year of volunteers" in Japan (Economic Planning Agency, 1999). Some 1.5 million volunteers in total engaged themselves in rehabilitation works following the earthquake. This is regarded as the first event that volunteers were involved in resolving social problems at a large scale.

To help these organizations to smoothly conduct activities such as gaining juridical personality, the Act to Promote Specified Non-profit Activities was enacted in 1998. Over 2,000 NPOs that engage in disaster management have been registered at the Cabinet Office as of 2011. These organizations are actively conducting relief and rehabilitation works following the Great East Japan Earthquake in 2011. Over 200 NPOs and NGOs participate in the Japan Civil Network for Disaster Relief in East Japan as of April 4, 2011, which is a broad coalition of Japanese NPOs providing disaster relief.

LESSONS FROM JICA PROJECTS

Approach

The JICA is shifting an engineering-oriented approach to an integrated approach including CBDRR (Ishiwatari, 2010). It focused on mainly structural measures, such as constructing dykes and dams, and providing monitoring and communication facilities for about half a century. It announced a new approach in disaster management in 2008, which defines community as the main actor in disaster management, and government agencies and other organizations concerned as supporting actors to the communities (JICA, 2008). One-third of technical assistance projects in disaster management include the activities of CBDRR following the new approach announced, while a few projects covered them before 1990 (Oi & Mimaki, 2010).

The JICA experts, who are mainly engineers for structural measures, replicate CBDDR of Japanese style in developing countries. They have developed capacities of government organizations in CBDRR, such as transferring technology to staff, and establishing organizations and budgetary systems. The projects often include construction of small-scale structure measures, such as evacuation centers and routes, and prevention works as a project component in addition to nonstructural measures. These community-scale structures had been common practices in CBDRR in Japan.

The communities had played a crucial role in coping with disasters before the miraculous economic development in Japan, when the government had limited capacities and budget. In developing countries where governments have limited capacities and budgets, the JICA has mobilized community's resources in DRR.

Nepal

The JICA has supported Nepalese efforts to mitigate flood and sediment disasters for over two decades. Sustainability of disaster management was secured through institutionalizing the government department, creating a budgetary system, and accumulating knowledge and experience in the department. To institutionalize the objectives and achievements of the projects supported by JICA, the Department of Water Induced Disaster Prevention was established in 2000 under the Ministry of Water Resources. The department created field offices throughout the country, assigned professional staff, and is managing budgets for CBDRR under severe budgetary constrains.

The JICA has supported the department to establish a model of CBDRR. The JICA experts worked together with Nepalese engineers to organize CBOs, to develop intermediate technology that communities can utilize, to conduct awareness program at school, to develop early warning and evacuation systems at a community level, and to develop capacities of the communities.

A pilot project at Kabilash village aims at reducing sediment disaster risks through a participatory approach, and avoiding loss of human lives by early warning and evacuation systems. The JICA experts produced hazard maps indicating risks of sediment disasters. By utilizing these hazard maps, the awareness was spread in total 7 schools, 175 students, and 429 villagers. The education program for pupils at school was effective to raise the awareness of not only pupils but also their parents and communities. The pupils imparted the knowledge that was gained at school to their parents at home. Since the program is included in their curriculum, the school is conducting the program even after the project.

Trainer trainings were conducted for school teachers, engineers of NGOs, and government engineers. The JICA experts supported the communities to produce plans of DRR and forestation. A simple early warning system was installed by providing monitoring equipment and a personal computer.

Low-cost technology was developed for CBDRR. These are bamboo fences and gabion boxes to stabilize sloops and mitigate sediment disasters. The community members are engaged in constructing these structures at their community. Although cost is low from a Japanese point of view, the developed technology is still high from a Nepalese point of view to widely replicate the technology to other areas.

Kenya

The JICA has supported the Water Resources Management Agency (WRMA) and the Ministry of Water in Kenya to develop their capacities in flood management and to conduct CBDRR against floods in the Nyando River Basin since 2006. No government agency had clear mandate for flood management in Kenya before the JICA support.

The WRMA became the implementing agency of flood management, while the Ministry of Water is responsible for policy. The WRMA supervises structure construction and assists communities in mobilizing CBOs, securing land for facilities, implementing environmental impact assessment clearance, and establishing O&M of facilities constructed. Based on these experiences, the WRMA developed a project cycle for CBDRR.

The JICA is taking an approach integrating structural and nonstructural measures at a community level. The projects aim at mitigating flood damages and improving people's evacuation, which continues for a month during severe floods. The structural measures include small-scale protection works for river erosion, river banks with ramps for cattle, raising local roads as evacuation routes, and the construction of evacuation centers with roof water catchments, toilets, and wells. The nonstructural measures include establishment of CBOs, training in organizational operation, community flood management plans, coordination procedures with disaster management committees, signboards for community flood hazard maps indicating evacuation routes and dangerous areas, evacuation training and drills, and education program at school.

CONCLUSION

This chapter shows that government roles are crucial to strengthen a community's capacities of DRR. The Japanese government has provided immense support to the CBOs of Suibo-dan, Syobo-dan, and Jisyubo for centuries.

The relationship between governments and communities has changed in Japan during its development and modernization for the last two centuries. Japanese experiences are regarded as the transition of this relationship from developing to developed countries. Various external factors, such as centralization or decentralization of government, modernization of state and society, peoples' life styles, and urbanization, have affected government roles in CBDRR. As the economy has developed, contribution of people to CBOs has decreased while that of the government has increased. Also, new forms of organizations such as NPOs and NGOs have emerged.

This chapter found that the approach of supporting government organizations in CBDRR is useful. Regardless of development stages, governments have important roles in CBDRR. The JICA has supported the governments of Kenya and Nepal to develop their capacities to support communities in DRR by replicating Japanese experiences. Organizations, budgetary systems, and staff capacities in governments should be created and strengthened to establish sustainable mechanisms in CBDRR.

Various factors that affect government roles should be examined to formulate CBDRR projects. Currently these examinations are implicitly conducted. Further studies are required to identify the factors to be examined, and to establish methods for the examination.

The Great East Japan Earthquake in 2011 reminds us that community can play crucial roles in disaster management. The only effective measure against the unexpected tsunami was evacuation, as the sea dykes were destroyed by the tsunami. Shobo-dan issued warnings for community members, instructed communities to be evacuated, and monitored the tsunami. Detailed studies are required to evaluate CBO's functions during this earthquake.

REFERENCES

Bajek, R., Matsuda, Y., & Okada, N. (2008). Japan's Jishu-bosai-soshiki community activities: Analysis of its role in participatory community disaster risk management. *Natural Hazards, 44*(2), 281–292.

Cabinet Office. (2010). *White paper on disaster management.* Oita: Saeki.

Committee on Strengthening Syobo-dan. (2010). *Report on Strengthening Syobo-dan [Syobodanno Jujitsu Kyokanituiteno Kentokai]* (in Japanese). Tokyo: Fire and Disaster Management Agency (FDMA).

Economic Planning Agency. (1999). *White paper on national life.* Tokyo: Government Printing Bureau, Ministry of Finance.

FDMA (2007). *Handbook on Jisyubosai-sosiki [Jisyubosaisosiki no Tebiki]* (in Japanese). Tokyo: FDMA.

FDMA. (2010). *White paper on fire fighting.* Oita: Saeki.

Hada, Y., et al. (2009). Increasing coping capacity of local community against disasters with coproduction between residents and public administration [Jumin Gyosei Kyodoniyoru Chiikibosairyoku kojonikansuru Torikumi] (in Japanese). *Proceedings of Chikianzen-gakkai,* 24, 31–34.

Haddad, M. A. (2006). Civic responsibility and patterns of voluntary participation around the world. *Comparative Political Studies, 39*(10), 1220–1242.

Haruyama, S., & Tujimura, A. (2009). Possibility of community-based activities for disaster prevention: Lessons learned from 2004 Toyoka Flood [Saisyotannitosihteno chikuno bosaikatsudo: 2004 Toyokasuigaino Jireikara] (in Japanese). *E-journal GEO, 4*(1), 1–20.

Hisada, Y., Murakami, Y., & Zama, S. (2008). Quick collection of earthquake damage information and effective emergency response by collaboration between local government and residents. *Proceedings on the 14th World Conference on Earthquake Engineering.*

Inoue, J., & Morita, B. (1980). *Handbook on suibo technology for practitioners [Jitsumusyano-tameno Suibogijutsu Handobukku]* (in Japanese). Tokyo: Sankaido.

Ishiwatari, M. (2010). Review of disaster rehabilitation methodologies following the Indian Ocean Tsunami from a human security perspective. *Asian Journal of Environment and Disaster Management, 2*(3), 275–288.

Japan Water Forum (JWF). (2007). *Flood fighting in Japan.* Tokyo: JWF.

JICA. (2003). *Disaster management and development. [Bosaito Kaihatsu]* (in Japanese). Tokyo: JICA.

JICA. (2008). *Issue-specific guidelines, disaster reduction.* Tokyo: JICA.

Kamee, K. (2010). Situation and issues of warning and evacuation for sediment disaster [Dosyasaigainitaisuru Keikai Hiantaiseino Genjoto Kadai] (in Japanese). *Chisui to Sabo,* 196.

Katada, T., Kodama, M., Kanai, M., Iwasaki, T., & Teshima, S. (2004). Process of attitude and behavior modification by delphi survey about disaster prevention consciousness [Saigaitaioishiki Derufaityosawo Motiita Juminno Taidokodohenyokateino Tsuiseki] (in Japanese). *Proceedings of Dobokukeikakugakukenkyu.*

Katada, T., & Kanai, S. (2010). Communication design for establishing evacuation system lead by residents against sediment disasters [Dosyasaigaiwo Taisyotosita Juminsyudougata Hinantaiseno Kakuritunotameno Komunikesyon Dezain] (in Japanese). In *Dobokugijutusya Jisenronbunsyu*, 1, 106–112.

Kawabata, H., & Fukuwa N. (2009). Consideration about the subsidization at the time of starting of community disaster mitigation activities. [Bosai Machizukurino Shidojiniokeru Katsudojoseikinno Yakuwarinikannsuru Kosatsu] (in Japanese). *Proceedings on Annual Meeting of Architectural Institute of Japan* (pp. 487–488).

Kawata, Y. (2010). *Tsunami disaster [Tsunamisaigai]* (in Japanese). Tokyo: Iwanamisyoten.

Kazama, T. (1985). Organization and system of suibo in Edo Era [Edojidainiokeru Suibono Soshikito Taisei] (in Japanese). *Proceedings on 5th Nihon Dobokushikennkyuhappyokai*, 163–168.

Kazama, T. (1988). System and preparedness of levee protection in the present age [Gendainiokeru Suibono Soshikito Taisei] (in Japanese). *Proceedings on 8th Nihon Dobokushikennkyuhappyokai*, 184–192.

Kida, A., Miyamura, T., & Takahashi, N. (1992). Significance and form of suibo [Suibono Igito Arikata] (in Japanese). *Proceedings of Technical Research Conference of Kanto Region, JSCE* (pp. 160–161).

Kikuchi, S. (2004). A study on establishment and transition of traditional community-based organization of river [Kawanikakawaru Dentotekisoshikino Seirituto Hensennikansuru Ichikosatsu] (in Japanese). *Doshisha Univ. Policy and Management 6*, 173–186.

Kuroda, H. (1998). The history and possibilities of voluntary disaster prevention organizations in neighborhood, [Jisyubosaisosiki Sono Keii to Tenbo] (in Japanese). *Proceedings of Institute of Social Safety Science*, 252–257.

Matsuki, H. (2010). Tripod scheme for flood disaster prevention and technical transfer. In R. Shaw (Ed.), *Community, environment and disaster risk management* (pp. 51–67). Bingley, UK: Emerald.

Ministry of Land, Infrastructure, Transport and Tourism (MLIT). (2009). *White paper on land, infrastructure, transport and tourism in Japan*. Tokyo: MLIT.

Miyamuara, T. (1985). *Suibo*. Tokyo: Cyuokoronsya.

Miyamura, T. (2000). Formation between flood control and suibo [Chisuito Suibono Kozu] (in Japanese). *Kasen, 652*: 14–19.

Motoyoshi, T. (2006). Public perception of flood risk and community-based disaster preparedness. In S. Ikeda, T. Fukuzono & T. Sato (Eds.), *A better integrated management of disaster risks – Toward resilient society to emerging disaster risks in mega-cities* (pp. 121–134). Tokyo: TERRAPUB.

Ogawa, H. (2009). *The present condition and problem of floods system in the area zero-meters above sea level [Kaibatsu zerometoruchitainiokeru Suibotaiseino Genjoutokadai]* (in Japanese). Research Paper of Gifu Women College, 58.

Oi, H., & Mimaki, J. (2010). Policy transitions in Japanese ODA for disaster risk reduction in developing countries. *Asian Journal of Environment and Disaster Management, 2*(3), 275–288.

Okuma, T. (1988). *River history of floods and flood management [Kouzuito Chisuino Kasenshi]* (in Japanese). Tokyo: Heibonsha.

Okuma, T. (2010). Technology has autonomy, too [Gijutunimo Jichigaaru] (in Japanese). In T. Uzawa & T. Okuma (Eds.), *River as Social Common Capital [Syakai Kyotsushihonntoshiteno Kawa]*. Tokyo: Tokyo University Press.

River Bureau, MLIT, Flood fighting activities and flood fighting organizations [Suibokatsudo Suibodannituitte] (in Japanese). Tokyo: MLIT.

Shaw, R., & Goda, K. (2004). From disaster to sustainable civil society: The Kobe experience. *Disasters, 28*(1), 16–40.

Shaw, R., & Okazaki, K. (2004). *Sustainable community based disaster management practices in Asia: A user's guide.* Kobe: UNCRD.

Shibata, A. (2003). Our disaster and Jisybo [Watashidomono Saigaito Jisybosai] (in Japanese). *Kasen, 59*(2), 54–68.

Sumi, T. (2006). *Enact of suibo law after the Second World War [Sengosuigaito Suibohono Seitei].* 1947 Kathryn Typhoon, Report of Expert Panel on Lessons of Disaster [Cyasurin 1947 Kasurintaifu, Report on Saigaikyokunnno keisyonikansuru senmonchosakai] (in Japanese). Tokyo: Cabinet Office.

Takahashi, Y. (2004). Public-private partnership as an example of flood control measures in Japan. *International Journal of Water Resources Development, 20*(1), 97–106.

Twigg, J. (1999). The age of accountability?: Future community involvement in disaster reduction. *Australian Journal of Emergency Management, 14*(4), 51–58.

Uchida, K. (1994). History of floods and community in modern Japan [Kindai Nihonno Suigaito Chiikino Syakaishi] (in Japanese). Tokyo: Kokinsyoin.

UN International Strategy for Disaster Reduction. (2005). *Hyogo declaration.* Geneva: UNISDR.

Watanabe, Y. (1939). General figures of Suibo [Wagakunino Suiboshisetsuno Gaikyo] (in Japanese). *Suiri to Doboku, 20*(5), 44–57.

Yamada, F. (2008). Implementation of risk communication for enhancement on community flood risk mitigation [Suigainitaisuru Chiikibosairyokukoujowo Mezashita Risukuko-minyukesyonno Jisentekikenkyu]. *Journal of JSDN, 27*(1), 25–43.

CHAPTER 3

ROLE OF NGOS IN COMMUNITY-BASED DISASTER RISK REDUCTION

Takako Izumi and Rajib Shaw

INTRODUCTION

The community-based disaster risk reduction (CBDRR) approach has been taken by nongovernmental organizations (NGOs) as a common approach to build resilient communities in their disaster risk reduction (DRR) efforts. The approach has been initially implemented in the developing world by NGOs, followed by international organizations like the International Federations of Red Cross and Red Crescent (Benson, Twigg, & Myers, 2001; Maceda, Gaillard, Stasiak, Le Masson, & Le Berre, 2009). The approach is now increasingly promoted among local governments in order to strengthen the links between the official disaster management system and community-based organizations (Kafle & Murshed, 2006). There are many case studies of DRR projects with community-based approaches by NGOs and local governments, and there are many variations as well (Heijmans, 2009).

According to Heijmans (2009), toward the end of the 1990s, the approach became an alternative to top-down approaches in disaster management. With this approach it succeeded in raising people's awareness of disaster risks by using intimate local knowledge and recognizing preexisting local

Community-Based Disaster Risk Reduction
Community, Environment and Disaster Risk Management, Volume 10, 35–54
Copyright © 2012 by Emerald Group Publishing Limited
ISSN: 2040-7262/doi:10.1108/S2040-7262(2012)0000010009

capacities and institutions. Therefore, it became possible to improve the position of impoverished, vulnerable, disaster-affected people by addressing the root cause of their vulnerability and by recognizing their fundamental right to participate in decisions that impact their lives. At the same time, the capacity development of the community is also critical in this approach to assess the risk, identify risk reduction measures, and plan and implement the measures (Delica-Willson, 2005).

The effectiveness and reasons of promoting community participation and involvement are not only for adopting local knowledge and addressing the root causes of their vulnerability, but also sustaining the community-level initiatives for disaster reduction. External agencies such as government and NGOs often initiate and implement community-level programs before and after disasters. However, such initiatives many times discontinue once the external support is withdrawn. There can be many reasons behind this lack of sustainability, some of which may be the lack of partnership, participation, empowerment, and ownership of local communities. Unless the disaster risk management efforts are sustainable at individual and community level, it would be difficult to reduce the vulnerability and losses. It is therefore important to involve people in decision-making on policies and strategies that should be followed for their development in the community (Kafle & Murshed, 2006; Shaw & Okazaki, 2004).

However, this approach does not highlight only the importance and effectiveness of the community involvement. In DRR, the government shapes policies and institutional frameworks, while civil society actors play a complementary role in supporting vulnerable communities. Primary responsibilities for implementation of the Hyogo Framework for Actions (HFA)[1] rest with states, but the collaboration and cooperation among all stakeholders, including NGOs, will be crucial in order to improve the resilience of communities (Heijmans, 2009; UNISDR, 2005). Each stakeholder has its own role to play in the DRR process, and by the leadership and initiatives of governments and NGOs, the CBDRR approach becomes possible.

The purposes of this chapter are to review the case studies of CBDRR by Asian NGOs to observe the roles of NGOs in CBDRR projects in Malaysia, Cambodia, and India; to address the issues and challenges that Asian NGOs face in the process of CBDRR implementation; and to discuss the way-forward and innovative way for the future CBDRR. Each case study has a different focus in the program, and it showcases the variety of CBDRR programs and different roles of NGOs in CBDRR.

NGOS AND CBDRR

Definition of NGOs

The definition of NGO varies. Streesen (1997) defines NGOs as professionally staffed organizations aiming at contributing to the reduction of human suffering and to the development of poor countries. It is also defined as a formal (professionalized) independent societal organization whose primary aim is to promote common goals at the national and international levels (Martens, 2002). Shaw (2003) stressed that the diversity in tasks, goals, and activities strains any simple definition of NGOs. It can be stated that the NGO includes a wide range of groups, which are independent of government and characterized by preliminary humanitarian activities, with focus on citizens' needs and demands.

Not only the definition but also the roles of NGOs include different perspectives. NGOs have been occupying the role of main service providers. Often replacing the role of the government on the ground, especially in remote rural areas, NGOs have traditionally assumed a gap-filling role that has sometimes created conflicting relations with governments (Clayton, Oakley, & Taylor, 2000; Ulleberg, 2009) Furthermore, NGOs have important functions and advantages such as (1) being good at reaching and mobilizing the poor and remote communities, (2) helping to empower the poor people to gain control of their lives and working with and strengthening local institutions, (3) carrying out projects at lower costs and with more efficiency than the government agencies, and (4) promoting sustainable development (Streesen, 1997).

Nikkhah and Redzuan (2010) emphasized the major role of NGOs for sustainable community development. According to them, NGOs have many programs, functions, and roles that assist the community to become empowered, and eventually attain sustainable development. In their discussion, in order to attain sustainable development, NGOs have to work on capacity development for communities. The CBDRR approach includes strengthening the preparedness capacity of communities (Benson et al., 2001). The NGOs appear to be well placed to play a significant role in DRR. They tend to work with poorer and more marginalized groups in society. Moreover, the participatory approach pursued by many NGOs offers them an opportunity to examine the nature of communities' vulnerability and, on the basis of this analysis, to incorporate appropriate DRR measures into their work.

On the other hand, the lack of sustainability of NGOs activities and programs can be a negative factor to attain the sustainable development of community resilience. Shaw (2009) stressed that many of the NGO activities face the problem of sustainability over a longer period of time, especially once the NGO withdrew from the field. Continuation of community activities over a longer period of time needs a policy environment at local level, as well as local institutions to continue the activities. At the same time, he emphasized the importance of linking NGOs and local government activities, and involving them in policy making.

The capacity development program through the CBDRR approach consists of numerous steps staring from different types of assessment and focus group discussions and requires follow-up activities such as impact assessment and simulation exercises and drills. The NGOs need to strengthen their capacity in many ways for successful and sustainable CBDRR programs: (1) fund-raising capacity to implement a longer-term project, (2) inclusion of both national and local governments to lead mainstreaming DRR into a policy, and (3) ensuring community empower-ment in DRR in their programs to initiate the DRR measures by communities.

In the following section, three case studies of CBDRR by NGOs in Malaysia, Cambodia, and India are included. The case study in Malaysia is on the community-based preparedness designed to require the involvement of the local government. The case study of CBDRR in Cambodia is a program that includes a livelihood activity that resulted in achieving stable income as well as poverty reduction. The last case study from India is the CBDRR project linked with environmental management.

Case Studies of CBDRR by NGOs

Case Study (Malaysia)

Malaysia has not faced any major disaster till date. However, it has been hit by a number of floods every year and there is an urgent need to strengthen the preparedness capacity among communities. According to the Malaysia country report by Views from the Frontline[2] by MERCY Malaysia, the average score of the DRR capacity at local level was 2.8 in Malaysia, which is higher than the midpoint (2.5), reflecting that a foundation in DRR exists. This indicates that the DRR capacity at local level in Malaysia is moderate and there are already initiatives and steps that have been taken toward DRR. However, the information and knowledge has not yet reached the communities. In general, community representatives feel they do not have enough information, tools, and capacity to materialize the five priorities plus cross-cutting issues at community level (MERCY Malaysia, 2009).

MERCY Malaysia initiated their DRR programs in 2008 especially for school children and communities in the flood-prone areas. The community-based preparedness program started when Johor state was hit by a massive flood in 2006–2007. The program emphasized the importance of the involvement of the local governments and their capacity development as well as the communities. It was considered that the program and community preparedness could be sustainable by the commitment of both communities and local governments. The identification of the target villages was made in consultation with the Malaysian National Security Council (Majlis Keselamatan Negara) and the Johor state office (MERCY Malaysia, 2010).

The Johor community-based preparedness programme (JCPP) aimed to build a culture of disaster preparedness and resilience in the target communities and to strengthen multistakeholder partnerships between local government agencies and local communities. Three districts in Johor were selected that were most hit by the flood in 2006–2007: Batu Pahat, Segamat, and Kota Tinggi. The program consists of three steps: (1) DRR seminars, (2) town watching (TW) workshops, and (3) community consultation and CBDRR projects (Table 1).

As the first step, the DRR seminars were conducted for the local government officials and the community members in Johor in order to promote the DRR concept, provide an insight into the previous DRR activities in Malaysia, and share the program plan to obtain their support and understanding to the program (MERCY Malaysia, 2010).

Second, the two TW workshops were conducted in each district for the local government officials and for the community members. The local government officials trained at the first workshop participated in the TW for communities as facilitators. It was to prepare the government officials to conduct further TW exercises in their communities, encourage them to incorporate DRR into policies and other activities, build relationships between different agencies, and encourage information sharing on existing hazard maps and disaster management plans. TW was originally used as a tool for urban planning, but it is now being used for disaster prevention as well. After the participants walk around the community, they identify both good and bad points and risks to disasters. Through this exercise, disasters are recognized as their concern and the awareness of disaster prevention is increased and actual disaster prevention activities are promoted (Shaw & Takeuchi, 2009).

Table 1.   Overview of the JCPP Project.

	Activity	Target	Outputs
Phase 1	DRR seminar	State and district government officials from three districts (Batu Pahat, Segamat, and Kota Tinggi)	- Government officials gained knowledge and awareness on DRR - Government officials learned the MERCY Malaysia's DRR project in Johor
Phase 2	Two Town watching workshops at each district	1. District government officials 2. Communities	- District government officials and communities learned the town watching methodology - Problems against disasters in each village were identified
Phase 3	Community consultation	Communities	- Disaster preparedness tools were identified: posters, signboards, brochures - Disaster preparedness activities were identified and implemented: first aid training, school watching workshop

Through the TW exercises, the participants identified concrete action plans to reduce disaster risks and discussed how to implement them. The actions recommended in the plan became the CBDRR projects supposed to be carried out by the community in the next six months. MERCY Malaysia worked with and supported the communities to conduct the activity. The projects selected by the communities at each district included: (a) developing posters and signboards with DRR messages, (b) conducting a community first-aid training session, (c) conducting a school watching workshop, and (d) developing a DRR brochure that included local knowledge on disaster preparedness as well as basic first-aid tips, and all the projects completed within six months after being identified (MERCY Malaysia, 2010).

The JCPP required the participation by both local government officials and community members from the beginning until the end of the projects. In each consultation, the local government officials were invited to the meetings with the community members and MERCY Malaysia. By the end of the program, the target communities and local government officials in each district had a clear picture and understanding on the hazards that they may face in the future, and a series of the preparedness activities have been completed with the involvement of the communities and local governments.

Case Study (Cambodia)
The Battambang province is one of the highly drought affected and vulnerable province in Cambodia. The community members lost their rice crops every year due to drought. The lack of climate-adapted agriculture made the community more vulnerable.

Save the Earth Cambodia (STEC) is a national NGO based in Cambodia. They initiated the community-based drought residence project through microinsurance. The project aimed at developing the capacity of the local government officials and community members on climate change and DRR, raising awareness on a climate change adaptation (CCA) measure in particular for drought, and establishing the mechanism of drought-resilient community through climate-adapted farming and other livelihood programs (Fig. 1). This program included four steps: (1) training workshops for the local government officials and community members, (2) developing drought risk management plan, (3) adapting climate-resilient farming, and (4) initiating poultry farming through microinsurance and home-gardening (Moolio, 2010).

In the Battambang province, rice-growing is the most common occupation. When crops failed, other problems emerged such as migration

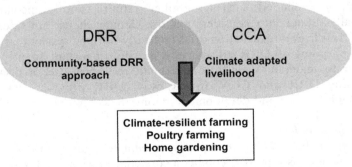

Fig. 1. Outputs from the DRR/CCA Project in Cambodia.

and school dropouts. STEC worked with the village community to identify their vulnerabilities and the risks they faced with droughts. The discussion involved persons with disabilities and children. The villagers were trained in climate risk mapping and drafted a risk reduction action plan. The Department of Agriculture provided technical support to the village to develop a farming calendar that applied specifically to their drought-affected community. The community learned about climate-adapted farming and replaced rice plantations with drought-resilient crops that grew faster than rice. The villagers started planting vegetables that could be harvested within a month instead of waiting for five months to harvest rice. The villagers continue using the training and information and sharing it with neighboring communities (Moolio, 2010).

The project included an activity of poultry farming and home-gardening. It was mainly to support women-headed households to have their livelihood through these activities. For poultry farming, the government officials from the Agriculture Department of the District Office provided training to the villagers on farming. The home-gardening program provided technical knowledge on gardening, seeds, and tools. The villagers learned the green vegetables grown by organic fertilizers are more economical and environment-friendly as well as healthier. This project was examined by an external consultant; the report highlighted that women's involvement in earning livelihood provided the families with stable income and fresh nutritious foods, and contributed to decrease of migration in particular of younger women to a city center for work and poverty reduction (STEC, 2010).

Disasters cause a heavy impact on livelihoods. In order to secure their living after being hit by disasters, it is important for DRR programs to include the livelihood element. It can be a transformation of the current planned crops such as from rice to vegetables and establishment of new scheme of livelihood such as poultry farming and home-gardening. Especially taking into consideration the climate change, in addition to saving their lives by evacuation drills and early warning system that are also major purposes of DRR efforts, it is equally important to provide the support to maintain their lives and build resilience after a disaster by combining DRR and CCA. In this way, DRR program can achieve sustainable income and development among the communities.

Case Study (India)
The need to build adaptive capacity to climate change into project and policy planning is rapidly becoming a core concern (Pelling & High, 2005). The environmental community has increasingly seen the relevance of

environmental management and good resource use for hazard control and reduction. It has been stimulated by the impacts of large-scale events that clearly revealed the relationship between environmental degradation and hazard occurrence. Equilibrium and resilience of ecosystems offer natural protection from natural hazards and reduce the likelihood of new hazards generated by processes of environmental degradation (UNDP, 2002).

Around the globe, land-use and land-cover changes are eroding the natural buffers that protect communities from hazard risk. These same changes often erode people's capacity to recover from disasters. Environmental management will reduce the risk, improve the resilience, and build capacity of the local communities. SEEDS India implemented a project to strengthen resilience of the local coastal communities in the Lighthouse Panchayat in Tamil Nadu in 2008 by establishing a multilayered and multispecies bioshield as an appropriate mitigating mechanism to encounter the possible disasters and minimize the extent of damage. The coastal line of Tamil Nadu is constantly facing threat due to sea-borne calamities. Natural disasters such as cyclones and heavy rains with floods have become an annual feature along the coastal districts. Beach erosion, seawater intrusion, and destruction of fragile ecosystem along the coastal districts are the other risks that need to be tackled along the coast. These characteristics bring the coastal areas under pressure to plan and develop mechanisms to mitigate the possible disasters and strengthen the ecological security and resilience of the local communities residing along the coast (SEEDS India, 2009).

The overall approaches of the project are science based, community centered, and partnership and process oriented. The major process of the project includes (1) situation analysis and community mobilization, (2) community-based institution building, (3) preparation of microplan and implementation of the activities, and (4) monitoring and evaluation. By adapting to the above approaches, five major activities were identified (Table 2).

Table 2. Major Activities of the Bioshield Project in India.

Activity
1   Village meeting to explain the objectives and seek their support and cooperation
2   Identification of the areas for plantation through biophysical survey with local support and obtaining permission for the plantation from the land owner
3   Assessment of damage to sand dunes in the project villages
4   Identifying and selecting suitable species for plantation
5   Developing a microplan and management of bioshield and sand dune restoration

The bioshield is established in the village common land. A microplan for the bioshield was developed and is being implemented with the active partnership of local communities and local bodies. A thorough biophysical survey was conducted by a hired expert helped to design the plots for each of the village and to conduct consultation with the community for the identification of the species and suitability of the species. It was also critical to include economically important species such as coconut. A series of community meetings were conducted on how to and who will take care of the plants. The initiative and ownership of the communities were the most important for program sustainability (SEEDS India, 2009).

According to the senior project manager in SEEDS India, the most challenging issue in this project was to convince the community that the project brings both disaster preparedness capacity and incomes, and eventually make the community agree to take the ownership to continue and manage the project. A number of community discussions were required to obtain their understanding and support. Currently, the project has been fully managed by the community and they are able to get a small amount of incomes from the products, that is, by selling coconuts.

Lessons Learnt from Case Studies
These three DRR projects have different focuses. The project in Malaysia put the priority on capacity development of local authorities as well as communities, taking into consideration its effectiveness for program sustainability. What needs to be highlighted in this project is it included the local government officials into all the processes. It is often difficult to have their participation in DRR activities by NGOs; however, if the coordination and understanding by governments are strong, it becomes possible. This will be one of the models of pure and typical CBDRR projects focusing on preparedness aspects.

The projects in Cambodia and India include an additional aspect such as CCA to regular DRR activities. Climate change is clearly happening, and it is important to prepare for the increased number and intensity of global disasters (IASC, 2010). Over the past years and decades, the DRR has been strengthened by a large portfolio of experiences, instruments, and methods to predict weather-related hazards, and must be acknowledged as a toolkit to create long-term resilience. In order to scale-up DRR from the current capacity, the present study addresses the urgent need to link DRR and CCA (Birkman & von Teichman, 2009). The projects in Cambodia and India managed to enhance regular DRR projects to the level of CCA including the aspects of livelihood and environmental management to DRR.

In countries such as Cambodia and India, the frequency and scale of meteorological disasters are much worse than a country such as Malaysia. It will be easier for Cambodia and India to develop CCA and DRR projects as the need of linkage is easier to be understood. However, in Malaysia, DRR efforts are still at an initial stage, while awareness raising on DRR is the major activity in disaster preparedness. Differences exist among countries in the speed of development and transformation of DRR and CCA activities. However, the activities and project focuses should be determined in community discussions and based on various types of assessments as the needs vary from country to country. Most importantly, NGOs have a role to identify the critical needs and design a project to be most suitable to the community needs.

The challenge highlighted in all three projects was to gain the community ownership for each project. All three projects organized a series of community consultations and discussions to obtain their understanding and support. No matter how a project is scaled-up, the most critical approach is community-based. The approach of CBDRR needs to be maintained even if it is transformed to CCA or combined activities.

CHALLENGES AND WAY FORWARD OF CBDRR BY NGOS

In order to discuss the challenges and way forward of CBDRR by NGOs, interviews and surveys were conducted with eight NGO staff from six organizations in six countries (Afghanistan, Cambodia, India, Indonesia, Malaysia, and Philippines) that are conducting the CBDRR projects. Afghanistan was selected to see the views and perspectives from a country that is still suffering from recovery and reconstruction from the internal and external conflicts. India, Indonesia, and Philippines are known as countries prone to various kinds of disasters, and a number of CBDRR projects have been conducted by governments and international and national NGOs. Cambodia is suffering from drought every year as well as poverty issues. Malaysia has no experience of a devastated disaster event and the DRR capacity is still limited. However, it has been hit by floods every year and the preparedness program for the frequent floods is considered critical.

Five questions were asked: (1) value and benefit of the CBDRR conducted by NGOs and why the involvement of NGOs in CBDRR is important, (2) major challenges and problems in conducting CBDRR, (3) how NGOs could tackle these issues, (4) innovative ideas to improve and scale-up the current CBDRR programs to apply to more complicated situations and conditions, and (5) new elements need to be included in the current CBDRR efforts.

Value and Benefit of the CBDRR Conducted by NGOs and Why the Involvement of NGOs in CBDRR is Important

The answers mainly included five values (Table 3). NGOs should have professional skills to address issues and develop projects and programs to improve a situation. The ideas such as CCA and microinsurance are the strategies and methodologies brought in and introduced by NGOs in their programs. Furthermore, as NGOs are considered impartial and neutral, it is easier for them to bring all the stakeholders together on the same platform and the support to and understanding of their activities are easily gained. They are not politically based or influenced; rather they work closely with communities. The fact would allow no biasness in the project or project site. The community feels more comfortable in voicing out their problems and concerns in DRR. NGOs are more independent and their voices can be easily heard without biases.

It was also highlighted that NGOs can play a role to bridge the gaps between community needs and current policies. NGOs are working in frontline with communities and expected to grasp the community needs efficiently and address them to higher levels. Especially, in their advocacy role, it was emphasized by an NGO in Malaysia that NGOs have a greater role in nondisaster-prone countries. In such countries, governments hardly advocate DRR and put in no efforts to conduct the capacity development programs of communities in DRR. If the community has no support or very little support from governments, NGOs involvement is more critical.

Table 3. Values of NGOs Intervention in CBDRR.

	Values	Countries
1	Skills, technical knowledge	Cambodia, Indonesia, Malaysia
2	Impartiality	Cambodia, Malaysia
3	Bridging gaps between governments and community (advocacy)	Indonesia
4	Capacity development for communities and government	Cambodia, Indonesia
5	Translating knowledge to the field	India, Philippines

Furthermore, NGOs can develop the capacity of communities to manage the risks while reducing vulnerabilities and having a critical role in advocacy. They have an important role of transferring the knowledge to the communities.

Major Challenges and Problems in Conducting CBDRR

Four major challenges were identified (Table 4). NGOs from Malaysia and Philippines pointed out the same issue: the challenge in community organization. It is important to establish a good relationship and trust with communities; however, there are not many trained and dedicated facilitators and local mechanisms that could invest time to strengthen community solidarity and ownership.

Another challenge for Malaysia is that the community does not have any urgency and need for preparedness as it does not have an experience of being struck by a heavy disaster. This will not be a challenge only for Malaysia; rather most of the nondisaster prone countries share this difficulty when they conduct the DRR activities. Given the risk of climate change, all the countries and communities have equal needs to learn how to prepare themselves for disasters, and NGOs particularly in nondisaster-prone countries have a role to strongly raise this point as governments do not have any particular strategy at national level.

Other answers included the lack of sustainability of funds to the projects. DRR requires a longer-term effort; however, the funds to the project can last only for one year most of the time. In such a short period, it is not possible to change the mindset of the communities and introduce the new concept of DRR to them. In addition, a contradiction of the strategy, plan, and message between governments and NGOs causes confusion in communities. Although NGOs clearly promote DRR and sustainable development, the activities and plans by governments and corporate sectors

Table 4. Major Challenges for NGOs in CBDRR.

	Major Challenges	Countries
1	Community organization	Malaysia, Philippines
2	No sense of preparedness need	Malaysia
3	Lack of funds sustainability	Cambodia, India
4	Lack of localized approach	Afghanistan

sometimes lead to an opposite direction. The lack of knowledge and understanding on DRR among governments and corporate sectors is one of the most difficult challenges to NGOs.

An NGO from Afghanistan raised an issue that the common DRR approach and practices such as CBDRR are not applicable to Afghanistan under such a conflict situation, and thus they require a unique and localized approach to be adaptable by the communities and local culture.

How to Tackle These Challenges

In order to tackle the challenges addressed, the NGOs underscored six ideas (Table 5).

The enhancement of advocacy efforts was stressed by Afghanistan and Indonesia. The advocacy needs are especially amongst multistakeholders including media, donors, corporate sectors, and governments. The NGOs from Malaysia and Philippines raised the common challenges of the complexity of community organization. In order to improve the situation, measures such as to identify the most effective local mechanism with traditional leaders, teachers, and religious leaders and to maintain frequent meetings and discussions with the communities were suggested. In addition, from the NGO side, it is important to allocate sufficient staff to manage the CBDRR programs to organize regular dialogues with the communities on the need of preparedness and of their support in project planning and implementation.

Given the complex situation, Afghanistan highlighted the need for the theories and practices to be developed in the context of the Afghan

Table 5. How to Tackle the Challenges in CBDRR.

	How to Tackle Challenges	Countries
1	Enhancement of advocacy efforts	Afghanistan, Indonesia
2	Identifying and using most effective local mechanism	Malaysia, Philippines
3	Sufficient staff allocation to conduct the DRR project	Malaysia
4	Developing strategy and measures that can be adaptable to their local context	Afghanistan
5	Giving the ownership to communities	Cambodia
6	Bridging the gap between knowledge and practice	India

environment, circumstances, and its disaster-coping mechanism and capacity. For a country like Afghanistan, in addition to strong advocacy to emphasize the importance and need of DRR efforts and measures in the country, an actual action plan, strategy, and measures that can be adapted to their local context are urgently needed.

Innovative Idea

Seven ideas were addressed (Table 6). It was recommended to accelerate the research on DRR tools and technology for more complicated needs in each country. At the same time, it was also emphasized to consider how the local culture and DRR activities can be mixed and localized. Furthermore, the need to develop a new media campaign for DRR was highlighted. Climate change became a trend and popular term when the seriousness of the issue was reinforced by various corporates, media, and governments. Many corporate sectors created the goods and items to promote the campaign and it influenced to make green culture a trend. It would be ideal if the term and concept of DRR can also become as popular as climate change. In order to do that, the advocacy of corporate sectors and media is critical.

An NGO from Afghanistan suggested that the DRR efforts should have a close link and be integrated into the projects in other sectors such as agriculture, infrastructure, health, livelihood, water, and sanitation. Afghanistan is facing various issues and DRR is not their priority under the current situation. Unless the DRR project is designed as an integrated project with other sectors, it would be very difficult to gain support and active participation by the communities and governments.

Table 6. Innovative Ideas in CBDRR.

	Innovative Ideas	Countries
1	Research and technology	Indonesia
2	Microinsurance for livelihood resilience	Cambodia
3	Localization of project	Malaysia
4	Linking different agencies and ministries for DRR	Malaysia
5	Media campaign for wider awareness raising	Malaysia
6	Mainstreaming DRR into other projects	Afghanistan
7	Integrating DRR with the need of the day	India

Table 7. Elements That Need to Be Included in CBDRR.

	Elements That Need to Be Included	Countries
1	Active involvement of media and private sectors	Indonesia
2	Participation of women, children, and persons with disabilities	Malaysia
3	Linkage of DRR and other issues	Malaysia
4	Integration of DRR knowledge into local practices	India

Elements to be Included in the Current CBDRR Efforts

Four elements were suggested to be included in the current CBDRR (Table 7). The media can play a very important role to influence the decisions of policy makers and governments. The NGO who raised this concern plans to initiate the awareness raising and capacity development project for media. In many cases, the participation of women, children, and persons with disabilities in dialogues and sessions remains weak. The situation depends on the culture and lifestyle of a country as well and it will not be easy to change the situation immediately. However, it is critical for NGOs to continue advocating the importance and need of wider stakeholders and family members, otherwise, the real goal of CBDRR will not be achieved.

Lack of communications and linkage among the line ministries that deal with disaster issues, environment, education, health, and public works to manage disaster risks may cause the delay of developing systematic and holistic action plans at national level. The last point highlights the importance of collaboration between practitioners and academics. Both research result and experiences and knowledge of practitioners need to be brought down to the grassroot level to maximize the effectiveness and efficiency of the expertise, and NGO can be a coordinator among these parties.

CONCLUSION

There are various key players in CBDRR such as governments, UN agencies, international and regional organization, research institutions, academics, communities, as well as many types of civil society organizations including NGOs. One of the remarkable characteristics of NGOs is that they are closer to communities, and are thus familiar with local culture and easily understand the importance of the community-based approach.

There are many case studies of DRR projects with community-based approaches by NGOs and local governments, and there are many variations as well. The current CBDRR program includes different focuses such as capacity development, livelihood, climate change, gender, and health. From the case studies from Malaysia, Cambodia, and India, the major roles of NGOs will be:

- Capacity development of local stakeholders (government, communities, Civil Society Organizations (CSOs))
- Establishing a good network and partnership with local stakeholders, resulting in a smooth coordination in DRR activities
- Identifying local needs, and designing and developing a project with new elements such as climate change
- Creating a sense of program ownership among community members for program sustainability.

Furthermore, through the survey and interviews with the NGO staff, more critical roles of NGOs were identified. The roles of NGOs have to be determined based on their values such as technical knowledge, impartiality, capacity development, advocacy, and translating knowledge into field. At the same time, NGOs themselves acknowledge the need of new innovative ideas and elements required to be added into current DRR tools, and how and in what roles they can contribute to fulfill the need. They have strength in building a network and communications with local governments as both of them know local culture, contexts, and critical needs, and NGOs can enhance the technical knowledge of local authorities providing inputs on developing local strategy and mechanism. At the same time, NGOs can expand the network to other stakeholders such as media, private sectors, and academics. Through collaboration with academics and NGOs, technical knowledge and scientific data can be incorporated in local projects and the required field of research becomes clear. Based on the NGOs' familiarity with local situation, their inputs are critical to mainstream cross-cutting issues into various projects. The additional roles of NGOs are summarized as below:

- Playing a role of facilitator and moderator among local stakeholders as they have a value of impartiality and bridging a gap in communications
- Advocating local needs
- Assisting in and working together with local governments in developing local strategy/mechanism

- Inviting various stakeholders in a DRR framework such as media and private sectors and highlighting the cross-cutting issues in various projects
- Addressing the need of specific field that requires research and technology together with academics and identifying innovative methodology and tools.

NGOs are also facing various challenges and difficulties in the process of CBDRR such as lack of funds sustainability and lack of localized approach. In particular, a country such as Afghanistan has more urgent issues due to conflicts and unique culture and obviously they require a different approach from other countries.

The NGOs have more advantages than other stakeholders in CBDRR and clearly have unique values. By making the best use of these advantages and values, NGOs are expected to further strengthen the CBDRR projects and develop and implement innovative CBDRR and CBDRR/ CCA programs in the future and have a significant role to share their experiences and advocate the local needs to higher levels. No matter how the projects are scaled-up and multidimensional approaches are required, the community-based approach is one of the most critical elements and foundation of any type of project.

NOTES

1. HFA, adopted by 168 states, sets a clear expected outcome – substantial reduction of disaster losses, of lives as well as the social, economic, and environmental assets of communities and countries – and lays out a detailed set of priorities to achieve this by 2015 (UNISDR, 2005).

2. Views from the Frontline is a participatory multistakeholder engagement process designed to monitor, review, and report on critical aspects of "local governance" considered essential to building disaster-resilient communities. The Global Network of Civil Society Organizations for Disaster Reduction (GNDR) organized the global survey on the progress of UN "Hyogo Framework for Action" at local level. MERCY Malaysia is selected as national coordinating organization for Malaysia and it conducted the national survey.

ACKNOWLEDGMENTS

The findings of this project were only made possible through the kind support and cooperation of NGOs based in Asia including MERCY Malaysia, Save the Earth Cambodia, and SEEDS India by sharing their case studies. Furthermore, the cooperation of the NGO staff in Afghanistan, Cambodia, India, Indonesia, Malaysia, and Philippines by answering the questionnaires is highly appreciated.

REFERENCES

Benson, C., Twigg, J., & Myers, M. (2001). NGO initiatives in risk reduction: An overview. *Disasters, 25*(3), 199–215.

Birkman, J., & von Teichman, K. (2009). Addressing the challenge: Recommendations and quality criteria for linking disaster risk reduction and adaptation to climate change. German Committee for Disaster Reduction (DKKV).

Clayton, A., Oakley, P., & Taylor. J. (2000). *Civil society organizations and service provision, civil society and social movements program.* Paper Number 2, United Nations Research Institute for Social Development.

Delica-Willson, Z. (2005). Community-based disaster risk management: Local level solutions to disaster risks. *Tropical Coasts, 12*(1), 66–73.

Heijmans, A. (2009). *The social life of community-based disaster risk reduction: Origins, politics and framing, disaster studies.* Working Paper 20, Aon Benfield UCL Hazard Research Center.

Inter-Agency for Standing Committee. (2010). *Addressing the humanitarian challenges of climate change: Regional and national perspective.* World Food Programme (WFP), International Federation of Red Cross and Red Crescent Societies (IFRC), and United Nations Office for the Coordination of Humanitarian Affairs (UNOCHA).

Kafle, S. K., & Murshed, Z. (2006). Community-based disaster risk management for local authorities. Participant's Workbook, Asian Disaster Preparedness Center (ADPC), Pathumthani.

Maceda, E., Gaillard, J., Stasiak, E., Le Masson, V., & Le Berre, I. (2009). Experimental use of participatory 3-dimentional models in island community-based disaster risk management. *The International Journal of Research into Island Cultures, 3*(1), 72–84.

Martens, K. (2002). Mission impossible? Defining nongovernmental organizations. *International Journal of Voluntary and Nonprofit Organizations, 13*(3), 271–285.

MERCY Malaysia. (2009). The Malaysia country report of Views from the Frontline.

MERCY Malaysia. (2010). Annual Report for 2009.

Moolio, P. (2010). *Enhancing drought resilient community development processes through micro insurance in Cambodia.* External Evaluation Report, Save the Earth Cambodia.

Nikkhah, H., & Redzuan, M. (2010). The role of NGOs in promoting empowerment for sustainable community development. *Journal of Human Ecology, 30*(2), 85–92.

Pelling, M., & High, C. (2005). *Social learning and adaptation to climate change.* Disaster Studies Working Paper 11, Benfield Hazard Research Center.

Save the Earth Cambodia. (2010). Presentation on linking DRR and climate change adaptation for sustainable development.

SEEDS India. (2009). Securing our shores: People participation and environmental management.

Shaw, R. (2003). Role of non-government organizations in earthquake disaster management: An Asian perspective. *Regional Development Dialogue, 24*(1), 117–129.

Shaw, R. (2009). *Role of local actors in community based disaster risk reduction: Perspectives in disaster management.* Middle East Technical University Disaster Management Implementation and Research Center, Ankara, Turkey, 121–145.

Shaw, R., & Okazaki, K. (2004). *Sustainable community based disaster management (CBDM) practices in Asia: A user's guide.* Disaster Management Planning Hyogo Office, United Nations Center for Regional Development (UNCRD).

Shaw, R., & Takeuchi, Y. (2009). *Town watching handbook for disaster education, enhancing experimental learning.* European Union, United Nations International Strategy for Disaster Reduction and Kyoto University.

Streesen, P. (1997). Non-governmental organizations and development. *Annals of the American Academy of Political and Social Science, 654,* 193–210.

Ulleberg, I. (2009). *The role and impact of NGOs in capacity development: From replacing the state to reinvigorating education.* United Nations Educational, Scientific, and Cultural Organization (UNESCO).

United Nations International Strategy for Disaster Reduction. (2005). *Words intoaction: A guide for implementing the Hyogo Framework.* United Nations.

United Nations Development Programme. (2002). *A climate risk management approach to disaster reduction and adaptation to climate change.* UNDP Expert Group Meeting Integrating Disaster Reduction with Adaptation to Climate Change.

CHAPTER 4

UNIVERSITIES AND COMMUNITY-BASED DISASTER RISK REDUCTION

Rajib Shaw, Yukiko Takeuchi, Ramasamy Krishnamurthy, Joy Jacqueline Pereira and Fuad Mallick

INTRODUCTION

Education has been there for ages. Need of education for sustainable development is stated in Chapter 36 of Agenda 21 (1992) as follows:

> Education, including formal education, public awareness and training, should be recognized as a process by which human beings and societies can reach their fullest potential. Education is critical for promoting sustainable development and improving the capacity of the people to address environment and development issues. While basic education provides the underpinning for any environment and development education, the latter needs to be incorporated as an essential part of learning. Both formal and non-formal education is indispensable to changing people's attitudes so that they have the capacity to assess and address their sustainable development concerns.

The Hyogo Framework for Action (HFA, 2005–2015) also re-emphasized the need and urgency of disaster-related education. While there has been quite active awareness raising and training for different sectors, formal higher education has been less dominant in disaster reduction field.

Community-Based Disaster Risk Reduction
Community, Environment and Disaster Risk Management, Volume 10, 55–66
Copyright © 2012 by Emerald Group Publishing Limited
All rights of reproduction in any form reserved
ISSN: 2040-7262/doi:10.1108/S2040-7262(2012)0000010010

Only after 2004 Indian Ocean Tsunami, an increasing trend is observed to develop and deliver disaster management courses in the universities targeting undergraduate and postgraduate students.

Education is considered one of the key mainstreaming tools for any subject. There have been several attempts to mainstream risk reduction in development practices. However, the real mainstreaming starts from formal educational institutions, including schools, colleges, and universities. The mode and method of education should be one of the important issues to make positive impacts. Disaster risk reduction (DRR) being a multi-disciplinary subject needs a combination of theory and practice. Possibly, more emphasis should be given to field practice and learning from experiences. Thus, the academic and formal education should go beyond the traditional boundaries of the school and/or university compound, and communicate more with the communities, and learn from their experiences.

When disaster education is mentioned, the usual focus is more on the school or family or community education. Very little focus has been given so far on higher education. However, higher education (in college and university) is the key to develop professionals in the subject. Higher education in disaster management is still lacking in most of the countries and regions. In this context, the lessons of environment or the field of sustainable development can provide useful tips. Not only the curriculum, but also the approach or mode of delivery in higher education is equally important. To develop an appropriate higher education a system of educational governance is required (COE 2005). Given the role of education has for the overall societal and economic development, there is a necessity to ensure the responsiveness of higher education to the changing needs and expectations of society. In this respect, it is important to ensure participation of external actors in the governance of higher education and to allow the flexibility to accommodate the continuous change in the needs and requirements over time. COE (2005) made several recommendations for higher education, which can be considered as the base of the disaster education in colleges and universities. These include serving the need and expectation of the society, having appropriate academic freedom, process of setting up long-terms goals and developing appropriate strategies for achieving them, providing reasonable scope of innovation and flexibility in research, promotion of good educational governance through regional and international networks, and ensuring quality control of teachers and students (Shaw, Mallick, & Takeuchi, 2011).

In this chapter, roles of universities in the community-based disaster risk reduction (CBDRR) projects are described, followed by evolution of university network and its education research agenda in the Asia Pacific region.

PROACTIVE FIELD-BASED APPROACH: EXAMPLE OF SELAMAT PROJECT

In 2004, Indonesia, Sri Lanka, India, and Maldives were the four nations to be directly impacted by the Indian Ocean Tsunami, where local communities even today are highly vulnerable and exposed to future disasters. The post-tsunami reconstruction efforts are still underway in most of the affected communities, yet most risk reduction initiatives are only at the level of pilot projects. The nongovernmental organizations (NGOs), community-based organizations (CBOs), and community groups at work do not have access to adequate knowledge resources and tools to address their local risks. Project Selamat recognizes the community and its educational institutions as the most crucial stakeholders for building resilience to disasters such as tsunami.

As a direct implementation of the HFA, the project aims at building community-level coping capacities toward long-term resilience. The objectives of the project include making tsunami-threatened communities aware of their risks and of actions needed, training local stakeholders in appropriate skills, establishing community-based infrastructure, and preparing and using IEC material for awareness, training, and advocacy. In this setting, the project aims to bring together the NGOs, the academic institutions, and the governments to work on a collaborative model of locally appropriate process of institutionalizing risk reduction process. NGOs have direct field access and experiences in grassroot project implementation. However, these experiences are not properly reflected in the educational curriculum. Thus, the Selamat project aims at bridging academic research, education, and field practice.

The project objective was to build capacity of local communities at risk to tsunamis and other coastal hazards. Some of the highlights of the university–NGO cooperation were:

1. Quality of knowledge and information: All participating universities in the targeted countries are esteemed organizations in the field of disaster risk management. Therefore, it brings high-quality knowledge and information.
2. Extensive network: The four universities have largest networks in the tsunami-affected areas, and thus ensure that the knowledge product will have largest circulation in future.
3. Ensuring sustainability: Through development of the certificate courses and customized courses, young professional development will be ensured, which is linked to the sustainability of the disaster preparedness activities in the targeted countries and communities.

The project targeted on three specific achievements:

- Education mainstreaming in the curriculum: Through development of courses and making it part of the regular curriculum of the universities.
- Linkages to field practice: Linking the courses with the NGO project learning.
- Participatory learning: Academic learning through participation and experiences (Fig. 1).

The project was developed through a series of consultations with the universities, local and national governments, partner NGOs, and school communities, especially in the tsunami-affected areas. The project was coordinated by Kyoto University Graduate School of Global Environmental Studies, in cooperation with Institute of Technology Bandung [ITB for Indonesia], University of Madras [UOM for India and Maldives], and University of Peradeniya [UOP for Sri Lanka]. The NGO coordination was done by SEEDS India, in cooperation with other NGOs in respective countries. Fig. 2 shows the process of action learning through three steps: see, learn, and act.

As a part of community learning process, eight training modules were developed based on the experiences from the local NGOs' activities. These are described in Table 1, which shows the linkage to the university curriculum in three respective universities.

A questionnaire survey was conducted among the graduate students in three universities to understand the need and interest in higher education in DRR, as well as to understand their willingness to take the above eight courses. Fig. 3 shows the results of the questionnaire survey. It shows that there are differential perceptions of the students based on the universities. While the students from UOM are more interested to study the disaster management subjects for use in emergency, the ITB students are interested

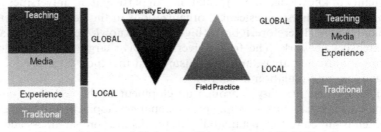

Fig. 1.   Linkage of University Education and Field Practice.

Fig. 2.   Process of Action Learning in Selamat Project.

in the subject, and the UOP students want to learn this for the future (Fig. 3a). For the interest in disaster management modules, the key interest is in module 2 [climate change adaptation], followed by 4 [community-based information system], 7 [postdisaster environmental impacts], and 1 [school safety]. One of the key issues of sustainability of these modules is the link to the existing courses in the respective universities. This shows a clear relationship of linking the community practice to the higher education in the universities.

CONTEXT OF HIGHER EDUCATION IN DRR

Disaster impacts are increasing across Asia, and disasters are becoming increasingly complex, which includes so many different dimensions. The traditional DRR approach is under pressure. There is a need to be more proactive in DRR. It is seen that the number of catastrophic disasters and

Table 1. Links of Training Modules to University Curriculum.

Modules	University of Madras (including its affiliated colleges and Anna University)	Institute of Technology Bandung	University of Peradeniya
1. School safety	Elective course introduced by applied geology (ongoing)		
2. Climate change adaptation	Certain components already incorporated in elective course of Master degree in applied geology – course begins from July 2009		Introduced in PG and UG courses
3. Community-based coastal zone management	Elective course introduced by applied geology (ongoing)	Courses in oceanography and urban regional planning	
4. Community-based information system	Elective course introduced by applied geology (ongoing)		
5. Participatory urban risk management	M.A. (town and country planning), M.A. (geography)	Introduced in urban planning at master's level	
6. Leadership training program for NGOs	M.A. (social work), M.A. (sociology and anthropology) can be offered as value added certificate courses		
7. Postdisaster environmental impact assessment	M.Sc. (environmental studies), B.E. (civil engineering) (offered by Anna University)	Elective courses offered in School of Environment	Courses offered by the Environmental Studies Department for UG students
8. Flood risk management	Core and elective courses are currently offered by Department of Applied Geology for postgraduate students		Climate hydrology for 50 students. Watershed management for UG students

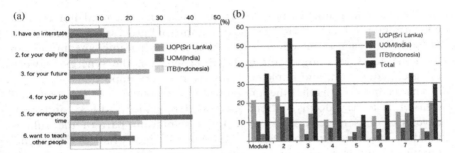

Fig. 3. (a) Left: Interest in Disaster Management Education among the Students, and (b) Right: Interest among the Students for Respective Modules.

their consequences have been increasing in spite of the advancements in technology. For example, Japan is one of the leading countries in DRR, but in the 1995 Kobe Earthquake (The Great Hanshin Awaji Earthquake) more than 6,400 people were killed. The most damaged in this earthquake were the nonengineered constructions. There exists engineering knowledge, but there is still a need for social processes to transfer that knowledge into practice. This shows the importance of multidisciplinary research.

The 2004 Indian Ocean Tsunami had a lead-time of more than two and half hours, but the early warning information could not reach the people in most affected countries. Therefore, there is a need for educational knowledge, research, and practice in DRR. How to bring university knowledge beyond the university context to the community is a big challenge. Many school buildings collapsed in Pakistan and India in the 2005 Kashmir Earthquake. The basic policies on DRR are extremely important. How to bring about policies that are more focused on the safety of schools is an important issue to work on. In the 2006 Sidr Cyclone, Bangladesh, the death toll was less than expected. It is argued that this was because of the advancement of the early warning systems in Bangladesh during the past three decades. However, the number of people killed by the cyclone was still very high. In the case of the 2008 Nargis Cyclone, Myanmar, the agencies got the early warning information three days in advance. However, the information could not be sent to people in the vulnerable areas due to limited physical and communication access, and they could not be evacuated out of the cyclone areas. The 2008 Wenchuan Earthquake, China, saw similar consequences like the 2005 Kashmir Earthquake. Many school buildings were damaged and lives lost due to lessons not learnt from past disasters in other areas.

The above-mentioned examples show that there is a need not only of educational products in DRR but also of improved process implementation. How the outreach of the educational product to actual implementation can be achieved is very important in DRR. Therefore, the synergy between research, education, and implementation is also very important.

The second point is that the link between development, environment, and disaster is a very deeply entrenched one. Unplanned, ad-hoc, and poor development is directly responsible for a significant part of the vulnerabilities observed in the region. Large-scale industrial developments unmindful of related risks and pollution considerations, rise of high-density settlements with inadequate infrastructure, nonengineered buildings, all have contributed to high levels of risk. The intermediary in this process is often the environment, as can be seen clearly in the case of climate change that has been established to have arisen out of anthropological causes. Thus, environment disaster linkage is crucial to address the development-related problems.

An enhanced understanding of community-based vulnerability and risk that has evolved over the past two decades throws light on the critical links related to disaster impacts. Instead of viewing disasters as time-specific events leading to loss of lives and property, they are now seen increasingly as disruptions in livelihoods that perpetuate poverty and vulnerability unless specific efforts are made to break the cycle. This has lead to far greater importance being attached to issues of access to resources, fulfillment of basic needs, creation of assets, addressing discrimination, and of course reducing shocks and stresses. Such a holistic understanding is highly applicable to the emerging threats of climate-change-related disasters, importantly including the long-term and day-to-day stresses that poor and vulnerable communities have to endure. Such understanding has emerged only due to concerted academic and research efforts by leading institutions. Most of this research has been the result of work by academicians in close partnership with civil society actors and vulnerable communities themselves. Concepts and tools such as town watching, participatory rapid appraisal (PRA, also in variant forms as participatory learning and appraisal or PLA, action-oriented learning or AOL), and community action planning have emerged through such efforts. Hence, an informal and formal network to share the educational product, experiences, and actual implementation can strengthen this synergy. In the education sector, the field-based campus is very important. Therefore, there is a need to go beyond the traditional educational institutions to work with local NGOs, local government, and international organizations.

EVOLUTION OF A UNIVERSITY NETWORK

The Asian University Network of Environment and Disaster Management (AUEDM) is a unique initiative of prominent Asian universities that come together to share knowledge resources related to environment and disaster risk management among themselves and with the larger group of stakeholders working on these issues, in addition to conventional national and thematic boundaries (Shaw et al., 2011). The AUEDM members work in close collaboration to conduct education and research, share findings, and find ways forward in a region that is increasingly at threat due to climate change impacts. It also works closely with governments, international agencies, and corporate and civil society organizations to establish collaborations that eventually lead to resilient communities. It reflects each member's commitment to implementation-oriented education and research in the field of environment and DRR. As of October 2011, the AUEDM has 25 university members from 17 countries and regions in the Asia Pacific area.

The objectives of the AUEDM are:

1. To share and work together (bilaterally or multilaterally) in promoting environment and DRR in higher education (focusing on, but not restricted to, postgraduate education)
2. To collaborate on field-based and policy-oriented research focusing on different aspects of DRR and environmental management
3. To broaden the scope of education and learning in the environment and DRR field through collaboration with diverse stakeholders including NGOs and local governments
4. To document, develop, and disseminate knowledge products in the field of environment and DRR
5. To provide a forum for consultation, information sharing, and cooperation among universities on matters and themes of common interest
6. To enhance recognition of the vital role of universities in implementation-oriented education and research in environment and DRR

The AUEDM has been conceived and pursued by its member organizations based on this common understanding and motivation. It has come about from felt needs that appear to be crucial for the survival of millions of poor and vulnerable men, women, and children living on the margins of society in Asia. The AUEDM members come together for reasons of educational, research, and networking imperatives.

- Educational imperative: To discuss the status and scope of environment and/or disaster management curriculum in the higher studies in each university. Each country has its own perspective. Some countries have full two-years DRR master program. Some universities have some modules of DRR in the postgraduate programs. Therefore, the attempt is not to standardize the program, but to learn and understand the process in DRR. The challenge is how effective the process can be customized into each context.
- Research imperative: To discuss the possibility of climate change adaptation as the key entry point of collaborative research. Each country has a high prevalence of impacts of climate change being borne by the most vulnerable communities. Impacts are most visible on coastal, mountain, urban poor and migrant communities. Since adaptation is a relatively new subject, heavy investments need to be made in research on effective local adaptation as a means for coping with imminent climate change impacts and linked disasters.
- Network imperative: To discuss the establishment of the Asian Universities network. While there are integral commonalities in the vulnerability context and the nature of impacts, the local setting and contextual nuances are highly varied across Asian countries. Networking is the only way to share knowledge and experiences, and to draw lessons based on principles derived from practices. The network is thus expected to go a long way in the development of a regional knowledge base, making it accessible for practitioners, and using it to influence the policy environment.

THE WAY AHEAD

The interface between science and governance requires research that is multidisciplinary, interdisciplinary, and transdisciplinary in approach (Pereira, Pulhin, & Shaw, 2010). Multidisciplinary approaches refer to the study of an issue from the perspective of several disciplines, with minor changes in methodology of individual disciplines (goal-oriented). Interdisciplinary approach involves the transfer of methodology from one discipline to another, at advanced levels leads to changes in epistemology. In transdisciplinary approaches, there is simultaneous integration of knowledge from various disciplines and perspectives, involving various stakeholders. Researchers and practitioners create synergies, drawing on explicit, tacit, and indigenous knowledge as well as inputs from stakeholders to develop various policy (regulatory, economic, voluntary etc.) communication and assessment tools. The goal is knowledge that is policy relevant, which facilitates informed decision-making at various levels (i.e., international, regional institutions, federal, state and local, organizational). Stakeholders include government, industry, investors, NGOs, CBOs, scientific organizations, and professional bodies, among others. Peers in academia are also a stakeholder and play a critical role in quality assurance for the research through the production of reviewed journals.

In order to consolidate the research agenda of AUEDM, the members initially focused on identifying gaps and opportunities for regional research. For this purpose, a series of workshops are conducted. The next phase is focused on strengthening the research agenda by seeking funds for bilateral and multilateral projects. For this purpose, research themes, expertise of AUEDM members, and potential funding agencies need to be identified. Another aspect to be focused on is sharing of experience and capacity building for research. This can be implemented through technical meetings and exchange of researchers including postgraduates. Publication and information dissemination is also an important area of concern. For this purpose, members are strongly encouraged to initiate or support initiatives to publish books, research monographs, or guidelines on topics of common interest. Members are also urged to strongly support the *Asian Journal on Environment and Disaster Management* (AJEDM).

The AUEDM is still at its inception stage. The target of AUEDM is not to increase the number of member universities, but to establish a network with strong commitment and uniqueness. To establish the unique approach, a few specific approaches have been undertaken as follows:

1. First, a strong relationship is established with the Asian Disaster Reduction and Response Network (1991), which is the network of national and local NGOs. ADRRN has a strong presence in the community levels in the Asian countries, and the network members possess several community-based projects on different aspects of DRR as well as postdisaster recovery. These projects can be considered as field laboratories, from where different education and research elements can be obtained. The cooperation of collaboration of local civil society and local university would be extremely important.

2. The second point is the collaboration among different universities. Ideally, a south-south collaboration needs to be established among the universities, where the students can conduct joint projects on a similar cross-boundary topic. This is considered to be effective for solving local

problems collectively from different universities. This will also be a good educational process for the young researchers and graduate students.
3. The third point is the collaboration with the cities network. CITYNET is the local government network in the Asia-Pacific regions, and has a disaster cluster, which focuses on the disaster-related activities in the urban areas. Many of the urban–risk-related research is not utilized into action due to lack of linkages to the city administration. The AUEDM has started strong collaboration with CITYNET to provide training to the local government officers from the member cities, and undertake participatory risk reduction projects in selected cities in the Asia Pacific region. This will ensure the link of the research into practice and policy.

REFERENCES

Chapter 36 of AGENDA 21, on 'Education, Awareness and Training' (1992).
COE. (2005). Council of Europe: Higher education governance between democratic culture, academic aspirations and market forces: Considerations and recommendations, Available at: http://www.coe.int/t/dg4/highereducation/governance/GOV_recommendations_EN.pdf. Accessed on February 2011.
Pereira, J., Pulhin, J., & Shaw, R. (2010). AUEDM: Generating knowledge through policy related research. AUEDM Fourth workshop in Chulalongkorn University, Bangkok, Thailand, 22–24 February, 2010.
Shaw, R., Mallick, F., & Takeuchi Y. (2011). "Essentials of higher education in disaster risk reduction: Prospects and challenges," Disaster Education, 95–113, Emerald Publisher, Bingley, UK.

CHAPTER 5

CORPORATE COMMUNITY INTERFACE: NEW APPROACHES IN DISASTER RISK REDUCTION

Rajib Shaw

INTRODUCTION

When a natural disaster happens, it is sometimes thought that it is the role of the government and national authority department to tackle it. But as seen in virtually every disaster incident, it is the local community that is hit and impacted the most. And unless the community reduces its vulnerability and followed with quick recovery, corporate activities get undoubtedly impacted. Moreover, while occasional large catastrophes such as earthquakes, volcanic eruptions, and cyclones continue to occur in various parts of the world, the rapid increase in disaster loss is due almost to an exponential increase in the occurrence of small- to medium-scale disasters associated with socio-natural hazards such as landslide, flood, drought, and fire.

Facing such a change of the pattern of disaster occurrence, community-based approaches can offer the only alternative for managing and reducing risks in developing regions. In many cases, even though a number of disaster risk reduction projects were undertaken in many parts of the world, once the donor community loses interest, such projects cease to exist. It is the aim of this handbook to promote community-based disaster management where its people do not rely on donor resources but instead continue to build their

Community-Based Disaster Risk Reduction
Community, Environment and Disaster Risk Management, Volume 10, 67–87
Copyright © 2012 by Emerald Group Publishing Limited
ISSN: 2040-7262/doi:10.1108/S2040-7262(2012)0000010011

own capacity. When it comes down to it, initiatives to involve the corporate sector in disaster risk reduction should take into account the local and current reality and not from the perspective of an imported agenda.

One of the major obstacles faced among practitioners in the field of disaster risk reduction is the issue of sustainability of a project. Because most of the disaster risk reduction-related projects are funded by some donor agencies, achieving the sustainability of a project is a constant challenge to them. Those projects that are funded by private sector companies, for example, may face an equal challenge because to assure the sustainability of a project, it requires a long-term planning supported by appropriate institutional and funding structures, which is not the case with the private sector funding scheme. Such conventional corporate sector interventions tended to be one-off interventions rather than strategic plans, which confirm that it is hard to obtain private sector funding for broad-based, collaborative, and long-term initiatives, and this has led to the situation where local capability is not built and thus creating a constant "dependent" syndrome to their incident-based donations.

However, in fact, the sustainability of the community where a company operates should be the utmost priority for the company and its business continuity. Many private companies have already started to raise awareness toward disasters, but they are limited to some internal trainings and workshops, while the company's operations are in fact very dependent on the community and the people's safety and resilience.

Any company that has operations in any part of the world has its roots traced to the communities it belongs to; that is through their employees and their families; and they are the ones who provide stable performance and thus bring profit to the company. While a company gains from the community and its people, at the same time, they acquire their wage through the company. Thus, with this strong bondage, one should not ignore this strong bondage particularly when considering disaster risk reduction activities where it requires persistent and long-term cooperation together to tackle disaster risks that now are a danger virtually to all the corporate companies in the world.

This basic hypothesis is the core of this chapter. The chapter is intended to show some key responsibilities in the corporate sectors, starting from the top-level decision makers, mid-level managers, and employees.

REDEFINING CORPORATE ROLES

The traditional way of thinking toward disaster management is focusing only on the aspect of disaster relief. However, after experiencing the recent decade's exponential increase in the occurrence of small- to medium-scale disasters that are associated with socio-natural hazards such as landslides, floods, droughts, and fires, more attention has started to be given to the interconnection between disaster management and developmental approach. Such transformation in tackling measures is considered to be a paradigm shift, from the relief model to a more holistic developmental model. Moreover, top-down disaster programs sometimes fail to address the specific local needs of vulnerable communities, overlook the potential of local resources and capacities, and may even increase people's vulnerability (Bhatt, 2002). What is important here is to integrate disaster management from the community level; and such community-based disaster management element is the core of the Corporate Community Interface (CCI).

In dealing with such developmental approach, the role of the corporate sector is crucial. Its role is already central to the lives of the developing countries and has the power to make their lives better, leading toward sustainable development. It is particularly true as more and more developing countries move to privatization in such key sectors as water, waste disposal, electric power, and transport. The very scale and intensity of the sustainable development challenge requires heavy reliance on technological solutions, for which the corporate sector is the primary vehicle. Fig. 1 shows the basic links between corporate and community at different levels (Miyaguchi & Shaw, 2007). While the connection is very weak in the headquarter level, it is very strong in the small and medium enterprises, and especially for the corporate sectors, which have different sites.

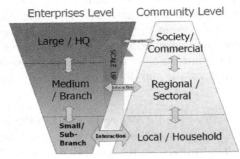

Fig. 1. Corporate Community Interface at Different Levels.

The role of the corporate sector in development can be categorized into three activity types (Nelson, 2002). These are:

- Core business activities: In the workplace, marketplace, and along the supply chain, like production of safe and affordable products, creating jobs, developing human resources, building local businesses, supporting technology development, and establishing physical and institutional infrastructure, etc.
- Social investment and philanthropy activities: This is supporting education, training, environmental, and health projects in local communities, building capacity of community leaders, training local technical specialists, building the voice of local civil society groups, establishing microcredit programs, and small business support, etc.
- Engagement in public policy dialogue and advocacy activities: This includes working with governments by supporting health care and education reform, addressing environmental regulatory policies with government and civil society, engaging in such issues as climate change and biodiversity, etc.

Considering their resources, expertise, network, and political decision power, the corporate sector has the strength and huge potential to become a central axis for community-based disaster management characterized by the developmental approach.

NEEDS AND CONCEPT OF CCI

There are some researches and studies that focus on the role of the corporate sector and their role in disaster risk reduction; however, there are three major challenges recognized in this new field. They are: (1) lack of empirical data; (2) difficulty in assessing the impact; and (3) limited lesson sharing, either domestically or internationally. A development handbook was created in order to contribute to answering such questions. There are several characteristics of the development handbook that are described below.

- *Working closely with corporate sector:* To develop the best user interface with regard to CCI, the handbook has been developed through close cooperation with corporate sector companies. It is the result of the collaborative arrangement that has been established with the corporate sector and accumulated practical know-how from the corporate–community relationship.

– *Wider stakeholder involvement:* A community is not merely made up of its residents, but also of the local government, the education sector, local businesses, and community-based organizations. In developing activities that benefit all of these community sectors, it is necessary to work with them. The handbook helps generating a learning environment where a wide range of stakeholders share and discuss their opinions and types of corporate strategies on disaster risk reduction activities.

– *Field- and time-tested:* All the case studies in the handbook are from the field level in which real voices from corporations and communities are captured. In addition to previous cases of corporate experiences, what is unique in the handbook is that it also includes ongoing experiences between corporations and the community. For this, a number of case studies from the Indian Tsunami-affected communities and other hazard-prone regions are conducted. By learning what is going on currently, the awareness becomes clearer about what more can be done to help the communities.

– *Layer-specific:* Corporate–community relationship is built not only through CEOs and their wives, but also through mid-level managers and all employees and their families. By focusing on each of these persons and hierarchies, the handbook is tailored and has been able to depict a clear picture as to how each of these players can improve their behavior and action.

– *Wide range of audience:* The CCI concept has the potential in shaping the developing countries in terms of economic, societal, and environmental dimensions. International actors from the donor community and development agencies have participated, and by bringing such a wide range of audience, the CCI concept helps to increase the momentum in shaping the next stage of corporate–community relationship in disaster risk reduction and also paves its way toward an effective, long-term approach toward sustainable development.

There are two dimensions of the CCI (Fig. 2), internal and external dimension. Internal dimension of the CCI concept deals with direct safety measures for corporation, including business continuity planning, on-site and off-site planning, and training and awareness building. This dimension is to secure the security of the corporate properties and human resources and other indispensable assets of a company.

The other dimension is that of the external one. This dimension is to do with the external environment beyond the company's direct safety measures.

Fig. 2. Dimensions of CCI.

It includes such elements as corporate social responsibility, public–private partnership, corporate volunteerism, and corporate motivation for community intervention. The concept of CCI is to emphasize both these dimensions. Internal measures must be first acknowledged as the highest priority for a company particularly operating in a disaster-prone region, and sound and sustainable relationship with the external environment is crucially important to secure a corporation's long-term economic activity.

DISASTER ISSUES FOR CEO AND CORPORATE DECISION MAKERS

For the CEO of a company or Director of a business association, their crucial role is to create a vision and indicate future direction for an institution or group of people that you manage or chair. To create a strong vision, they need to consider numerous factors in their daily management, including long-term sustainability of business, positioning in industry, brand management and public relations, and so on. And such elements are precisely related to disaster and its impacts. There are three dimensions of damage and impact from natural disasters that need to be considered; economic, social, and environmental dimensions. Nowadays, there is more and more evidence that these three dimensions are interrelated and influence each other either simultaneously or in the future; therefore, they need to be taken into consideration as a whole and not to be treated separately.

Economic Consequences to Company

First, economic losses to a company are rather intuitive in the sense that natural disaster affects and damages such physical infrastructure as plants and laboratories, commercial equipment, and also intangibles such as insurance coverage and business continuity planning. The indirect effects are those impacting output of goods and services, for example, there will be lower output from factories that have been destroyed or damaged. The magnitude of such economic loss has been increasing over this last decade amounting to as much as $575.2 billion (Munich Re, 2005). And the cost is rising with an increase in the number and severity of weather incidents, and more people are now at risk. There have been a number of studies of business recovery in disaster areas. One says that 40 percent to 60 percent of businesses affected by such disasters never reopened. Of those that do reopen, 40 percent to 60 percent close within two years (Daniel, Holly, Mittler, & Nagy, 2001; FEMA, 2006). Consequences are easily imagined; employees lose their jobs, their homes, and personal possessions, some of which can never be recovered. The magnitude of economic loss and impact from natural disasters should never be underestimated.

Social Consequences to Company

Second, the social dimension of disaster impact and influence is also multifold. There have been a number of efforts made to calculate such a loss in at the social level (ERM, 2005). However, as of now there has not yet been an agreed-upon methodology as to how to exactly to quantify or monetize such loss. Social losses to the corporate sector due to natural disaster are, for example, job loss, displaced households, huge decrease in consumption, business, labor activities, and biggest of all, human casualties. They can all be considered a kind of indirect economic loss to the community, but social impacts remain longer than those of direct economic loss. The main indirect social effects are increase in stress symptoms or increased incidence of depression, disruption in school attendance, disruptions to the social fabric, and loss of social contacts and relationships; direct economic losses could sometimes be remedied by simple insurance coverage and compensation. However, since social dimension is to do with societal structure as a whole, that is, how people behave and lead their life, restoring to the original level may take so much longer time than simple economic recovery. When considering the social dimension, building up the resilience of the community should be paid careful attention to for companies and associations to sustain their operations and activities.

Environmental Consequences to Company

The potential loss is not just confined to the economic and social dimension. The third dimension of the loss is that of environmental and, subsequently, public health. The risks that workers and their families may face from a disaster event are the potential disruption of water supplies and sewage systems, which leads to contamination and further transmission of some diseases. Floods, for example, have been known to prompt outbreaks of leptospirosis in areas where the organism is found in water sources. When water and sewage systems have been disrupted, safe water and food supplies are of great importance in preventing enteric disease transmission. During natural disasters, technological malfunctions may release hazardous materials, such as release of toxic chemicals from a point source displaced by strong winds, seismic motion, or rapidly moving water (PAHO, 2000). The risk for such environmental and health hazard must be lessened as much as possible; it is crucially important to raise awareness of and educate workers and their families in this respect. If things mentioned above are rather direct environmental and health issues, those of indirect issues are related to wide-ranging air pollution. For example, uncontrolled forest fires have many times caused widespread pollution over vast expanses of the world. Natural or manmade disasters resulting in massive structural collapse or dust clouds have caused the release of chemical or biological contaminants, for example, asbestos (Noji, 1996).

Overall, the role of environmental degradation and, more broadly, human modification of the natural environment, plays an important role in floods, agricultural and meteorological droughts, and landslides. Particularly for droughts, water use and water management practices directly affect the preconditions for hydrological drought. In other words, sensitive attention to continuous sound environmental management is a crucial part of disaster risk reduction. Once environmental management is neglected, it is the community and the workers within who will suffer when the disaster does happen. Such environment management prior to the disaster stage is also indispensable to shorten the recovery and rehabilitation process. Without proper environmental management, ecological and physical vulnerability of the community will remain critically low. The important message is that virtually in all operating sites, there is always associated disaster risks and vulnerability (particularly the operation sites are located in the vulnerable community). And the important task for CEOs and Directors is to direct and raise awareness among workers, their family members, as well as surrounding community residents. It is to set the right vision and create an enabling environment for them in order that they can be well prepared and mitigate future impact of disasters, minimizing the otherwise long-lasting, devastating effect of disasters. There are a number of ways that CEOs and Directors can contribute in a concrete way; for example:

- Organizing awareness building workshops or seminars by inviting experts and those who have experienced disasters;
- Involving labor unions to expand the information loop regarding disaster risks and develop mutual dialogues;
- Encouraging its employees and their families to engage in various community events, to forge deeper relationship with community residents, and active information exchange on a frequent basis; and
- Developing and checking company and association's both on-site and off-site planning.

DISASTER-RELATED ISSUES FOR MID-LEVEL MANAGERS

When CEOs or Directors of business association hold an important role as vision creator and direction setter, mid-level managers hold some different responsibilities and roles. Overall, there exist three kinds of differences on which expected roles and important disaster issues for mid-level managers can be drawn (Institute for Business Home Safety (IBHS), 2002).

Decision Making

The first difference is that mid-level managers are there for decision making, as opposed to vision creation done by CEOs and Directors. When a framework of the entire company or association is set and designed by CEO or Director, it is the mid-level manager's job to further shape the framework and make important decisions to further define various works that are associated under such framework. In other words, such decision making is to do with setting up actual planning, regulation, and codes of conducts of a company or association. The first set of important disaster issues that mid-level manager need to take care are thus:

(1) Making sure the right building code is used;
(2) Checking and planning the right land use plan; and
(3) Forming business recovery alliances.

The reason for (1) is to ensure both current and future construction and development meet the best standards for resisting natural hazard impacts. And for this purpose, measures that can be taken are:

(a) Adopting the latest version of the model building codes as the minimum code,
(b) Promoting code enforcement for any new construction and rehabilitation of existing structures; and
(c) Developing recommendations to amend local codes to incorporate disaster safety measures into standards for repair, remodeling, or rehabilitating existing structures.

The reason for (2) is to reduce vulnerability by siting development and redevelopment out of harm's way. And for this purpose, measures that can be taken are such as:

(a) Addressing relevant hazards and the risks they pose in all land use development decisions,
(b) Encouraging adoption of local land use plans that incorporate hazards into decision making,
(c) Documenting changes to local comprehensive planning guidelines for inclusion of natural hazards
(d) Documenting potential loss reduction benefits of land use planning decisions that eliminate or reduce placement of property in harm's way

The reason for (3) is to establish a public–private link to reduce potential impact and losses, as well as speed recovery. And for this purpose, measures that can be taken are such as:

(a) Assessing business recovery needs and institutionalizing a communication framework between the private and public sectors, in cooperation with major business associations, local government associations, national associations, and lifeline and representatives of businesses that form the core of the economy,
(b) Reaching out to businesses to provide tools for loss reduction and recovery,
(c) Developing strategies to measure business actions that decrease vulnerability.

Closer Interaction with Employees and their Families

The second difference is that, since mid-level managers work with the employees on a daily basis, they naturally have closer interaction with employees and their families than with CEOs and Directors. As a manger, s/ he has bigger responsibility of their performance, behavior, as well as their direct safety. In other words, managers are in charge of in-site company issues and all inside company matters. The second set of important disaster issues that mid-level manager need to take care are thus:

(1) Developing response and recovery plans
(2) Developing a system for lifeline protection
(3) Organizing professional training, mock drills, and awareness building
(4) Creating incentives and disincentives

The reason for (1) is to enhance the company and association's ability to respond to a natural disaster event and accelerate recovery. And for this, measures that can be taken are:

(a) Maintaining an emergency response plan,
(b) Developing appropriate interlocal and regional mutual aid agreements for response, recovery, and rebuilding,
(c) Developing a business contingency plan that incorporates priorities of local post-disaster recovery plans,
(d) Providing technical assistance to communities for development of local recovery plans,
(e) Documenting the number of communities that have developed pre-disaster mitigation as well as post-disaster recovery plans, and monitoring their implementation.

The reason for (2) is to minimize damage and disruption of lifeline utilities, such as electricity water, infrastructure, such as roads, and critical facilities, such as hospitals. And for this, measures that can be taken are:

(a) Encouraging public and private owners/operators of lifelines and critical facilities to incorporate natural hazard protection into capital improvement budgets, maintenance and/or rehabilitation, and new construction,
(b) Encouraging publicly and privately owned lifelines, such as utilities, health care facilities, food distribution companies, also to participate in business recovery alliances.

The reason for (3) is to educate their employees and their families, as well as building design and construction professionals, on disaster-resistant behavior, techniques, and standards. And for this, measures that can be taken are:

(a) Supporting mitigation and prevention training and conducting mock drills
(b) Raising awareness among employees and their families by disseminating updated information to employees and their families on disaster and its impact, disaster-resistant technique, and behavior

The reason for (4) is to encourage behavior that reduces vulnerability from natural hazards. And for this, measures that can be taken are:

(a) Identifying the existing incentives and disincentives that may help individuals, businesses, and associations to become more disaster resistant at such a level as regulatory and policy from regional as well as community levels, social values, and financial/economic sectors.

Closer Interaction with Community

The third set of difference from CEO and director is closer relationship with the local community. Relationship with the local community is somewhat transitional from the fact that mid-level managers are more in touch with employees and their families who, undeniably, are an important part of the local community after they return home. Relations with them means relations with the local community. Thus, this is not external relations per se, but encompasses both internal and external relationship, and decision making that is associated with them. The third set of important disaster issues that mid-level manager need to take care are:

(1) Building community-level disaster resistance
(2) Building public awareness and outreach
(3) Protecting childcare centers.

The reason for (1) is to create an environment that encourages local activities to reduce vulnerability. And for this, measures that can be taken are:

(a) Implementing pilot projects and activities in communities that incorporate disaster resistance and resilience into their daily practices,
(b) Coordinating with and initiating local disaster-resistant community activities.

The reason for (2) is to make individuals and organizations aware of their vulnerability and to motivate behavior change to reduce losses. And for this, measures that can be taken are:

(a) Identifying target audiences for awareness messages, with behavior change objectives for each audience,
(b) Developing regular messages for each audience and strategies to deliver the message,
(c) Implementing the public awareness strategy for the identified target audiences, document results, and measure effects.

The reason for (3) is to protect a particularly vulnerable population and to educate parents and employees about disaster safety and loss reduction. And for this, measures that can be taken are:

(a) Working with local, as well as national, childcare agencies with authority and accountability for child health and safety to integrate nonstructural retrofit of childcare centers into their programs
(b) Working with childcare networks, for example, YMCAs and Boys and Girls Clubs, to integrate nonstructural retrofit of childcare centers into their programs
(c) Working with business groups to support nonstructural retrofit of childcare centers, necessary for disaster recovery
(d) Conducting various educational outreach programs on disaster safety for parents.

ACTIVITIES RELATED TO EMPLOYEES

Education, training, and awareness building has a pivotal role in promoting a culture of safety and prevention. Trained managers and aware employees and communities would form the front line against disaster risks. Such individuals would know what procedures to follow and actions to take to reduce the social, economic, and environmental vulnerabilities and to mitigate hazard impact. Industry managers can undertake a number of actions to promote education, training, and for awareness raising in their units and in adjacent communities, as the following:

– Support the integration of disaster risk education in the curriculum of schools and colleges in the vicinity;
– Train the industry staff on firefighting, evacuation, medical first aid;

- Establish and train search and rescue teams in the vicinity of the industry;
- Publish and disseminate awareness materials; for example, posters, brochures, pamphlets, booklets, videos about disaster risks and risk reduction;
- Organize rallies and walks on a periodical basis to raise awareness of communities;
- Hold exhibitions on disaster preparedness;
- Organize seminars and workshops with various community groups about disaster preparedness;
- Face to face meetings and groups discussions can be very effective in thoroughly discussing issues and finding solutions to local disaster risks.

To undertake effective awareness raising activities, it is important to assess the existing knowledge of local communities about disasters and risks and identify their information needs regarding disaster preparedness. This can be done through surveys or meetings with community groups. It is also essential to identify locally relevant channels of communication that are easily accessible to the majority of the community. Locally influential communicators may include teachers, priests, imams, pundits, sportsmen who can influence people's opinion. Get help from these communicators in order to influence people's opinion.

TYPES OF INTERVENTIONS OF CORPORATE SECTORS

Although we have not seen quite a large number of corporate practices in the field of disaster management and risk reduction, its number has been growing since 1990. Because it is important to be aware of the overall categories of these practices and get to know which kind of practice that a company or business association is or would like to be involved in. By categorizing the types of corporate practices, there seems to exist four kinds of organizations (Miyaguchi & Shaw, 2009). All four types can be drawn as in the figure below (Fig. 3). The vertical axis represents the relevance to the core business, that is, the degree to do with making money and/or investment. The horizontal axis represents the degree of "activeness," that is, whether activities are jointly implemented (active involvement), as opposed to being contracted out (non-active involvement).

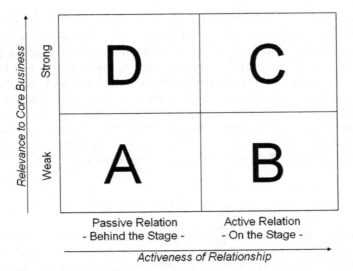

Fig. 3. Types of Interventions of Corporate Sectors

Type A: Resource Distribution

The first category is about giving out a company or association's resources –
be it monetary assets, technical assistance, or human resources. Within this
category, there is a subcategory of either "monetary contribution" or "in-
kind contribution." The monetary resource give-out is simply known as
donation and whatever the theme to which the donation is given. The
resource provider considers how relevant the theme is to them and decides
whether such donation is worthwhile from their mission or their corporate/
association image. There are a number of companies and associations that
pledged millions of dollars for post-disaster and humanitarian relief. The
biggest of its magnitude was seen in the event of Indian Ocean Tsunami
where reportedly as much as $5 billion was donated by private individuals
and companies (*The Economist*, 2005).

The other subcategory is known also as "in-kind contribution," through
such forms as donating equipment, physical infrastructure, sending
employee volunteers, and human technical assistance. Compared to simple
money donation, in-kind contribution happens only if the opportunity is
considered to be more relevant to the company or association's core asset.

Examples are such as providing medical products (by pharmaceutical companies), building materials (by construction companies), telecommunication equipment and services (by cell and telecommunication companies), logistical and shipping services (by logistics companies), and so on.

The characteristics of this type A are that their resource distribution is rather reactive than proactive, and since it is strictly about giving out resources, it does not generate much of business revenues from it; type A interventions are done mostly with the purpose of image enhancing or public relation purpose, as so often witnessed by mainstream activities under the concept of "corporate social responsibilities (CSR)."

Type B: Network/Cooperative

The second category is about formulation of some kind of cooperative or group of like-minded companies and/or associations for disaster management. The primary purpose is to raise awareness, exchange information, and forge strong mutual relationships among participating members to minimize disaster impact and maximize the impact of disaster relief. This category is further divided into two subcategories; either "loose/diverse" or "focused/professional." The "loose/diverse" type of network building is to build an informal environment where a diverse range of individuals and stakeholders are expected to participate and exchange information regarding disaster and its risks. The purpose of such informal, but extensive network is to raise general awareness, lowers transaction cost which might otherwise obstruct or impede during possible disaster event. It is to establish a common ground whereby a wide range of stakeholders will have opportunities to coordinate with others in case of emergencies. The characteristic of this kind, however, is that participating groups or individuals do not necessarily pledge to actively involve themselves in minimizing the impact by, for example, utilizing their professional resources. Loose associations among local municipalities, together with private companies, are a prime example of this kind.

The other subcategory is of focused/professional type. It is about a group of companies and members of a certain kind of business association in formulating a cooperative which is a group of companies with the same professional theme and interest. The main difference of this subcategory from the "loose/diverse" type is that they are actually committed to contributing their resources before and after emergencies. Since the members gather under a specific thematic focus, they are expected to contribute their professional resources, such as specific business knowledge and know-how, rather than just monetary contribution.

This subcategory is exemplified by an organization established by a group of construction companies that are dedicated to coordinating among member companies to effectively distribute their professional staff and resources before and after emergent incidences. Since this second subcategory requires members to invest their resources, including time and human resources, on a continuous basis, it is less common than "loose/diverse" types of association.

Type C: Core Business

The third type has to do with relevance to core business activities. It is whether activities before and after emergency are precisely what a company does for their usual business operation. It is about the activities that cover a range of their day-to-day business operations, and not just one-off or one-point intervention. For example, to illustrate the point, in the case of give-away of medicines by pharmaceutical companies, even though their products are being distributed and thus with relevance to their core business, such give-away is only one-off donation in case of emergency; thus their activities are not considered in the core business type, but categorized rather as type A: resource distribution. This category is equally divided into two subcategories: one is "philanthropic/simple cooperation" and the other is "investment/profiting making."

The philanthropic/simple cooperation activities are often demonstrated by a partnership between humanitarian relief organization and a logistic/delivery company. What is characteristic is that a series of a company's daily business operations are fully integrated with that of a humanitarian organization where, for example, a logistic company deals with controlling incoming requests, stocktaking and management of inventory, tracking information control, international administrative support, and other daily business operations. Such partnerships are seen with such humanitarian aid organization as World Food Program, UNHCR, and International Red Cross. On the other hand, one characteristic of this subcategory is that the participating company does not get profit or revenue from cooperating with such an organization, at least in the short term. All is done purely by pro-bono basis.

The other subcategory of core business type of activities is "investment/profit making." With relevance to the core business operations, this type of practice is more progressively business oriented. It is often characterized by an inflow of investment in disaster-hit areas by construction or building equipment companies; in this case, while helping the local community revitalize their investment, their activities can be somewhat, if not totally, business oriented in that it can expect the return on investment and grasp future business opportunities through establishing a firm relationship with various local stakeholders. Since this kind of activity can be seen as strictly business, it is often exercised unilaterally by one or a group of companies sharing the same interest.

Type D: Research Work

The fourth category is supporting and funding a series of research activities. It is a soft type of contribution when it comes to disaster management field. The main purpose is to foster deeper understandings of disaster-related risk and know-how of management and also to raise awareness among the public and professional community over such an issue. One subcategory of this type is "relevance to business." If the research that is funded by the company studies the topic in which the company operates, of course, it has direct relevance to business. For example, we have seen a number of insurance companies that have funded researches on disaster mitigation and prevention, simply because they are the ones who are affected the most – it is reported that the insured losses are as much as $176.0 billion from 1995–2005, which have skyrocketed from $7.1 billion just in the 60s globally (Munich Re, 2004) – and simply put, insurance in itself is a form of disaster preparedness. Insurance and reinsurance companies are the principal sponsors of disaster reduction, especially of research work. Such sponsorship, however, can be put as an unequal partnership because the sponsor controls the funds and therefore the agenda and scope of the research.

The other subcategory is "non-relevance to business," the opposite one from the former subcategory. It is often seen by a foundation of a big, multinational corporation. Its purpose is broader than the insurance company sponsorship in that the research work topic can vary, as long as such work is associated with a set of themes on which the foundation puts emphasis, for example, peace building, conflict resolution, and sustainable development. Although such sponsorship to research work contributes significantly to academic research and awareness raising, in both of the subcategories described above, the common trait is that a company's involvement is rather passive. They merely fund and sponsor research work and does not get involved with implementation dimension.

CATEGORIZATION OF LOCAL RESOURCES IN COMMUNITY LEVEL

Local communities in vicinity of an industrial unit may have a range of resources to reduce risks, and prepare for and respond to catastrophic events, when they occur. It is imperative for middle-level industry managers to explore the extent of resources available locally with communities and build partnerships with local communities to benefit from local resources for implementation of industry and community-level risk reduction activities. A brief overview of resources that might be available in a community is given below.

Knowledge of past disasters, vulnerabilities, and capacities: Through their direct past experience, the local communities may have accumulated wealth of knowledge about various types of hazards that occur in the area, their seasonality, frequency, and intensity, and they would have knowledge of social groups who suffered the most. They would also know the strategies that were deployed by local people and government to deal with disaster situations. This knowledge of local communities can be utilized in a beneficial manner through the participation of communities in risk assessment and risk reduction planning processes.

Knowledge of preparedness and mitigation actions: Communities would also have developed coping mechanisms to reduce the impact of disasters through mitigation activities and preparedness measures. The industry management can benefit from experiences of communities in mitigating disaster risks, and preparing for them. This could be done by involving communities in planning and implementation processes and systems. Some coping strategies and institutional mechanisms developed by local communities could also be deployed to deal with industrial hazards as well; for example, developing a local early warning system,

Community organizations and volunteers: Communities frequently confronted with disasters tend to develop organizational and volunteering mechanisms in order to deal with disaster risks. Such organizations might be comprised of locally elected committees, local youth volunteers (e.g., Red Cross volunteers), women's associations, panchayats (in India), religious organizations, or mass associations; for example, women's unions, elderly unions, youth unions in Cambodia, Lao, and Viet Nam. Industry management should develop partnerships with such community groups and organizations to mobilize local resources for risk reduction and disaster preparedness.

Technical experts: Safer construction experts in the form of masons/ engineers, medical workers to provide first aid after disasters, firefighters, and boat makers, may be available in disaster-prone communities. There might also be experts who may have knowledge on hazard resistant sources of livelihoods; e.g,. drought resistant crops etc. It would be important to develop relations with such experts and their organizations to benefit from their services for disaster risk reduction, preparedness, and response.

Physical resources and equipment/tools: Communities also may have a number of physical resources and equipment and tools that could be deployed for disaster risk reduction and preparedness. For example school building, temple, mosque, or church can be used as evacuation centers after disasters. Such institutions could also be used for awareness raising, education, and activities to organize communities. Other community resources related to disaster preparedness and response may include boats and vehicles that could be used for evacuation. It would be essential to understand about the ownership of these resources. Resources owned by certain families and individuals may not be available for the benefit of the general community. Resources that are common property might be more easily available. However, it would be important to understand the management regimes of such resources as well.

Local natural resources (bamboo, forests, water, land, etc.): A range of natural resources may exist within communities that could be utilized for disaster risk reduction and preparedness activities; for example, forests, plant species like bamboo, lakes or water channels, etc. Common property resources may be available relatively easily for common use. Individually owned resources will have to be negotiated for their utilization for common interest, either through buying them or paying rental costs, etc.

REFERENCES

Daniel, J. A., Holly, J. N., Mittler, E., & Nagy, R. (2001). *Organizations at risk: What happens when small businesses and not-for-profits encounter natural disasters.* Fairfax, VA: Public Entity Risk Institute.

Bhatt, R. M. (2002). *Corporate social responsibility and natural disaster reduction: Local overview of Gujarat* (67 pp.). Ahmedabad, India: Disaster mitigation institute.

Environmental Resources Management. (2005). *Natural disasters and disaster risk reduction measures: A desk review of costs and benefits.* Department for International Development. UK and Yoshiaki Kawata and Yuka Karatani. 2002. *Study on indirect loss estimation of the social value due to heavy casualties.* Kyoto University.

Federal Emergency Management Agency (FEMA). (2006). Retrieved from http://www.fema. gov. Accessed on October 2011.

Institute for Business & Home Safety (2002). *Showcase state model for natural disaster resistance and resilience: A guidebook for loss reduction partnership* (34 pp.). Florida, USA.

Miyaguchi, T., & Shaw, R. (2007). Corporate community interface in disaster management: A preliminary study from Mumbai, India. *In Risk Management, 9,* 209–222.

Miyaguchi, T., & Shaw, R. (2009). Corporate sectors and disaster risk reduction: A community focused approach. In R. Shaw & R. Krishnamurthy (Eds.), *Disaster management: Global challenges and local solutions* (pp. 567–585). Hyderabad, India: University Press.

Munich, Re. (2004). *Topics geo. Annual review: Natural catastrophes* 2004 (60 pp.). Munchen, Germany.

Munich Re. (2005). *Topics geo. Annual review: Natural catastrophes* 2005 (52 pp.). Munchen, Germany.

Nelson, J. (2002). *Building partnerships: Cooperation between the United Nations system and the private sector.* New York, NY: United Nations.

Noji, E. K. (Ed.). (1996). *The public health consequences of disasters.* New York, NY: Oxford University Press.

Pan American Health Organization. (2000). *Natural disasters: Protecting the public's health.* Washington, DC: PAHO.

The Economist. (2005). Relief but little rebuilding. *The Economist.* Retrieved from http://www.economist.com/PrinterFriendly.cfm?story_id=5327849

PART II
ASIAN EXPERIENCES

CHAPTER 6

BANGLADESH EXPERIENCES OF COMMUNITY-BASED DISASTER RISK REDUCTION

Umma Habiba and Rajib Shaw

INTRODUCTION

According to the Ministry of Environment and Forest (MoEF) (2008), Bangladesh is the most vulnerable country to natural hazards and disasters due to its geography, high population density, and poverty. The country is exposed to a variety of recurring natural hazards such as floods, cyclones, droughts, earthquakes, and riverbank erosion (Ministry of Food and Disaster Management (MoFDM), 2007). Furthermore, Harmeling (2010) mentioned that Bangladesh heads the list of countries most at risk for floods. Bangladesh has suffered from 93 large-scale natural disasters in the period from 1991 to 2000 that killed 0.2 million people and caused loss of property valued at about 59 billion dollars in the agriculture and infrastructure sectors (Climate Change Cell, Ministry of Environment and Forest, Bangladesh, 2009). Fig. 1 represents different natural hazard-prone areas of Bangladesh.

Natural hazards and disasters are very common in Bangladesh. But over four decades ago, local people were not as aware of these catastrophic events and they were not well educated about the likelihood of disaster. Currently, people are increasing information and enhancing their capacity to prepare and respond to disasters with the help of different organizations. This is only

Community-Based Disaster Risk Reduction
Community, Environment and Disaster Risk Management, Volume 10, 91–111
ISSN: 2040-7262/doi:10.1108/S2040-7262(2012)0000010012

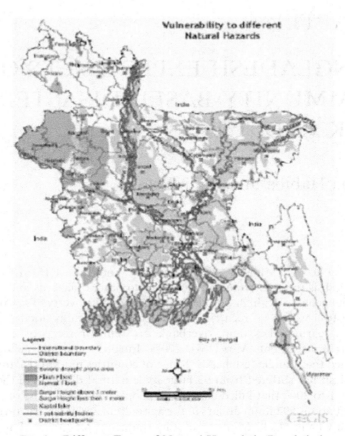

Fig. 1. Different Types of Natural Hazards in Bangladesh.
Source: CEGIS.

possible today due to the induction of Community Based Disaster Risk
Reduction (CBDRR). The concept of CBDRR is relatively new. It is a
multi-disciplinary agenda for community development; it is a different
paradigm (long-term) that builds on the intrinsic relationship between
disasters and development. In Bangladesh, it evolved in the aftermath of the
most destructive cyclone, named Bhola, in 1970. This cyclone caused
massive destruction as well as the deaths of 500,000 people. But the
introduction of the Cyclone Preparedness Program (CPP) in the coastal
districts in 1972 drastically reduced the casualty rate because of its strong

consideration for the people in the community. For instance, in a 1991 cyclone, 150,000 people lost their lives, but in the 2007 cyclone Sidr, only 3,363 people lost their lives. The CPP is responsible for activities such as the formation of village disaster preparedness committees, development of an extensive awareness-raising campaign, training of the community in disaster preparedness, community first aid, and cyclone warning signals, shelter maintenance, and implementation of disaster preparedness measures such as installation of drinking water and food shortage facilities and construction of poultry sheds (Yodmani, 2001).

Among south Asian countries, Bangladesh was the first to start the process of CBDRR through CPP. On the other hand, India started its disaster risk management (DRM) in 2002. Other south Asian countries have started CBDRR recently. In almost all countries, CBDRR has been taken up largely through the initiative of international/national NGOs and in some countries in collaboration with the national governments. In this regard, CPP in Bangladesh was started by the International Federation of Red Cross and Red Crescent Societies (IFRC) while India, Afghanistan, Bhutan, and Nepal have started DRM by United Nations Develop Programme (UNDP).

In every disaster, it is the people at the community or village level who suffer the most adverse effects. The poor within the communities especially face this disaster impact and they are the front-line responders who react spontaneously pre-, during, and post- disaster events. In this regard, CBDRR provides an opportunity to dovetail indigenous knowledge for disaster risk reduction and settle strategy to mainstream risk reduction at the community level. Therefore, current community-based disaster risk reduction is increasingly being recognized by NGO, governmental agencies, and international organizations and it is emerging as a key response to adapting to these natural disasters. Based on the above discussion, this chapter intends to explore major disasters in Bangladesh and their impact. Then the focus shifts to how the community develops innovative approaches to deal with these disaster risks, how the CBDRR approach can be institutionalized, and finally, concluding remarks.

OVERVIEW OF THE MOST SEVERE DISASTERS IN BANGLADESH

Bangladesh is highly susceptible to different climatic disasters and therefore, the impact of these climatic events will likely be the most critical for the lives and livelihood of people in this country. This section tries to highlight the most severe disasters in Bangladesh that frequently take place and how these disasters have an effect on different sectors of Bangladesh in different manners.

Floods

Bangladesh is well known as being the world's most flood-prone country. Regular river floods affect 20% of the country, increasing up to 68% in extreme years. Approximately 37%, 43%, 52%, and 68% of the country is inundated with floods of return periods of 10, 20, 50, and 100 years, accordingly (National Plan for Disaster Management, 2010). On the contrary, Mirza (2002) mentioned that one-fifth of the country is flooded every year and in extreme years, two-thirds of the country can be inundated. Flood is a regular phenomenon in Bangladesh and tends to occur between April and May and September and November (NAPA, 2005). During the last 50 years, at least 7 mega-floods occurred, affecting about 35% to 75% of the land area. Table 1 gives a summary of the adverse effects of the most

Table 1.   Adverse Impacts of Major Floods in Bangladesh During the Last 50 Years.

Events	Impact
1954 floods	Affected 55% of the country
1974 floods	Moderately severe, over 2,000 deaths, affected 58% of the country, followed by famine with over 30,000 deaths
1984 floods	Inundated 52,520 sq. km, estimated damage US$1.0 billion
1987 floods	Inundated over 50,000 sq. km, estimated damage US$1.0 billion, 2,055 deaths
1988 floods	Inundated 61% of the country, estimated damage US$1.2 billion, rendered more than 45 million homeless, between 2,000 and 6,500 deaths
1998 floods	Inundated nearly 100,000 sq. km, estimated damage US$2.8 billion, rendered more than 30 million homeless, damaged 500,000 homes, heavy loss of infrastructure, 1,100 deaths
2004 floods	Inundated 38% of the country, estimated damage US$1 billion, affected nearly 3.8 million people, 700 deaths
2007 floods	Inundated 32,000 sq. km, estimated damage over US$1.0 billion, over 85,000 houses destroyed and almost 1 million damaged, approximately 1.2 million acres of crops destroyed or partially damaged, 649 deaths

Source: Cited in Rahman et al. (2008).

recent extreme floods in Bangladesh. During this period, major flooding was recorded in 1988, 1998, 2004, and 2007. These different intensities of floods caused massive destruction and serious damage to agriculture along with infrastructure such as houses, roads, bridges, schools, and rural health centers, thereby affecting basic shelter for people. The floods also affected communication and education systems, and health care provision as well.

Cyclones

Bangladesh regularly suffers another serious disaster, tropical cyclones, that often with storm surges. Due to its funnel-shaped coast, Bangladesh normally becomes the landing ground and breeding place of catastrophic cyclones that form in the Bay of Bengal. These cyclonic storms generally appear in the Bay of Bengal in the months of April and May and the mid-September to mid-December periods. From 1797 to 1998, 67 major cyclone storms and storm surges have been reported in Bangladesh. A list of devastating cyclones is given in Table 2. In this table, it is revealed that the most deadly cyclone hits in Bangladesh were on November 13, 1970 and April 29, 1991 causing causalities of at least 500,000 people and 150,000 people, respectively. Furthermore, most recently the cyclone Sidr struck Bangladesh on November 15, 2007 and killed and injured over 3,363 and 55,282 people, respectively. It is also reported that 563,877 houses were totally destroyed and 955,065 houses were partially damaged. It was also reported that 186,883 hectares of crop areas were fully and 498,645 hectare areas partly damaged by Sidr (National Plan for Disaster Management, 2010).

Droughts

Another insidious onset disaster, drought, takes place in Bangladesh more frequently than in the past because of climate change (National Drought Mitigation Center (NDMC), 2006). Every year Bangladesh experiences a dry period for seven months, from November to May, when rainfall is normally low. During the last 50 years, Bangladesh experienced drought conditions about 20 times. Of these, the droughts in 1971, 1973, 1978, 1979, 1981, 1982, 1992, 1994, 1995, 2000, and 2006 were particularly severe.

Moreover, depending on the intensity, the drought caused annual damage of 2.32 million hectares of cultivable T-aman (rice variety) in kharif season and 2.2 million hectares of rabi crops in rabi season (the three cropping

Table 2. Major Cyclones that Hit Bangladeshi Coast.

Date		Maximum Wind Speed (km/h)	Storm Surge Height (m)	Casualty
May 11–12	1965	162	3.7	19,279 people
December 14–15	1965	210	4.7–6.1	873 people
October 1	1966	146	4.7–9.1	850 people, 65,000 cattle
November 13	1970	222	10.6	500,000 people
May 24–25	1985	100	3.0–4.6	11,069 people, 135,033 cattle
November 24–30	1988	162	4.5	5,708 people, 65,000 cattle
April 29–30	1991	225	5.0–8.0	150,000 people, 70,000 cattle
November 21–25	1995	210	–	650 people, 17,000 cattle
May 16–19	1997	225	3.05	126 people
November 15	2007	250	5.0	3,363 people
May 25	2009	120	3	121 people

Source: List of Bangladesh tropical cyclone – Wikipedia, the free encyclopedia, accessed on January 25, 2011.

seasons in Bangladesh are locally known as pre-kharif, kharif, and rabi) (Climate Change Cell of Bangladesh, 2009) (Table 3). In addition, Rahman et al. (2008) highlighted that the recent 2006 drought caused 25% to 30% crop reduction in the northwestern part of Bangladesh. Therefore, it curtailed the country's food chain, food stock, and agro-based production systems.

Apart from the above discussion, it is clear that Bangladesh is the center for a variety of climatic disasters that frequently take place in this country almost every year. Therefore, it is of the utmost importance to take immediate action against these recurring disasters. Although climatic disaster cannot be prevented, damage can be mitigated through proper disaster risk reduction planning and active participation of different levels such as from the local level to national levels in a country. In this regard, community-based disaster risk reduction will be a landmark that can successfully reduce the impact experienced by these disasters. The next section attempts to address different stakeholders of Bangladesh involved in the disaster risk reduction process.

Table 3. Impacts of Annual Drought in Bangladesh.

Classification of Drought	Area Affected (Million Hectare)		
	Rabi season (November–February)	Pre-kharif season (March–June)	Kharif season (July–October)
Very severe	0.446	0.403	0.344
Severe	1.71	1.15	0.74
Moderate	2.95	4.76	3.17
Slight	4.21	4.09	2.9
No drought	3.17	2.09	0.68
No T-aman	–	–	4.71

Source: Climate Change Cell (2009).

MAJOR STAKEHOLDERS RELATED TO DISASTER RISK REDUCTION IN BANGLADESH

At the National Level

The concept of developing national preparedness toward disasters evolved after the devastating flood in 1988 and the cyclone in 1991. At these times, it was evident that disaster preparedness could be integrated into the socio-economic development process at household, community, regional, and national level; thus it will give the community long-term capability to mitigate disaster risk and vulnerability. This idea also helped the Government of Bangladesh (GoB) to undertake action against disaster preparedness.

Since then, the Bangladesh government has established the MoFDM in 1993, changing the Ministry of Relief and Rehabilitation. This ministry is responsible for the formulation and implementation of a national DRM policy along with co-ordination of all disaster management activities within the country. Additionally, the Disaster Management Bureau (DMB) and Directorate of Relief and Rehabilitation (DRR) also belong to this ministry. DMB coordinates the DRM efforts of government institutions and NGOs, and provides professional and technical support to all levels of DRM policy and practice in Bangladesh including "facilitating improved information collection and warning dissemination". Moreover, DMB receives early warning messages from Bangladesh Meteorological Department (BMD) and Flood Forecast and Warning Centre (FFWC) by fax and email, and disseminates information also by fax and email through District Relief and Rehabilitation Officers (DRROs) under Deputy Commissioners (DC) in 64 districts of Bangladesh. The information also starts flowing down through other various levels up to field levels (i.e., District Disaster Management Committee (DDMC), Upazila Disaster Management Committee (UzDMC), Union Disaster Management Committee (UDMC)) under the framework of disaster management guidebook, that is, Standing Orders on disaster.

Furthermore, to increase resilience at the national to community level and to reduce damage and losses from natural disasters and the impacts of climate change, the Comprehensive Disaster Management Program (CDMP) was launched in 2003 to assist MoFDM in achieving government vision, mission, and objectives. The program encompasses all aspects of risk management with an objective to strengthen the capacity of Bangladesh disaster management system. Adding to this, Climate Change Cell under MoEF was designed to address CCA issues in disaster management. Beside these, the Ministry of Water Resources (MoWR) implemented various development works such as flood control and drainage (FCD), riverbank erosion control, and delta development through Bangladesh Water Development Board (BWDB), Water Resources Planning Organization (WARPO), and the River Research Institute. On the other hand, the Local Government Engineering Department (LGED) under the Ministry of Local Government also is constructing and maintaining cyclone and flood shelters in the affected area along with Fire Service and Civil Defense search-and-rescue activities after earthquakes.

United Nations and International Donors

Several international donors such as UNDP, Department for International Development (DFID), EU, and World Bank showed their commitment to initiatives of the GoB with regard to disaster reduction. The IFRC is involved in preparedness activities at the community level through Bangladesh Red Crescent Society (BDRCS) which is responsible for disseminating cyclone warnings to the coastal area's people who are at risk for cyclones through a network of more than 40,000 volunteers. USAID works with a number of NGOs and universities to support institutional capacity building activities as well as community disaster response simulation drills. AusAid integrates DRR in all their aid programs and supports advocacy and programming for disaster risk. Other donor organizations like DANIDA, SIDA, CIDA, and countries like Saudi Arabia as well as other Arab countries and private donors have earmarked substantial funds for the construction of multi-purpose disaster shelters in Bangladesh with the collaboration of the GoB.

International and National NGOs

Several international NGOs such as Oxfam, Care International, Concern Universal-Bangladesh, Action Aid, as well as Bangladesh Rural Advancement Committee (BRAC), Bangladesh Disaster Preparedness Centre (BDPC), Center for Natural Resource Studies (CNRS) and other as national NGOs are focusing on pre-disaster awareness and preparedness at the household and community levels. These activities mainly include prevention, mitigation, preparedness, responses, recovery, and rehabilitation work. Some local NGOs such as Caritas, Care Bangladesh, World Vision, BRAC, and others also involved in the construction of cyclone and flood shelters (SDC, 2010). For instance, Concern Universal-Bangladesh has initiated and implemented a Community-Based Disaster Preparedness project through radio spots with the help of Dhaka Ahsania Mission. The use of radio spots is a concept that gives information to the people by using this medium and reducing the losses of despised and endangered vulnerable people in disaster-prone areas. The radio set and megaphone is placed in Gonokendro, union parishad and school where people from a selected area can listen to weather-related information and protect themselves by using disaster preparedness, prevention, and warning signs in extreme weather situations. Radio spot managers are community volunteers with a specific mandate to disseminate and act upon early warning system (Concern Universal-Bangladesh, 2011). Another example is from a local NGO named Care Bangladesh in which they implemented a number of community-based initiatives. They utilized food-for-work to help communities with community "flood proofing" after the 1998 floods. This included the raising of house plinths to a 5-year flood level, schools and community centers to a 20-year flood level, raising hand pumps, and building foot paths as well as village-level saving schemes that are used as a safety net in a disaster to meet immediate relief needs.

Private Sector

The private sector is increasingly taking a role in Disaster Risk Reduction. Grammen Phone (private) and Teletalk, two mobile companies in Bangladesh, have started to make disaster early warning alerts by sending message to their subscribers in two districts, Shirajgang (flood prone) and Cox's Bazar (cyclone prone). They intend to expand it across the country in a later stage.

Academia

Recently BRAC University has started a post-graduate Disaster Management course. Other universities all over Bangladesh such as Dhaka University and the International Center for Climate Change and Development (ICCCAD) have incorporated Disaster Risk Reduction and Climate Change issues in their curricula. The UNDP Comprehensive Disaster Management Project (CDMP) also has initiated a few disaster risk reduction programs in selected universities in Bangladesh. Besides this, a number of experienced and worldwide recognized scientists are actively involved in participating research activities in DRR. Among them, the Bangladesh Center for Advanced studies (BCAS) and the Center for Environmental and Geographic Information Services (CEGIS) are doing significant research related to disaster risk in Bangladesh.

Media

Media also play a key role for disseminating early warnings all over the country. Due to the low literacy rate in Bangladesh, most of the people preferred electronic media rather than print media. Therefore, Bangladeshi television (TV) and Bangladeshi radio are the government's sole private

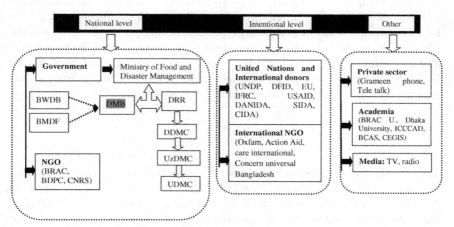

Fig. 2. A Flow Diagram Shows Various Stakeholders Involved in Disaster Risk Reduction in Bangladesh.

channel that only receive early warning messages from BMD and FFWC, and broadcasts this information throughout the country. Fig. 2 indicates the various stakeholders' involvement in different levels through which they are performing disaster risk reduction activities in Bangladesh.

INNOVATIVE APPROACHES FOR CBDRR

Bangladesh has a long history of community-based approaches for disaster risk reduction. As climate-related disasters frequently happen in Bangladesh, the rural communities have built up a variety of innovative approaches in collaboration with different international as well as governmental organization or NGOs, through which they hope to survive these disaster events. For example, a floating garden is one of the good practices that is extensively used in southern Bangladesh to improve the people's food resources during flooding periods. Similarly, cyclone preparedness programs and rainwater harvest are significant because these community-based approaches help the community sustain their livelihood successfully during cyclones and droughts, respectively. Therefore, this section seeks to give an idea of how these approaches are efficiently carried out by the community and also by organizations in different areas to cope with these devastating disasters.

Floating Gardens

Problem
The south central part of Bangladesh is prone to extended flooding and waterlogging due to both high tides and river water. This area is generally flat and land elevation is below the mean sea level. Furthermore, erratic rainfall behavior and temperature as a consequence of climate change affects agriculture, homestead vegetable cultivation, fish culture, and hampers livelihood activities of this region.

Stakeholders
The floating garden is mainly practiced in some communities of the southern wetlands of Bangladesh. But in the recent years, it has generated huge interest in the agricultural field and also it has had a positive contribution in improving livelihood and food security, so that it is now expanding into northern Bangladesh by the Practical Action, Strengthening Household Abilities for Responding to Development Opportunities (SHOUHARDO)

program by CARE Bangladesh in northeastern Bangladesh, Research on Innovative and Strategic Policy Options (RIPSO) by APEIS in southern Bangladesh. The National Action Program for Adaptation (NAPA) has listed floating garden as one of the 15 major projects, but as yet no pragmatic steps have been taken to implement it.

Innovative Approach
To overcome this problem, the community has developed and established a sustainable community-based floating garden that helps to protect them from the devastating effects of floodwater and allows farmers to grow crops in a floating platform. According to need, people of different parts of Bangladesh have adopted, modified, and named this practice differently such as *baira, boor, dhap, gathua, gatoni, geto, kandi,* and *vasoman chash* and floating agriculture (Asia-Pacific Environmental Innovation Strategies (APEIS) 2004; Irfanullah, Adrika, Ghani, & Khan, 2007; Islam & Atkins, 2007).

Usually people of this region use bamboo to make the floating base which helps avoid damage due to wave action or drifting (Fig. 3). Various local materials are used to construct the floating layer. The most commonly used material is water hyacinth that is piled and then covered with soil and cow dung to form a seed bed for planting different types of crops. The main

Fig. 3. Floating Garden
Source: Aarjan Dixit (2011).

crops cultivated in the floating gardens are okra, cucumber, bitter gourd, tomato, cauliflower, chili, amaranth, taro, pumpkin, turmeric, and others. The community practices this floating cultivation during the winter season as well as the monsoon season (mainly June to August).

Lessons Learned

- Floating gardens provide an alternative option to grow vegetables on the floating bed by reducing pressure on the arable land or by turning the flooded and waterlogged areas into productive lands.
- It generates income for the rural poor, and also leads to significant and substantial increase of food production in that rural area.
- It provides a proper gender balance by involving men and women in maintaining these activities.
- As it is mostly practiced in the coastal area of Bangladesh, this proven approach should be scaled up by different organizations and also by governmental institutions to adapt it to the country level whenever it will be applicable.

Volunteer activities in the cyclone preparedness program

Problem
Cyclones cause more devastation and death in Bangladesh than any other disaster, so it is a top priority in Bangladesh that needs to be addressed properly. The cyclones of 1965, 1970, 1985, and 1991 that hit the coast affected people in 32 regions and caused massive destruction.

Stakeholders
After the devastating cyclone of 1970, the UN General Assembly requested the League of Red Cross (now known as International Federation) undertake the leading role for pre-disaster planning in Bangladesh. Afterward, the CPP of the BDRCS was introduced in Bangladesh in 1972. Now, the CPP is jointly operated by the Red Crescent Society and the Ministry of Disaster Management and Relief in Bangladesh. It carries out disaster preparedness activities with 11 million people residing in the 710 km long coastal areas through an efficient volunteer network. Moreover, the designated warning signal for approaching cyclone comes from the BMD and transmits this information from a zonal office to upazila level offices through high frequency (HF) radios. The upazila office further passes this information to

village unions and lower levels through very high frequency (VHF) radios. At present, CPP extends their activities in 32 upazilas (sub-district) in 274 unions (village level) divided into 2,845 units.

Innovative Approach

The CPP of the BDRCS, together with its volunteers, play a leading and crucial role in disseminating the cyclone warning, evacuation, rescue, first aid, and emergency relief works to the grass-roots level in the coastal and offshore areas, with the people under the supervision of local administration. The volunteers are the backbone of CPP and are responsible for alerting people by megaphones and microphones, house-to-house contact, raising danger signal flags, rescue of survivors, first aid to the wounded, post-cyclone security measures, distribution of relief materials, and surveying damages caused by cyclones and reporting these to their local headquarters (Fig. 4).

Additionally, the CPP undertakes other awareness programs such as public awareness programs, cyclonic drills, publicity campaigns, radio and TV programs, posters, leaflets and booklets, and the staging of plays for rural communities for better preparedness activities, leading to successful implementation.

Lessons Learned

- The CPP is a unique, remarkable, and successful example of CBDRR in this sub-continent. This shows the dedication of protecting the population along with building capacity for community activities.
- Volunteers are the backbone of CPP; they exhibit a high level of commitment for their program and readiness to meet the community requirements for better disaster preparedness.
- Volunteers come from the community and remain in the community.
- The CPP involves the community with full participation, increased awareness of the community, in order to have a practical approach for reducing risks and losses.
- Achievements of cyclone preparedness programs are significant and impressive, and they can be replicated elsewhere.
- This idea provides lessons to improve capabilities to meet disaster challenges.

Fig. 4. CPP's Poster for Raising Public Awareness.
Source: Bangladesh Red Crescent Society.

Rainwater Harvesting in Bangladesh

Problems
The coastal belt of Bangladesh suffers from a scarcity of drinking water because of its salty ground water, as well as drought that causes a major water problem in this area. Additionally, most of the hand tube-wells in this area are inoperative because of presence of high levels of salt, arsenic, and iron.

Stakeholders
Rainwater harvesting practice was first carried out at the community level in Dacope upazila of Khulna districts with the help of Bangladesh Agricultural University in 1988. After that, with the support from Department of Public

Health Engineering, UNICEF extended this rainwater harvesting practice in Chittagong hill tract and then extended it in coastal belt areas. But due to contamination of wells with arsenic, an alternative option for drinking water was necessary. WHO and Swiss technology transfer agent SKAT agreed to identify the feasibility of this technology in 1998. At the same time, International Development Enterprises (IDE) offered locally acceptable, affordable technologies for the community. Furthermore, Oxfam, CARE, and Bangladesh University of Engineering and Technology (BUET) were also involved in this rainwater harvesting system.

Innovative Approach
Rainwater harvesting refers to the collection and storage of rainwater *in situ* or within the vicinity of rainfall. In Bangladesh, it is mainly used for drinking and cooking purposes. It provides a viable option than the other technologies because annual rainfall in Bangladesh is 2350 mm that does not uniformly distribute in all areas of the country. For instance, the amount of annual rainfall in the northeastern part is about 5,500 mm, whereas in the southwestern part, it is around 1,200 mm. Again, most of the rainfall occurs from July to October. Depending upon the scarcity of drinking water, various types of rainwater harvesting models are used at the household and community levels. Among them, cement/mortar jars, ferro-cement tanks, and R.C.C. ring tanks are used at the household level and constructed underground rain water harvesting systems are used at the community level (Fig. 5). Besides these, there is an indigenous process of rainwater harvesting system that is practiced in different parts of Bangladesh called the do-it–yourself construction model (motka). While using these models, hazardous aspects such as contamination of water, mosquito breeding, and so forth should be kept in mind.

Lessons Learned

- The rainwater harvesting in rural areas seems to be an alternate water source especially in the arsenic, salinity, and drought-affected areas.
- Although the number of rainwater harvesting systems is rapidly increasing, time is needed to maintain the pH value and checking of water quality.
- During the dry season, the situation becomes worse, because most of the water tanks start to empty. This situation causes the local people to collect drinking water from ponds using the filtering technology.

Fig. 5.   Rainwater Harvesting in Bangladesh.
Source: Author.

- Rainwater harvesting and its judicious utilization for agriculture and municipal use would be essential in future life.

The above discussion proves that the community people are the key actors for disaster reduction and these best practices can be carried out by vulnerable communities in any disaster-prone area to endure the adverse effects of disasters. Furthermore, it is notable here that community people can utilize their local resources and share indigenous knowledge to resolve the disaster impact.

INSTITUTIONALIZING CBDRR IN BANGLADESH

With the increasing frequency and intensity of disasters in Bangladesh, CBDRR is an important issue for empowering community people in terms of disasters. It has been recognized that to reduce the risks of natural hazards, community awareness, and capacity building must be raised through integrating disaster preparedness into development process. As the objective of CBDRR is to build the capacities of communities and local authorities to assess disaster risks and vulnerabilities and to come up with appropriate risk reduction measures, therefore, it is high time to institutionalize CBDRR into government policy-making and programs as it has significant value. It is reported that the Bangladesh government developed a "National plan for disaster management (2007–2015)" by MoFDM in which they recognized community empowerment through CBDRR as one of the six key results with the following elements:

- Capacity building of local disaster management committees.
- Development of community-based early warning system.
- Community risk assessment at the union level.
- Development of risk reduction action plan at the union level.
- Development of contingency plan at the union level.
- Bottom-up mainstreaming of risk reduction action plans into local development plans.
- Local DRR funding mechanisms for implementation of community risk reduction actions.

Moreover, institutionalization of CBDRR needs legislation that supports CBDRR activities and must be incorporated into government framework and plan of action of all development stakeholders. The government must mention the role of NGOs and other organizations for CBDRR and recognize the need for involving communities and community groups in disaster risk reduction work into their development plans and policies. In addition, local governments need to institutionalize CBDRR in investment programming and project design, budgeting, and revenue generation. At the same time, it needs to take pragmatic steps to address the lack of activities between national, sub-national, and community levels. Therefore, the institutionalization of CBDRR requires the following as its precondition:

- A guideline for disaster risk reduction
- Integrate into National Disaster Management Framework
- Strong policy support
- Institutionalized budget
- Definite role of stakeholder
- Transparency and accountability of the framework

CONCLUSION

According to Shahid and Behrawan (2008), Bangladesh is one of the most disaster-prone countries in the world. UNDP (2004) further identified

Bangladesh as the most vulnerable country in the world to tropical cyclones and the sixth most vulnerable country to floods. It is evident from the study that Bangladesh is one of the most highly vulnerable countries in the world due to the climate change effect. Therefore, it is the community that receives help last in every disaster and the poor within the communities that are the most vulnerable to disaster risk.

To reduce the disaster risk, a number of CBDRR programs have been undertaken by various stakeholders in Bangladesh. Among these, some of the good CBDRR practices are mentioned previously. The key success factors such as applying best practice methodologies of community development through community-based disaster mitigation, organizational contribution and mechanisms, and capability building activities of the community people and volunteers have been highlighted. Furthermore, this will help give an idea how CBDRR effectively supports the vulnerable communities to withstand such disasters.

On the other hand, CBDRR shifts from a top-down to a bottom-up approach. The community-based approach corrects the defects of the top-down approach in development planning and disaster risk reduction which failed to address the local needs, ignored the potential of indigenous resources and capacities, and may have been increased people's vulnerabilities. In this regard, community-based activities will be effectively reduced the disaster risk, as they can emphasize their needs and prioritize their responsive measures toward disaster. Therefore, the best CBDRR practices should be scaled up and practiced into other disaster-prone areas where applicable.

According to the Asian Disaster Preparedness Center (ADPC), community action for disaster risk reduction is a crucial element in promoting a "culture of prevention" and creating safer communities. Community actions make the disaster reduction most effective, because it meets the local needs. Moreover, in order to make the community more resilient to disasters, more emphasis should be given to community level disaster risk reduction, including reaching people with appropriate early warning, awareness raising, capacity building, small scale disaster mitigation, livelihood support and disaster risk reduction in floods, cyclones, and earthquake-prone areas.

Although the communities are central in disaster management, they need more awareness information, encouragement, and support during disaster events from government and other actors, particularly from NGOs. Moreover, community participation and control is essential for any successful implementation, orientation, and maintenance of any disaster risk reduction project. Aside from the above, we can conclude that a community driven disaster risk reduction approach will be more reliable and effective as people directly involved in this process will be sustained for a long time. Therefore, CBDRR will serve as a bridge among communities, governments, donors, and other stakeholders in any successful disaster risk reduction program.

ACKNOWLEDGMENTS

The first author gratefully acknowledges the support from GCOE-ARS program of Kyoto University. The author especially thanks the Graduate School of Global Environmental Studies for her research in Kyoto University, Japan, for support as teaching and research assistantship, and also support in the form of a JASSO scholarship.

REFERENCES

Aarjan Dixit. (2011). *Adapting to climate change in Bangladesh*. Retrieved from http://www.wri.org/stories/2011/04/adapting-climate-change-bangladesh

Asia-Pacific Environmental Innovation Strategies (APEIS) and Research on Innovative and Strategic Policy Options (RIPSO). (2004). *Floating agriculture in flood-prone or submerged areas in Bangladesh (Southern Regions of Bangladesh)*. Retrieved from http://www.iges.or.jp/APEIS/RISPO/inventory/db/pdf/0146.pdf

Climate Change Cell. (2009). *Department of environment*. Bangladesh: Ministry of Environment and Forests.

Concern Universal Bangladesh. (2011). Retrieved from http://www.concern-universal.org.bd

Harmeling, S. (2010). Global climate risk index 2010. Who is most vulnerable? Weather-related loss events since 1990 and how Copenhagen needs to respond. Briefing paper, Germanwatch.

Irfanullah, H. M., Adrika, A., Ghani, A., & Khan, Z. A. (2007). Introduction of floating gardening in the North-eastern Wetlands of Bangladesh for nutritional security and sustainable livelihood. *Renewable Agriculture and Food Systems, 23*(2), 89–96.

Islam, T., & Atkins, P. (2007). Indigenous floating cultivation: A sustainable agricultural practice in the Wetlands of Bangladesh. *Development in Practice, 4*(1), 130–136.

Ministry of Environment and Forests. (2008). Bangladesh climate change strategy and action plan 2008. Ministry of Environment and Forests, Government of the People's Republic of Bangladesh, Dhaka.

Ministry of Food and Disaster Management. (2007). National plan for disaster management 2007–2015. Ministry of Food and Disaster Management, Government of the People's Republic of Bangladesh, Dhaka.

Mirza, M. M. Q. (2002). Global warming and changes in the probability of occurrence of floods in Bangladesh and implications. *Global Environmental Change, 12*, 127–138.

National Adaptation Programme of Action (NAPA). (2005). Final report. Ministry of Environment and Forest, Government of the People's Republic of Bangladesh, Dhaka.

National Drought Mitigation Center (NDMC). (2006). *What is drought? Understanding and defining drought.* Retrieved from http://www.drought.unl.edu/whatis/concept.htm

National Plan for Disaster Management 2010–2015. (2010). Disaster Management Bureau, Disaster Management and Relief Division, Ministry of Food and Disaster Management, Dhaka.

Rahman, A., Alam, M., Alam, S. S., Uzzaman, M. R., Rashid, M., & Rabbani, G. (2008). Risks, vulnerability and adaptation in Bangladesh. Human Development Report 2007/08, Human Development Report Office Occasional Paper, 2007/13.

Shahid, S., & Behrawan, H. (2008). Drought risk assessment in the western part of Bangladesh. *Natural Hazards: Journal of the International Society for the Prevention and Mitigation of Natural Hazards, 46,* 391–413.

Swiss Agency for Development and Corporation (SDC). (2010). Disaster risk reduction programme for Bangladesh 2010–2012. Directorate of Humanitarian Aid and SHA, CH-3003 Bern.

UNDP. (2004). Reducing disaster risk: A challenge for development. A global report. United Nations Development Programme, Bureau for Crisis Prevention and Recovery, New York, NY.

Yodmani, S. (2001). Disaster risk management and vulnerability reduction: Protecting the poor. Social Protection Workshop 6: Protecting communities – Social funds and disaster management. Under the Asia and Pacific Forum on Poverty, Manila.

CHAPTER 7

COMMUNITY-BASED RISK REDUCTION APPROACHES IN URBAN INDIA

Sunil Parashar and Rajib Shaw

INTRODUCTION

Disasters being common in Indian cities, communities have created and utilized their own coping mechanism to deal with such situations and strengthen their resilience by adopting methods to adjust to the risk situation. For example, during the Mumbai Floods in 2005, slum communities, with the support of social organizations, were able to adopt ways to cope well with the risk situation (Chatterjee, 2010). This chapter particularly focuses on community-based approaches in urban India.

Several institutions around the world including nongovernment organizations (NGOs), international nongovernment organizations (INGOs), and national and local governments (LGs) have recognized that a community-based approach is essential for building resilient communities. The Government of India (GOI), with the support of United Nations Development Programme (UNDP), implemented the world's largest CBDRM program (2002–2009) in 176 multi-hazard prone districts across 17 states of India (ADPC, 2010). The key component of this program was to strengthen the capacity of the local people and institutions by integrating community-based disaster preparedness into local government development

Community-Based Disaster Risk Reduction
Community, Environment and Disaster Risk Management, Volume 10, 113–130
ISSN: 2040-7262/doi:10.1108/S2040-7262(2012)0000010013

plans (ADPC, 2010). The program specifically focused on disaster risk management (DRM) and covered broad areas like awareness generation, capacity building, institutionalization, involvement of community, gender mainstreaming, and convergence and partnerships (UNDP, 2010). For example, in Delhi, disaster preparedness month was celebrated to raise awareness of communities and local governments (UNDP, 2010). Similarly, a program on "school safety through education and building safer school" was implemented in 38 project cities (UNDP, 2010). In addition, several activities on building disaster preparedness and mitigation at the central, state, and local levels were implemented in targeted districts. For example, around 10,000 masons, 900 engineers, 50 architects were trained in earthquake resistance in 13 districts and six cities of Uttar Pradesh (UNDP, 2010). In addition, emergency operation centers (EOCs) were created in the targeted district under this program. Apart from capacity building, the GOI institutionalized disaster education in school curriculums. The Central Board of Secondary Education (CBSE) introduced disaster management in the school curriculum (UNDP, 2010). Involvement of communities in the GOI-UNDP program was felt necessary. Therefore, communities, such as the National Service Scheme (NSS), National Cadet Corps (NCC), Nehru Yuva Kendra Sangathan (NYKS), and Bharat Scout and Guides were trained in targeted districts. In Delhi, 30 volunteers from NYSK and Civil Defense were trained on community-based disaster management planning (UNDP, 2010). This helped later in preparation of documents including district disaster management plan, and evacuation plans.

Apart from the GOI-UNDP initiatives, several other institutions in India including NGOs, community-based organizations (CBOs) have implemented CBDRR in India's urban areas. For example, Earthquake Safety Initiative by SEEDS, India (NGO), targeted Himachal Pradesh, one of the earthquake and landslide prone states of India. Communities including parents, masons, governments, and neighborhoods were trained on disasters through schools (UNICEF, 2009). Similarly, FOCUS Humanitarian, an affiliate of Aga Khan Development Network (AKDN), implemented the "School Safety" initiative in Gujarat, a multi-hazard prone state of India (UNICEF, 2009). The objective was to make schools safer from disasters through the CBDRR approach. The school community including both teachers and children were involved in disaster risk reduction (DRR)-related activities such as preparing school disaster management plan, formation of school emergency management committees, task force formation, among others (UNICEF, 2009).

In recent years, several measures to improve the CBDRR approach in India have also been taken by Humanitarian agencies. One such program was organized in Delhi by Sphere India in January 2009 (Sphere India, 2010). Sphere India organized a national conference on good practices in community-based DRR. One of the objectives was to enhance the knowledge and awareness about CBDRR models among the DRR practitioners, government agency, and NGOs (Sphere India, 2010). From the field, best practices on CBDRR were shared with participant members. In spite of several initiatives on CBDRR, there are several challenges, especially in urban areas, that need more consideration. The following section discusses some urban issues and the need of a CBDRR approach.

URBAN ISSUES AND NEED OF CBDRR APPROACH

The Global Assessment Report 2009 clearly states that disaster risks in urban areas are increasing very rapidly. This is mainly due to two important factors – unplanned urbanization and poor urban governance (UNISDR, 2010). Today, over half of the world's population lives in cities. Following which, infrastructures and other services are becoming deficient. This situation is very clearly visible in Indian cities as well as in third world countries. Indian cities are typically exposed to poverty, inequality, environment, and health problems. On the one hand, cities like Delhi, Mumbai, Kolkata, Chennai, and other metropolitans are centers of economic growth and social development. On the other hand, they are also vulnerable to disasters because of their haphazard physical growth, inadequate infrastructure, and development of slums, where poor people live with poor economic assets, inadequate water supply, poor sanitation, polluted air, poor waste management, and several environmental problems. Thus, the urban poor are often badly affected when disaster strikes. However, not all urban poor are equally vulnerable due to their different religion, employment, region, gender, language, and demographic composition. In Mumbai Floods 2005, not all slums were equally affected (Chatterjee, 2010). For example, new residents (less than 10 years) and old residents (more than 20 years) living in slums were more vulnerable than medial residents (10–20 years) (Chatterjee, 2010). Medial residents had greater access to the social networks during the flood and that helped in their quick rehabilitation and recovery (Chatterjee, 2010). Similarly, religion also played an important role in determining their vulnerability. Christian families were supported by formal institutions, whereas Hindu and Muslim families were mainly dependent on their social connections (Chatterjee, 2010). Therefore, they were more vulnerable than Christian families. In addition, families of Maharashtra state origin had greater access to resources and decision making than non-Maharashtra state origin (Chatterjee, 2010). Therefore, region also played an important role in determining their vulnerability. Similarly, employment was an important factor in recovery. In the recovery stage, family members with formal jobs were capable of safeguarding formal means of shelters and resources, whereas informal sector workers were more vulnerable due to the lack of proper livelihood opportunity after the flood (Chatterjee, 2010). The above example of Mumbai Flood clearly shows how urban areas are complex and composed of heterogeneous groups. Their disaster vulnerabilities are determined by social, political, and global forces (Chatterjee, 2010).

In recent years, CBDRR practitioners have encountered several challenges while implementing CBDRR in urban India. Some of them are: lack of time and interest in CBDRR programs, heterogeneous community, problems faced every day, among others. One of the main reasons behind these challenges is the urban characteristics and associated social problems. For example, anonymity is an integral component of an urban community, which means people do not know each other in a city. It creates lack of social bonding and trust among neighborhoods. It further leads to social problems, such as tremendous mental pressure and tensions because of which people hardly show any interest in participating in community-level activities for social welfare. Similarly, social problems such as population congestion, crime, shortage of resources, and services like water, electricity, among others create additional barriers for implementing CBDRR in urban India.

Therefore, urban areas need a special dimension of DRR activity, which can enhance the resilience of an urban community. An approach like CBDRR should be created in such a way that it can address urban complexity and vulnerability of heterogeneous groups. This can be done by greater community involvement, especially urban poor in the CBDRR process. For example, urban communities must be included in all stages of CBDRR such as community profiling, community risk assessment, detailing formulation of counter disaster plan, implementing and monitoring, and evaluation and feedback (Yodmani, 2001). In addition, community-based initiatives that address urban risks can also be used for making CBDRR effective and sustainable. Finally, involvement of the local government is also essential. It will help in meeting some challenges of CBDRR implementation such as lack of funding, institutionalizing CBDRR in national development plans, among others. Successful practice from CBDRR can be useful to advocate or influence policies at the national level. The following section discusses some examples of community involvement in urban risk reduction process. These examples also show how greater involvement of a community can address the urban risk issues effectively, especially in Indian cities.

ILLUSTRATIVE EXAMPLES OF COMMUNITY INVOLVEMENT IN URBAN RISK REDUCTION

Advance Locality Management (ALM) Scheme

The advance locality management (ALM) is a community–government partnership in Mumbai that first started in 1996 (Baud & Nainan, 2006; Surjan & Shaw, 2010). The main objective of this movement was to address the neighborhood problems and growing localized risks due to environment degradation, waste generation, among others (Surjan & Shaw, 2010). Thus, the focus was to improve the garbage collection and to maintain the street lights, drainage systems, and railways (Sivaramakrishnan, 2000). Initially, this initiative started in an environmentally degraded low and middle income neighborhoods. It was a collective initiative by volunteers themselves, who contributed to the functioning of this movement (Surjan & Shaw, 2010). Later, the solid waste department of Mumbai Corporation of Greater Mumbai (MCGM) came forward to form a partnership with this initiative due to its increasing benefits of a growing movement. Finally, in 1997, the ALM program was initiated by MCGM through a partnership approach, where citizens were involved in setting up a system for improving the solid waste management in an environment friendly manner (Mahadevia, Pharate & Mistry, 2005).

The ALM is composed of two groups: (i) residents of the locality and; (ii) administration of the MCGM (Mahadevia et al., 2005). Among the residents, the ALM committee is formed with members (residents and shopkeepers) of group housing societies or one group housing society. The committee members of ALM are selected democratically. For example, one member from each building is a representative in the ALM. Thus, the size of the committee depends on the number and size of housing societies or population. The committee members generally include designers of housing societies, social workers, retired civil servants, traders, local corporators, among others (Mahadevia et al., 2005). The committee meets once in a week to discuss their problems and they keep a register to note complaints.

The residents are also required to maintain the waste by separating them into wet-waste (biodegradable waste) and dry-waste (recyclable waste) (Mahadevia et al., 2005). Later, through vermin-composting, the wet-waste is converted into compost, and the dry-waste is disposed through ragpickers.

At the local government level, the ALM society is registered with the Local Municipal Ward Office. The ward office appoints a Nodal Officer to collaborate with the ALM. The nodal officer acts as facilitator and coordinates with other MCGM departments to solve the complaints registered by the ALM. In addition, a common fund is created and treated as "Maintenance Fund," where residents have to contribute Re. 1 per apartment per day. Thus, all expenses of maintenance are incurred from this fund. However, no salary is paid to the member of the ALM. Moreover, ALM representatives also interact with assistant municipal commissioner (AMC) through monthly meetings, where unresolved issues of the ALM are discussed.

According to the CDP report, there are 584 ALM committees in the city (Surjan & Shaw, 2010). Around 375 societies are registered covering a population of around two million (Mahadevia et al., 2005). The number of ALMs has increased since 1997, when the scheme started with one locality.

Apart from waste segregation, the ALM also addresses issues related to clearance of garbage, damaged roads, encroachment, nuisance reduction, watchdog, gardening, recreation, maintenance and repair, cultural activities, celebration of festivals, and religious get-togethers. In addition, the ALM also provides livelihood opportunity to the rag-pickers. Rag-pickers can effectively engage in collecting recyclable waste and can earn their livelihood.

The contribution of the ALM is very significant in segregation of solid waste at the household level. Moreover, with the increase in waste segregation practices, the habit of throwing garbage has reduced significantly. Dustbins are removed from the roads, improving the look of the streets. Streets have become clean and hygienic for the residents. Similarly, the collection and usage of organic waste has improved the concept of solid waste management in the city. For example, around 55% of the organic waste is used as organic manure for gardening (Mahadevia et al., 2005). Similarly, the burden of collection and disposal of solid waste to dumping sites has been significantly reduced because of the ALM. The scheme provides an effective platform to citizens to improve the city's environment. With the success in solid waste management, the scope of ALM activities has also increased. Some ALMs have also taken the responsibility to maintain open spaces such as *Juhu* beach (Kundu, 2005). The concept of ALM has also influenced the corporate sector, and now many corporate houses are engaged in improving their solid waste management, roads, sanitation, among others (Mahadevia et al., 2005).

There are some challenges of the ALM schemes. Several ALMs in the city are not functioning efficiently. There are conflicts between the ALM and MCGM on the issues of collection and recycling of biodegradable waste (Mahadevia et al., 2005). For example, some ALMs did not want to recycle organic waste. The vermin-composting in neighborhoods give out foul odor. Therefore, some ALMs want MCGMs to collect and recycle the biodegradable waste.

Environmental Improvement Initiatives in Puri

The section here discusses some examples of environmental improvement initiatives in Puri, a coastal city situated in the state of Orissa. With an area of 16.84 km², the city is growing with a density of 7,435 persons per sq. km (2001) (Surjan & Shaw, 2008). The city is regarded as one of the most revered and pilgrimage spots in India. Every year millions of pilgrims and tourists visit this place. Around 24 festivals are celebrated every year (Surjan & Shaw, 2008). Being a coastal city, the construction activities have not followed the norms and regulations of coastal zone management plan. The city has a master plan. However, the decisions to construct houses and infrastructure are taken on an ad hoc basis. Consequently, the physical environment and living condition in the city have deteriorated. The city's low-lying areas and wetlands are rapidly transformed into mix-land uses. The city also lacks in open and recreational spaces. In addition to this, the city is also vulnerable to various kinds of natural hazards such as cyclones, earthquakes, floods, and tsunami, among others. The disaster management plan is predominantly focused on rural areas and hardly provides adequate attention to the urban areas. Consequently, the urban areas of Puri are vulnerable to both environmental risks as well as to disaster risks. On the other hand, there are some good initiatives led by the community to improve the city's environment. The following section briefly discusses some initiatives led by the community.

The Sahi Community

The word "Sahi" is used to denote a kind of settlement in Puri (Surjan & Shaw, 2008). These settlements are mostly old and situated around the temples (Surjan, Takeuchi, & Shaw, 2011). People living in this kind of settlements are called "Sahi Community" (Surjan & Shaw, 2008). They are mainly engaged in temple activities and provide their services for daily rituals and annual ceremonies. Sahis are also recognized as a traditional community, having lifelong strong belongingness with temples. They have preserved their old characteristics by maintaining the old structure and functioning system including old houses, open spaces, water harvesting, heritage building and complexes, street network, among others.

The two most important characteristics of Sahis are: "*Chhakas*," which are road intersections and "*Choupals*," which refer to a platform or building that is similar to a temple (Surjan & Shaw, 2008). These two characteristics have brought strong community bonding, trust, and shared interest among the people. In addition, the people have strong bonding with the places of their forefathers and they played an important role in preserving their neighborhood heritage identity, open spaces, water harvesting elements, and gardens. Sahis are also proactive in responding to calamities or disasters. For instance, they showed strong community participation after the Gujarat Earthquake and Orissa Super cyclone (Surjan & Shaw, 2008). The example of Sahi clearly shows the success effort of the community role in environment preservation. One of the biggest challenges of the Sahi community is rapid urbanization. Rapid urbanization has reduced the size of open spaces, parks, space for plants, among others. Consequently, the traditional neighborhoods are increasingly getting threatened.

Indigenous Community Institutions
Jagaghars are community-based institutions in Puri (Surjan & Shaw, 2008). Traditionally, they were set up as recreational centers to integrate local people. A typical Jagaghar consists of a temple, a pond, coconut and herbal trees, a sand pit, and a gymnasium (Surjan & Shaw, 2008). They all are enclosed within a boundary wall. Jagaghars are also recognized as democratic, community-owned, and nonpolitical but proactive institutions that aim to maintain recreational facilities and open spaces through indigenous knowledge. Today, Jagaghars are considered as an important institution in Puri. They provide better opportunities and a platform for the interaction of local people. In addition, Jagaghars also have traditional knowledge, which they use to preserve natural resources such as water, flora, fauna, among others. For example, maintenance of ponds significantly contributes in the recharge of ground water and keeps the water table high. Thus, Jagaghars institutions show an effective example of environmental conservation through local indigenous knowledge.

Nirmal Shreekshetra *(Community-Based Waste Management)*
Nirmal Shreekshetra is a program of solid waste management, implemented by three CBOs (Surjan & Shaw, 2008). The main goal of this program is to

implement the strategies for solid waste management that are economically and environmentally sustainable. During the pilot stage, the program was launched in three zones. These zones had different kinds of land use including residential areas, commercial areas, among others. The activities organized in the pilot stage include surveys, awareness campaigns, sanitation programs, and street plays. It was felt that the pilot stage had contributed in the 60–70% success in the segregation and collection at the local level (Surjan & Shaw, 2008). In addition, the medical centers recorded reduction in the number of cases of malaria, water and vector-borne diseases in the pilot areas. Later, this project received huge support from the local administration as well as from the temple. The important aspect of this program is the community's presence. Involving the community makes this program self-sustainable, partnership oriented, and consensus based. Integrating such a program with the city's waste management plan can improve the scope of such a program in penetrating all localities.

District-Level Hyogo Framework for Action (HFA) Forum in East Delhi

District (HFA) forum was established in East Delhi on March 1, 2011, by the Alliance for adaptation and disaster risk reduction (AADRR) group with the strong support from Deputy Commissioner of East Delhi (AADRR, 2011). The AADRR is a national coalition of experts from civil society organizations (CSOs), Government bodies, UN agencies, Disaster Management experts, and concerned stakeholders in the field of DRR and climate change adaptation (CCA) (AADRR, 2011). The main objective of this forum is to enhance the disaster resilience of the community through DRR measures. East Delhi is vulnerable to several kinds of natural and man-made hazards such as floods, earthquakes, extreme temperature, water scarcity, bomb blasts, fires, among others. For example, in the past, there were floods in this district in 1967, 1971, 1975, 1976, 1978, 1988, 1995, 1998, 2008, and 2010 (DDMA, 2005). Thus, the district needs more attention to address disaster-related issues. This forum is based on "Hyogo Framework for Action (2005–2015): Building the resilience of nations and communities to disasters" (UNISDR, 2005). In 2005, it was negotiated and a 10-years plan was adopted by 168 member states of the United Nations to reduce the vulnerability to natural hazards (UNISDR, 2005).

This forum was launched through a consultation workshop on DRR in East Delhi. The workshop was that of multi-stakeholders and brought together 32 members from NGOs, CBOs, Residential and Welfare

Associations (RWAs), District Disaster Management Authorities (DDMA), among others. The workshop was seeking to address three core issues – disaster risk issues in East Delhi; a brief discussion, and people's reaction to the recent building collapse in Lalita Park, East Delhi; and discussion and proposal to establish a district HFA forum to address disaster risks.

The proposed forum structure is composed of partners from the core group AADRR; local administrative (DM/SDM, ward committees); local citizens (RWAs, women groups); NGOs, schools, hospitals, and volunteers as shown in Fig. 1. The forum aims at promoting localization and institutionalization of HFA priorities and placing communities and women groups at center stage. It is an instrument to implement DRR activities and seeks to improve the resilience of vulnerable communities.

Setting up of the district HFA forum went through a long discussion. The main discussion points in the workshop were: viability of the district forum; consensus on the activities/output of the forum; organization structure; expected support from AADRR; and other issues. The experts from the AADRR and key stakeholders/participants recognized the need of this kind of forum at the district level. The experts acknowledge that this forum will act as a vehicle to connect the community with the government. Moreover, several recommendations were provided based on individual understanding. Some of the recommendations from the discussion were:

• the forum will be crucial in guiding on the first initiatives to be resorted by the communities at times of disasters;

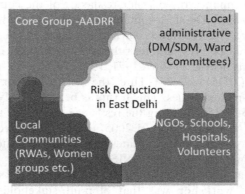

Fig 1. Proposed Structure of HFA Forum During the Workshop.

- it will also be handy in keeping a check on the engineers, passing the buildings without certifying that they are earthquake resistant and structurally fit for public usage;
- the forum would also be handy in training the communities to act as first respondents and intervene efficiently at the time of disasters;
- it will empower or train and strengthen communities and identify volunteers, who can respond well at the time of disasters;
- the forum can guide in setting up a training wing, and also acknowledge the contributions of the communities at the time of an eventuality; and
- the forum could function as a research group and provides its technical input.

Several discussion points were raised about the power, funding, and resources of the forum. However, no consensus was made in the workshop. In addition, it was felt that funds are now available at the district level for preparedness of the administration. In case the forum agrees, then those funds could be utilized effectively. It was also felt during the discussion that a DDMA forum does exist, which is facilitated by the government. However, there are no representatives from the civil society. So, this forum will be facilitated by a network of civil society and backed by government officials. The forum will not be a duplication of the work but provide support to the DDMA through public participation. East Delhi was the first district to initiate this kind of forum at the district level.

Re-Building Resilience after Floods: The Case of Surat

With an area of 7,761 sq. km, Surat is the second-largest populated district after Ahmedabad (Oza & Chauhan, 2010). The total population of Surat is 6.07 million (Surat Census, 2011). Surat is also recognized as the commercial capital city of Gujarat and one of India's eighth largest metropolitan cities. The city is largely recognized for its textiles and diamond business. Geographically, the city is situated on the left bank of Tapti River. The river is known for floods due to depression that originate from the Bay of Bengal and travel from East to West causing rainfall in the upper catchment areas and resulting floods along its course. This river is a main source of water for Surat. However, in the past, Surat was affected heavily following floods in Tapti River. The worst flood occurred in 2006 when large quantities of water was released from Ukai dam, situated on Tapti River (Oza & Chauhan, 2010). The flood caused huge damage to lives, livelihoods, and property. For example, more than 2 million people were trapped in their own houses or neighbors' houses without food and basic services for four days and nights (Oza & Chauhan, 2010). Around 150 people lost their lives (Oza & Chauhan, 2010). The total economic loss recorded was more than 0.21 trillion (Oza & Chauhan, 2010). The flood also caused huge damages to the other districts of Gujarat. Kheda, Vadodara, and Anand districts were the worst affected by this flood. Several national and international NGOs including Oxfam, Action Aid, World Vision, CARE provided relief and responded in the Flood-affected districts. Several organizations worked together with local community organizations by providing food, hygiene kits, basic domestic utensils, and health services. However, local organizations were struggling in expanding relief and recovery from communities to the poor people. Later, it was felt that relief and recovery should be done in a decentralized way. However, recovery efforts remained a major issue in all small towns.

The initiative aimed at reducing the vulnerability of low-income communities through their own actions and efforts. The All India Disaster Mitigation Institute (AIDMI), an action research organization based in Ahmedabad (Gujarat), initiated this work in eight slums of Surat (Oza & Chauhan, 2010). The initiative aimed at reducing vulnerability of the affected community by focusing on various measures such as economic recovery, safer shelter, better area development, and disaster preparedness. The overall goal was to build resilience against flood and other hazards of low-income communities.

This initiative provided opportunities to the affected community to do their own need assessment, provided services to affected families, relief distribution, setting priorities for planned recovery for income, assets, shelters, among others. The AIDMI provided financial and technical support to the targeted areas (Oza & Chauhan, 2010). A committee of affected community was formed in each targeted slum, which was led by women. The committee was involved in activities such as assessment of the low-income communities, assessing the situation after the floods, loss of livelihood assets such as shelters, and other infrastructure. In some slums a cash-for-recovery program was initiated for new livelihood opportunity. Later, community resources centers (CRCs) and community infrastructure projects (CIPs) were initiated in the targeted slums to provide the basic services such as food, education, health, and employment (Oza & Chauhan, 2010). For better and safer recovery, the AIDMI introduced a disaster insurance scheme that covered 19 eventualities including earthquakes, floods, cyclones, landslides, droughts, among others. Overall, the initiative utilized the community-based approach in the relief and rehabilitation of affected communities in targeted slums.

The initiative led to several positive impacts in the targeted slums. Some of them were: economic recovery of the affected community because of livelihood support, awareness and preparedness for future hazards, protection against future risks resulting from disaster insurance by the AIDMI, the community's vision expanded from hazard protection to the vulnerability reduction, among others (Oza & Chauhan, 2010). Similarly, the flood response expanded to multi-hazards response, preparedness, and recovery as development activities. Finally, the recovery process became more of an urban poverty reduction and development activities (Oza & Chauhan, 2010).

LESSONS LEARNED AND FUTURE PERSPECTIVE

The case examples discussed in the previous section clearly show community involvement is important for urban risk reduction. Their active involvement was seen in all case examples. For instance, the community was proactively engaged in developing plans as well as in the decision making process. Thus, the community has been empowered by having greater access to resources, greater participation in decision making, and enjoying greater benefits of a healthy environment. The examples discussed are community driven with minimum intervention of the state or local government. However, involvement of nation, state, and local governments are essential for making these initiatives long-term and effective. The following section analyzes these examples on the basis of key parameters such as stakeholders, duration (timeframe), ownership, potential for upscaling, incorporation of disaster risk, and connections with urban governance and development.

Stakeholder Participation

Stakeholders are important components of any program. They are often those that affected or benefited by the outcome of the program. The case studies involve a broad range of stakeholders including the local government (MCGM), NGOs, CBOs, residents, Schools, Hospitals, local community, among others as shown in Table 1 involving a broad spectrum of stakeholders such as institutions with indirect interest helps in addressing the larger development concern. For example, the case example of environmental improvement initiative in Puri has the community as their

Table 1. Showing Stakeholders, Duration (Timeframe), Ownership, Potential Of Up Scaling, Incorporation Of Disaster Risk, And Linkages with Urban Governance and Development in Four Case Examples.

Case Examples	Advance Locality Management (ALM) Scheme	Environmental Improvement Initiatives in Puri	District Level Hyogo Framework for Action (HFA) Forum in East Delhi	Rebuilding Resilience after Flood: The case of Surat
Stakeholder participation	Residents and Local government (MCGM)	Sahi community, Jagaghars community, and CBOs	AADRR group, Local administrative committees, NGOs, schools, hospitals, volunteers, and local citizens	AIDMI, slum community, and government of Gujarat
Duration (time frame)	1996 onward	N.D.	2011 onwards	N.D.
Ownership	Residents and Local government (MCGM)	Community and CBOs	Administrative Committees and local citizens	Slum community
Potential of up scaling	*State level* programmes of MHADA, MMRDA; *National schemes:* JNURM, SCP, IDSMT	*State level* programmes of BDA, Puri municipality; *National schemes:* JNURM, EDP	*State level* programmes of DDMA, DDA, MCD; *National schemes:* GOI-UNDP Disaster Risk Reduction Programme (2009–2012); Risk Mitigation Projects	*State level* programmes of GSDMA, SUDA, DDMA; *National schemes:* GOI-UNDP Disaster Risk Reduction Programme (2009–12); Risk Mitigation Projects
Incorporation of disaster risk	Not explicitly	Not explicitly	Specifically focusing on DRR	Specifically focusing on DRR
Linkages with urban governance and development issues	Part of the national urban development programs	Part of national and state level urban development programs	State level urban development programs	Part of state level and city level of urban development issues

MHADA: Maharashtra Housing and Area Development Authority; *MMRDA:* Mumbai Metropolitan Region Development Authority; *JNNURM:* Jawahar Lal Nehru National Urban Renewal Mission; *SCP:* Sustainable Cities Programme; *IDSMT:* Integrated Development of Small and Medium Towns; *BDA:* Bhubaneswar Development Authority; *EDP:* Eco-city Development Plan; *DDA:* Delhi Disaster Management Authority; *DDA:* Delhi Development Authority; *MCD:* Municipal Corporation of Delhi; *GSDMA:* Gujarat State Disaster Management Authority; *DDMA:* District Disaster Management Authority; *SUDA:* Surat Urban Development Authority; N.D.: No Date.

main stakeholder. However, the outcomes of their program also affect or benefit Puri Municipality. The city municipality also deals with the issues that are addressed by the local community such as solid waste management, environment improvement, among others. Thus, incorporating Puri Municipality as one of the stakeholders in the community-based schemes will help in addressing larger development concerns of Puri city.

Duration

The duration or timeframe of a program is important for its sustainability. Most of the case examples shown in Table 1 are ongoing. In the future, their effectiveness can be evaluated by developing some key indicators for their long-term sustainability. Beaudoux, Crombrugghe, Douxchamps, Guenuea, and Nieuwkert (1992) suggest a number of quantitative and qualitative indicators that can be used. Some of them are: technical indicators, economic indicators, operating or organizational indicators, social indicators, and environmental indicators. For example, environmental indicator can be very useful in analyzing the impact of environment improvement initiatives in Puri, India. It can be done by assessing the impact of improved solid waste management on people's health.

Ownership

Table 1 shows different kinds of ownership from case examples. The case of environment improvement initiative in Puri and the case example of Surat show greater community ownership. They show a clear example of ownership by insiders, which means partnership by the local community, residents, among others. Another kind of ownership is the involvement of outsiders such as local governments (MCGM), NGOs, among others. For example, the case examples of the ALM scheme and district HFA forum show ownership of both the local government and community. A greater community ownership contributes to people empowerment. The implications will lead to the people of the community themselves planning and implementing projects by mobilizing resources, setting the key agenda, and integrating and expanding the outcome of the program. Therefore, case examples like the ALM scheme and district-level HFA forum in East Delhi can be improved further by fostering greater ownership by the community in the future.

Potential for Upscaling

There are a number of ways of upscaling community-level programs. One such way of upscaling is by implementing the community-level or micro-level program at the state level. This can be done by incorporating the community-level program in broad national or state-level programs such as the JNNURUM scheme of the GOI, the SCP program, IDSMT, and several other programs (see Table 1) that are based on the similar theme of the case examples. Thus, the community-level program becomes the integral component of national or state-level schemes. Similarly, community-level programs can also be expanded by including more themes. For example, the ALM scheme of solid waste management can be expanded by incorporating DRR components into their main activity. Similarly, the community-level initiative in Puri can also be expanded by incorporating some disaster preparedness measures such as developing a cyclone disaster management plan at the community level.

Incorporation of Disaster Risks

As cities in India are regularly affected by disasters, it is essential to include disaster risk in all community development or city development programs. For example, ALM Schemes in Mumbai and Environment improvement initiatives in Puri can expand their activities by including disaster risk into their regular programs. They can sensitize people about the local disaster risk through awareness building activities, hazard mapping, etc. Moreover, they can also promote people to develop their local area disaster management plan. Integrating disaster-related issues in these initiatives will make community prepared for future disasters.

Linkage with Urban Governance and Development Issues

The examples discussed highlights development issues of Indian cities such as environmental issues, solid waste management problem, and disasters, among others. On the other hand, these examples also show a kind of urban governance structure, where communities and the local government work together to solve some development issues. Thus, it is necessary to promote lessons learned and good practices from these small-scale initiatives. These practices can be documented and disseminated to governments, national partners, large audiences. Later, they can be used to advocate or influence policy making and planning at the national level.

ACKNOWLEDGMENTS

The first author acknowledges the support of the Japanese Government (Monbukagakusho: MEXT) for scholarship and Kyoto University's Environmental Management Leadership Programme (EML). Support from Global Center of Excellence (GCOE) program "Human Security Engineering for Asian Megacities" is also acknowledged.

REFERENCES

AADRR. (2011) Consultation workshop on disaster risk reduction in East Delhi, alliance for adaptation and disaster risk reduction, Secretariat, New Delhi.

ADPC. (2010). Implementing national programs on community-based disaster risk reduction in high risk communities: Lessons learned challenges and way ahead. Working Paper, Version 2. Bangkok, Thailand.

Baud, I., & Nainan, N. (2006). "Negotiated Spaces" for representation in Mumbai: Ward committees, advanced locality management and the politics of middle-class activism. Paper presented to the IDPAD end symposium, Hyderabad, India, November 1–3, 2006. Retrieved from http://www.idpad.org/html/hyderabad.htm

Beaudoux, E., Crombrugghe, G. de., Douxchamps, F., Guenuea, M.-C., Nieuwkert, M., et al. (1992). *Supporting development action from identification to evaluation*. London: Macmillan Press.

Chatterjee, M. (2010). Slum dwellers response to flooding events in the megacities of India. *Mitigation and Adaptation Strategies for Global Change, 15*, 337–353.

DDMA. (2005). *District disaster management plan – East Delhi*. East Delhi: Office of Deputy Commissioner.

Kundu, D. (2005). Elite capture in decentralized governance in metro cities: Lessons from the Delhi experience. Paper presented at Workshop on Inclusive Mega Cities in India? – Learning's from Mumbai, organised by Centre for Development Alternatives (CFDA) and Institute of Social Studies, The Hague.

Mahadevia, D., Pharate, B., & Mistry, A. (2005). *New practices of waste management – Case of Mumbai*. Working Paper No. 35. School of Planning, CEPT University, Ahmedabad.

Oza, S., & Chauhan, V. (2010). Big floods in small towns: How communities rebuild resilience? In SAARC (Ed.), *Urban risk management in south Asia* (pp. 101–108). Retrieved from http://saarc-sdmc.nic.in/pdf/Publications/URM/URM-final.pdf

Sivaramakrishnan, K. C. (2000). Confronting urban issues with a metropolitan view in Mumbai, India. In B. A. Ruble, R. E. Stren, J. S. Tulchin & D. H. Varat (Eds.), *Urban governance around the world* (pp. 13–17). Washington, DC: University of Toronto Press: Toronto.

Sphere India. (2010). *Turning the tide national conference on "good practices in community based disaster risk reduction"*. New Delhi: Sphere India.

Surat Census. (2011). Retrieved from http://www.census2011.co.in/census/district/206-surat.html. Accessed on October 5, 2011.

Surjan, A., & Shaw, R. (2010). Enhancing disaster resiliency through local environment management: Case of Mumbai, India. In SAARC (Ed.), *Urban Risk Management in south Asia*. (pp. 79–90). Retrieved from http://saarc-sdmc.nic.in/pdf/Publications/URM/URM-final.pdf

Surjan, A., Takeuchi, Y., & Shaw, R. (2011). From disaster and climate risk to urban resilience: Approaching through community based environmental improvement, RPS, Singapore (282 pages).

Surjan, A. K., & Shaw, R. (2008). 'Eco-city' to 'disaster-resilient eco-community': A concerted approach in the coastal city of Puri, India. *Sustainability Science, 3*, 249–265.

UNDP. (2010). Good practices in community based disaster risk management. New Delhi, India.

UNICEF. (2009). Conference on community-based disaster risk reduction. New Delhi, India.

UNISDR. (2005). *World conference on disaster reduction 18–22 January 2005, Kobe, Hyogo, Japan*. Retrieved from http://www.unisdr.org/2005/wcdr/intergover/official-doc/L-docs/Hyogo-framework-for-action-english.pdf

UNISDR. (2010). The Incheon declaration: Building a local government alliances for disaster risk reduction. In SAARC (Ed.), *Urban risk management in south Asia* (pp. 144–148). Retrieved from http://saarc-sdmc.nic.in/pdf/Publications/URM/URM-final.pdf

Yodmani, S. (2001). Disaster risk management and vulnerability reduction: Protecting the poor. Paper presented at the Asia and Pacific Forum on Poverty, 5–9 February 2001, Philippines. Retrieved from http://www.adpc.net/infores/adpc-documents/PovertyPaper.pdf

CHAPTER 8

CIVIL SOCIETY ORGANIZATION AND DISASTER RISK REDUCTION IN INDONESIA: ROLE OF WOMEN, YOUTH, AND FAITH-BASED GROUPS

Farah Mulyasari and Rajib Shaw

INTRODUCTION

The understanding of the term "civil society" has been given in many references. One reference is given by the London School of Economics Centre for Civil Society (2011), and its working definition is rather illustrative. Civil society, according to them, refers to the arena of collective action around shared interests, purposes, and values. The civil society commonly embraces a diversity of spaces, actors, and institutional forms, and varies in the degree of formality, autonomy, and power. Civil societies are often populated by organizations such as registered charities, development nongovernmental organizations (NGOs), professional associations, and community groups, such as women, youth, and faith-based or religious organizations. Those groups are seen as the nearest to the grassroots level and therefore could best accommodate their aspirations and needs. These groups are referred hereafter as Civil Society Organizations (CSOs).

Community-Based Disaster Risk Reduction
Community, Environment and Disaster Risk Management, Volume 10, 131–150
Copyright © 2012 by Emerald Group Publishing Limited
ISSN: 2040-7262/doi:10.1108/S2040-7262(2012)0000010014

The CSO owns base characters, which highlights the participation of the community from earlier mentioned different types of community groups. Those groups are considered to be effective in bringing about change within the community at large, due to its nature of collective action around shared interests. Bringing the change within the community includes the reduction of risk toward disasters or simply disaster risk reduction (DRR). Combining the nature of CSO and DRR, then Community-Based Disaster Risk Reduction (CBDRR) is formed to fulfill the needs of and deliver services to the community and to mainstream DRR activities. As described by Clayton, Oakley, and Taylor (2000), providing social services has been a critical role that CSOs have traditionally played, both in industrialized and developing countries. However, the key change that has taken place in recent years is that CSOs no longer just provide services to people that the government has failed to reach, but they are now far more in the mainstream of development activities. The nature (close to the grassroots level), scale, and profile of CBDRR have been acknowledged and recognized by the government, and those recognitions enable them to mainstream and conduct activities in reducing the disaster risks, targeting the beneficiaries for the communities.

Although the CBDRR certainly plays an important role and contributes positively to the communities, there are shortcomings that could hamper their steps. For an example, the limited coverage – although the CBDRR could reach wider public, according to Robinson and White (1997), one of the shortcomings of the CSO service provision is underlined by the limitation of coverage. CSOs may be able to aim service delivery to poor people, but the scale of their operations is limited and consequently many people do not benefit from them. The critical issue would be how to scale-up CSO interventions in order to reach more people and second, how to improve coordination between CSOs and government in service provision, respectively in DRR. The CSOs might be notoriously weak on coordination. In relation to service provision, however, this is essential to ensure that CSOs do not duplicate each other's efforts or concentrate all their efforts in the same geographical areas. Another example that could be a shortcoming is the quality of provision, which includes technical capacity and a quite significant amount of motivation to the communities that are critical issues to the delivery of services. Noted again by Robinson and White (1997), the massive increase in the role of CSOs in service provision in recent years raises questions about the capacity of CSOs to deliver high-quality services. However, there is little evidence from developing countries on which a general statement could be made about whether CSOs can provide better-quality services than the government. Despite a number of studies that draw attention to the shortcomings of government provision in health-care, there have been few studies on the quality of health-care services provided by CSOs. Green and Matthias (1997) mentioned also the cases of CSOs providing higher-quality health-care than the government are generally due to greater access to resources, not to any intrinsic comparative advantage. They point out that the converse is also true and that when funding levels for CSOs drop, the quality levels of health-care also tend to fall.

In spite of those examples of the shortcomings, CSOs are definitely regarded as contributing and bringing change to the communities. The chapter aims to describe the example of the participation of different CSOs for CBDRR in Indonesia as the lessons learned; how to capitalize the CSOs for effective CBDRR, as well as exploring the issues on how to mobilize those CSOs for CBDRR in tailoring the needs and enhancement for the future.

CHARACTERIZING THE CIVIL SOCIETY ORGANIZATIONS IN INDONESIA

The example of the participation of different CSOs for CBDRR in Indonesia is described below. Generally, the CSOs in Indonesia could be distinguished into three major groups:

- Women Welfare Associations (*TP PKK/Tim Penggerak Pemberdayaan Kesejahteraan Keluarga*),
- Youth unions (*Karang Taruna*) and KNPI (*Komite Nasional Pemuda Indonesia*), and
- Faith-based or religious organizations (*DKM/Dewan Keluarga Masjid and Pesantren*/Islamic Boarding Schools).

Those groups are typical CSOs that could be found in Indonesia and are mostly working with the grass-roots level. Because they are working together with and for the grass-roots level/communities at large, those CSOs have access to vast human resources and have great influences to bring about change within the community. Their current status has shifted from the implementer (the extended hand of local government) to the conception/ creator and mainstreamer of community development activities. Their contributions to the communities are varied in many ways. From the family planning campaign, health and sanitation education, women's empowerment, organizing national independence commemoration events, and public religious education and volunteering. Their efforts in supporting the government to reach the wider public has been recognized and labeled as community educators, intermediaries, and community facilitators. Each of those CSOs is characterized below.

Women's Associations

The Women Welfare Associations or better known as TP PKK, (*Tim Penggerak Pemberdayaan Kesejahteraan Keluarga*) has been classified as one of major CSOs in Indonesia. These associations are found throughout Indonesia. They are established in different administrative levels of governance hierarchy, from the national level to the smallest administrative units at wards (in the cities) and village levels (in rural areas). At the national level, the women's association is headed by the wife of the Minister of Home Affairs, at the provincial level is headed by the wife of the Governor, at the city level is headed by the wife of the mayor, at the sub-district level is headed by the wife of the head of the sub-district, and at the ward level is headed by the wife of the ward leader. These positions in return will be changed once in a five-year election, in line with their husbands' regional leadership elections.

This women's association (TP PKK) is unique; it works independently, an independent and nonprofit social institution that is not affiliated to any particular political party; yet is subsidized by the government. Referring to their historical roots in 1967, according to Central Secretariat of TP PKK (2011), TP PKK was established behind the motivation to improve the condition of Indonesian families. More than 50% of Indonesia's population is women, especially those who are living in rural areas. And most of them could be found in the low economic status and education levels. This is one of the factors that caused the low rate of life expectancy, which is for 63 years for males and 67 years for females. The maternal mortality rate (MMR) is quite high at 307 per 100,000 live births, and the infant mortality rate (IMR) is also significant high: 46 per 1,000 births. Recognizing these, the TP PKK moved to increase its activities, particularly for the efforts of decreasing the MMR and IMR rates. Seeing the unfortunate condition of the Central Java Province people, the wife of the Central Java Province Governor, Madame Isriati Moenadi, pioneered the establishment of Family Welfare Movement (TP PKK) as a community movement that aims to address "family welfare, on the awareness and skills that family own." TP

PKK is a movement that grows from the bottom of the development, for and managed by the community toward the realization of a safe, healthy and prosperous family as their vision.

In order to achieve its vision, TP PKK has adopted 10 main programs, including the efforts to meet the basic human needs, namely in fulfilling the physical, mental, and social aspects. Those ten main programs are as follow: (1) appreciation and implementing the *Pancasila* (foundation of the Indonesian state of ideology); (2) mutual cooperation (which are attitudes that are rooted in tradition, culture, local wisdom/indigenous knowledge, community life, etc.); (3) food; (4) clothing; (5) housing and household management; (6) education and skills; (7) health; (8) development of cooperative life; (9) environmental sustainability; and (10) planning a healthy life (TP PKK, 2006).

Basically, the aforementioned characters of this women's association/TP PKK could be highly regarded as a potential driver and change of agent for DRR activities within the communities. It is seen not only from their possible programs, but from the women's spirit and strong will to improve their life, families, and surrounding community).

Youth Unions

The youth movement in Indonesia more or less has the same characteristics as the women's associations. They are established from the largest to the smallest administrative unit. The youth in Indonesia, according to the Ministry of Youth and Sports of Indonesia (2010) ranges between 16 and 30 years old. Commonly, the smallest unit of youth union is founded at the ward level, the so-called *Karang Taruna,* endorsed by the Ministry of Social Affairs of Indonesia. According to Department Social Affairs (2006), *Karang Taruna* is the umbrella organization for the youth. *Karang Taruna* or the Youth Union is a coordinating institution of which several programs are carried out involving all the components and potential in youth of urban as well as rural areas. These youth unions are working in the field of social welfare and community development. The youth unions as far as possible should be able to demonstrate their function and role optimally. As an organization, it has a board of management and a full member of youth participation. Each member can carry out their functions in their respective sectors and are able to work together with the local administration. Having clear activity programs in accordance with the needs and problems that exist around the youth and surrounding community, those programs are institutionalized and sustained, focusing and involving all elements of the younger generation.

In the urban areas, one of the Youth Union's strengths is the ability to raise funds that comes from the government and NGOs for the implementation of community program activities. As a case example of particular events, such as yearly national independence commemoration day (August 17) and religious festivity, the youth within the ward gathered and developed plans for organizing and holding the event. It started by raising the funds from the community, organizing and implementing the event for the community. The youth that are gathered in the Youth Union are volunteers and considered as a motor engine in running the activities within the community. This organization is independent from nature with voluntary work as its base. In the rural areas, the youth applied another approach to serve and participate in the rural community development, especially in the field of raising social welfare. One of many components that the youth play an important role for rural development is the community empowerment organization (*LPM/Lembaga Pemberdayaan Masyarakat*). *LPM* is a public institution, representing the aspirations of all communities in the rural development in a holistic manner (ideology, political, economic, social, cultural, religious, security, and defense) and has the task of organizing meetings in the village; hence the Youth Union has the coordination, consultation, correction task, and gives criticisms/suggestions together with the *LPM*. Thus the Youth Union has the main task of empowering the youth with *LPM* program to jointly address the social welfare issues with the local government, as a form of community participation (Ministry of Social Affairs of Indonesia, 2011).

In accordance with each Youth Union's conditions, it is expected to respond and handle the social welfare problems of the youth and community. In general, *LPM* as a vehicle for community participation (including the Youth Union) will always give the spirit, encouragement, and support the community development through programs that have been planned for the youth. With the provision of their capability and reliability, the Youth Union will be able to optimally tackle the social welfare issues. Thus via the LPM's programs, the Youth Union is able to contribute to the youth and community optimally and increase the social solidarity among them. Other issues beneficial to the community that are covered by the Youth Union are the prevention of juvenile crime and delinquency as well as drug and alcohol abuse. As a form of community participation and volunteering, delivering social services and rehabilitation such as: environmental protection and sanitation, support for vulnerable groups such as children, the disabled, women, the elderly, and disaster victims, are handled by the Youth Union as well. Other socioeconomic activities such as economic development through cooperation with existing social organization, such as the formation of the joint business group, enhancing skills, and entrepreneurship are examples that are explored and done by the Youth Union at the national level.

Specifically targeted for disaster emergency and response, the Ministry of Social Affairs has formed *Tagana* (*Taruna Siaga Bencana*/Disaster Preparedness Youth) with the personnel of more than 30,000 people throughout Indonesian provinces. It is enacted by Law No. 11 year 2009 about Social Welfare and Ministry Regulation No. 82/HUK/2006. Its membership is mostly the youth, but it is not limited to any age (Ministry of Social Affairs, 2011).

Other type of the youth union, which can be found at the national and provincial level, is the so-called *KNPI* (*Komite Nasional Pemuda Indonesia*/ Indonesia National Youth Council). KNPI is an umbrella organization of youth assembled and is the core of the strength of Indonesia's youth. In line with the KNPI paradigm shift, the role and main duties of KNPI are to oversee the changes in society toward the creation of the Indonesian people who are a qualified, dignified, just, and prosperous society in an egalitarian and democratic life (KNPI, 2011). It addresses the youth's issues on global scale, as an example, the KNPI is acted as a host for International Youth Forum on Climate Change for the year 2011.

Faith-Based or Religious Organizations

Many religious organizations or groups are forming within the country; some of them have a strong and long historical background, dating from old colonial times. Many of them were established as a means of promoting the social welfare as well as education of their members, as an alternative to those provided by the colonial ruler. Several of them have strong roots among the population spread in most parts of the country. In many cases, they have charismatic, respected leaders, which represent informal leadership within the communities and often act as the counterpart of the government officials in the daily social and political activities. They are often considered as having a strong potential power to implement disaster reduction awareness programs among their followers. Implementing CBDRR activities among their communities can be considered as an attractive challenge, as many of them have been involved in many disaster relief and recovery activities during disaster situation. Partnered with an academic or research institution that can act as their technical support, these organizations can develop a potential capacity for conducting and implementing CBDRR programs.

Nahdlatul Ulama and *Muhammadiyah*, two big Islamic organizations with long history in Indonesia, have been implementing CBDRR activities involving school children and *pesantren* (Islamic religious boarding school) students, youth Islamic organizations, and communities around *pesantren*. A research institution of ITB (Institut Teknologi Bandung), named the Center for Disaster Mitigation (CDM), under a collaboration scheme with those two organizations, provided technical support in the capacity building, developing, planning, and implementing their CBDRR programs (CDM-ITB, 2007). Those two religious organizations are putting effort for building disaster risk awareness among the community as well as their members, by organizing community workshops and training and by conducting participatory activities related to understanding hazards in the areas where they live. Facilitation is carried out to bridge the hazard knowledge gap of the people and to develop common sense regarding safety culture among the people. The programs are designed such that the beneficiaries will include people who lives in rural as well as urban area, as they are both vulnerable to various hazards due to lack of knowledge, lack of access to infrastructure and services, as well as lack of opportunity and resources which impede the implementation of DRR initiatives.

Another vulnerable group are the children, who are often considered as a potential target for disaster awareness program, as they represent the future generation of the country, as well as the fact that they can act as ambassadors or media to communicate the information to their parents and older member of the families. *Nahdlatul Ulama* designed the program to include *pesantrens* (Islamic boarding schools), which count for more than several thousand spread out around Indonesia as their capacity building target, because these *pesantrens* are expected to act as the local center of excellence in disaster information and as the development agent within their community. *Muhammadiyah* organization targets elementary schools and youth organizations under its jurisdiction for the disaster awareness programs, and expects that the two entities can act as agent of development in building the safety culture among their communities.

To develop the capacity of the religious organizations in implementing CBDRR processes, at the outset the CDM-ITB established a clear objective of their programs, who will be the targets and who will be the main actors.

Expected output and outcomes as well as tangible, auditable, and accountable performance indicators are identified. Need assessment was done in order to gain the information regarding what kind of knowledge do they need, what kind of skill they should have, and what capacity in the first place they already have. Once the needs have been analyzed, the transferring process is started. Training and training of trainers (ToT) are carried out as the first step necessary to strengthen the capacity of the religious organizations to develop and implement their own CBDRR programs as well as their own facilitators. Relevant dissemination materials are developed to use in the CBDRR implementation programs, such as the materials of introduction and concept of disaster management, knowledge of hazards (earthquake, flood, tsunami, landslides, volcanic eruption, tornado, and fire); methods on how to deliver disaster awareness materials to school children with special characteristics in Islamic teaching; and CBDRR techniques and tools (community participatory hazard and vulnerability assessment, community action planning, psychology, how to communicate with children and adults as well). Simulations, drills, exercises, and experiments are used to enhance the training delivery.

As for monetary issues, funding is always one of the crucial issues raised by the community organizations for sustaining CBDRR programs. The strategies to deal with the financial issue include building the capacity to develop sound proposals, seeking and developing networks with national, regional, and local government and NGOs, including international multi-lateral and bilateral aid agencies. Realizing the two-year program, a strong and well-managed project organization within the implementing agencies (the religious organizations) with adequate human resources supported by appropriate leadership and good communication are indispensable to the successful implementation of these programs. A strong commitment from related stakeholders will ensure the sustainability of the initiatives.

Another type of faith-based or religious organization is *DKM* (*Dewan Keluarga Masjid*/Mosque Council) that can be found at any major mosque at the sub-district and ward levels. These Mosque Councils are independent, yet have an organization structure that is headed mostly by the elderly or community leaders. Their activities are mainly fundraising for the poor and organizing religious events, such as providing the religious materials and educating the young as well as holding a men's and women's forum for conveying and discussing not only the religious matter, but to address social issues as well. Table 1 below provides the summary of the mentioned CSOs in Indonesia.

Table 1. Summary of Community Society Organizations in Indonesia.

Community Society Organizations (CSOs) Type	Characters
Women's Associations/TP PKK	• Women's participation • Independent • Yearly subsidized budget • Headed by the wives of appointed administrative leaders • Established from National to Ward level • Focusing on Family Welfare
Youth Union/Karang Taruna, KNPI	• Youth participation • Volunteer • Fundraising from community and donors • Headed by the elected youth leader • Established in urban as well as in rural areas • Focusing on the socio-economic issues
Faith-based or Religious Organizations/Pesantren, DKM	• Not limited age of participation • Independent and volunteer • Fundraising and small amount of government subsidy • Headed by community leader (high influenced person) • Focusing on educating religious and social issues

LINKING THE CIVIL SOCIETY ORGANIZATIONS' ACTIVITIES WITH DISASTER RISK REDUCTION

Several types of existing CSOs in Indonesia have been described in the previous section. The question that would next arise is how to link their activities with DRR. Those CSOs are the women's associations, youth unions, and faith-based or religious organization, which can be termed the pioneer and agent of change for CBDRR. Firstly, those CSOs are regarded as the potential catalysts for triggering the DRR activities within the community, as they existed within the neighborhood and rooted for years. Secondly, those CSOs are seen as the organizations that are capable of bearing the responsibilities and have taken form as the role models, because most of the highly influential people are the members of it (wives of the administrative leaders, high-end persons, community and religious leaders, etc.). In order to be successfully linked with DRR, several factors need to be infiltrated in their activities. The linking factors for example are in the form of principles that are chalked out and offered by UN-ISDR (2007), and can be adopted as guidelines. Many of them are explicitly recognized and emphasized in the Hyogo Framework of Action (HFA). Past experiences in DRR have led to the development of those basic principles, underpinning the achievements of effective DRR. Those factors are: linking and integration into development planning; capacity development, decentralization; public–private partnership; and community participation.

At first, primary responsibility for implementing measures to reduce disaster risk is done by the government. DRR has to be an essential part of a government's investment in sustainable development. The guidelines set by UN-ISDR (2007) have also mentioned that the government has the power as well as the responsibility to protect their citizens and their national assets by reducing the risk of losses from disasters. The government, however, cannot do the work alone. Effective DRR relies on the efforts of many different stakeholders, including regional and international organizations, civil society including volunteers, the private sector, the media, and the scientific community. Particularly at this, CSOs should point out and raise their voices to be heard and noticed and be engaged by the government. The first factor is that DRR must be integrated into development activities. Past disaster events are destroying lives and livelihoods and trapping many people in poverty. The government can minimize such losses by integrating DRR measures into development strategies, assessing potential risks as part of development planning, and allocating resources for risk reduction sector-wise. At this certain point, an opportunity gap exists that can be filled by the CSOs to link and integrate those development strategies in their daily routine activities and programs. By introducing those strategies to the communities by means of chain reactions, wider public participation in DRR could be obtained.

Capacity development could be another entry point to link CSOs' activities with DRR, as it is a central strategy for reducing disaster risk. Capacity development is needed to build and maintain the ability of people, organizations, and societies to manage their risks successfully. This requires not only training and individuals to recognize and reduce risks in their localities. It also includes sustainable technology transfer, information exchange, network development, management skills, professional linkages, and other resources. Thus capacity development needs to be sustained

through institutions that support capacity building and capacity maintenance as permanent ongoing objectives. CSOs can be such institutions to
have DRR invested in their activities and programs.

The following factor is decentralization, where responsibility for DRR
ought to be decentralized. Many DRR activities need to be implemented at
provincial, municipal, and local levels, as the hazards faced and the
populations exposed are specific to particular geographic areas. Similarly,
the administrative responsibilities to manage key risk factors, such as land-
use zoning regulations are often devolved to such scales. In order to
recognize and respond to these locally specific characteristics, it is
necessary to decentralize responsibilities and resources for DRR to
relevant sub-national or local authorities, as appropriate. Moreover,
decentralization can also motivate increased local participation. Therefore, the CSOs along with improved efficiency and equitable benefits from
local services are suitable actors in communicating DRR to the
communities at large.

Closing public–private partnerships are also an important tool for DRR
and linking factor of CSOs activities with DRR. Public–private partnerships
are voluntary joint associations formed to address shared objectives through
collaborative actions. These collaborative actions may involve public
organizations such as government agencies, professional and/or academic
institutions, NGOs, and CSOs together with business organizations such as
companies, industry associations, and private foundations. Because the
threats from natural hazards affect both public and private interests alike,
private–public partnerships can offer opportunities to combine resources
and expertise to act jointly to reduce risks and potential losses. They can
thereby improve the resilience of communities. In general, closing a
partnership with the authorities and business sector can be another factor
in linking CSOs' activities with DRR.

Additionally, the foremost factor among them is that effective DRR
requires definitely community participation. CSOs can better gather and
mobilize the community to be participated in short amount of time, are the
CSOs. CSOs are close to the grass-roots people and are actually in the midst
of communities. In addition, they have members that are considered to be
prominent within the society and regarded as role models that could
influence the behavior and perceptions of community at large and trigger
risk reduction actions collectively.

In summary, Table 2 shows the matrix on how those linking factors of
DRR attribute to the three previously identified CSOs.

Table 2. CSOs and Attributing Factors for DRR.

CSOs	Attributing Factors for DRR				
	Integration into development planning	Capacity development	Decentralization	Public–Private partnership	Community participation
Women's Welfare Associations	Evaluating the disaster management plan with ward and sub-district officers	Women disaster awareness courses	Collection and communication risk data at wards	Micro-credit and soft-loan system for women-headed households	Cultural events organization for fundraising
Youth Unions	Mobilizing youth in the participation of disaster management plan review	Youth disaster drills	Set-up disaster unit office with ward government	Engagement of private sector for young entrepreneurs	Mobilization of youth in volunteering
Faith-Based Organizations	Engage the community in the participation of disaster management plan review	Training of Trainers for community safety campaign	Collective cooperative schemes at ward level	Linkage of rehabilitation and reconstruction subsidy	Informal community gathering for planning

CAPITALIZING THE CIVIL SOCIETY
ORGANIZATIONS FOR EFFECTIVE CBDRR

Previously, different types of CSOs in Indonesia have been mentioned and their characteristics have been described, followed by possible factors that enable their activities link with DRR. A further step would be how to capitalize all above mentioned to be an effective CBDRR. In detail, how those characters, benefits of the CSOs can be captured and utilized in mobilizing the efforts and attempts of the community to reduce the underlying risks. Clearly, the CSOs are the social capitals and marked as potential "vehicle" for the community to address their needs and participation in DRR.

Before elaborating how to capitalize the CSOs for CBDRR, one may ask why the CSOs are important social capitals. The following argument has been made by Putnam (2000): First, social capital allows the communities to resolve collective problems more easily. People often might be better off if they cooperate, with each doing her/his share. Second, social capital greases the wheels that allow communities to advance smoothly; where the people are trusting and trustworthy, and where they are subject to repeated interactions with their fellow citizens, in everyday business and social transactions that are less costly. A third way is that social capital improves the lot, by widening the awareness of the many ways in which the fates are linked. When the people lack connection to others, they are unable to test the veracity of their own views, whether in the give or take of casual conversation or in more formal deliberation. Without such an opportunity, people are more likely to be swayed by their worse impulses. The networks that constitute social capital also serve as conduits for the flow of helpful information that facilitates achieving the goals. Social capital also operates through psychological and biological processes to improve individual's lives. Community connectedness is crucial, whereas being connected is nowadays a demand.

In order to capitalize the CSOs for effective CBDRR, as has been mentioned earlier, the CSOs could at the first place regarded as facilitators, intermediaries, and public educators or informal educators. Again, Putnam's (2000) discussed the social capital that provides informal educators with a rationale for their activities. The classic working environment for the informal educator is the group, club, or organization, or the CSOs. Several backing reasons that pointed out by Putnam (2000) are as follows.

First, the simple act of joining and being regularly involved in organized groups has a very significant impact on individual health and well-being.

Working in the appropriate manner that people may join groups – whether they are organized around enthusiasms and interests, social activity, or economic and political aims – can make a considerable contribution in it. Encouraging the development of associational life can also make a significant difference to the experience of being in different communities, for example, the case of schooling is highlighted. Educational achievement is likely to rise significantly, and the quality of day-to-day interaction is likely to be enhanced by a much greater emphasis on the cultivation of extracurricular activity involving groups and teams. As Shaw and Takeuchi (2009) have also proposed that the education in risk reduction should go beyond textbooks and should also involve experiential learning. The books may provide the knowledge, but it is more important to transform the knowledge into practice in the form of practical training such as disaster drill, capacity building, and experiential learning through people, community, and CSOs.

Second, informal education's longstanding concern with association and the quality of life in associations and CSOs can make a direct and important contribution to the development of social networks as well as the relationships of trust and tolerance that is usually involved. Informal educators' interests within CSOs are in dialogue, conversation, and the cultivation of environments, in which people can work together, take them to the heart of what is required to strengthen and develop social capital and civic society. A focus on tolerance and the acceptance of differences is required. Within CSOs, there are places for bridging, bonding, and linking the social capital. Such informal education activities can be implemented for example through town watches, disaster drills, cultural performances, parents, and local community involvements. These activities can be distinguished in their learning process and tools (Mulyasari, Takeuchi, & Shaw, 2011). Basically, those activities bring communities into contact with other community members, forge a bond, and eventually form a social capital, society networks, and society organizations or community society organization.

Third, according to Putnam's (2000) analysis, for example, crime can be reduced, educational achievement can be enhanced, and better health can be fostered through the strengthening of social capital. Significantly, this entails working across communities – and in particular, sustaining the commitment and capacities already involved in community organizations and enthusiast groups, which are the CSOs, and encouraging those on the cusp of being actively involved. Last but not least, interaction within the CSOs enables people to build communities and to commit themselves to each other and knit the social fabric. There have been a number of definitions of social capital; Begum (2003) had summarized the following: "Social capital is a resource, private and public, inherent in the structure of relationships in organizational social networks and interpersonal relationships." Begum (2003) also mentioned that according to this view, social capital is not a characteristic that can be looked at in isolation; rather, it achieves meaning relative to other forms of capital, such as physical, financial, human, and cultural; and community resources at large, such as infrastructure, government social spending and public investment, and the role of private business. In addition, according to what Putnam (2000) has mentioned earlier that social capital entails working across communities, Begum (2003) stated that social capital can also be used to promote objectives of participation and community involvement that are key to many government regeneration initiatives. This means that the renewed focus on community involvement is part of systematic efforts to establish greater links between the community and the government.

The issues mentioned above describe how the existence of the CSOs as a social capital can be captured and capitalized as the motor engine for the community to commonly undertake DRR activities.

WAY FORWARD

One of the community empowerment strategies is based on community participation (Kieffer, 1984; Paton & Bishop, 1996). Once the basis for empowerment is established, the next stage involves the identification of a community change agent. The involvement of community members provides mutual support and opportunities in lobbying the authority. Those can be found in the CSOs, where collective efficacy might be a good indicator of the level of cooperation and assistance available within a community and this in turn may be a measurement of the likelihood of the success of mitigation and risk reduction strategies. These all require a collective and coordinated action to be adopted and implemented.

After elaborating the CSOs issues and their details, there is no doubt that CSOs are important in contributing the DRR. This is emphasized by Victoria (2009) that whether a disaster is major or minor, of national or local proportion, it is the people at the community who will suffer most its adverse effects. People, collectively, use coping and survival strategies to face and respond to the situation long before outside help from the government or NGOs arrives. The final step, after capitalizing the CSOs for

DRR, would be how to effectively mobilize those (CSOs) so that it is tailored to the community's needs and improved toward enhancement.

One of the tailoring issues is gender. Gender is a core factor in disaster risk and in the implementation of DRR. Gender is a central organizing principle in all societies, and therefore women and men are differently at risk from disasters. As Enarson (1998) argued that gender relations play clearly a role in the political economy of disaster, organizational relief and response, community leadership and mobilization, household preparation, and family recovery and disaster survival strategies. Moreover, Enarson (1998) also argued that more equitable social relations also support the development of more democratic and participatory disaster resilient communities. In all settings, at home, at work, or in the neighborhood, gender shapes the capacities and resources of individuals to minimize harm, adapt to hazards, and respond to disasters. Gender terrain of disaster can help communities live more safely with hazard, respond to crisis, and reduce the impact of future disasters (Enarson, 1998). It is evident from past disasters that low-income women and those who are marginalized due to marital status, physical ability, age, social stigma, or caste are especially disadvantaged. At the grass-roots level, on the other hand, women are often well positioned to manage risk due to their roles as both users and managers of environmental resources, as economic providers, and as caregivers and community workers. For these reasons, it is necessarily correctly targeted at the most vulnerable groups and is effectively implemented through the roles of both women and men. That is exactly the entry point for one of the CSOs, such as women's associations, to come into play.

Another tailoring issue is that DRR within CSOs needs to be customized to particular settings. The CSO in one area varies greatly in political, socioeconomic, cultural, environment, and hazard backgrounds with other organizations. Measures that succeed in reducing risk in one setting may not work in others. Customizing involves making use of others' experience, for instance by reviewing the context of particular measures and the nature of good practices and lessons learned, and then tailoring these to implement policies and activities that are appropriate for the local contexts. An important aspect of customizing is an awareness of cultural diversity, recognizing the differences among groups of people in language, socio-economic, and political systems, religion, ethnicity, their indigenous knowledge, and in their historical relationship with nature. Understanding the patterns and behavior of social organizations within society is crucial in promoting positive perception and action for disaster education as part of DRR (Takeuchi, Mulyasari, & Shaw, 2011). In addition, local sociopolitical

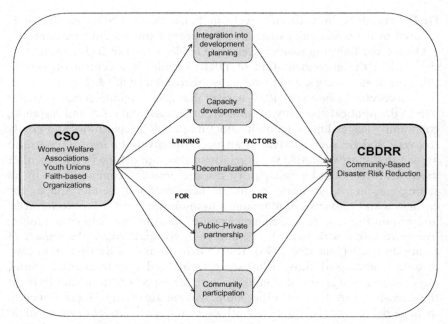

Fig. 1. The CSO and the Five Linking Factors for CBDRR.

structures and cultural conditions, such as kinship arrangements, customary rights, community and family networks, and systems of leadership, nearly always persist during times of stress, such as disaster. It is important to take these factors as a starting point and to build on them when designing and implementing new policies and practices for community-based DRR.

Those above-mentioned issues are necessary for the CSOs to be worked in mobilizing the community for creating at the end the culture of safety and building safer communities through community-based DRR. Fig. 1 shows the overview of CSOs and the five linking factors for CBDRR.

ACKNOWLEDGMENTS

The authors are thankful to the Japanese Government (Monbukagakusho: MEXT) Scholarship and GCOE-HSE Program of Kyoto University for support extended for this study to the first author.

REFERENCES

Begum, H. (2003). Social capital in action: Adding up local connections and networks. A pilot study in London. Centre for Civil Society (CCS), London School of Economics, UK. Retrieved from http://eprints.lse.ac.uk/29402/1/Social_Capital_in_Action.pdf. Accessed October 2011.

CDM-ITB. (2007). Technical support for capacity development of Nahdlatul Ulama and Muhammadyah organizations in implementing community based disaster risk mitigation. Annual Report, CDM-ITB and Ausaid.

Central Secretariat of TP PKK. (2011). History of TP PKK. Retrieved from http://tp-pkkpusat.org/index.php?option=com_content&view=article&id=62&Itemid=75. Accessed March 2011.

Clayton, A., Oakley, P., & Taylor, J. (2000). Civil Society Organizations and Service Provision. Civil Society and Social Movements Program Paper No.2. United Nations Research Institute for Social Development/UNRISD, Geneva, Switzerland.

Department of Social Affairs. (2006). Youth empowerment program LPM. Retrieved from http://www.depsos.go.id/modules.php?name=News&file=article&sid=355. Accessed March 2011.

Enarson, E. (1998). Through women's eyes: A gendered research agenda for disaster social science. *Disasters, 22*(2), 157–173.

Green, A., & Matthias, A. (1997). *Non-governmental organizations' and health in developing countries*. Basingstoke: Macmillan.

Kieffer, C. (1984). Citizen empowerment: A developmental perspective. *Prevention in Human Services, 3*, 9–36.

KNPI. (2011). *Komite Nasional Pemuda Indonesia*/Indonesia national youth council. http://knpi.net/index.php?option=com_frontpage&Itemid=1. Accessed March 2011.

London School of Economics and Centre for Civil Society. (2011). What is civil society ministry of social affairs of Indonesia (2011). *Taruna Siaga Bencana*. Retrieved from http://tagana.depsos.go.id/?profile/history. Accessed March 2011.

Ministry of Social Affairs of Indonesia. (2011). Pemberdayaan Karang Taruna dengan Program LPM. Retrieved from http://www.depsos.go.id/modules.php?name=News&file=article&sid=355. Accessed October 2011.

Ministry of Youth and Sport of Indonesia. (2010). Strategic planning of the ministry of youth and sport of Indonesia 2010–2014, Jakarta, Indonesia.

Mulyasari, F., Takeuchi, Y., & Shaw, R. (2011). Implementation tools for disaster education. In R. Shaw, K. Shiwaku & Y. Takeuchi (Eds.), *Disaster education, community, environment and disaster risk management, Volume 7* (pp. 137–151). Bingley, UK: Emerald Books.

Paton, D., & Bishop, B. (1996). Disasters and communities: Promoting physiological wellbeing. In D. Paton & N. Long (Eds.), *Psychological aspects of disaster: Impact, coping, and intervention*. Palmerstone North: Dunmore Press.

Putnam, R. (2000). *Bowling alone: The collapse and revival of American community* (pp. 288–290). New York, NY: Simon and Schuster.

Robinson, M., & White, G. (1997). *The role of civic organizations in the provision of social services: Towards synergy*. Helsinki, Finland: World Institute for Development Economics Research.

Shaw, R., & Takeuchi, Y. (2009). Town watching handbook for disaster education. Enhancing experiential learning. European Union (EU), International Strategy for Disaster Risk Reduction (ISDR), and Kyoto University, Japan.

Takeuchi, Y., Mulyasari, F., & Shaw, R. (2011). Roles of family and community in disaster education. In R. Shaw, K. Shiwaku & Y. Takeuchi (Eds.), *Disaster education. Community, environment and disaster risk management, Volume 7* (pp. 77–94). Bingley, UK: Emerald Books.

TP PKK. (2006). PKK Cadre Handbook Year 2006, PKK Movement of West Java Province. Buku Saku Kader PKK. Tim Penggerak PKK Provinsi Jawa Barat Tahun 2006.

UN-ISDR. (2007). A set of guiding principles for implementing disaster risk reduction. Words into action: A guide for implementing the Hyogo framework, United Nations secretariat of the International Strategy for Disaster Reduction (UN-ISDR), Geneva, Switzerland, pp. 4–5.

Victoria, L. (2009). Community capacity and disaster resilience. In R. Shaw & R. R. Krishnamurthy (Eds.), *Disaster management: Global challenges and local solutions* (pp. 338–351). Chennai, India: Universities Press.

CHAPTER 9

PARTNERSHIP BETWEEN CITY GOVERNMENT AND COMMUNITY-BASED DISASTER PREVENTION ORGANIZATIONS IN KOBE, JAPAN

Yuki Matsuoka, Jonas Joerin, Rajib Shaw and Yukiko Takeuchi

INTRODUCTION

The importance of community-based organizations to support relief works in the aftermath of disasters is widely recognized as indispensable in providing quickly the needed help for affected populations (Bajek, Matsuda, & Okada, 2008; Nagasaka, 2008; Norris, Stevens, Pfefferbaum, Wyche, & Pfefferbaum, 2008; Shaw & Goda, 2004; Suzuki, 2006). Although communities' involvement in rescue operations is essential, their role in rehabilitation and future disaster preparedness activities is equally important in the process of forming a disaster-resilient society (Nagasaka, 2008). Furthermore, the level of interaction between local authorities and communities within different phases (preparedness, relief, and rehabilitation) of the disaster management cycle requires attention to effectively implement community-based disaster risk reduction (CBDRR).

Community-Based Disaster Risk Reduction
Community, Environment and Disaster Risk Management, Volume 10, 151–184
Copyright © 2012 by Emerald Group Publishing Limited
All rights of reproduction in any form reserved
ISSN: 2040-7262/doi:10.1108/S2040-7262(2012)0000010015

After the devastating Great Hanshin-Awaji earthquake on January 17, 1995, which left heavy traces of destruction on various infrastructures and resulted in the loss of more than 6,400 human lives, the voluntary support of many surviving residents in Kobe in rescue operations highlighted the potential of well-functioning communities. The inherent characteristics of communities to provide a network among people strengthen their social capital and ability to respond to potential disasters (Nakagawa & Shaw, 2004; Shaw & Goda, 2004). Bajek et al. (2008) emphasize on this event as it marked the beginning of a paradigm shift on how the Japanese government and society perceived the management of disasters. This was exemplified in the adoption of the White Paper on Disaster Management (2007) where a disaster was not anymore seen as being solely prevented through technical and engineering solutions, but much more in a multidisciplinary approach through the involvement of different actors such as communities (Nagasaka, 2008). For example, the rehabilitation efforts following the earthquake in Kobe were characterized by increased involvement of communities in the reconstruction planning of the city (Shaw & Goda, 2004).

The heightened participation of communities in disaster-related voluntary-based organizations following the earthquake in 1995 in Japan is shown by Bajek et al. (2008). According to them, since 1995, the number of autonomous organizations for disaster reduction, named Jishu-bosai-soshiki (short Jishubo), functioning at the community level in form of neighborhood organizations, have increased from 43.8% in 1995 to 62.5% in 2004. The percentages imply the rate of households participating in such organizations in Japan. However, Bajek et al. (2008) assume that the increase in number of participating households is largely due to the existence of community councils all over Japan, named Chonaikai in Japanese, which trigger a "compulsory participation" for people to take part in their activities. As the Chonaikai's are historically manifested in the Japanese society, their influence goes beyond the gathering of their people, but they also work together with other units of the local government such as the police or civil servants (Bajek et al., 2008). Thus, even though they are the smallest administrative unit in the municipal administration in Japan, they have the potential to exert a considerable amount of power within their communities.

Although communities are perceived as integral actors in the management of disasters and recent trends show that more people in Japan participate in voluntary-based organizations, the question arises to what extent their activities in implementing disaster risk reduction (DRR) is coordinated with the local authorities. In this chapter, the role of the Bosai Fukushi Komyunithi (BOKOMI), in implementing CBDRR, established in the city of Kobe after the Great Hanshin-Awaji Earthquake in 1995, is examined by assessing the level of partnership between the 191 BOKOMIs, formed in the 191 school districts of the city, and the Kobe City Government.

This chapter analyzes the concept and level of partnership between a community and a local government through theoretical aspects described in a partnership framework. The developed partnership framework is applied to evaluate a potential partnership between communities, called "BOKOMIs" (Disaster Prevention Welfare Communities), and the local government of Kobe City.

THE CONCEPT OF PARTNERSHIP BETWEEN A COMMUNITY AND A LOCAL GOVERNMENT

As social capital (e.g., strong ties, networks, and trust) among people is regarded as a key feature to support the well-functioning and resilience of a community in times of a disaster (Murphy, 2007; Shaw & Goda, 2004), the establishment of community-based organizations during pre-disaster times may have the potential to implement CBDRR (Patterson, Weil, & Patel, 2010). However, the efficacy of community-based organizations to implement DRR may depend on two factors: firstly, the participation level of people within a community, and secondly, the relationship between such a community and the government it belongs to. Fig. 1 shows, on the left, the different stages of power citizens may get, but depending on the behavior of the government, this level of participation is higher or lower (middle and right parts) (Arnstein, 1969; Pretty, 1995). For example, in an autocratic political system, the level of people's participation in decision-making processes is fully dependent on the terms defined by the ruling government, and thus, people are likely being manipulated and may not participate.

The opposite would be that citizen gain full control in decision-making processes and do not rely anymore on an authority or government that may prescribe certain rules. Since this latter scenario demands a high control within communities to function effectively, in order not to end up in anarchy, governments throughout the world take the lead in guiding communities. However, what is the most favorable relationship between these two actors in relation to implementing DRR? From the perspective where communities are regarded as valuable sources for sharing indigenous knowledge, a certain level of power given to communities may have positive impacts in the overall decision-making process. Fig. 1 shows that the level of

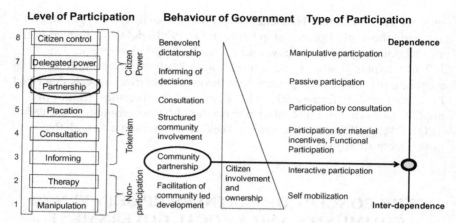

Fig. 1. Level and Type of Participation between a Community and a Local Government.

participation leading to a partnership relationship between communities and a government is proposed as an ideal and effective solution where both parties act upon agreed terms.

Definition and Characterization of Partnership

As communities can provide valuable knowledge about their people's needs and concerns, a local government may not have sufficient access to these types of information, which favors the involvement of communities into the overall decision-making process. Thus, a more participatory-based decision-making process may result in more widely accepted decisions and solutions. In the field of DRR, this has particular importance if so-called soft adaptation measures are aimed to be implemented.

According to Vasconcellos and Vasconcellos (2009, p. 135), a "partnership contains the sense of cooperation, mutual trust and synergy between stakeholders to achieve a common objective." This characterization of partnership addresses similar issue compared to how social capital is perceived as a successful partnership can mobilize different actors to generate added value that goes beyond an individual actor's space of action. Based on further extensive literature review, attention needs to be given to the following aspects of a partnership: firstly, it forms relationships between two or more stakeholders and aggregates different resources to pursue a joint approach to achieve common goals (Lewis, 2000; McQuaid, 2000; Penrose, 2000); secondly, a partnership can build an organization in which mutual trust among the participating actors is essential for its success (Harriss, 2000; Postma, 1994).

Partnership Framework

By linking the theoretical aspects of a partnership, a framework is developed where five key factors determine and summarize the understanding of this term. This framework is based on literature review (Arnstein, 1969; Harriss, 2000; Lewis, 2000; Patterson et al., 2010; Postma, 1994; Pretty, 1995; Vasconcellos & Vasconcellos, 2009) and reveals that all aspects of a partnership need to be equally shared and responsibility taken.

- A: Common objectives (shared interests, benefit, values, and priorities among partners)
- B: Shared decision-making (partners take decisions mutual consent)
- C: Regular interaction (maintenance and support between partners)
- D: Level of control (partners meet agreed deadlines of projects/ activities)
- E: Ownership (partners have shared responsibilities and resources)

Applying this theoretical partnership framework into a potential community–local government relationship, the factor E gains particular importance. In this partnership framework, it is not only expected that both parties have common objectives, shared decision-making, regular interaction, but also ownership in their activities. Thus, communities may receive responsibility or ownership that is usually held by the local government. This means entrusting people to carry out activities independently gives people higher affiliation in the implementation of activities. In the context of CBDRR, this form of coexistence between two bodies (communities and local government) may be an ideal form to stimulate more bottom-up-driven development in the field of disaster preparedness (Mayo, 1997). Providing communities to share their views and ideas in the decision-making process demands a flexible government and a certain amount of freedom given to people if such a partnership aims to become successful. However, common objectives and ideas may have to be evolved from an iterating process where both parties not only share their individual ideas but also have to fight for them. Again in the context of implementing the Hyogo

Framework for Action and pushing for DRR, the application of a shared type of relationship in form of a mutual partnership between communities and local governments is one way CBDRR can be implemented. This partnership framework also has the aspiration to function as a tool to measure sustainability between two partners. Thus, if both, communities and local government agree on all the five factors, their relationship is not only successful, but may also trigger sustainable solutions.

Types of Partnership

A partnership can last for any type of time period. Fig. 2 shows that the identified types of partnership between communities and their local government are split into three key types based on the time scale: single-event, based on agreement, and institutionalized.

The institutionalized type of partnership is expected to take the form of an accepted coexistence of communities and local government with a sharing of power. This type requires additional trust between the two partners to enter into that stage as only after several years this level may be achieved. In the following part, the abovementioned partnership framework is applied in a case study between BOKOMIs and the Kobe City Government.

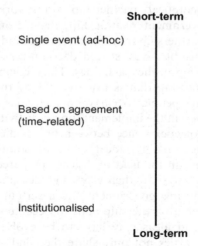

Fig. 2.   Types of Partnership between a Community and a Local Government.

EXPERIENCE OF THE GREAT HANSHIN-AWAJI EARTHQUAKE IN 1995

On January 17, 1995, the Great Hanshin-Awaji Earthquake occurred at 5:46 a.m. and caused devastating damage in the region of western Japan named Hanshin-Awaji, including Kobe City. This powerful earthquake reached 7.2 on the Richter scale and registered 7 on the Japanese Meteorological Agency seismic intensity scale. Its epicenter was 14 km below and about 25 km from central Kobe. This was the first major earthquake that hit a Japan urban area after the World War II.

The total number of dead people was 6,434. In the Hyogo Prefecture, the total number of death was 6,402 people, which included 4,571 in Kobe City. The total number of persons injured was 43,792. In the Hyogo Prefecture, the total number of casualties was 40,092, which included 14,678 in Kobe City. According to the official record announced by Kobe City Government, 59% of the total number of death was people of over 60 years. Forty-nine percent of the total number of death was people of over 65 years. Completely or partially collapsed houses and buildings account for 122,566. The evacuees at peak were 236,899 people.

A large number of houses and buildings, train tracks and bridges, and elevated expressways were destroyed by the earthquake, which triggered fires in many places. Due to the narrow streets in the old neighborhoods and wooden houses, as fires were fed, rescue units and firefighting units had difficulties to operate their emergency activities in many parts of Kobe City. According to a survey conducted by the Kobe City Government, 97% of the buried or confined people who were rescued replied that they were rescued by their family members or neighbors, or saved themselves, while rescue workers had difficulties to reach them (Fig. 3).

Analysis of Impacts in Nine Wards in Kobe City

Kobe City consists of nine wards: Higashinada, Nada, Chuo, Hyogo, Kita, Nagata, Suma, Tarumi, and Nishi wards (Fig. 4). Nishi ward and Kita ward are located at the inland side of Kobe City, which include mountainous area and wide residential areas and do not border the sea. From Tarumi ward located at the west end of the city to Higashinada ward located at the east end, all other wards are along the coastal area of Kobe City.

Table 1 summarizes comparative data from the nine wards, in particular, focusing on the death toll of the age group of persons over 65 years with

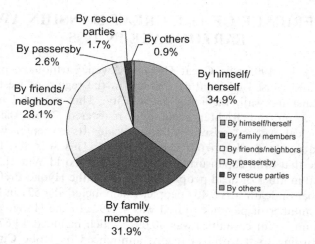

Fig. 3.   Who Rescued Buried or Confined People in Kobe City When the Great
Hanshin-Awaji Earthquake Occurred. *Source*: Kobe City Government.

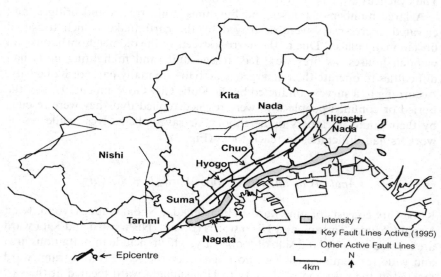

Fig. 4.   Map of Kobe Consisting of Nine Wards, Showing the Epicenter and Its
Intensity Scale. *Source*: Kobe City Government.

Table 1. Data of Losses of Human Lives among Nine Wards, the Age Group of People of over 65 Years and Destroyed Houses among Nine Wards.

	Higashinada	Nada	Chuo	Hyogo	Kita	Nagata	Suma	Tarumi	Nishi	Total
Population in 1995	191,716	124,538	111,195	117,558	217,166	129,978	188,949	237,735	201,530	1,520,365
Over 65 (1990)	20,498	18,340	15,657	20,766	18,515	22,494	18,179	22,294	12,573	169,316
In % (1990)	10.8	14.2	13.5	16.8	9.3	16.4	9.7	9.5	7.9	12.0
Population density 1995 per km²	6,315	3,966	3,911	8,085	898	11,342	6,298	8,841	1,462	2,757
Ranking of population density	4	6	7	3	9	1	5	2	8	
Death (total)	1,470	934	243	556	13	921	399	26	9	4,571
% of death (total)	0.767	0.750	0.219	0.473	0.006	0.709	0.211	0.011	0.004	0.301
Ranking of number of death (total)	1	2	6	4	8	3	5	7	9	
Ranking of number of death (total)	1	2	5	4	8	3	6	7	9	
Overs 65 years	589	420	117	251	4	506	200	6	3	2,096
% of death over 65 years	42	46	51	50	50	58	55	75	43	
Ranking of number of death (>65)	1	3	6	4	6	2	5	7	9	
Ranking of % of death (>65)	9	7	4	5	5	2	3	1	8	
Total number of destroyed houses	14,269	15,252	8,367	12,796	1,294	17,509	10,135	561	1,500	81,683
% of destroyed houses	24.9	23.2	13.5	20.9	1.5	39.2	17.1	3.6	1.6	15.10
Ranking of % of destroyed houses	2	3	6	4	9	1	5	7	8	

Source: The Kobe City Government.

population data from Kobe City. Table 1 also summarizes comparative data of destroyed houses among the nine wards. The ranking of population density, absolute number of total death, percentage of total death, absolute number of death of people of over 65 years people, percentage of people over 65 years, and percentage of destroyed houses among nine wards are mentioned in Table 1 with the purpose to show which wards resulted in being more impact than the others.

Analysis of the damages and comparison of the data shown in Table 1 among nine wards in Kobe City provided the following key findings:

- According to the 1990 National Census, the percentage of the population over 65 years was between 9.3% and 16.8% in the nine wards, which is similar to other major cities in Japan such as Nagoya City and Kyoto City (Japanese average of population of over 65 years in 1990 is 12%). However, the age group of persons over 65 years had high percentages of total death tolls (between 42% and 75%) in all nine wards, which may indicate that elderly people are one of the most vulnerable population group in case of a disaster.
- High population density does not equal to high death toll. Tarumi ward (the ranking of population density is 2) had one of the lowest death toll among the nine wards.
- More affected areas by reviewing these rankings noted in Table 1 are the following four wards: Higashinada, Nada, Hyogo, and Nagata.
- Higashinada, Nagata, and Hyogo wards have high population densities and also have a high elderly population (over 65 years). The population densities (Japanese average 2,731 persons/km^2) are high in Nagata (11,342/ km^2) and Hyogo (8,085/km^2) with also high elderly (over 65 years) population (Nagata 16.4% and Hyogo 16.8%) (Japanese average 12%).
- Higashinada, Nagata, and Nada wards that had concentration of old wooden buildings show highest percentages of destroyed houses and death tolls among the 9 wards (Kobe Institute of Urban Research and Kobe City Government, 2000).
- Kita, Nishi, and Tarumi wards with high population densities and relatively new constructed houses and building had lower death tolls.

From the Hanshin Awaji-Earthquake, it is obvious that the age group of over 65 years is one of the most vulnerable groups, in particular, living in the density area with old houses. Learning from these findings, the Kobe City Government has been conducting an important initiative for developing "BOKOMI" with the aim to building resilience of its communities against disasters.

In the next section, how BOKOMI as community-based DRR organizations has been established and developed will be described including some analysis of BOKOMI development in each of the nine wards.

BOKOMI CONCEPT AS AN EXAMPLE OF PARTNERSHIP BETWEEN CITY GOVERNMENT AND COMMUNITIES

Japanese Law to Promote Community-Based Disaster Management

Before the details of the specific case of Kobe City, it is worth describing how the Japanese domestic law addresses and promotes community-based DRR activities in general. Within the Japan Disaster Countermeasure Basic Act, there are the following several articles and clauses included regarding responsibilities of municipalities and residents to promote voluntary disaster prevention organizations.

• Responsibilities of municipalities

Article 5: "To protect lives, livelihoods and property of the concerned areas of municipalities and residents from natural disasters, municipalities as the basic local governments are responsible for formulating disaster reduction plans for the concerned areas of municipalities and implementing them based on the laws in collaboration with the related agencies and other local governments" (Japan Fire and Disaster Management Agency of the Ministry of Internal Affairs and Communications, 2003).

Clause 2: "To accomplish the responsibilities said in the previous clause, the mayors are obliged to develop organizations such as firefighting and flood-fighting teams and improve disaster reduction related organizations such as public groups in the concerned areas of municipalities and 'voluntary disaster reduction organizations' building on the spirit of neighbor cooperation among the residents. The mayors ought to demonstrate the full functioning of all the municipalities have" (Japan Fire and Disaster Management Agency of the Ministry of Internal Affairs and Communications, 2003).

Clause 3: "Firefighting organizations, flood-fighting teams and other municipal agencies are obliged to cooperate each other to fully accomplish the responsibilities of municipalities said in the clause 1 when conducting the necessary clerical work" (Japan Fire and Disaster Management Agency of the Ministry of Internal Affairs and Communications, 2003).

- Responsibilities of residents
  Article 7: "The public groups in the areas of local governments, managers of facilities that are important for disaster reduction, and those who are responsible for disaster reduction by law ought to fulfill their obligation in sincerity by law or the local disaster management plans" (Japan Fire and Disaster Management Agency of the Ministry of Internal Affairs and Communications, 2003).
  Clause 2: "Besides the specified in the previous clause, the residents residing in the local governments ought to take measures to get prepared for natural disasters themselves and contribute to disaster reduction by participating in voluntary disaster reduction activities and so forth" (Japan Fire and Disaster Management Agency of the Ministry of Internal Affairs and Communications, 2003).

- Consideration for disaster reduction in countermeasures
  Article 8
  Clause 2: "The national and local governments are obliged to implement the followings to prevent disaster occurrence or expansion of disasters" (Japan Fire and Disaster Management Agency of the Ministry of Internal Affairs and Communications, 2003).
  Clause 13: "Development of voluntary disaster reduction organizations, development of environment for disaster reduction activities by volunteers, and promotion of other citizens' voluntary disaster reduction activities" (Japan Fire and Disaster Management Agency of the Ministry of Internal Affairs and Communications, 2003).

In addition, in the Japanese Fire and Disaster Management Organization Act, there is the following article.

Article 26 – 2: (partially amended in June 2003)
Clause 2: "The national and local governments are obliged to take necessary measures to provide the opportunities of education and trainings on firefighting to those who compose the disaster reduction organizations in order to promote the activities that contribute to fire fighting conducted by the residents' voluntary disaster reduction organizations" (Japan Fire and Disaster Management Agency of the Ministry of Internal Affairs and Communications, 2003).

With these domestic laws promoting citizen and community DRR activities, the Kobe City Government has taken further steps and developed the

BOKOMI system. By recognizing BOKOMI as the equivalent and enhanced modality of the citizen voluntary disaster prevention activities specified in the national law, strong support from the Kobe City Government is ensured.

Establishment of BOKOMI in Kobe

The Preamble of the Outline for Development Program of Disaster Prevention Welfare Community (BOKOMI) in Kobe City (from the revised version of 2010 March 31) is described as follows:

> The Great Hanshin-Awaji Earthquake caused unprecedented damage to Kobe and deprived the lives of many people in a moment. We have learned lots of lessons from the experience of this earthquake, including the importance of the lives, cooperative help and preparedness. After the earthquake, many disasters such as earthquakes, storms and floods sill occur frequently in our country, and the people endlessly suffer from disaster damage throughout the world. We ought to convey our experiences and lessons learnt from the earthquake to the future generations to inherit safety and security to children. The disaster-safe welfare community (BOKOMI) is exactly what was created building on the experiences and lessons learnt from the earthquake. The citizens, enterprises and city (Kobe City) declare hereby that we, based on the spirit of collaboration and participation, strive together for activating and succeeding the disaster-safe welfare community activities building on the basic principles of self-help, cooperative help and public help.

Behind BOKOMI establishment, there are three principles based on the experience of the Great Hanshin-Awaji Earthquake: "self-help," "cooperation-help," and "public-help" (Fig. 5). Promotion of BOKOMI establishment and developing its activities are for the purpose of fostering all of these three principles in Kobe City.

While professional rescue workers had difficulties to reach at many disaster sites, rescue operations were to a large extent conducted by citizens after the earthquake hit Kobe City. For example, citizens battled the fires by forming budget brigades to carry water to the fires. However, they did not have enough equipment to act in an organized manner nor did they get appropriate training before. Learning from the Hanshin-Awaji Earthquake, Kobe City recognized the strong need of developing and enhancing voluntary community-based organizations for disaster prevention throughout the city. Specific needs for support are also identified, such as distributing various disaster prevention equipment and materials, supporting emergency drills, and offering them subsidies to conduct disaster prevention activities (JICA Hyogo, Kobe City Government, 2010).

Since 1995 after the earthquake, Kobe City started to develop community disaster prevention groups named "Disaster-Safe Welfare Community" in

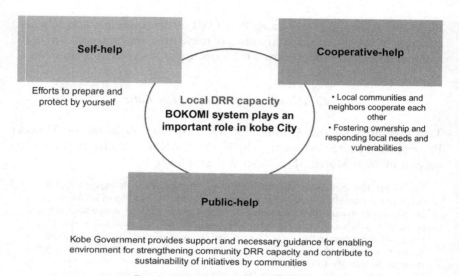

Fig. 5.   Principle Behind BOKOMI.

11 districts of Kobe, as pilot districts. The Kobe City Government then referred to these groups as community-based disaster prevention organizations. The short name for Disaster-safer Welfare Community is "BOKOMI," which is the abbreviation of its Japanese name "Bosai Fukushi Komyunithi" (JICA Hyogo, Kobe City Government, 2010), as mentioned earlier.

After the pilot phase in 11 districts, the BOKOMI concept was formalized in 1997 according to the Mayor's decision and mainstreamed in all the school districts of Kobe City. BOKOMIs are established based on municipal elementary schools districts in Kobe City. The total number of municipal elementary schools is 191. As shown in Fig. 6, the number of BOKOMI steadily increased and reached a 100% coverage in 2008. The reason why BOKOMIs are based in elementary school districts is because "welfare-community" groups were already established in each elementary school district, and thus, disaster prevention activities could be integrated into these existing groups. In addition, elementary schools are designated as evacuation sites for communities in emergencies in Japan. These are the key reasons why BOKOMIs are established in each elementary school district (JICA Hyogo, Kobe City Government, 2010).

The first policy outline for Development Program of Disaster Prevention Welfare Community (BOKOMI) in Kobe City was adopted as the Mayor's

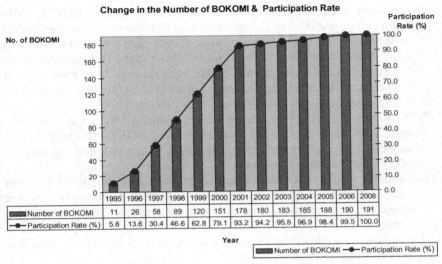

Change in the Number of BOKOMI & Participation Rate

	1995	1996	1997	1998	1999	2000	2001	2002	2003	2004	2005	2006	2008
Number of BOKOMI	11	26	58	89	120	151	178	180	183	185	188	190	191
Participation Rate (%)	5.8	13.6	30.4	46.6	62.8	79.1	93.2	94.2	95.8	96.9	98.4	99.5	100.0

Year

Number of BOKOMI —●— Participation Rate (%)

Fig. 6.   Pace of the Establishment of BOKOMI in Kobe City.

decision as of June 20 in 1997. Since the adoption of the first outline, the policy outline has gone through several revision and improvement by applying needs and demands identified during these years of implementation from practical perspectives. For example, such revision and improvements include an establishment of a subsidy system for innovative BOKOMI project proposals, which will be described in the next section.

Detail Activities of BOKOMI and Support from Kobe City

The process of establishing BOKOMI in a district is based on multi-stakeholder consultation in the district. Firstly, the establishment of a BOKOMI is discussed and agreed by local government organizations, including the local city office (ward office) and fire station, together with leaders of local residents and other local multi-stakeholders. BOKOMI is a community-based organization comprised of local residents' associations, women's associations, elderly associations, child committee member, youth associations, PTA, local fire station, and local business entities. In order to support activities of BOKOMIs, the Kobe City Government provides various support measures as described below.

(1) Provision of disaster prevention materials and equipment for BOKOMIs when they are established, based on a list of 54 items (machinery and other materials). When BOKOMI was formed, each BOKOMI can select items from the list according to their needs. Those items include firefighting equipment such as small pumps, rescue equipment including shovels and crowbars, and first aid equipment such as folding stretchers, as well as helmets and hand-held loud speakers, and so on.

(2) Provision of subsidies for activity expenses through Kobe City's funding system by receiving project proposals from BOKOMIs, in order to support their disaster reduction activities such as drills and the renewal of disaster reduction equipment.

(3) Support to develop a citizen's disaster prevention leader. Kobe City has implemented training for civil disaster reduction leaders who arrange disaster reduction activities for neighborhood residents (30–50 households).

(4) Support of area firefighting officers and volunteer fire corps (for town watching, risk identification, coorganization of disaster drills, and fire-aid training).

Main activities by BOKOMIs have two perspectives: disaster prevention and risk reduction activities and welfare-related activities. These activities are combined and carried out together. Disaster-prevention and risk reduction activities by BOKOMI:

- Disaster drills and training
- DRR education program with schools
- BOKOMI junior team (fostering children's teams to lead and work on DRR activities)
- Public awareness event
- First-aid seminar and checking emergency materials and equipment
- Town watching and preparation of community safety map and risk reduction activities with rescue workers and firefighters (identification evacuation root, removal of object blocking these roots, fixing furniture, etc.)

Combining with welfare activity:

- Regular communication within communities to form their unity, so that they can take action, when emergency/disaster happens, considering needs of vulnerable groups such as elderly and disabled people.
- Leaning how to support the people with special needs during disasters (elderly people and handicapped people).

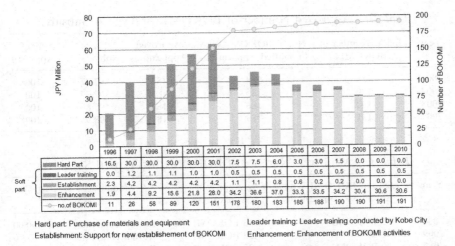

	1996	1997	1998	1999	2000	2001	2002	2003	2004	2005	2006	2007	2008	2009	2010
Hard Part	16.5	30.0	30.0	30.0	30.0	30.0	7.5	7.5	6.0	3.0	3.0	1.5	0.0	0.0	0.0
Leader training	0.0	1.2	1.1	1.1	1.0	1.0	0.5	0.5	0.5	0.5	0.5	0.5	0.5	0.5	0.5
Establishment	2.3	4.2	4.2	4.2	4.2	4.2	1.1	1.1	0.8	0.6	0.2	0.2	0.0	0.0	0.0
Enhancement	1.9	4.4	9.2	15.6	21.8	28.0	34.2	36.6	37.0	33.3	33.5	34.2	30.4	30.6	30.6
no.of BOKOMI	11	26	58	89	120	151	178	180	183	185	188	190	190	191	191

Hard part: Purchase of materials and equipment   Leader training: Leader training conducted by Kobe City
Establishment: Support for new establishement of BOKOMI   Enhancement: Enhancement of BOKOMI activities

Fig. 7.   Kobe City's Annual Budget History to Support BOKOMI between 1996 and 2010.

To support BOKOMI activities, Kobe City has maintained a certain allocation within its annual budget as shown in Fig. 7. When a BOKOMI is established, equipment and materials were provided by Kobe City. The budget for this initial installation cost by providing hard part such as equipments and materials accounted for the majority of its BOKOMI-related annual budget for the early years between 1996 and 2001, reflecting on the increase in the number of established BOKOMI. After all the 191 BOKOMIs were established in Kobe City, the focus of the BOKOMI-related budget was put on the enhancement of BOKOMI activities and leader's training, which is considered as soft part. The absolute size of annual budget within Kobe City allocated to support BOKOMIs has been decreased during the last several years especially since 2002. However, considering the economic sluggish in Japan and also the fact that 16 years have passed since the Hanshin-Awaji Earthquake, it is considered as still positive to maintain a certain level of annual budget to support BOKOMI.

To support BOKOMI activities, Kobe City has currently two types of subsidies. Type A is to support the regular management and operation of BOKOMI by supporting cost for materials, equipment, meeting cost, training expenses, and so on. Under the Type A subsidy, all the established BOKOMI are eligible to submit applications every year. By submitting an application for this subsidy, maximum JPY 140,000 per one BOKOMI per year can be

Table 2. Approved Number of BOKOMI for Type A Subsidy.

Year	Eligible Number of BOKOMI	No. of BOKOMI Who Submitted Applications	Approved Applications	% of Submission	% of Approval
2006	188	184	184	97.87	100
2007	190	185	185	97.37	100
2008	190	186	186	97.89	100
2009	191	189	189	98.95	100

Table 3. Approved Number of BOKOMI for Type B Subsidy.

Year	No. of BOKOMI Who Submitted Applications	Approved Applications	Modality	%
2008	35 BOKOMI	35 BOKOMI	Review committee	100.00
2009	40 BOKOMI	35 BOKOMI	Review committee	87.50
2010	29 BOKOMI (49 projects)	25 BOKOMI (29 projects)	Review committee	86.20

approved. As the Table 2 summarizes, 100% BOKOMIs have received this subsidy if they submit applications. This is useful approach adopted by Kobe City in order to maintain regular function of each BOKOMI.

Type B, started since 2008, is to support concrete and innovative projects by BOKOMIs through approving project proposals. BOKOMIs can submit concrete project proposal applications to Kobe City according to its Guideline. Then, through the Review Committee consisting of nine officials from several departments and sections of the Kobe City Government, submitted project proposals will be reviewed and selected. By submitting a project proposal application for Type B subsidy, maximum JPY 200,000 per one BOKOMI per year can be approved. The Guideline with the selection criteria (Table 4) for Review Committee is available on the web site of the Kobe City Government. The approval rates for the Type B for the last three years (Table 3) are lower than ones of the Type A (Table 2). However, the approval rates for the Type B are considered as relatively high (86.2% in the year 2010). At the same time, the number of applications is increasing every year, which has resulted in raising high competitiveness among submitted applications for Type B. A certain level of competition is important to inspire innovative ideas on activities by BOKOMI, which is the purpose of the Type B system. The list of criteria for the Type B (Table 4) includes the element of innovation as well as other important elements such

Table 4. The Criteria for Review Committee for Type B Subsidy.

Criteria	Point	Breakdown	Details
1 Local characteristics	20	20	Is the project considering local characteristics? such as -Geographical consideration -Human and social consideration (elderly people, foreigners and -Physical consideration (infrastructure and buildings)
2 Innovation	20	10	Is the project based on new ideas?
		5	Any innovate measures to promote local citizen participation?
		5	Applicable to the current situation?
3 Community	10	10	Does this project mach with local needs? -Number of citizens who benefit from this activity or/and size of areas which benefit from this activity -Contribution of promotion of alarm utilization or cleaning activities to the areas, etc.
4 Effectiveness and relevance	15	10	Is this effective when disaster happens? -Such as dissemination or improvement of disaster prevention -Such as dissemination of disaster prevention and risk reduction -Such as concrete measures to prevent fires or to address tsunami
		5	Is the impact of the subsidy clear? Is the impact of the project relevant?
5 Synergy and cooperation	15	5	Is the promoting the cooperation between local citizen and local organizing body? -Such as close communication among partners, local NGOs and volunteer groups, others
		5	Is this contributing to the unity of the local community and promoting their network?
		5	Linkage between welfare activities and disaster prevention activities are included?
6 Future perspective	10	5	Is the considering sustainability of activities?
		5	Is it promoting children's and youth participation?
7 Feasibility	10	10	Is the project well planned and feasible?
Total	100		
8 Others	10	10	Any other specific local consideration to be evaluated

Source: Kobe City.

as application of local characteristics, community focus, effectiveness and relevance, synergy and cooperation, future perspectives, and feasibility.

Analysis on BOKOMI

In the section on Analysis on Impacts in Nine Wards in Kobe City, impacts of the Hanshin-Awaji Earthquake in each nine wards and most affected four wards (Higashi-Nada, Nagata, Hyogo, and Nada) among them were described. In the section on Establishment of BOKOMI in Kobe, how BOKOMIs were established through the last 15 years was described. Depending on the size of population of each ward, the number of BOKOMIs is different from each ward as described in the Table 5. This section tries to review how active each ward is in terms of BOKOMI activities, by looking at two indicators for active level: years of establishment of BOKOMIs in each ward and the number of applications to the Type B subsidy system in each ward.

Looking at these years of BOKOMI establishments in each of the nine wards (Fig. 8), Higashinada that was one of the four most affected wards quickly completed their establishment of BOKOMIs for the first four years. Nagata that was also one of the four most affected wards took longer time to complete BOKOMI establishments. Therefore, it cannot be said that more devastated areas have more incentives and speed to establish community-based DRR organizations. This may imply that most devastated areas such as Nagata needed more time to recover and needed more time to have their residents to come back to the areas to settle again than other areas. On the other hand, Kita and Suma wards, which were less damaged, established BOKOMIs in their wards relevantly quickly. It can be regarded as positive sign since less affected areas such as Kita ward also took actions seriously as for the need of establishing the community-based by learning from the Great Hanshin-Awaji Earthquake.

Early establishment of BOKOMIs can be regarded as one of the indicators for active level. The other active indicator is active submission of proposals to the Type B subsidy. Table 5 notes the number of BOKOMI in each of the nine wards and number of percentage of approved projects through Type B subsidy system in the years 2009 and 2010. According to this indicator of active level, Suma ward is the most active ward, followed by Hyogo, Kita, and Tarumi wards. Therefore, again, it cannot be said that more devastated areas have more active in terms of project proposals for BOKOMI activities. Through the experience of the Great Hanshin-Awaji

Table 5. Numbers of approved proposals for Type B subsidy in 9 wards.

	Higashinada		Nada		Chuo		Hyogo		Kita		Nagata		Suma		Tarumi		Nishi		Total
	2010	2009	2010	2009	2010	2009	2010	2009	2010	2009	2010	2009	2010	2009	2010	2009	2010	2009	
No. of BOKOMI	13		16		18		17		33		19		21		24		30		191
Active criteria: Type B approved proposal	2	4	1	1	1	3	4	7	2	7	2	1	7	9	2	6	4	2	65
Total approved projects	6		2		4		11		9		3		16		8		6		65
% of approved project/No. of BOKOMI	15.38	30.77	6.25	6.25	5.56	16.67	23.53	41.18	6.06	21.21	10.53	5.26	33.33	42.86	8.33	25.00	13.33	6.67	–
Average % of approved project/ No. of BOKOMI	23.08		6.25		11.11		32.35		13.64		7.89		38.10		16.67		10.00		–
Ranking	3		9		6		2		5		8		1		4		7		–
% of approved project/total approved projects	9.2		3.1		6.2		16.9		13.8		4.6		24.6		12.3		9.2		100
Ranking	5		9		7		2		3		8		1		4		5		–

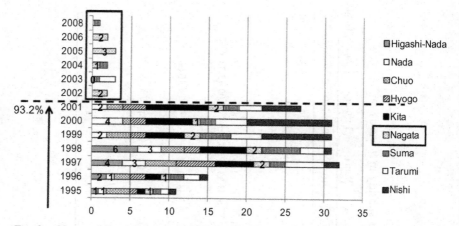

Fig. 8. Years of Establishment of BOKOMIs in Nine Wards (Higashinada, Nada, and Nagata Wards Are Attached with Numbers of BOKOMI Established in Each Year to Show Their Comparison).

Earthquake and lessons learnt, the level of awareness on the need for community-based DRR activities has been widely recognized throughout Kobe City regardless of the level of damage by the earthquake. This is an encouraging point in terms of promoting CBDRR and its wider application. Because this fact exemplifies that incentives to take actions for CBDRR can be learnt actively from other communities.

In terms of the contents of BOKOMI activities, activities mentioned in these approved projects in the years 2009 and 2010 are categorized according to the five priority areas specified in the Hyogo Framework for Action (Table 6).

"Hyogo Framework for Action 2005–2015: Building the Resilience of Nations and Communities to Disasters" (HFA) adopted at the 2nd United Nations World Conference on DRR, held in January 2005 in Kobe City, now serves as the universal guideline on DRR policies. Substantive reduction of disasters losses is expected through the implementation of HFA by UN Member States and other relevant multi-stakeholders. HFA has five Priorities for Action as mentioned below.

HFA Priority 1: Making DRR a Priority
HFA Priority 2: Improving Risk Information and Early Warning
HFA Priority 3: Building a Culture of Safety and Resilience

Table 6. Project Contents Categorized into HFA 5 Priority Areas.

		Higashinada	Nada	Chuo	Hyogo	Kita	Nagata	Suma	Tarumi	Nishi	Total	%	Ranking
HFA 2	Technical related and developing risk mapping	2	2				1	1	1	1	8	7.14	5
HFA 3	DRR education focusing on children	2	2		4	7		8	1	3	27	24.11	3
HFA 3	Public awareness raising	1	2	1	4	2	2	6	10	2	30	26.79	1
HFA 4	Considering the people with special needs and welfare aspect	4	6		1	1		3	1	2	18	16.07	4
HFA 5	Disaster drills	4	2		8	2	1	5	4	3	29	25.89	2

HFA Priority 4: Reducing the Risks in Key Sectors
HFA Priority 5: Strengthening Preparedness for Response

By looking at contents of these approved projects that received Type B subsidy from Kobe City, these contents are categorized according to these five priority areas of the HFA (Table 6). The main focus of BOKOMI projects are along with HFA 3 (more than 50% of approved projects are related to this area) and HFA 5 (approximately 26% of approved projects are related to this area). These projects focus on DRR education targeted at children by working with schools, public awareness-raising activities, and conducting disaster drills. Focusing on children is important to ensure that experiences and lessons from the Hanshin-Awaji Earthquake are passed onto the younger generation who did not directly experience the disaster, while those who experienced it directly are getting old and have difficulties to lead CBDRR activities.

DISCUSSION

Perspectives from Kobe City Government

In the section on Partnership Framework, the framework with following five key factors was described. These five key items are utilized to analyze the BOKOMI case as summarized in Table 7. Factor A "Common Objectives" is strong and positive aspect for the Kobe BOKOMI case. The objective to strengthen community capacity is based on their actual experiences of the major disaster at both the community side and the City Government side. Both the BOKOMI side and the City Government side clearly share the major focus of BOMOKO activities on awareness and education, which leads to the strong focus on preparedness activities through regular disaster drills.

Factor B "Shared Decision-Making" has both positive and negative aspects. Formulation of project proposals is done by BOKOMIs according to the guidelines, but the selection is done by the Review Committee that consists of only Kobe City Government officials without having a representative from BOKOMI side. It may be recommended to have representatives from BOKOMI side within the Review Committee for having more opportunity to reflect perspectives from BOKOMI side on its decisions.

Factor C "Regular Interaction" has also both positive and negative elements. Regardless of different degree, active participation can be observed in all nine wards. It shows that almost 100% of Type A subsidy application rate and that

Table 7. Analysis of BOKOMI According to Five Factors of the Partnership Framework from Perspectives from the Kobe City Government.

	Factors (in relation to DRR activities)	Findings	Evaluation
A	Common objectives	BOKOMI concept was established at the bottom-up and supported by Kobe City Government	+
		• Majority of conducted projects are related to HFA priorities 3 and 5	
B	Shared decision-making	• Formulation of project is done by BOKOMIs according to mutually agreed guidelines.	+/−
		• Decisions for approved project involving funding is done by Kobe City Government	
C	Regular interaction	• BOKOMIs in Higashi-Nada are most active in relation to participation	+/−
		• BOKOMIs in Suma are most active in relation to project application/approval	
		• All BOKOMIs apply for Type A funding	
		• Overall funding for BOKOMI project is maintained by Kobe City Government	
D	Level of control	No data	N/A
E	Ownership	• Kobe City Government and BOKOMIs have own human resources and knowledge to formulate and carry out projects	+/−
		• BOKOMIs can carry out projects independently, but depend on Kobe City Government for funding approval	

all nine wards have several BOKOMIs with approved projects for Type B. Also, for BOKOMI activities, they have regular contact with their firefighting offices in particular when they conduct drills. This ensures interaction between Kobe City officials and BOKOMIs. However, similar to the above factor B, subsidy mechanisms are fully managed by the Kobe City Government. Having representatives from BOKOMI side involved in funding mechanisms will have more opportunity to reflect perspectives from BOKOMI side.

Factor D "Level of Control" does not have much data and information available to evaluate.

Factor E "Ownership" has also both positive and negative aspects. The positive side is to have own human resources and knowledge at both Kobe City side and at BOKOMI side. BOKOMIs can implement projects and carry out activities independently, but at the same time, they highly depend on the Kobe City Government for funding approval. It is important for the Kobe City Government to maintain its initiative and annual budget allocation for ensuring enabling environment for BOKOMIs to sustain its activities. At the same time, if BOKOMI could enhance their funding support from business sector by themselves, the ownership from BOKOMI side would be enhanced and expected to be stronger.

Regarding the type of partnerships described in the section on Types of Partnership in terms of time period, BOKOMI case can be categorized as an institutionalized type of partnership, which is based on an accepted coexistence of communities and a local government with a sharing power. BOKOMI exists already for 16 years and has been enhanced and evolved during these years through building on acquired trust between BOKOMIs and the Kobe City Government.

There are certain limitations of this research approach since partnership framework may not be necessarily applicable for other types of partnership. The above result focused on perspective and available data mainly from the Kobe City Government. It is important to review the perspectives and evaluations directly gained from BOKOMI side as well. For the purpose, the other analysis was conducted to explore the views and perspectives from the community side for further improvement of the partnership modality of this BOKOMI case.

Perspectives from Community

Kobe Institute of Urban Research (KIUR) in cooperation with Kobe City Government conducted a questionnaire survey targeted at all the

191 BOKOMIs, as part of its area management research between November 2010 and March 2011 (Kobe Institute of Urban Research, 2011). The purpose of this survey was to assess the level of community development by asking community-based organizations/groups to reply to a questionnaire. Target groups were BOKOMIs and Community development councils (MACHI-ZUKURI KYOGIKAI and FUREAI-MACHI-ZUKURI KYO-GIKAI). According to the report of the survey by the KIUR, 79 BOKOMI replies were received out of the total 191 BOKOMIs (rate of reply = 41.3%). These replies from BOKOMIS are analyzed as the perspectives from the community side in this section, by applying to the partnership framework developed and presented in the section on Definition and Characterization of Partnership, and by comparing the perspectives between Kobe City Government and BOKOMIs. By using the available elements as the survey results by KIUR, three parameters under each five factors are identified for further detail analysis, and the available elements are categorized into the five factors as Table 8 notes.

Analyses of the survey result by the KIUR are conducted by authors. Findings as perspectives from community side toward BOKOMIs are summarized in Table 9.

Factor A "Common Objectives" shows that strong shared common objectives for disaster prevention exists in partnerships between BOKOMIs and Kobe City Government. However, there are several areas for improvements as described below.

To increase transparency, BOKOMIs can do more efforts on disseminating their decisions and plans to residents by sharing discussion and results from committee meetings, in combination with current active knowledge sharing and activity information to residents, as described under the parameter "Transparency" of Factor A and "Dissemination of information" of Factor C. More efforts on innovations and improvements on BOKOMI activities are needed. Kobe City Government should do more promotion of its project-based subsidy, and BOKOMIs need to make further efforts on this aspect, considering that the rate of Type B subsidy submission is currently low. This innovation for new activities is crucial area for BOKOMIs, in particular because the society is changing after 16 years since the Kobe Earthquake. Lessons learned and experiences are at risk of fading out. This would require further involvement of younger generation and also innovative measures and continuous efforts at BOKOMIs as shown under "Efforts on innovations and improvement" of Factor B. In addition to regular meetings and annual general assembly meetings, enhanced modality of receiving feedback from residents is an important area for improvement for BOKOMI activities, as

Table 8. Partnership Framework with Five Factors and Three Identified Parameters.

Factors	Common Objectives	Sharing of Decision-Making	Regular Interaction	Level of Control	Ownership
Parameters	Shared themes of activities	Transparency	Frequency of interaction	Structure of funding system	Existence of physical base
	Origin of establishment	Efforts on innovations and improvement	Interaction with community members	Level of independence in planning process of activities	Community involvement
	Consultation	Influence in decision-making processes	Dissemination of knowledge and information	External support in implementation process of activities	Resource mobilization

Table 9. Analysis of BOKOMI Under Five Factors and Three Parameters of the Partnership Framework from Community Perspectives.

Factors	Parameters and Findings	Evaluation
A Common objectives	(*Shared themes of activities*): Disaster prevention is the core and shared theme along with KCG's objective and its guideline. Activities are also linked with other issues such as children and elderly welfare etc (+) (*Origin of establishment*): More than 70% is based on KCG advocacy, which provided good triggers and facilitation for the establishment (*Consultation*): Committee members are the main actors involved in the consultation process for activity planning, BOKOMIs get primarily advices from KCG as the main partner, but also others (+/−)	(+/−)
B Shared decision-making	(*Transparency*): Regular participation rate for committee meetings are that 97% members are attending more than half. (+). But less than 50% of BOKOMIs are producing and disseminating minutes (−) (*Efforts on innovations and improvement*): KCG is promoting innovative activities to be developed by BOKOMIs through providing project-based subsidies (+). But, almost half of them are not making efforts on innovation and improvements (−) (*Influence in decision-making processes*): Committee members are the main body for decision making. Nearly 56% are done by majority of committee members, and 27% are committee members with others. Only 17% is relying on specific committee members. (+) This demonstrates that ownership for planning of activities belongs to committee members, but are at the same time open for other resident to be engaged	(+/−)
C Regular interaction	(*Frequency of interaction*): More than 90% of all BOKOMIs organize an annual GA and almost 70% have a meeting once every two months (+). Internal communication is regularly organized (*Receiving feedback from residents*): 50% has mechanism to receive feedbacks (−) (*Dissemination of knowledge and information*): Frequent (nearly 70% are doing PR activities more than twice a year) promotion and disseminations within the	(+/−)

Table 9. (*Continued*)

Factors		Parameters and Findings	Evaluation
		BOKOMI, which contribute public awareness aspect as well (+)	
D	Level of control	(*Structure of funding pattern*): 82% are based on subsidies and donations without much own income generation. Strong support from KCG subsidies (+). It could be interpreted as high dependence on partners (in this case KCG) and less control by themselves in terms of generating own financial resources (−)	(+/−)
		(*Level of independence in planning process of activities*): Have good level of internal resources and at the same time get advice from external partners (+). KCG (73%) is the largest partner for this. Strong partnership between KCG and BOKOMIs exists, at the same time, not relying on only KCG, but have other partner groups within the BOKOMI area (+)	
		(*External support in implementation process of activities*): Have good level of internal resources for implementation and at the same time have a wide range of partners who provide support for implementation (+). KCG (73%) is the largest partner for this. Strong partnership between KCG and BOKOMIs exists, at the same time, not relying on only KCG, but has partner groups within the BOKOMI area (+)	
E	Ownership	(*Existence of a physical base and its utilization*): Nearly 90% of BOKOMIs have physical bases for activities (+), most of them are owned by Kobe City (−), which could increase dependence on KCG	(+/−)
		(*Community involvement*): Less than 60 years old is only 32.8. Less than 40 years old is only 2.1%. Nearly 70% is retired age. Less involvement by younger generation and female (−). Good collaboration with various actors (+)	
		(*Resource mobilization*): Strong support from KCG (+), but could be regarded as strong reliance on subsidies by KCG (−), BOKOMI's own income generation for widening financial resources is limited (−)	

shown in "Receiving feedback from residents" of Factor C. To enhance regular interaction and knowledge dissemination to residents by BOKOMIs, there is potential for improvement by utilizing social media, which may target the younger generation to get involved under Factor C. Although strong partnerships exists between BOKOMIs and Kobe City Government, at the same time, BOKOMIs should seek multiple sources of funding, to avoid relying only on the city. This would enhance the sustainability of BOKOMI activities, as implied under "Level of control" of Factor D. Building on current partners, BOKOMIs should seek wider range of involvement from different generations and female. Also, enhanced engagement with different actors, such as private sector, would be a potential area for BOKOMIs to seek in terms of multiple funding and nondependence on only Kobe City Government, as implied under "Community involvement" and "Resource mobilization" of Factor E.

Level of partnerships depends on the maturity and cohesion of society. Strong DRR awareness needs to be fostered toward a more self-initiated community DRR organization. However, during the initial phase, more support and guidance from local governments are needed and helpful, as demonstrated in the case of the Kobe City. Culture of partnership and wide participation of society (generations and multi-stakeholders) are prerequisite for sustainable activities and enhancing DRR capacity. Kobe City Government and BOKOMIs partnership is a viable approach to implement DRR with communities living in urban areas. BOKOMI is a kind of partnership that can enhance five factors of partnership frame. Continuous efforts (innovation and improvements) are crucial by responding to changing society and its needs. By evaluating the BOKOMI through the partnership frame according to both perspectives of the Kobe City Government and communities, it can be said that a partnership between Kobe City Government and BOKOMIs exist and institutionalized.

CONCLUSION

The principle of "Self-help, Cooperative-help and Public-help" behind BOKOMI shown in Fig. 5 is important to strengthen all the three areas, not relying on a local government only nor only on the individuals themselves. BOKOMI is an effective way of community participation in an urban area where it is challenging to keep the ties beyond generations and transfer lessons from past disasters to younger generations. This principle can be applied to many other cities and communities. Long-term and sustainable efforts by the Kobe City Government to support CBDRR can be a good example of partnership between a city government and communities. At the same time, there may still be room for improvement as suggested under the section on Discussion. However, continuous and sustainable efforts for improvement need a solid basis within a community, to which BOKOMI type partnership can contribute.

There are other examples of community DRR partnership in an urban area. Risk reduction in cities of fast-developing nations is both an opportunity and a big challenge. It is an opportunity because cities are considered efficient spatial forms of human habitation where smart interventions can be optimized. However, involvement and ownership of urban society is a big challenge (Surjan, Redkar, & Shaw, 2009). One of the examples is from Mumbai, which is the largest city in India. Similar to the BOKOMI example from Kobe city, the example of the Advance Locality Management (ALM) from Mumbai also demonstrated citizen–government partnerships emanating from community-based small-scale initiatives for improving neighborhood's environment by concluding that there are enormous benefits in scaling up the participatory approaches, which result in reducing vulnerabilities and enhancing resilience of cities (Surjan et al., 2009). BOKOMI from Kobe city and ALM from Mumbai city may give a very innovative idea in urban context, and similar examples may exist in different cities. However, it is worth mentioning that these cities both in developing countries and in developed countries have similar challenges in urban areas to address social vulnerabilities to disasters. For the purpose of tackling the challenges and scale up the efforts on DRR, a partnership between communities and a local government through participatory approaches is demonstrated as an effective approach of urban governance, as shown through both Kobe and Mumbai cases. This approach has a potential to be replicated in other urban cities and contribute to building urban resilience against disasters.

The effort to apply this BOKOMI case to other part of the world has been already attempted in cooperation between the Kobe City Government and the Japan International Cooperation Agency (JICA) by sharing the activities of BOKOMI. It has been promoted in several countries already such as Turkey (2007), Sri Lanka (2008), Costa Rica (2009), and Indonesia (2010). In particular, the Kobe City Government in conjunction with JICA Hyogo Office has created a training course focusing on CBDRR using BOKOMI case for participants involved in disaster management in other countries. BOKOMI-type partnership is expected to be recognized as good CBDRR approaches further widely in the world with the aim at building resilience of communities against disasters in urban and aging societies.

ACKNOWLEDGMENTS

The authors highly acknowledge the cooperation extended from the Kobe City Government, in particular, the Kobe City Fire Bureau for providing information related to BOKOMI. Support from the Global COE Program "Human Security Engineering for Asia Megacities" is highly appreciated.

REFERENCES

Arnstein, S. R. (1969). A ladder of citizen participation. *Journal of the American Institute of Planners, 35*(4), 216–224.

Bajek, R., Matsuda, Y., & Okada, N. (2008). Japan's Jishu-bosai-soshiki community activities: Analysis of its role in participatory community disaster risk management. *Natural Hazards, 44*, 281–292.

Harriss, J. (2000). Working together: The principles and practice of co-operation. In S. P. Osborne (Ed.), *Public-private partnerships: Theory and practice in international perspective*. London: Routledge.

Japan Fire and Disaster Management Agency of the Ministry of Internal Affairs and Communications. (2003). Manual for voluntary disaster prevention organization – Community and disaster prevention. Ministry of Internal Affairs and Communications, Tokyo.

JICA Hyogo Disaster Learning Center (DRLC). (2010). BOKOMI guidebook – Sharing lessons learned by the City of Kobe from the Great Hanshin-Awaji Earthquake. JICA Hyogo Disaster Learning Center (DRLC).

Kobe Institute of Urban Research. (2011). Report of the Area Management Policy, Kobe.

Kobe Institute of Urban Research and Kobe City Government. (2000). *The great Hanshin-Awaji Earthquake Kobe reconstruction journal*. Kobe: Kobe Institute of Urban Research and Kobe City Government.

Lewis, D. (2000). Building 'active' partnership in aid-recipient countries: Lessons from a rural development project in Bangladesh. In S. P. Osborne (Ed.), *Public-private partnerships: Theory and practice in international perspective*. London: Routledge.

Mayo, M. (1997). Partnerships for regeneration and community development: Some opportunities, challenges and constraints. *Critical Social Policy, 17*, 3–26.

McQuaid, R. W. (2000). The theory of partnership: Why have partnerships?. In S. P. Osborne (Ed.), *Public-private partnerships: Theory and practice in international perspective*. London: Routledge.

Murphy, B. L. (2007). Locating social capital in resilient community-level emergency management. *Natural Hazards, 41*, 297–315.

Nagasaka, T. (2008). New problems in the study of disaster prevention based on disaster risk governance. *Quarterly Review, 27*, 77–92.

Nakagawa, Y., & Shaw, R. (2004). Social capital: A missing link to disaster recovery. *International Journal of Mass Emergencies and Disasters, 22*(1), 5–34.

Norris, F. H., Stevens, S. P., Pfefferbaum, B., Wyche, K. F., & Pfefferbaum, R. L. (2008). Community resilience as a metaphor, theory, set of capacities, and strategy for disaster readiness. *American Journal of Community Psychology, 41*, 127–150.

Patterson, O., Weil, F., & Patel, K. (2010). The role of community in disaster response: Conceptual models. *Population Research and Policy Review, 29*, 127–141.

Penrose, A. (2000). Partnership. In D. Robinson, T. Hewitt & J. Harriss (Eds.), *Managing development: Understanding inter-organizational relationships*. London: Sage; The Open University.

Postma, W. (1994). NGO partnership and institutional development: Making it real, making it intentional. *Canadian Journal of African Studies, 28*(3), 447–471.

Pretty, J. N. (1995). *Regenerating agriculture: Policies and practice/or sustainability and self-reliance*. London; Washington, DC: Earthscan Publications; National Academy Press.

Shaw, R., & Goda, K. (2004). From disaster to sustainable civil society: The Kobe experience. *Disasters, 28*(1), 16–40.

Surjan, A., Redkar, S., & Shaw, R. (2009). Community-based urban risk reduction: Case of Mumbai. In R. Shaw, H. Srinivas, & A. Sharma (Eds.), *Urban risk reduction: An Asian perspective* (Vol. 1, pp. 339–354). Bingley: Emerald Group Publishing Limited.

Suzuki, I. (2006). Roles of volunteers in disaster prevention: Implications of questionnaire and interview surveys. In S. Ikeda, T. Fukuzono & T. Sato (Eds.), *A better integrated management of disaster risks: Toward resilient society to emerging disaster risks in mega-cities* (pp. 153–163). Tokyo: Terra.

Vasconcellos, M., & Vasconcellos, A. M. (2009). Partnership, empowerment and local development. *Interacoes, 10*(2), 133–148.

CHAPTER 10

REACHING THE UNREACHABLE: MYANMAR EXPERIENCES OF COMMUNITY-BASED DISASTER RISK REDUCTION

Mitsuko Shikada, U Than Myint, U Ko Ko Gyi, Yuko Nakagawa and Rajib Shaw

INTRODUCTION

Geographical Background and Hazards of Myanmar

The Union of Myanmar is located in mainland Southeast Asia and shares borders with India, China, Lao PDR, Thailand, and Bangladesh. It is situated between the Himalayan ranges and the Bay of Bengal. Due to these diversified geographical features, Myanmar is highly vulnerable to different kinds of hazards, and has experienced many kinds of disasters in the past, according to the Hazard Profile of Myanmar (2009), such as cyclones, floods, storms, landslides, earthquakes, tsunamis, droughts, and fires. For the general public, cyclones are considered the major menace in the country, however the recent earthquake with a magnitude of 6.9 in Shan state on March 24, 2011 made inhabitants realize that they are living with the risk of earthquakes as well. According to New Light of Myanmar (the State-run newspaper) on March 26, 2011, the earthquake resulted in 73 deaths

Community-Based Disaster Risk Reduction
Community, Environment and Disaster Risk Management, Volume 10, 185–203
Copyright © 2012 by Emerald Group Publishing Limited
ISSN: 2040-7262/doi:10.1108/S2040-7262(2012)0000010016

(official record of the country). Besides earthquakes and cyclones, there have been many victims of landslides, and the people at coastal areas face the risk of tsunami in the case of earthquakes that occur in the Indian Ocean. In 2004, 61 people were killed in Myanmar by the Indian Ocean tsunami according to the Hazard Profile of Myanmar (2009). Furthermore, the year of 2011 witnessed chronic and severe floods all over the country.

Cyclone Nargis and Need for Disaster Risk Reduction

According to the Hazard Profile of Myanmar (2009), the biggest disaster of Myanmar within recorded history was the cyclone Nargis in May 2008, which struck coastal areas of the country with high-speed winds of up to 250 kilometers per hour and a 3.6 meter storm surge. The cyclone resulted in 138,373 people dead or missing, and 2.4 million people affected by loss of family members, properties, and livelihoods. Compared to other neighboring countries such as Bangladesh, Myanmar had never before experienced such damage by natural disasters until the cyclone Nargis hit in May 2008.

Post-disaster analysis by PONREP I–IV (2008–2010) showed that the main cause of tragedy was that communities were not fully aware of the danger of the cyclone. Even though an announcement from the Department of Meteorology and Hydrology was broadcast, many disregarded the impact of the cyclone, and others did not have any idea how to prepare and where and when to evacuate. By the time the affected communities realized the danger of the approaching cyclone, it was too late. People did not have any means to help themselves from the 200 to 250 kilometers per hour winds or the tidal storm surge of 3.6 meters, which they had never seen or experienced before.

Another major cause for the extensive damage was the problem of logistics for relief supplies. Main roads and rivers were full of debris, and therefore the delivery of relief materials was considerably delayed, further impacting the affected communities. Many people died during this time because of the shortage of drinking water and food, especially in remote villages.

Human losses could have been reduced if the community was more aware of the risk of cyclones and storm surges, possessed knowledge on how to respond to them, and took precautions much earlier. The extent of the damage and loss made the authorities, as well as aid agencies working for disaster risk reduction (DRR), realize and reiterate the importance of education programs for DRR and community-based DRR to prepare for future disasters through various approaches and methods.

Disaster Management in Myanmar

Myanmar is a signatory of the Hyogo Framework for Action (HFA-2005–2015) and is also a signatory of the ASEAN Agreement on Disaster Management and Emergency Response (AADMER). However, specific plans for national disaster management were not fully developed until the cyclone Nargis struck the country, as Myanmar Action Plan for Disaster Risk Reduction (MAPDRR) was prepared in 2009 by a taskforce comprising 12 ministries of government, Myanmar Red Cross Society, UNOCHA, ASEAN and ADPC. Although the cyclone Nargis severely affected local communities, it provided an impetus to develop disaster management plans and DRR activities for future disasters, and this was possible because recovery agencies advocated and promoted the principal of "build back better."

Immediately after cyclone Nargis, the national government of Myanmar organized the Tripartite Core Group (TCG) to respond to the emergency, consisting of the Government of Myanmar, the Association of Southeast Asian Nations (ASEAN), and UN agencies, which initiated assessments, relief arrangement, reviewing the situations, and coordinating the work of all aid agencies from Myanmar and outside. The TCG published a recovery implementation plan called PONREP[1] (Post-Nargis Recovery and Pre-paredness Plan) in 2008 and facilitated the process of relief-to-recovery efforts of many organizations. PONREP was reviewed several times and PONREP II,[2] PONREP III,[3] and PONREP IV[4] were developed in 2009–2010 to monitor and update the situation of affected communities for humanitarian response, and to make more informed, strategic decisions for long-term recovery.

As PONREP II–IV illustrated, there was noticeable progress on the relief-to-recovery process through the considerable efforts of different organiza-tions. However, there was still a need to fill the gap in response and recovery, and many services and training for various issues and topics were deemed necessary for the affected people. There are many agencies which are still working for the effected region three years after cyclone Nargis. The existing institutional arrangements at the national level, divisional level, district level, and township are reviewed in "Institutional Arrangements for Disaster Management in Myanmar," published in 2009 by the Ministry of

Social Welfare Relief and Resettlement, Relief and Resettlement Department (MoSWRR-RRD), and Asian Disaster Preparedness Centre (ADPC). The Government of Myanmar institutionalized a well laid out disaster management system, especially after cyclone Nargis.

In 2009, the Myanmar National Disaster Preparedness Committee (NDPC), chaired by the Prime Minister, was set up and the National Disaster Preparedness Management Working Committee (NDPMWC) was organized under NDPC, which is chaired by Secretary of State Peace and Development Council to reach out to the village level. Ten thematic subcommittees each headed by a respective Minister were also set up under the NDPMWC and the Ministry of Social Welfare was designated as the line ministry to collaborate and coordinate with academic institutions/ specialists and NGOs. NDPC was reconstituted in April 2011, and reformed into two organizations, one is the renewed NDPC[5] and the other is the Myanmar National Search and Rescue Committee[6] (English translation only available as a tentative version by UNDP) to formulate preparedness plan and to cope with emergency response more effectively. The Union Minister of MoSWRR has been designated as Chairperson of NDPC (made up of 14 members from concerned ministries), which mainly acts to provide guidance and supervision in the preparedness program, and relief and rehabilitation activities such as planning, coordinating, documenting, and monitoring. Regarding the Myanmar National Search and Rescue Committee, the Union Minister from Ministry of Home Affairs has been assigned as Chairperson of Myanmar National Rescue Committee, consisting of 22 members. The duties are mainly to conduct risk assessments and operate taskforces to save lives.

In order to make the coordination among the agencies smoother, the "Standing Order on Natural Disaster Management in Myanmar" was also stated in 2010 by NDPC, which clarified the duties and responsibilities among the agencies in accordance with timelines; during the pre-disaster phase, during disaster, relief, rehabilitation, and reconstruction. Additionally, the Myanmar Inter Agency Contingency Plan (IA-CP) is being developed as of October 2011. The planned tasks of IA-CP are to identify the risks faced by different areas, to define the key agencies and its contacts, and to detail the preparedness and response plans, coordinated by UN, INGOs, and LNGOs with RRD. The organizations of technical groups were also facilitated to disseminate knowledge for DRR in Myanmar. A key output was the development of the Hazard Profile of Myanmar, published in 2009 July. All these were the major contributions as a part of process of pursuing HFA and MAPDRR, which was published in 2009, mentioned above.

MKRC AND WKRC FOR "REACHING THE UNREACHABLE"

The Need for MKRC and WKRC

The main lesson learned from cyclone Nargis was the need for better awareness on DRR at the community level in Myanmar so as to encourage community people to take action properly to prepare to mitigate disaster risks. In order to strengthen resilience of communities that are at risk for natural disasters, the need for a knowledge resource center was strongly felt and shared among the aid agencies. However, the main challenge was the logistics of implementing and delivering effective training. After discussion with local counterparts, stakeholders, and specialists, a unique DRR education project called "Mobile Knowledge Resource Centre (MKRC) and Water Knowledge Resource Centre (WKRC)," with the mission of "Reaching the Unreachable" was developed by SEEDS Asia with local counterpart, the Myanmar Engineering Society.

Due to logistics and resource issues, some areas remained unreachable. Thus, the approach was to circumvent the lack of accessibility by making the MKRC in the form of a mobile truck, and the WKRC as a ship, in order to be able to reach people in remote areas. The goal of the MKRC and WKRC is to increase the awareness of communities on disaster risks and hazards, and to enhance individual, family, and neighborhood level actions (SEEDS Asia, Reaching the Unreachable, 2010). Thus, educational materials of different types and topics were mounted on the MKRC and WKRC in order to make it mobile and enable its transport to different locations. This enabled children and community members to understand the importance of DRR more easily with its practical activities and visual presentation of posters, videos, and miniature models for understanding hazards and risks of disasters.

The KIDA Approach

In order to realize the aim that people will be able to take appropriate measures to prepare for emergency, the KIDA (Knowledge-Interest-Desire-Action) tree model was adapted for developing the MKRC and WKRC.[7] The KIDA approach is based on the AIDMA (Attention-Interest-Desire-Memory-Action) model, which is used in the field of advertising to consider

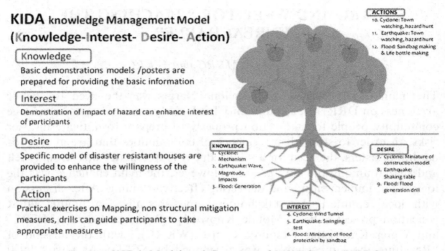

KIDA knowledge Management Model
(Knowledge-Interest- Desire- Action)

Knowledge
Basic demonstrations models /posters are
prepared for providing the basic information

Interest
Demonstration of impact of hazard can enhance interest
of participants

Desire
Specific model of disaster resistant houses are
provided to enhance the willingness of the
participants

Action
Practical exercises on Mapping, non structural mitigation
measures, drills can guide participants to take
appropriate measures

Fig. 1. KIDA Model and Contents of MKRC and WKRC.
Source: 1-2-3 of Disaster Education, Kyoto University (2009).

the process of the consumer attraction to, and purchasing of, a product.
DRR requires people to have appropriate knowledge and to take action.
KIDA emphasizes knowledge, interest, and desire to promote action, and
actual actions are significant outputs of disaster education. Therefore, the
contents of the MKRC and WKRC were developed and classified based on
the KIDA model (see Fig. 1).

MKRC and WKRC are developed on a truck and a ship, respectively,
with colorful decorations and local child-friendly illustrations. Posters and
machines are also considered to attract people to enjoy learning, and to
achieve a strong impact in reminding them with messages. These are
considered very important points to disseminate and locate the culture of
preparedness (see Fig. 2).

Main Targets of MKRC and WKRC

Schools are recognized as a key window for a community to gain
knowledge. Through enhancing the awareness of the school students and
teachers, a message can be further disseminated to parents and family
members (SEEDS Asia, Let's Make Schools More Resilient, 2009). With the

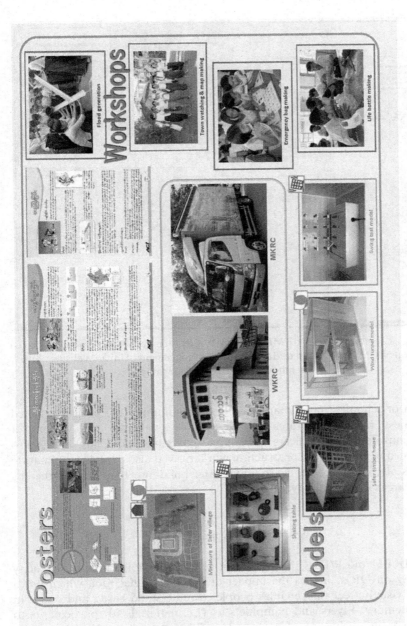

Fig. 2. Contents of MKRC and WKRC at a Glance.

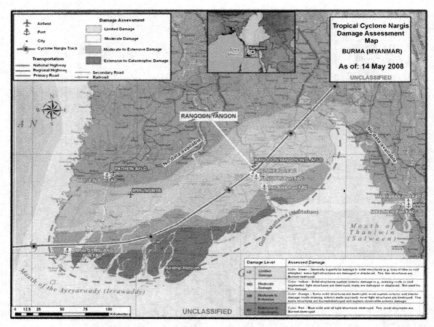

Fig. 3. Target Locations of MKRC and WKRC (circled area). *Source*: Affected Map on MIMU (Myanmar Information Management Unit) Website: http://themimu.info/Affected/index.php

notion of school to family, and family to community, the project targeted awareness raising programs in the schools, with the involvement of Township Education Officers (TEOs) and government officials. It was also envisaged to be used for construction workers, as it also contained miniature models of construction to learn about safer buildings. Fig. 3 shows the key target areas in coastal Myanmar.

Sustainable Training System

The MKRC and WKRC is an attempt at sustainable learning for capacity building on DRR: first is the impact of an educational tool, which has a strong visual effect that enables people to understand easily and retain in their memory. Flyers and pamphlets as IEC materials for participants to learn continuously are also provided. The second is that the target participants are mainly schools, and conducting train-the-trainer programs for teachers ensures the knowledge and skill for teaching mechanism, effects, and things to be prepared are developed. The teachers are expected to teach DRR to students continuously to make their community resilient. The third is synchronization of existing school subjects, which is linked with topics that MKRC and WKRC introduces. Causes and effects of risks and hazards can easily be explained by utilizing the MKRC and WKRC. The fourth is to provide trial visit service and rental service for other organizations. Trial visit service is to introduce MKRC and WKRC to an organization such as DRR-related NGOs or government agencies on a request basis for the first time. If they find MKRC and WKRC useful to integrate with their own activities, they can rent the MKRC and WKRC on a per-day basis. By establishing the institutional linkage among the DRR working group, MKRC and WKRC can cover a considerably larger area and reach a larger number of people to provide disaster education, compared to conventional approaches.

ACHIEVEMENTS AND KEY OBSERVATIONS

Since the launch of the MKRC and WKRC, 8914 people participated in its training sessions in Ayeyarwady and Yangon regions during November 17, 2009 and December 31, 2010. The opening ceremony of each of MKRC and WKRC session saw government officials attending and sharing with all stakeholders of the project. Support from the government is a key element to implement, develop, and continue the project, which was facilitated by the project's local counterpart, the Myanmar Engineering Society.

Results of Training of Trainers

MKRC and WKRC firstly conducted Training of Trainers (ToT) for teachers, who then utilized the MKRC and WKRC to teach DRR to students. This process enhanced involvement of teachers so that their understanding the knowledge on mechanisms and effects of hazards, safety tips, how to conduct town watches to make hazard/resource maps and so forth increased, and by teaching to students by themselves, the knowledge and skill would remain with them (Fig. 4). Thus it was felt that the understanding of the MKRC and WKRC by teachers was a key factor to deliver the message to children. There has been regular evaluation

Fig. 4. A Teacher Trains Students Utilizing MKRC Contents.

Table 1. Brief Profile of Teachers.

	Brief Profile of Teachers
Target	Teachers in 5 Training targeted Townships (AYD: Dedaye, Kyailet, Pyapon, Bogale, + YGN Hlaing Tar Yar T/S)
Methods	Questionnaires at before/after
N	234 teachers who attended ToT
Gender	$M = 31\%$, $F = 79\%$

conducted after training in the form of questionnaire and individual hearing, part of which is described below.

Questionnaire data presented here was taken during the MKRC and WKRC training conducted in July–December 2010. A total of 234 teachers attended the ToT program from the townships of Dedaye, Kyailet, Pyapon Bogale (these three are in the Ayeyarwady Region), and Hlaing Thar Yar (Table 1). Of the respondents, 31% were male and 79% were female (most of the teachers in Myanmar are female). The detail and findings are as follows.

Before training, teachers were asked whether they had attended any DRR training by any agencies. According to the survey, it was found that 60% of teachers had never attended any DRR training from any other organizations, and 40% had received DRR training before, more than once (Fig. 5). Among the target areas; Dedaye, Kyailet, Pyapon, Bogale in Ayeyarwady region, and Hlaing Thar Yar in Yangon region were highly damaged by cyclone Nargis,

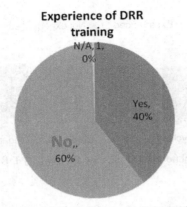

Experience of DRR training

N/A, 1, 0%

Yes, 40%

No, 60%

Fig. 5. Questionnaire Result of ToT (before training) "Have you attended any DRR training before?"

and many aid agencies provided DRR education and related projects. This result shows there is still a shortage of resources to provide DRR education for all teachers. At the same time, this question enabled us to sort and compare the knowledge level on DRR between those who received DRR training and those who had not, which will be shown later.

As a pre-training question, the teachers were asked whether they could explain the mechanism of major hazards such as cyclone, flood, earthquake, and tsunami, or not. The result came out that almost 73–74% of teachers could explain the mechanism of cyclone, flood, and earthquake, but the remaining 26%–27% could not. As for tsunami, 70% of teachers could explain, but 30% could not. This inability to explain tsunami mechanism was relatively high compared to the other hazards. Broadly, we can say that more than one in four teachers in the target area was incapable of explaining the hazards to their students. This can be considered serious as one schoolteacher teaches 40 students annually.

The question was then asked to those who answered "Cannot explain" on hazard in the previous question, whether they experienced DRR training. A clear result of this question was that among teachers who defined herself/ himself unable to explain the mechanism of hazards, most of them (92–97%) had never experienced DRR training. This shows that DRR training affects the ability of teachers to provide DRR knowledge to students in the areas (Fig. 6).

After the ToT, MKRC, and WKRC training have a session for teachers to explain the MKRC and WKRC contents by utilizing posters and miniature models as pre-demonstration to ensure their understanding,

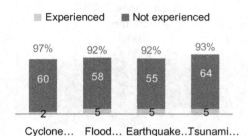

Fig. 6.   Inability to explain hazards among teachers by DRR education experience.

before teaching it to students. By this explanation, teachers enhanced their understanding of mechanisms, impacts, and safety tips against disaster. Knowing the mechanism helps people to think when and how to prepare, and knowing the impact can motivate people to take action for preparedness. As a result of the training, 100% of teachers who attended felt "improvement or increased of knowledge and/or capacity for DRR" and 99% of teachers could understand the basic concept of DRR: Risk of disaster can be reduced by increasing capacity and decreasing vulnerability.

The expected actions for them to take in the future classes, according to the response of the questionnaire, was to "teach mechanism of hazards to your students," "prepare emergency bags at school," "tell a disaster story you have seen from video to your students," "make a life-saving bottle at your class," "listen more carefully to the announcements or news from radio, TV, newspaper, etc.," "give safety tips for students which you learned from posters," "make evacuation routes around the school with other teachers and students." Fifty-four percent to seventy-two percent of participated teachers responded that they decided to conduct above DRR classes at their respective schools. Through this entire process, it was expected that the knowledge would remain with the teacher, to disseminate to students even in the long-term future.

It should be noted that the Ministry of Education has started introducing a "life skill" course in school curricula from 2010 aiming for students to learn how to cope with and respond to disasters. However, local teachers in the field have not yet been provided enough instruction on what and how they should teach their children on the subject, so teacher's understanding of the subject at local school levels must be enhanced. Through the interviews and questionnaires with local schoolteachers, it was confirmed that with the MKRC and WKRC DRR training, local schoolteachers became much more confident with more knowledge and experiences on what and how to teach their students about DRR. As the "life skill" course is official curricula, proper and long-term provision of DRR knowledge is expected.

Another point to note is that because MKRC and WKRC project target schoolteachers, many female participants were trained as a result because schoolteachers in Myanmar are mainly women, especially for elementary levels. Usually, participants of DRR training tend to be male, such as community representatives, due to cultural reasons in many Asian countries and sometimes this contributes a gender imbalance for proper DRR at community level. By targeting schoolteachers, awareness raising for women for DRR is achieved as byproduct.

Results of Training for Students and Villagers

Those teachers who attended ToT provided training to students of their own schools. MKRC or WKRC reached out to 33 schools during the survey period, and received 5132 participants (students/villagers/teachers). Among the all participants, questionnaires were collected from 3644 participants. The duration of the training was from July 1, 2010 to December 31, 2010. The results were collected through questionnaires (Table 2).

Similar to the ToT survey, students and villagers were also questioned whether they had a chance to attend any DRR training before. The result was that students and villagers had even less experience in attending DRR than teachers. Only 28% (999 people) had experienced, but 68% (2478 people) had not (Fig. 7). Again, the need for a long-term commitment to cover more areas and beneficiaries, to conduct training with cooperation with many agencies was seen.

For the purpose of knowing the level of awareness and understanding of students and villagers on hazards, the participants were requested to answer whether they knew "How the following (cyclone, flood, earthquake, and

Table 2. Brief Profile of Students and Villagers.

	Brief Profile of Students and Villagers
Target	Students and villagers in 5 Training targeted Township, 33 schools (AYD: Dedaye, Kyailet, Pyapon, Bogale, + YGN Hlaing Tar Yar T/S)
Methods	Questionnaires at before/after
N	Collected from 3,644 students/villagers who attended Training
Gender	$M = 48\%$ (1,743 people), $F = 52\%$ (1,891people)

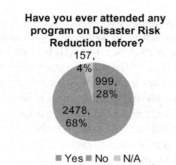

Fig. 7. DRR Experience Ratio Among Villagers and Students.

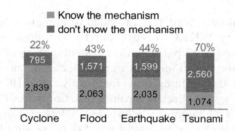

Fig. 8. Knowledge of Hazard Mechanisms Among Students and Villagers Before Training.

tsunami) hazards happen?" The results came out as follows. Cyclone: 22% answered "do not know how it occurs," although most had experienced cyclones. Flood: Floods are very common disasters along the rivers in the area, but 43% said they were unaware of the reason. Earthquake: 44% of people answered "don't know why it happens." Tsunami: 70% of people answered that they did not know the cause of it. Through the questions and the results above, it was clear that even though they experienced disasters, the respondents were not well informed on the causes of risks and hazards (Fig. 8).

While disaster education was not a focus before, the Ministry of Education of the country is now taking an initiative to incorporate DRR into the regular school curriculum. Thus it is now available in current classes in general science, language class (English), geography, and life skill subject to provide the knowledge on hazards and disasters. In order to assist teachers to teach and students to learn, MKRC and WKRC could be suitable materials to promote DRR education with the connection from science (knowledge) to action (life skill). The results of training are analyzed to see the effectiveness of the MKRC and WKRC as below.

There were remarkable improvements after training in the understanding of every hazard. Especially the result on the mechanism of tsunami showed a significant increase in knowledge where the number of respondents who answered "Don't know how it happens" decreased from 70% to 14%. DRR training contributed that more than 85% of targeted students and villagers could define themselves "I understand" the cause of each hazard." Another result also showed that 94% of participants of MKRC and WKRC training felt that they gained more knowledge and idea on where and how to prepare for each hazard, too (Fig. 9).

As shown in Fig. 10, participants answered their improvement at different levels and a total of 95% of respondents felt their improvement of their knowledge and capacity on DRR.

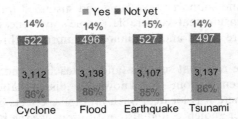

Fig. 9. Understanding of hazard Mechanisms Among Students and Villagers after Training.

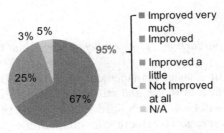

Fig. 10. Questionnaire Results on Improvement of Knowledge/Capacity for DRR after Training.

THE WAY FORWARD

Key Lessons

The crisis situation that cyclone Nargis created was unique and unprecedented, particularly for a developing country such as Myanmar. The impact of the cyclone was exacerbated by poverty and subsistence livelihoods of many of the affected households. These contexts within which the project was developed and implemented, clearly demonstrated the following key lessons:

- The importance of soft solutions (training and awareness raising) in addition to hard solutions (dykes, breakwaters, resistant building, etc.) for different stakeholders.
- The need for strong local partners/collaborators to ensure proper implementation of the project, and for the longer term sustainability of the project's outcomes, including financial (in this case, operation of the MKRC and WKRC). Such key local partners also ensure that political commitment and support is available and sustained for the project.
- The need to ensure that vulnerable people's awareness of disaster risks and hazards are raised and continuously improved through a variety of means.
- The facilitative role that schools (and its teachers and students) play in becoming an entry point for knowledge dissemination to the larger community where it is located. Such multiplier effects enable the project to reach a wider audience, and also institutionalize the knowledge gained.
- The need to target as many local communities as possible, and directly in the locations where they are located – necessitating the delivery of training packages and sessions that are mobile (in the case of this project, the MKRC and WKRC).

Wider Outreach in Terms of Beneficiaries and Contents

When we talk about disaster management, we tend to focus on hard issues including construction of dykes and strong infrastructures. However, there is no guarantee of safety with such hard solutions and there are limitations due to financial resources. To achieve safer communities, we need to balance with soft solutions such as generating and increasing awareness for DRR among local people. The MKRC and WKRC are examples of such efforts in this direction by SEEDS Asia and Myanmar Engineering Society. DRR training was provided to 10,085 people as of April 3, 2011. It should be noted that for many participants it is the first time to learn about disasters, and DRR itself and the impacts of MKRC and WKRC training is significant in terms of how to prepare for possible future disasters.

However, there are also some challenges. First, there was always limitation in number of people who could join the program of MKRC and WKRC due to the limitation of truck/ship size, place, time, and availability of IEC materials and fund. Therefore, the current activity has focused on the development of additional tools for disaster education in school and communities. The Ministry of Education has introduced "life skill curricula" in Myanmar from 2010. In order to fit and produce the synergies with formal education, MKRC and WKRC project continues its efforts to update education tools to fit in the formal education system, so that the sustainability of DRR education can be ensured.

Second is that so far the disasters that the MKRC and WKRC have focused on are cyclones, floods, earthquakes, and tsunamis. However, Myanmar has other natural hazards risks as well, such as tornados and landslides, and the risk of disasters is also considered to be high. These additional tools and information are required to develop for disseminating the knowledge effectively and to be shared as culture of preparedness.

Finally, to nurture the culture of DRR, MKRC, and WKRC training should be continued in the long run to reach more number of people in wider areas. MKRC and WKRC and its associated capacity building program are small steps toward to the long-term goal of building disaster-resilient communities and nations. The need of supporters and network will be essentials in the long run.

Toward Sustainability

SEEDS Asia, along with its partner organization MES, the Myanmar Engineering Society, has worked for community-based DRR through a unique action learning approach. The project has continued more than 3.5 years, and reached a considerable number of beneficiaries. For any outside intervention to be sustainable, it needs to be linked to the local system. The approach of MKRC and WKRC is no exception to this. Possibly the same approach needs to be continued for another one to two years, during which specific sustainable mechanisms need to be found. The essential part of sustainability would be to link with the existing education system, through relevant government ministries or departments. Over the last three years, there has been significant change in the DRR spectrum in Myanmar. Governments both at national and selected local levels have a higher degree of awareness and capacity to conduct risk reduction initiatives. The national government is strongly committed to the ASEAN framework and Hyogo Framework for Action for DRR. The national disaster day is widely celebrated with participation from top-level decision makers at the national level. Disaster education importance has been realized at the highest level. Therefore, it is possibly a key time to link the MKRC and WKRC based disaster education programs in the government schemes and ongoing programs to ensure sustainability. Township level education offices need to be linked with the usage of MKRC and WKRC in regular education programs, both for in-service and preservice teacher training as well as school based education programs. Private–public participation is another model which can be used to test the sustainability of the programs. The cost of operation of MKRC and WKRC is affordable at the local level, and cost-sharing programs need to be considered. The local people are well equipped with the knowledge and know-how of the programs, and therefore the knowledge sharing and transfer mechanisms are also in place. Possibly, the next two years would pave the way for sustainability of the program.

NOTES

1. Post-Nargis Periodic Review (PONREP) was published six months after Nargis, and the assessment was done in June, and refined in October–November 2008.
2. PONREP II, July 2009, focused on the worst affected townships and described the situation of: (1) Health (Health facilities, child health, WASH: water sanitation and hygiene); (2) livelihood, shelter, education; (3) Protected lives: women, children, persons with a disability, return, integration and resettlement.
3. PONREP III published in January 2010 was to follow 18 months after Nargis to assess the progress (the data covering area is almost same), and determined not to lose momentum toward recovery, especially livelihoods as fundamental for self-reliance.
4. PONREP IV was a final assessment to review and examine the status of households with the previous records of PONREP I–III to facilitate further support based on need.
5. Republic of the Union of Myanmar, President's office, Notification Number: 23/2011 2nd Warning of Tagu 1373 ME, April 20, 2011 "Reconstruction of Myanmar Natural Disaster Preparedness Committee."
6. Republic of the Union of Myanmar, President's Office, Notification Number: 17/2001 2nd warning of Tagu ME, April 20, 2011 "Myanmar National Search and Rescue Committee Reformation."
7. Adopted from "1-2-3 Disaster Education" by Kyoto University, 2009."

ACKNOWLEDGMENTS

The authors acknowledge the funding support from CWS (ACT Alliance), JPF (Japan Platform) and MOFA (Ministry of Foreign Affairs) Government of Japan Grassroots Fund for developing MKRC and WKRC and implementing the training programs. Cooperation from the national governments and local education boards, schools, and villages is deeply appreciated.

REFERENCES

Hazard profile of Myanmar. (2009, July). MES, MGS,MIMU,ADPC, DMH, and others.
Institutional Arrangements for disaster management in Myanmar. (2009). Department of Relief and Resettlement, Ministry of Social Welfare Relief and Resettlement, Government of Myanmar.
SEEDS Asia. (2009). Let's Make Schools More Resilient: Handbook on School Disaster Education for Teachers.
Post-Nargis Periodic Review. (2008, July). Tripartite Core Group (TCG) in Myanmar.
Post-Nargis Periodic Review II. (2009, July). Tripartite Core Group (TCG) in Myanmar.
Post-Nargis Periodic Review III. (2010, January). Tripartite Core Group (TCG) in Myanmar.
Post-Nargis Periodic Review IV. (2010, July). Tripartite Core Group (TCG) in Myanmar.
SEEDS Asia. (2010). Reaching the Unreachable: Mobile Knowledge Resource Center and Water Knowledge Resource Center.
Standing Order on Natural Disaster Management. (2009, January). Natural Disaster Preparedness Committee of Government of Myanmar (English translated version by ADPC).

CHAPTER 11

COMMUNITY-BASED DISASTER RISK MANAGEMENT EXPERIENCE OF THE PHILIPPINES

Glenn Fernandez, Noralene Uy and Rajib Shaw

CONTEXT AND IMPORTANCE OF CBDRM IN THE PHILIPPINES

Community-based disaster risk management (CBDRM) initiatives have strong roots in Philippine society not only because of the country's contributory vulnerability to disasters but also because of a culture of community cooperation known as *bayanihan* and a history of social movement driven by the citizens' discontent with bad governance leading to social injustice and environmental degradation (Heijmans, 2009). CBDRM in the Philippines has been a mechanism for change within civil society (Allen, 2006; Heijmans, 2009). In this way, community-based approaches are a fundamental form of empowerment of participants and a compelling strategy for enforcing the transmission of ideas and claims from the bottom up (Allen, 2006).

Philippines Disaster Profile

Due to its location along the western rim of the Pacific Ring of Fire and the Pacific typhoon belt, the Philippines is found to be naturally vulnerable to

Community-Based Disaster Risk Reduction
Community, Environment and Disaster Risk Management, Volume 10, 205–231
Copyright © 2012 by Emerald Group Publishing Limited
All rights of reproduction in any form reserved
ISSN: 2040-7262/doi:10.1108/S2040-7262(2012)0000010017

various disasters. The threat of natural hazards such as earthquake, tsunami, volcanic eruption, landslide, flood, tropical cyclones, and drought brings constant risks to vulnerable populations year after year. Table 1 identifies the Philippines as one of the Top five countries with the highest number of reported disaster events consistently in the last five years.

The Philippines is exposed to the Southwest monsoon, Northeast monsoon, North Pacific Trade winds, Tropical Convergence Zone, tail end of the cold front, easterly waves, the passage of tropical cyclones, and the El Nino Southern Oscillation (ENSO) phenomenon. The tropical maritime climate of the country is characterized by weather events influenced by numerous mountains and valleys, mountain ranges, and the surrounding sea. An average of 20 typhoons and storms enter the Philippines from the Pacific Ocean over the eastern seaboard every year. For the period 1900 to 2011, four of the Top 10 natural disasters in the Philippines, in terms of the number of people affected, happened in the last five years, all caused by typhoons (Table 2). The ranking points to the sad fact that a single disaster event can easily impact millions of Filipinos and might overwhelm national disaster management capacities. Hence, there is a need to develop and strengthen local disaster prevention, mitigation, response, and rehabilitation capacities to complement national capacities.

In addition to large calamities, there is an even larger number of unreported small hazard events that do not register on national news but that consistently wipe out the few assets of the poor, preventing their escape from the poverty cycle (World Bank & NDCC, 2005).

Table 1. Top 10 Countries Sorted by Number of Reported Disaster Events (in parentheses).

Rank	2010	2009	2008	2007	2006
1	China (22)	Philippines (25)	China (29)	United States (23)	China (38)
2	India (16)	China (24)	United States (22)	China (20)	United States (31)
3	Philippines (14)	United States (16)	Philippines (20)	India (20)	India (21)
4	United States (12)	India (15)	Indonesia (17)	Indonesia (17)	Philippines (20)
5	Indonesia (11)	Indonesia (12)	India (11)	Philippines (16)	Indonesia (20)
6	Australia (8)	Brazil (9)	Vietnam (10)	Pakistan (10)	Afghanistan (13)
7	Mexico (8)	Mexico (7)	Colombia (9)	Japan (8)	Vietnam (11)
8	Russia (8)	Australia (6)	Kenya (8)	Mexico (7)	Pakistan (9)
9	Pakistan (7)	Bangladesh (6)	Thailand (5)	Algeria (7)	Bangladesh (8)
10	Vietnam (7)	Vietnam (6)	Australia (5)	Haiti (7)	Romania (8)

Sources: EM-DAT: The OFDA/CRED International Disaster Database – www.emdat.be – Université Catholique de Louvain – Brussels – Belgium; Vos, Rodriguez, Below, & Guha-Sapir, 2010.

Table 2. Top 10 Natural Disasters in Philippines for the Period 1900–2011 Sorted by Numbers of Total Affected People, Per Data Accessed on April 4, 2011.

Rank	Disaster Type	Date	Affected Persons
1	Typhoon Mike (local name Ruping)	November 1990	6,159,569
2	Typhoon Ketsana *(Ondoy)*	September 2009	4,901,763
3	Typhoon Fengshen *(Frank)*	June 2008	4,785,460
4	Typhoon Parma *(Pepeng)*	September 2009	4,478,491
5	Typhoon Babs *(Loleng)*	October 1998	3,902,424
6	Typhoon Xangsane *(Milenyo)*	September 2006	3,842,406
7	Tropical Storm Vera *(Openg)*	November 1973	3,400,024
8	Typhoon Ruby *(Unsang)*	October 1988	3,250,208
9	Flood	July 1972	2,770,647
10	Typhoon Olga *(Didang)*	May 1976	2,700,000

Source: EM-DAT: The OFDA/CRED International Disaster Database – www.emdat.be – Université Catholique de Louvain – Brussels – Belgium.

Key Elements of CBDRM Practice in the Philippines

The tradition of CBDRM in the Philippines is considered to be homegrown because it is a response to vulnerability caused by natural disasters compounded by huge social inequalities in Philippine society (Heijmans, 2009). Because of this, community-based initiatives (often channeled through people's organizations) find ground in support of vulnerable sectors and communities. The Citizens' Disaster Response Network's (CDRN) community-based disaster management (CBDM) policy, for instance, is a critique of the top-down, single-event relief operations of the government. This approach is quite different from *Duryog Nivaran* in South Asia and from LA RED in Latin America, as both frame the problem of DRM as a lack of information, experience, and material for drawing up proper policy guidelines and insufficient research into alternative technologies (ibid.)

Some key elements can be identified in many CBDRM activities and programs in the country (Heijmans, 2009; Victoria, 2003; PDRSEA, 2008). These include:

- Recognizing disasters as a question of people's vulnerability, thus priority is given to the most vulnerable groups, families, and people in the community such as the urban poor and informal sector; the subsistence farmers, fisherfolk, and indigenous people; and the elderly, physically handicapped, children, and women

- Acknowledging people's existing capacities and coping mechanisms, hence activities aim to strengthen these
- Seeking to contribute to addressing the roots of people's vulnerability and to transforming or removing the structures generating inequity and underdevelopment through education and capacity building, gender sensitivity, and economic resilience building
- Considering people's participation essential to disaster management because community members are the main actors and initiators as well as the ultimate beneficiaries, thus commitment and accountability of multi-stakeholders are necessary
- Putting a premium on the organizational capacity of the vulnerable sectors through the formation of grassroots disaster response organizations
- Mobilizing the less vulnerable sectors into partnership with the vulnerable sectors in disaster management and development work and outsiders (e.g., NGOs) may have supporting and facilitating roles
- Being aware that risk reduction measures are community-specific and entail cultural appropriateness and sensitivity to local structures to encourage community ownership
- Using local knowledge about hazards and harmonization of local, indigenous, and scientific knowledge
- Blending community-based and top-down approaches
- Demonstrating transparency in procedures and processes
- Utilizing a communication design, which the community has the capacity of using such as early warning information and dissemination of such information
- Putting in place an exit strategy for external stakeholders as a sustainability mechanism to ensure that CBDRM initiatives continue even after outside funding support is terminated

EVOLUTION OF CBDRM IN THE PHILIPPINES

Even before the concept became a generally accepted approach by the international community at the end of the 1990s, Philippine grassroots organizations had already pioneered the development and implementation of CBDRM (Maceda, Gaillard, Stasiak, Le Masson, & Le Berre, 2009). With the passage of a new disaster management law in 2010, the government has officially adopted CBDRM as a model to engage communities in DRR undertaking, with the hope that heightened involvement would translate to communities being more responsive and self-managing when emergencies do arise (Ramos, 2011).

Trends in the DRM System

Fig. 1 summarizes some milestones in Philippine disaster management system. In the 1970s and 1980s, the aim was primarily disaster preparedness and response with emphasis on emergency operations (Heijmans, 2009). The enactment of Presidential Decree 1566 in 1978 was focused on a reactive approach to disasters in keeping with prevailing thinking during that time (Benson, 2009). As early as then, the capacity of local government units (LGUs) were being developed since they were tasked to take the lead on disaster response. The beginnings of a citizenry-based disaster response in the Philippines can also be traced back to the 1970s when people's organizations and students took the initiative to render support to peasants affected by floods in Central Luzon (Heijmans, 2009). This led to a growing social movement with a citizenry-based and development-oriented approach to disaster response, which the progressive nongovernment organization (NGO), Citizen's Disaster Response Network, follows.

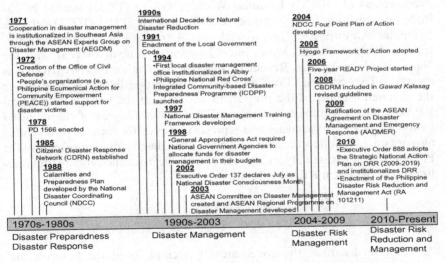

Fig. 1. Milestones in the Philippine Disaster Risk Management System.

As a strong advocate of CBDRM, the Philippine National Red Cross (PNRC) has adopted and implemented the Integrated Community Disaster Planning Program (1994), the Community-Based Disaster Management Program (2001–2004), the *Barangay* Disaster Action Teams (2005–present), and the Red Cross 143 Program (2008–present). The Red Cross 143 Program aims to have 44 volunteers (one team leader and 43 team members, hence 143) in each of the country's 42,000 *barangays* (villages) trained in disaster preparedness and response, in health and welfare, and voluntary blood donation advocacy, among others.

Starting in 2006, a five-year multiagency initiative called Hazards Mapping for Effective Community-Based Disaster Risk Mitigation or the READY Project is being implemented to cover 27 high-risk provinces of the country (Solidum & Duran-Alegre, 2011). The main aim of this project is to address the problem of disaster risk management at the local level. The READY Project has three components: (1) multi-hazard and risk assessment, (2) community-based disaster risk mitigation through the development of community-based early warning system (CBEWS) and the conduct of information, education, and communication (IEC) campaigns, and (3) mainstreaming disaster risk reduction into the local development. The Project is implemented by the National Disaster Coordinating Council (NDCC) through the Office of Civil Defense (OCD) as the executing agency, with the Collective Strengthening of Community Awareness for Natural Disasters (CSCAND, a subcommittee on Preparedness of NDCC) Technical Working Group (TWG) headed by the Philippine Institute of Volcanology and Seismology (PHIVOLCS) with the Philippine Atmospheric, Geophysical, and Astronomical Services Administration (PAGASA), the Mines and Geosciences Bureau (MGB), and the National Mapping and Resource Information Authority (NAMRIA) as members. The CSCAND TWG members are the responsible agencies to deliver the required outputs of the project. In addition, at the local level, a Local READY Team, composed of regional or local employees of the involved national government agencies and representatives of the local government, is also organized to follow up activities and assist in the coordination aspect of the Project. Further sustainability is ensured with the assistance and institutionalization of the Local READY Team.

The Government's Focus on and Promotion of CBDRM

As mentioned earlier, the government has emphasized the key role and exercise of leadership responsibilities of LGUs since 1978. This was reinforced with the passage of the Local Government Code in 1991, which devolved most of the national government functions to LGUs. The community level is considered to be the appropriate level for disaster preparedness intervention, where community members experience different degrees of access to community institutions and resources (depending on social status and social capital), which is reinforced by substantial social pressure to abide by rules and norms embedded in the community structure (Allen, 2006).

To raise the consciousness of Filipinos on disaster management, the first week of July of every year was declared Natural Disaster Consciousness Week in 1998. Recognizing the need for more time for agencies to implement their campaign programs, this was replaced by the National Disaster Consciousness Month, to run for the whole month of July each year.

In 1998 the NDCC initiated *Gawad KALASAG (KA-lamidad at Sakuna LA-banan, SA-riling G-aling ang Kaligtasan)* as a recognition scheme in search for excellence on DRM and humanitarian assistance. The Filipino word *kalasag* means shield. In a related manner, *Gawad KALASAG* promotes to protect or shield high-risk communities against hazards by encouraging the participation of various stakeholders in conceptualizing and implementing DRM programs. *Gawad KALASAG* provides the mechanism to obtain sustained commitment and support from the highest level of government by recognizing the exceptional contributions of the various DRM practitioners (Local Disaster Risk Reduction and Management Coordinating Councils at the provincial, city, municipal, and *barangay* levels; local and international NGOs; schools and hospitals; and heroic individuals and groups) in building the resilience of communities to disaster (National Disaster Coordinating Council (NDCC), 2008). At the same time, *Gawad KALASAG* aims to promote the spirit of volunteerism among agencies and individuals in DRM.

INSTITUTIONALIZATION AND GOVERNANCE MECHANISMS

Since CBDRM would utilize participatory tools such as participatory risk assessment, participatory identification of risk reduction measures, participatory planning, community-managed risk reduction programs and participatory monitoring and evaluation, an organization or a committee that will facilitate and coordinate the CBDRM process is important.

Institutional Structure

The National Disaster Risk Reduction and Management Council (NDRRMC) is the coordinating body for disaster risk management in the Philippines. It was established through PD 1566 and was then called the NDCC. The NDRRMC is the highest policy-making body on matters concerning disasters. It advises the President of the Philippines on the status of national disaster preparedness and management plans and recommends to the President the declaration of state of calamity and the release of the national calamity fund. The OCD was given a vital role in executing and monitoring the implementation of policies and programs and in providing secretariat support to NDRMMC. The NDRMMC is chaired by the Secretary of the Department of National Defense and includes other department secretaries, representatives of various national government agencies, the Secretary General of the PNRC, four representatives from other CSOs, and one representative from the private sector as members.

The NDRRMC has institutionalized the Cluster Approach as a coordination tool to ensure a more coherent and effective delivery of humanitarian assistance by mobilizing groups of agencies, organizations, and NGOs to respond in a strategic manner across all key sectors or areas of activity. As shown in Table 3, cluster leads have designated tasks related to

Table 3. Cluster Approach in the Philippine Disaster Management System.

Cluster	Government Lead Agency
Nutrition	Department of Health (DOH)
Water, sanitation and hygiene (WASH)	
Health	
Emergency shelter	Department of Social Welfare
Protection	and Development (DSWD)
Food	
Livelihood	
Camp coordination and management	Office of Civil Defense – Provincial Disaster Coordinating Council (OCD-PDCC)
Logistics	Office of Civil Defense (OCD)
Emergency telecommunications	
Early recovery	
Education	Department of Education (DepEd)
Agriculture	Department of Agriculture (DA)

Sources: NDCC Circular No. 5 (2007) and NDCC Memorandum No. 4 (2008).

their mandates. Their principal roles are (i) to craft cluster operational strategies covering pre- and post-event phases of a disaster that will provide a clear direction for cluster partners on how, what, when, and where to distribute, (ii) facilitate a process aimed at ensuring well-coordinated and effective humanitarian responses in the sector or area of activity concerned, and (iii) ensure continuous improvement in the implementation of the Cluster Approach in the country by identifying best practices and carrying out lessons learned activities either individually or in collaboration with other clusters. The cluster approach primarily focuses on the roles and responsibilities of agencies at the national level. However, cluster focal points at regional and provincial levels exist as ready coordination mechanisms by which assistance will be channeled through. At the *barangay* level, the Cluster Approach is replicated through assignment of committees per area of activity (Corporate Network for Disaster Response (CNDR), 2011b), as exemplified in Fig. 2.

In terms of organizational network, the NDRRMC spans across national, regional, provincial, city, municipal, and *barangay* levels. As shown in Fig. 3, every level of government has its own disaster risk reduction and management council or committee.

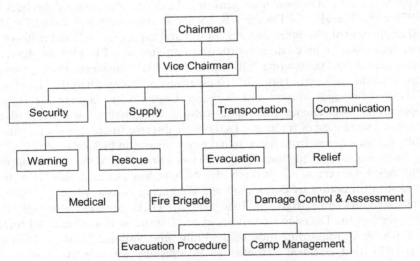

Fig. 2. Sample Organizational Structure of the *Barangay* Disaster Risk Reduction and Management Committee.

Fig. 3.   NDRRMC Organizational Network.

Policy Environment

The cornerstone of disaster management policy in the Philippines dates back in 1978 when Presidential Decree No. 1566 was enacted, which called for the strengthening of Philippine disaster control and capability and establishing the national program on community disaster preparedness. PD 1566 emphasized self-reliance by encouraging self-help and mutual assistance, thus, primary responsibility was placed upon LGUs especially officials such as the Governor, City or Municipal Mayor, and *Barangay* Captain. In planning and actual operations, inter-agency and multi-sectoral coordination was required to optimize utilization of resources. LGUs were directed to utilize local resources fully before support from the national government can be sought.

As a signatory to the Hyogo Framework for Action (HFA), the Philippine Government, through the NDCC has adopted the HFA five priorities for action by developing and enhancing current plans, programs, and activities on DRR. In June 2007, NDCC initiated, through the Partnership for Disaster Reduction in the Southeast Asia Phase 4 Project (PDRSEA 4), the formulation of the Philippine National Strategic Plan on CBDRM that outlined activities in establishing an effective system to promote CBDRM (NDCC, 2008).

In the same way, as a signatory to the ASEAN Agreement on Disaster Management and Emergency Response (AADMER), the Philippines adheres to the principles and objectives of the regional agreement and first ever HFA-related binding instrument in the world (Reyes, 2010).

In 2010 the Philippines Disaster Risk Reduction and Management Act (Republic Act No. 10121) was finally enacted. The new law provides for the development of policies and plans and the implementation of actions and measures pertaining to all aspects of disaster risk reduction and management, including good governance, risk assessment and early warning, knowledge building and awareness raising, reducing underlying risk factors, and preparedness for effective response and early recovery. Among its salient features include the following:

- Development, promotion, and implementation of the National Disaster Risk Reduction and Management Plan
- Mainstreaming of disaster risk reduction (DRR) and climate change adaptation (CCA) in development, peace, and conflict resolution processes
- Support to knowledge management and education (e.g., setting up of training institutes)
- Composition of National Council to include representatives from the national government, leagues of LGUs, private sector, and civil society organizations
- Renaming of previous disaster councils as National/Regional/Local Disaster Risk Reduction and Management Councils and the *Barangay* Disaster Coordinating Councils are now known as *Barangay* Disaster Risk Reduction and Management Committees and will fall under the *Barangay* Development Council
- Enhanced functions (e.g., monitoring and evaluation) and organizational structure of the OCD
- Establishment of permanent Local Disaster Risk Reduction and Management Offices

Funding Mechanism

Every year, a National Disaster Risk Reduction and Management Fund (NDRRMF, formerly called Calamity Fund) is appropriated in the national budget for the purpose of aid; relief, and rehabilitation services to communities and areas affected by man-made and natural calamities; repair and reconstruction of permanent structures, including other capital expenditures for disaster operation; and rehabilitation activities. The specific amount of the NDRRMF and the appropriate recipient agencies and/or LGUs vary every year upon approval of the President of the Philippines with recommendation of the NDRRMC. Based on data from the Department of Budget and Management, the approved NDRRM Fund for the years 2007–2011 was 9 billion pesos in 2007; 2 billion pesos in 2008, 2009, and 2010; and 5 billion pesos in 2011. Of this amount, 30 percent is allocated as Quick Response Fund (QRF) or standby fund for relief and recovery programs in order to normalize the situation and living conditions of affected people and areas as quickly as possible. The government agencies through which the NDRRMF is usually released for specific purposes are shown in Table 4. A declaration of a state of calamity of the disaster-affected areas is the basis for the release of NDRRMF by the President. The OCD, as lead agency for disaster risk reduction and management in the country, is allocated 1 billion pesos as its revolving fund.

At the local level, a Local Disaster Risk Reduction and Management Fund (LDRRMF) is appropriated amounting to not less than 5 percent of the estimated revenue from regular sources as mandated under the Local Government Code of 1991 to support disaster risk management activities such as, but not limited to, pre-disaster preparedness programs including

Table 4. Government agencies to which the NDRRMF is commonly allocated.

Government Department/Agency	Purpose
Department of Social Welfare and Development (DSWD)	Emergency relief and rehabilitation assistance to disaster victims
Department of Health (DOH)	Medical assistance to disaster victims
Department of Public Works and Highways (DPWH)	Immediate repair/restoration of damaged vital infrastructures (e.g., school buildings)
Department of Education (DepEd)	Replacement of totally damaged instructional materials and prioritization and restoration/repair of school buildings (including libraries, laboratories, and toilets) in coordination with DPWH
Department of Agriculture (DA)	Assistance to the agricultural sector
Department of Transportation and Communications (DOTC)	Repair/restoration of vial government transportation and communication facilities/infrastructures
Department of National Defense/ Armed Forces of the Philippines	Relief, rescue and evacuation activities and repair/ rehabilitation of public utilities
Other departments/agencies	Immediate repair/restoration of vital infrastructures/ facilities

Source: NDCC Memorandum Order No. 4 (1989).

training, purchasing life-saving rescue equipment, supplies and medicines, for post-disaster activities and for the payment of premiums on calamity insurance. In the same way as at the national level, 30 percent of the amount appropriated for the LDRRMF is allocated as QRF. Before 2010, most of the remaining fund was used for post-disaster activities. With the enactment of the disaster risk reduction and management law, it is now specified that 70 percent of the LDRRMF can be allocated for pre-disaster preparedness activities. This shift indicates that the government is gearing toward a more risk reduction-oriented agenda.

LINKAGES TO EDUCATIONAL SECTOR

Disaster education is one of the nonstructural mitigation measures implemented to address vulnerabilities in society (Victoria, 2009). Education and training are undertaken to enable community members to understand the risks they face and the tools and methods available to them to prepare for and extenuate the effects of disasters (Martin, 2008).

Importance of Community Disaster Education and Training

According to the Citizens' Disaster Response Center (CDRC), the key to its disaster management program is education. CDRC has developed education modules for disaster preparedness and management at the grassroots level (CDRC, 2001). Through CDRC's disaster education program, CBDM facilitators aim to help reinforce traditional community values such as self-help, resourcefulness, and cooperativism. CDRC is convinced that disaster preparedness does not simply require funding and material support. Funding and material support are necessary. But it is the people's managerial abilities, creativity, innovation, outlook, and values which make the real difference. This is the reason why CDRC emphasizes disaster education. Unless properly educated, the community would most likely waste or mismanage the funds and other material support intended to help it prevent or mitigate disasters.

In another example, training and education is an important tool applied in all six steps of the Integrated Community Disaster Planning Program (ICDPP) of PNRC (Falk, 2005). They are crucial to the promotion of a "culture of preparedness." For the local government staff, the ICDPP training focused on enhancing skills in planning and mobilizing resources for disaster management. Popular awareness-raising materials such as simple and colorful comic books and posters written in the Filipino language are proven very effective for disseminating information on disaster management, especially if the contents and situations are familiar to the local people.

In the area of training, NDRRMC has also been partnering with the World Bank Institute and the Earthquakes and Megacities Initiative since 2006 in implementing and delivering a series of online courses designed to build competency in DRM practice. One of the courses is specifically focusing on CBDRM. The target participants of the distance learning program are local chief executives, city, municipal and provincial government officers, members of local and regional legislative and development councils, administrators, disaster managers, emergency planners, and staff members of the planning, engineering, and disaster management offices. In addition, many NGOs such as DRRNet and Center for Disaster Preparedness (CPD) have developed and implemented various training programs that target different end users. The CDP, for instance, has sustained its CBDRM Training and Learning Circle through the years.

Finally, with the enactment of RA 10121, Disaster Risk Reduction and Management Training Institutes will be established to train public and private individuals, both at the local and national levels, in such subject as disaster risk reduction and management among others. The Institutes are expected to consolidate and prepare training materials and publications of disaster risk reduction and management books and manuals to assist disaster risk reduction and management workers in the planning and implementation of this program and projects. The Institutes will also be conducting research programs to upgrade knowledge and skills and document best practices on disaster risk reduction and management. The Institutes will also be mandated to conduct periodic awareness and education programs to accommodate new elective officials and members of the LDRRMCs (Republic Act No. 10121, 2010).

INVOLVEMENT OF THE EDUCATION SECTOR IN CBDRM IN THE PHILIPPINES

From 2007 to 2008, NDCC and DepEd, in partnership with the Asian Disaster Preparedness Center (ADPC), undertook a project to develop DRM modules for integration into the secondary school curriculum. The module includes information on disaster preparedness, prevention and mitigation of hazards and risks of natural events to vulnerable communities and areas. Disaster awareness has formed part of the learning core competencies under the Science and Social Studies subjects in public elementary and high schools (GFDRR, 2009). DepEd is continuing the implementation of the project on "Prioritizing the Mainstreaming of Disaster Risk Reduction Management in the School System and Implementation of Programs and Projects as mandated by Department Order No. 55 series of 2007" (Ramos, 2011). So far, public grade school and secondary school curricula have been updated to incorporate DRR. Lesson examplars and other learning materials to guide both teachers and school children have been developed. The teachers are also educated in DRR by including the concepts in the Teacher's Education Curriculum. At present, however, education in DRR is still limited in scope and education materials are still inadequate.

Moreover, as a member of the NDRRMC, DepEd provides assistance in public education and campaigns regarding disaster preparedness, prevention, and mitigation; makes school buildings available as evacuation centers; and trains education staff in disaster preparedness. Supporting the efforts of DepEd, a three-day seminar-workshop on natural hazards awareness and Public School Teachers preparedness focusing on earthquake and volcanoes is annually conducted for public school teachers of Metro Manila by PHIVOLCS since 2002.

In April 2010, the Philippines spearheaded and launched the Pledging Campaign for One Million Safe Schools and Hospitals Programs in Southeast Asia as a collaborative effort among ASEAN Committee on Disaster Management (ACDM) Focal Point, OCD, DepEd, and DOH. During the pledging, both DepEd and DOH pledged to make about more than 100,000 education and health facilities in the country safe from natural disasters. Regular drills in schools and hospitals for emergency preparedness are being conducted by DepEd and DOH. Lessons learned from these drills can be shared by students, teachers, and hospital staff to their household and their community.

Youth Participation in CBDRM

A survey conducted by a public opinion polling body found that 10 percent of the Filipino youth were connected to a youth organization (Economic and Social Commission for Asia and the Pacific (ESCAP), 2000). Six percent were members of arts, music, or educational organizations; three percent were part of a charitable organization; and one percent of the youth were affiliated to a political party, labor union, or professional association. The Filipino youth have been highly encouraged to participate in politics and governance, and the Philippines is the only nation in the world that has a mechanism of involving the youth sector in governance, through the *Sangguniang Kabataan* (Youth Council, SK). As a case in point, the Philippine Disaster Risk Reduction and Management Act of 2010 encourages the youth to participate in disaster risk reduction and management activities, such as organizing quick response groups, particularly in identified disaster-prone areas, as well as the inclusion of disaster risk reduction and management programs as part of the SK programs and projects.

Through the SK, young people between the ages of 15 to 21 can directly participate at all levels of governance: *barangay*, municipal, city, provincial, and national. There are around 41,995 youth councils all over the Philippines, corresponding to the total number of villages. Each SK has its own annual budget, which is 10% of the total *barangay* budget (Velasco, 2005). The SK Chairman automatically sits in the *Sangguniang Barangay* (Village Council) as ex officio member and as chairman of the Committee on Youth and Sports, one of the standing committees in the village council.

Examples of recent autonomous SK involvement in DRR include the comprehensive "Training/Workshop on Integrating Disaster Risk Reduction (DRR) and Climate Change Adaptation (CCA) into Local Development Planning" organized by the SK Provincial Federation of Quezon province in July, 2011, in coordination with Philippine Rural Reconstruction Movement (PRRM) (Sangguniang Kabataan Provincial Federation (SKPF), 2011); the SK participation in the "Life Boat Handling and Rescue Operations Training" organized by the municipality of Famy, Laguna, from June to July 2011 (Provincial Disaster Risk Reduction and Management Office (PDRRMO), 2011); the training on the basics of disaster risk reduction and management of 28 SK presidents of the municipality of San Jose, Antique, in May 2011 (Local Governance Regional Resource Center (LGRRC), 2011); and the SK participation in a one-day disaster preparedness seminar and earthquake drill organized by Yes Pinoy Foundation (YPF) on April 15, 2011 (Gonzaga, 2011).

Among the youth organizations that require a membership fee, some of the most popular are the Red Cross Youth councils and science clubs. The Red Cross Youth (RCY) is one of the six major services of the PNRC. Its mission is to educate and empower the children and youth in the spirit of Red Cross through constructive trainings and effective leadership and provide opportunities for directing and harnessing their energy and idealism into worthwhile humanitarian activities. Young people can join RCY councils in the school or in the community and participate in Disaster Management Trainings (DMT) as well as take an educator's course on HIV – AIDS Prevention and Education (HAPE) and Drug Abuse Prevention and Education (DAPE) and conduct dissemination sessions in schools and in the community. RCY allows the development of the spirit of humanitarianism and social service in the youth through active and direct involvement in Red Cross activities.

On the other hand, science club activities are an excellent example of how to supplement formal disaster education in the classroom, as shown in Fig. 4 (Shiwaku & Fernandez, 2011). In 2010, there were two DRR-themed national science camps. The first one was organized by PSYSC in cooperation with Kyoto University, the Asian University Network of Environment and Disaster Risk Management (AUEDM), the United Nations International Strategy for Disaster Reduction (UNISDR) Bangkok Office, the United Nations Educational, Scientific, and Cultural Organization (UNESCO) Jakarta Office, and the PHIVOLCS. The camp theme was "Alert Level 10: The RESCUE (Resilient, Empowered Science Clubs even Under Emergency)." Camp 2010 was about rethinking the way young people prepare for hazards and respond to disasters. Lectures included "Science of Disasters and Detection of Hazards" (explanation on the

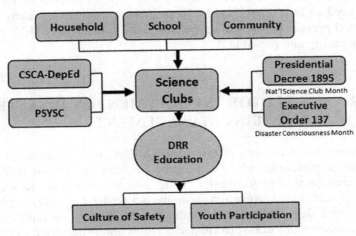

Fig. 4. Science Clubs as Vehicle for DRR Education.

different kinds of geological and hydro-meteorological hazards; recent major disasters in the Philippines; advances in Doppler radar and seismograph technology and other ways of knowing when a disaster is impending); "Community in Action: From Tragedy to Strategy" (impact of disasters on national development; CBDRM); and "Disaster Preparedness 101" (4 Rs of Disaster Management: Reduction, Readiness, Response, Recovery; thinking globally, acting locally: what science clubs can do to help in building the disaster resilience of their community).

Coincidentally, the 2010 Youth for Environment Summer (YES) Camp organized by the Center for Students and Co-curricular Affairs of the Department of Education (CSCA-DepEd) and the Department of Environment and Natural Resources (DENR) Youth Desk, in collaboration with the NGO *Kabataang Sama-samang Maglilingkod* (Youth Unified in Service), Inc. (KASAMA), also had a disaster risk reduction theme. The camp was held in Baguio City and the theme was *"Sagip Kalikasan, Sagip Buhay"* (Disaster Management through Environmental Protection). One of the objectives of the YES Camp was to "inculcate among students the critical role of environmental protection in preventing and coping with the effects of natural disasters such as typhoons, floods, earthquakes, and droughts."

Given their wide distribution across the country and their ability to integrate DRR in their activities, the SK, Red Cross Youth councils, and science clubs can contribute enormously to building a culture of safety and enhancing youth participation in CBDRM. Young people need organizations such as these three that provide positive, supportive environments. The youth need to have opportunities to contribute to society. Young people have great promise in addressing environmental concerns like DRR because of their energy and passion.

PRIVATE SECTOR INVOLVEMENT IN DISASTER RISK MANAGEMENT

The private sector consists of those entities that are not controlled by the state such as private firms and companies, corporations, private banks, and nongovernmental organizations, among others. In recent decades, the private sector has become increasingly active in the role it plays in international development and humanitarian relief as exemplified by a growing number of public-private partnerships and programs that promote social development and humanitarian relief (Warhurst, 2006). In addition, it is heavily involved commercially in DRR by way of engineers, consultants, software designers, insurers, transporters, and suppliers of various goods and services for whom risk and disasters are business opportunities (Twigg, 2001). In the Philippines, the rise of influential associations with strong business leadership in the 1970s led to corporate contributions for development initiatives, which later evolved beyond philanthropy to direct involvement in community projects including disaster relief and, recently, mitigation and preparedness activities (ibid.).

The private sector is recognized as important in the HFA. Priority 4 calls for the reduction of underlying risks of which one of the activities is to promote the establishment of public–private partnerships to better engage the private sector in disaster risk reduction activities; encourage the private sector to foster a culture of disaster prevention, putting greater emphasis on, and allocating resources to, pre-disaster activities such as risk assessments and early warning systems (ISDR, 2005). Although the private sector faces the challenge of competing priorities when considering involvement in DRM, there are ample opportunities for realigning investment and deeper engagement in DRM (World Economic Forum (WEF) World Bank, and United Nations International Strategy for Disaster Reduction, 2008).

Potential of Corporate Sector in Community-Based Disaster Risk Management

Businesses – whether large, medium, or small – are key actors in the communities in which they operate and can be involved in CBDRM on a number of levels (Warhurst, 2006). Corporate social responsibility (CSR) is often seen as the right vehicle for businesses to undertake DRM initiatives. However, the case for CSR is generally a blend of concerns about reputation management, risk management, employee recruitment, motivation and retention, investor relations, and access to capital brought about by the rising influence of institutional investors, new rules of competitiveness, the links between operational efficiency and resource use efficiency and cooperative relationships with local communities (ibid.). It is thus very rare for CSR activities on CBDRM to take on a proactive nature when most interventions are of the responsive, short-term, one-off, and post-disaster type (Twigg, 2001; Miyaguchi & Shaw, 2007).

It would seem that it is in the best interest of businesses to invest in preventive measures to ensure business continuity since capital assets – buildings, plant, and equipment – can be damaged and their supply chains disrupted by loss of infrastructure or transportation during a disaster. In addition, they may undertake CBDRM in response to the need to manage risk since they may find themselves operating in hazard-prone markets. Furthermore, external requirements or expectations of stakeholders including customers, suppliers, and local communities as well as those public interest groups that have interest in their operations and impacts may dictate that they "do the right thing" in their every day operations (Warhurst, 2006).

According to Miyaguchi (2008), the corporate sector can be an integral part of building disaster resilience because it (i) possesses substantial resources including human, material, technical, and financial, (ii) has a significant presence in every region of the world due to its economic activities, and (iii) possesses a vast amount of technical knowledge to better respond to and mitigate disasters. Also, businesses can contribute to DRM by (i) helping to reduce poverty and therefore vulnerability in the regions in which they operate; (ii) collaborating with local actors to assess disaster risk, engage in mitigation and preparedness activities, train their staff on first aid and disaster management, and contribute to disaster risk awareness raising; (iii) having specific resources and expertise that can be useful in preparedness for disaster response; (iv) having good local connections that can be extremely useful in responding to disasters, and (v) helping to recover from disasters by helping to ensure that – in the process of rebuilding - vulnerability is reduced through responsible planning and construction, therefore mitigating the risk of future natural hazards (Warhurst, 2006).

Noah's Ark Project: An Example of a Corporate-Led CBDRM Project

The Corporate Network for Disaster Response (CNDR) is a network of business groups, associations, corporations, and corporate foundations in the Philippines, which seeks to rationalize and institutionalize disaster risk management efforts of the business community. It started as a group coordinating the responses of the business sector to the 1990 Luzon Earthquake. From community disaster response, its services have evolved to the whole range of disaster risk management work including disaster preparedness and rehabilitation.

CNDR's community-based disaster preparedness projects aim to (i) enhance the capacities of the target communities to respond to disasters and reduce their vulnerabilities; (ii) strengthen institutional capacity of LGUs to engage in CBDRM activities and institutionalize DRR through local legislative plans and agenda, and (iii) strengthen the relationship between the corporate and public sectors for CBDRM and emergency preparedness (Corporate Network for Disaster Response (CNDR), 2011a). In addition, its thrusts include (i) providing service to the business sector by assisting its members in the development of appropriate disaster response programs and providing venues to raise disaster preparedness awareness in the business sector and (ii) facilitating private sector support in CBDRM activities by promoting Public–Private sector partnership in DRR.

In August 2010, CNDR, along with Ayala Foundation, Inc., and Habitat for Humanity Philippines, Inc., started implementing a community-based disaster preparedness project called "Building Noah's Ark in Flood Prone Communities" (Noah's Ark Project) in Malanday, Marikina City, one of the areas highly affected by Typhoon Ondoy (International Name Ketsana) in 2009. It aims to find a safe spot in a high-risk area and develop it into an evacuation center; retrofit schools and other public buildings into suitable evacuation areas, and develop capacities of vulnerable communities to prepare for flooding. CNDR handles the capacity-building activities for the project, which include the installation of community rain gauges and training on how to collect, analyze, and interpret rainfall data; formulation of contingency plan on security support, transportation, triage and medical and paramedic support, and simulation exercise to test the plan; and preparation of community-based disaster preparedness manuals on early warning system, communication protocol, and evacuation procedures.

A series of seminar workshops was undertaken by CNDR in the period September to December 2010 (CNDR, 2011b). The first workshop was held to reorganize the Local Disaster Coordinating Council into Local Disaster Risk Reduction and Management in pursuant of the recently approved Philippine Disaster Risk Reduction and Management Act. The output of the workshop was the organizational structure of the *Barangay* Disaster Risk Reduction and Management Committee of Malanday, which identified members and task unit leaders and reorientated them on their roles and responsibilities. The second workshop was on hazard awareness and disaster preparedness where participants did risk mapping and transect walk. The outputs of this workshop were the hazard map, vulnerable population map, and resources map of Malanday. The third workshop, community-based warning systems and evacuation procedures planning, tackled flood warning criteria, communication plan, inventory of communication equipment, evacuation plans, and sample advisories (in English and Filipino) as well as establishing the Warning, Communication, and Evacuation Committee structure. The fourth workshop conducted training on rain gauge installation and rain level observation and recording using the hydro-meteorological station rain observer report template. Finally, the fifth and sixth workshops undertook flood warning and evacuation drill planning where participants were provided with evacuation drill sequence guide, radio message template, public information campaign materials templates, and directory of relevant DRRM partners and the actual evacuation drill conducted.

TOWARD SUSTAINABLE CBDRM

In the Philippines, CBDRM has proven useful under different conditions: in mountainous areas, in coastal communities, and even in an urban community of semilegal garbage-collectors (Falk, 2005). However, involvement in community-based DRR initiatives entails short-term costs for local participants in terms of time, energy, and lost opportunities, which have to be weighed against potential (often long-term) benefits (Allen, 2006). Therefore, it is necessary to reflect on the lessons learned from past and present CBDRM practices in order to enhance the implementation of CBDRM and address the issue of sustainability.

Lessons Learned from CBDRM Implementation in the Philippines

Based on current good practices, Victoria (2009) notes down the following benefits of CBDRM:

1. Community process and participation builds confidence among community members, making them proud that they are able to make a difference and have capabilities to pursue disaster mitigation and preparedness and bigger development responsibilities at the local level. This leads to empowerment.
2. Community involvement in risk assessment and risk reduction planning leads to ownership, commitment, and individual and concerted actions in disaster mitigation, including resource mobilization.
3. Trusting and supporting the capacity-building process results in a wide range of appropriate and doable mitigation solutions.
4. Community-based disaster mitigation is cost effective and sustainable self-help approach even if it is time consuming.

Experiences in the Philippines affirm the effectiveness of involving communities in disaster preparedness and mitigation, making CBDRM a viable approach in addressing disaster risk and promoting sustainable development (Luna, 2007; Victoria, 2003). However, local communities admittedly cannot reduce all vulnerabilities on their own. While communities have built on local coping strategies and capacities to reduce some vulnerability, many necessary structural mitigation measures that involve big capital outlay are sometimes needed. More important, vulnerability is complex issue involving numerous conditions, factors, and processes, which can only be addressed through complementary and concerted action among multiple-stakeholders from various disciplines and levels of the disaster management and development planning system. This is why it is advisable to bear in mind that CBDRM is only a supplement to – not a substitute for – regional and national disaster capacities. CBDRM is best suited for reducing the impact of small-scale local hazards (Falk, 2005).

Moreover, CBDRM practice is very contextual to be effective, and therefore its outcomes are difficult to replicate in other localities. For example, what works in Mindanao for internal refugees may not be of priority for lahar-affected communities in Central Luzon (Heijmans, 2009).

Strengthening Mechanisms for Public-Private Partnerships in CBDRM

The inherent issues and problems of CBDRM serve as challenges that can be creatively responded to through innovative ideas. Effective mainstreaming disaster sensitivity and concerns in the local development planning is imperative if we do not want the products of our years of development go into waste due to a single disaster event (Luna, 2007). A mutual support system by all stakeholders can fast track the CBDRM approach in becoming a movement that can facilitate national and local actors to effect changes for more effective disaster risk reduction.

Partnership between the vulnerable and less vulnerable sectors is important. The less vulnerable sectors are able to contribute resources like finances, leadership, technical skills, intellectual thinking, and material resources, which are much needed to sustain CBDRM (Heijmans, 2009). To further enhance disaster risk reduction, it is acknowledged that CBDRM should integrate a larger array of stakeholders, not just community beneficiaries and NGO facilitators but including local governments, scientists, students, teachers, youth organizations, faith groups, women's groups, labor groups, mass media, etc. The participation of scientists and local governments in CBDRM is especially important to integrate indigenous and scientific knowledge, as well as bottom-up and top-down disaster risk reduction measures (Gaillard & Maceda, 2009).

Under the DRRM Act of 2010, a DRRM Institute will be established to cater to the needs of all stakeholders. There are also ongoing capacity-building activities sponsored by OCD and other NDRRMC member agencies such as the Department of Science and Technology (DOST), Department of Interior and Local Government (DILG), National Economic and Development Authority (NEDA), to name a few. As always, these capacity-building activities are hindered by resource constraints, although local expertise, knowledge and experience are widely available (Ramos, 2011). But the vibrant civil society organization (CSO) participation in the area of CBDRM indicates that capacity development for DRR is a high priority even among nongovernment actors. The initiatives of CSOs significantly complement the existing programs of the government. The academe also plays an important role in this regard, with their formal, informal, and nonformal education courses and training and outreach activities.

Institutionalization and Financial Support

With the enactment of the DRRM Act of 2010, the government has officially adopted CBDRM as a model to engage communities in DRR undertaking, although the government has been emphasizing the key role and exercise of leadership responsibilities of LGUs since 1970s. The passage of the Local Government Code in 1991 also devolved most of the national government functions to LGUs, including disaster preparedness interventions. To finance CBDRM, a Local Disaster Risk Reduction and Management Fund is appropriated amounting to not less than 5% of the estimated revenue from regular sources to support disaster risk management activities such as pre-disaster preparedness programs, post-disaster activities, and payment of premiums on calamity insurance.

Institutionalization and funding of CBDRM are very important for sustainability, as well as support from internal and external public and private institutions and the community members themselves. In the end, we must never underestimate local capacity. In the words of CBDRM advocate Zenaida Delica-Willison, "No matter how poor a community is, it can still generate resources through networking and provision of labor and local materials. Sustainability of efforts requires the cooperation of all stakeholders" (Delica-Willison, 2005).

ACKNOWLEDGMENTS

We would like to extend our gratitude to the Ministry of Education, Culture, Sports, Science, and Technology (MEXT) of Japan for Uy's and Fernandez's scholarship at Kyoto University and to the Global Center for Education and Research on Human Security Engineering for Asian Megacities (GCOE-HSE), and Global Center of Education and Sustainability/Survivability Science for a Resilient Society Adaptable to Extreme Weather Conditions (GCOE-ARS) Programs of Kyoto University for providing invaluable support. The kind assistance of the Corporate Network for Disaster Response is highly appreciated.

REFERENCES

Allen, K. A. (2006). Community-based Disaster preparedness and climate adaptation: Local capacity-building in the Philippines. *Disasters, 30*(1), 81–101. Oxford: Overseas Development Institute.

Benson, C. (2009). *Mainstreaming disaster risk reduction into development: Challenges and experience in the Philippines.* Geneva, Switzerland: ProVention Consortium. Retrieved from http://www.unisdr.org/files/8700_8700mainstreamingphilippines1.pdf

Citizens' Disaster Response Center (CDRC). (2001). *Disaster preparedness and management innovations in the Philippines.* Retrieved from http://ssc.undp.org/uploads/media/disaster.pdf

Corporate Network for Disaster Response (CNDR). (2011a). CNDR profile 2010. Pasig: CNDR

Corporate Network for Disaster Response (CNDR). (2011b). *Noah's ark project: Compilation of project materials.* Pasig: CNDR.

Delica-Willison, Z. G. (2005). *Community-based disaster risk management: Local level solutions to disaster risks.* Retrieved from http://www.pacificdisaster.net/pdnadmin/data/original/cbdrm_local_level_solutions_dr.pdf

Economic and Social Commission for Asia and the Pacific (ESCAP). (2000). *Youth in the Philippines: A review of the youth situation and national policies and programmes.* New York, NY: United Nations Publications.

Falk, K. (ed.). (2005). *Preparing for disaster – A community-based approach.* Copenhagen: Danish Red Cross. Retrieved from http://www.proventionconsortium.org/themes/default/pdfs/CRA/PNRC_CBDP_2005_meth.pdf

Gaillard, J.-C., & Maceda, E. (2009). *Participatory three-dimensional mapping for disaster risk reduction.* PLA 60, 109-118, IIED, UK. Retrieved from http://www.iapad.org/publications/ppgis/Gaillard_Maceda_PLA_2009.pdf

Gonzaga, C. (2011). *Yes Pinoy foundation involves youth in disaster preparedness.* Retrieved from http://www.preventionweb.net/english/professional/news/v.php?id = 18963

Heijmans, A. (2009). *The social life of community-based disaster risk reduction: Origins, politics and framing.* Disaster Studies Working Paper No. 20. Aon Benfield UCL Hazard Research Center, London, UK.

ISDR (International Strategy for Disaster Reduction). (2005). *Hyogo framework for action 2005–2015: Building the resilience of nations and communities to disasters.* Geneva, Switzerland: ISDR. Retrieved from http://www.unisdr.org/2005/wcdr/intergover/official-doc/L-docs/Hyogo-framework-for-action-english.pdf

LGRRC (Local Governance Regional Resource Center). (2011). *Antique SKs undergo disaster management training.* Retrieved from http://www.lgrrc6.org.ph/index.php?option=com_content&view=article&id=84%3Aantique-sks-undergo-disaster-management-training&catid=41%3Anews-and-updates&Itemid=2

Luna, E. M. (2007). Mainstreaming community-based disaster risk management in local development planning. Paper presented at the Forum on Framework-Building for Investigation of Local Government Settlement Planning Responses to Disaster Mitigation, January 17, 2007 sponsored by the Alternative Planning Initiatives (ALTERPLAN), Quezon City.

Maceda, E., Gaillard, J.-C., Stasiak, E., Le Masson, V., & Le Berre, I. (2009). Experimental use of participatory 3-dimensional models in island community-based disaster risk management. *Shima: The International Journal of Research into Island Cultures, 3*(1), 72–84. Retrieved from http://www.shimajournal.org/issues/v3n1/h.%20Maceda%20et%20al.%20Shima%20v3n1%2072-84.pdf

Martin, C. M. (2008). Incorporating community planning into local government development plans: The Philippine national red cross experience. Paper presentation at the 3rd Asian Ministerial Conference Disaster Risk Reduction in Kuala Lumpur, Malaysia, December 2–4, 2008.

Miyaguchi, T. (2008). *Climate Change Impact Reduction through Corporate Community Interface: Cases from India and Indonesia.* Unpublished graduate thesis. Graduate School of Global Environmental Studies, Kyoto University, Japan.

Miyaguchi, T., & Shaw, R. (2007). Corporate community interface in disaster management: A preliminary study from Mumbai, India. *Risk Management, 9*, 209–222.

NDCC (National Disaster Coordinating Council). (1989). *Policies and procedures in requesting, allocating, releasing and monitoring of calamity fund.* Memorandum Order No. 4, Series of 1989. Quezon City, Philippines: NDCC.

NDCC (National Disaster Coordinating Council). (2008). Revised guidelines on the "Gawad KALASAG": Search for Excellence in disaster risk management and humanitarian assistance. Memorandum Circular No. 1, Series of 2008. Quezon City, Philippines: NDCC.

PDRRMO (Provincial Disaster Risk Reduction and Management Office). (2011). *Life Boat handling and rescue operations training in Famy, Laguna Still ongoing.* Retrieved from http://www.laguna.com.ph/?q=content/life-boat-handling-and-rescue-operations-training-famy-laguna-still-ongoing

PDRSEA (Partnerships for Disaster Reduction-South East Asia). (2008). *Monitoring and reporting progress on community-based disaster risk management in Philippines.* Bangkok, Thailand: Asian Disaster Preparedness Center. Retrieved from http://www.adpc.net/v2007/Programs/CBDRM/Publications/Downloads/Publications/Philipines_Update.pdf

Ramos, B. (2011). *Philippines: National progress report on the implementation of the Hyogo Framework for Action (2009–2011) – Interim*. Retrieved from http://www.preventionweb. net/files/18619_phl_NationalHFAprogress_2009-11.pdf

Republic Act No. 10121. (2010). *Philippine disaster risk reduction and management act of 2010*. Retrieved from http://www.ndcc.gov.ph/attachments/045_RA%2010121.pdf

Reyes, M. L. (2010). *Presentation of AADMER work programme 2010–2015 at the IAP Meeting 24–26 March 2010*. Retrieved from http://unisdr-apps.net/confluence/display/iap09/IAP+Meeting+March+24-26%2C+2010

Shiwaku, K., & Fernandez, G. (2011). Role of school in disaster education. In S. Rajib, K. Shiwaku & Y. Teuchi (Eds.), *Disaster education*. Bingley, UK: Emerald Publishing.

SKPF (Sangguniang Kabataan Provincial Federation). (2011). *SKPF holds climate change adaptation, disaster risk management training*. Retrieved from http://www.skquezon.com/uncategorized/skpf-holds-climate-change-adaptation-disaster-risk-management-training

Solidum, R. Jr., & Duran-Alegre, L. (2011). Hazard mapping and assessment for effective community-based disaster risk management (READY) project. *Asian Journal of Environment and Disaster Management, 3*(1), 79–92.

Twigg, J. (2001). *Corporate social responsibility and disaster reduction: A global overview*. London: Benfield Greig Hazard Research Centre.

Velasco, D. (2005). Rejecting 'old style' politics? Youth participation in the Philippines. In B. Martin (Ed.), *Go! Young progressives in Southeast Asia*. Manila: Friedrich-Ebert-Stiftung. Retrieved from http://library.fes.de/pdf-files/bueros/philippinen/04526/countrypapers_philippines.pdf

Victoria, L. P. (2003). *Community Based disaster management in the Philippines: Making a Difference in people's lives*. Bangkok: ADPC.

Victoria, L. P. (2009). *Overview of community based disaster risk management in the Philippines*. Retrieved from http://www.jointokyo.org/files/cms/news/pdf/june_26_2009_ppt_4.pdf

Vos, F., Rodriguez, J., Below, R., & Guha-Sapir, D. (2010). *Annual disaster statistical review 2009: The Numbers and Trends*. Brussels: CRED.

Warhurst, A. (2006). Disaster prevention: A role for business. An exploration of the business case for reducing natural disaster risk in developing countries and for establishing networks of disaster prevention partnerships. International Federation of Red Cross and Red Crescent Societies, The ProVentium Consortium and Maplecroft.

World Bank and NDCC. (2005). *Natural disaster risk management in the Philippines: Enhancing poverty alleviation through disaster reduction*. Retrieved from http://siteresources.worldbank.org/INTEAPREGTOPENVIRONMENT/Resources/PH_Disaster_Risk_Mgmt.pdf

World Economic Forum (WEF), World Bank, and United Nations International Strategy for Disaster Reduction. (2008). Building Resilience to Natural Disasters: A Framework for Private Sector Engagement. Geneva: World Economic Forum.

CHAPTER 12

COMMUNITY-BASED DISASTER RISK REDUCTION IN TIMOR-LESTE

Jessica Mercer, Alberto dos Reis Freitas and Heather Campbell

INTRODUCTION

Timor-Leste is a small, island country situated between South East Asia, Australia, and the Pacific, where it shares a unique mix of climates from all three neighboring regions (Kirono, 2010). The country achieved independence in 2002 having suffered over 400 years of colonialism and foreign occupation, first by the Portuguese and then by the Indonesians (Sandlund et al., 2001). The post-referendum troubles in 1999 left Timor-Leste with seriously damaged infrastructure and relatively little economic activity (Hill, 2001). However, since 1999, the country has made significant steps forward and despite some upheaval in 2006 has significantly developed in terms of infrastructure and economic activity. Nonetheless, Timor-Leste, as a Small Island Developing State (SIDS) also has a number of other vulnerabilities and challenges to contend with including its mountainous region, relative isolation, dependence upon agriculture, and high levels of unemployment. Timor-Leste has a land mass of $14,874 \, km^2$ with a population of approximately 1 million, which is rapidly increasing

Community-Based Disaster Risk Reduction
Community, Environment and Disaster Risk Management, Volume 10, 233–254
Copyright © 2012 by Emerald Group Publishing Limited
ISSN: 2040-7262/doi:10.1108/S2040-7262(2012)0000010018

(Government of Timor-Leste, 2010). The country is dominated by the central Mountain range of Ramelau with as much as 44% of Timor-Leste's land having a slope of more than 40% and over 70% of the country's population dependent upon agriculture for their livelihood (Sandlund et al., 2001).

Timor-Leste is prone to a wide range of environmental hazards including drought, fire, floods, landslides, earthquake, tsunami, and storms. In addition, there is a high potential risk of social related hazards such as civil unrest and conflict. In response to these wide ranging hazards, disaster risk reduction (DRR) activities in Timor-Leste are centered around the National Disaster Management Directorate (NDMD) whose mission is to "consolidate a culture of prevention and to provide the Nation with means to prevent natural disasters and/or at least to minimize the effects of disasters" (2008). The NDMD is a government body existing under the Ministry of Social Solidarity with an office in Dili, the capital of Timor-Leste. The 13 districts in Timor-Leste then have a District Disaster Management Committee (DDMC) operating under the relevant District Government. As a new country, Timor-Leste is only just beginning to develop relevant policies and structures for disaster risk management (DRM). Such development has been heavily impeded upon by a lack of capacity and resources. However, a turning point for DRM in Timor-Leste occurred after the Indian Ocean Tsunami in late December 2004. This created a strong awareness among Timorese of their risk to earthquake and tsunami hazard. Consequently, this led to recognition of the need for a more proactive approach to reducing risk and managing disasters in Timor-Leste.

The current National Disaster Risk Management Policy (NDRMP) for Timor-Leste was developed in 2008. It provides a platform from which to develop programs and plans for DRM in line with internationally recognized approaches, notably the Hyogo Framework for Action 2005–2015, which Timor-Leste is a signatory to (NDMD, 2008). The NDRMP aims to respond to Timor-Leste's constitutional mandate to identify government priorities and strategies in order to guarantee the safety and security of Timorese people, their property, and natural resources (NDMD, 2008). It outlines plans to develop DRM programs including risk analyses, vulnerability monitoring, early warning, emergency management, post-disaster research and review, recovery and knowledge development, awareness raising, and human resource development (NDMD, 2008).

The capacity and resources available to develop and implement such an ambitious plan of action are however limited. Currently, less than 1% of the national budget is allocated to DRR, and there has been limited success in the setting up of a cross-ministerial working group to oversee the implementation of the NDRMP. In response, local and international non-governmental organizations (NGOs) in Timor-Leste have been working closely with the NDMD and DDMCs to strengthen capacity in Community-Based Disaster Risk Reduction (CBDRR) and improve coordination and communication at the local, district, and national levels. In this context, this chapter will report on CBDRR approaches undertaken by Catholic Relief Services (CRS) in partnership with local communities, NGOs, and government authorities in Timor-Leste. This is in order to identify how CBDRR processes are contributing to the overall goals of the NDRMP at the local level.

CATHOLIC RELIEF SERVICES, CARITAS BAUCAU, AND PROJECT AREA

CRS and Caritas Baucau have been working with communities in Baucau district since 1999. Baucau is one of 13 districts in Timor-Leste and is located in the Eastern part of the country, approximately 122 km^2 from Dili. The capital of the district, also called Baucau, is the second largest city in Timor-Leste with 20,362 inhabitants (Government of Timor-Leste, 2010). Baucau district comprises the subdistricts of Baguia, Baucau vila, Laga, Quelicai, Vemasse, and Venilale (formerly known as Vila Viçosa) with the main economic activity in the district consisting of agriculture (corn, rice, peanut, coconut, and horticultural crops). In Timor-Leste, sub-districts are comprised of Sukos (villages), which are the smallest administrative unit. These in turn are comprised of one or more Aldeias (sub-villages), which are further divided up into Bairos (hamlets).

Since 2009, CRS and Caritas Baucau have worked closely with Baucau DDMC to reduce risk to natural and man-made hazards through the program entitled "Hamutuk Hamenus Risko" or "Together Reduce Risk." Within this program, two overall objectives are outlined, which are designed to meet the overall goal of building community resilience. The objectives are (1) disaster management committees in Baucau district facilitate CBDRR in their areas and (2) pilot communities have increased resilience to natural and man-made disasters.

This chapter will specifically focus on CBDRR in two Sukos in Baucau district called Uma Ana Ico and Uma Ana Ulu. Uma Ana Ico and Uma

Ana Ulu are both situated within Venilale subdistrict of Baucau, which is situated 25 km south of Baucau town (see Fig. 1). Uma Ana Ico consists of four Aldeias namely Uaitunau, Betunau, Uaite, and Queleborouai and is made up of 405 households with a total of 1,544 inhabitants while Uma Ana Ulu consists of four Aldeias namely Ossogigi, Caihula, Venilale, and Nunodocu and is made up of 495 households with a total of 2,040 inhabitants. The two Sukos are annually affected by hazards including high winds, landslides, drought, pest infestation, and poor land use management practices such as use of slash and burn techniques. These have significant impact considering Uma Ana Ico and Uma Ana Ulu are dependent upon agriculture for their livelihood, with crops grown including vegetables such as mustard, tomatoes, garlic and cabbage, fruit trees, and cash crops such as peanuts and candlenuts. Within the two Sukos, three dialects are spoken – Waimua'a, Makasa'e, and Uaima'a, although the majority dialect spoken is Uaima'a. The two Suko's are quite closely knit with the Catholic Church forming a very important part of the community's identity. The Church also contributes significantly to the Suko's development and access to education as the Church coordinates three primary schools in the area. There is also one government run primary school.

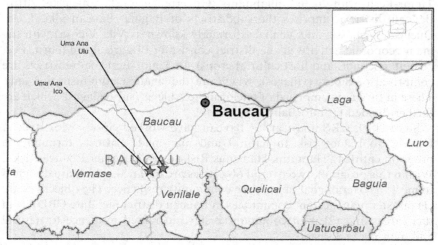

Fig. 1.   Map of Baucau District with Location of Sukos.
Source: Adapted from UNMIT (2007).

COMMUNITY-BASED DISASTER RISK REDUCTION IN SUKOS UMA ANA ICO AND UMA ANA ULU

The first steps involved in the CBDRR process within Uma Ana Ico and Uma Ana Ulu involved the socialization, formation of Suko disaster management committee's (SDMCs), and orientation of Participatory Disaster Risk Assessment (PDRA) teams. CRS and Caritas Baucau worked with Baucau DDMC and Venilale sub-district disaster management committee (SDDMC) to partner with communities identified by the DDMC and SDDMC as particularly vulnerable to environmental hazards.

PDRA teams consisted of a representative from the DDMC and SDDMC, Caritas Baucau staff and CRS staff members, representatives of "at risk" communities, and, once established, representatives from the SDMCs. Where possible the PDRA teams were balanced in terms of gender, composing of half male and half female members. In order to undertake the assessment, the PDRA team were made aware of and educated in Timor-Leste's NDRMP. The PDRA team were also introduced to terminology related to DRM and supported to translate these words into local dialects. This was in order to use them within the assessment in a way that community members would understand and that was suitable to the local context. These activities took place over a period of two weeks with all stakeholders involved including government, civil society, and community members (see Table 1 for a breakdown of CBDRR activities and stakeholders involved).

One of the first responsibilities of the PDRA team was to work with community members to establish a SDMC. This was in order that (a) there was a management body within the community, which could then be connected to established administrative structures and (b) to contribute to ensuring sustainability of the process through ownership by the community concerned. In partnership with identified SDMC members and other community representatives, detailed terms of reference (ToR) were developed, which outlined the main aims, objectives, and responsibilities of SDMCs, dependent on the specific context. Within each SDMC, various responsibilities were outlined. These included (a) a planning department whose responsibility is to ensure plans are updated regularly from household through to Aldeia and Suko levels; (b) a mitigation department whose responsibility is to address underlying community vulnerability and to ensure plans are implemented; (c) a logistics and preparedness department that are responsible for early warning systems, awareness raising activities, and contingency plans; (d) a mobilization department whose responsibility is to

Table 1. CBDRR Activities and Stakeholders Involved.

CBDRR Activities	Stakeholders and Associated Responsibilities
Establishment of Disaster Management Committees (DDMC, SDDMC, and SDMC)	NDMD and key local authorities at district, subdistrict, and Suko levels. – To formalize and establish terms of reference for DDMC, SDDMC, and SDMCs.
CBDRR process orientation and team preparation	NGOs, local authorities, and community leaders. – Team preparation and provision of Training of Trainers (ToT) program for key DMC members from across ministries, for example, health, education, police, fire brigade, agriculture, and others on terminology of disaster, CBDRR process and methodology.
Risk assessment	DMC members (Suko, sub-district, and district), NGO staff and community members including those most vulnerable such as youths, women, church representatives, elderly, and people with disabilities. – Undertake joint risk assessment at community level.
Integrated community action plan	DMCs members, NGO staff, and communities. – Development of joint action plan.
Disaster simulation and first aid training	DMCs, communities, and NGO staff.
Proposal development and financial training	Key DMC members at Suko, subdistrict, and district levels.
Implementation of action plan	Experts, NGO staff, community, government staff.
CBDRR study tour across district	At risk communities and DMC members, NGO project staff, and other relevant stakeholders within district, for example, neighboring communities.
Connecting with local-level government plans	DMC members at subdistrict and district levels.
Reviewing and evaluating	Communities and DMC members (Suko, subdistrict, and district levels).
Linking SDMC with SDDMC and DDMC	Coordinator of DMCs at different levels.

ensure community members are fully informed and involved in the process and know procedures in case of an emergency; and (e) a information and formation department whose task is to provide information on DRM at the Suko level for subdistrict, district, and national levels and to help coordinate linkages between these levels for an effective response at the Suko level. As with the PDRA team, SDMCs consisted of both male and female community members. This was to ensure both sexes were fairly represented given their often differing vulnerabilities and that all were directly involved in the process. An example composition of the SDMC established for Uma Ana Ulu is outlined in Table 2.

Once the PDRA team was established, the next step involved undertaking a hazard, vulnerability, and capacity assessment (HVCA) with the community using participatory rural appraisal (PRA) tools such as transect walks, historical timelines, seasonal calendars, hazard, resource and social maps, livelihood analysis, wealth ranking, problem tree analysis, and matrix and scoring tools such as pairwise ranking, Venn diagrams, and so on (Kumar, 2002). These activities were undertaken over a week's period within both Suko's. The PDRA team first undertook a transect walk around both Suko's with members of the SDMC's to identify issues of concern to community members. Information gathered and discussed during the transect walk then helped to inform the development of social maps, which outlined social demographics of each Suko. This was then followed by mapping of resources available to community members and finally discussions revolved around hazards, their location, and impact upon community members. Hazards were subsequently also marked on the maps

Table 2. The Composition of the SDMC Members for Uma Ana Ulu.

No	Position within SDMC	Institution
1	Coordinator of SDMC	Suko Chief
2	Secretary	Suko council secretary
3	Finance/treasurer	Woman's group representative
4	Advisor	Suko council advisor
5	Planning department	Youth representative
6	Planning department	Teacher
7	Mitigation department	Aldeia Betunau Chief
8	Mitigation department	Nurses
9	Logistics and preparedness department	Woman's group representative
10	Logistics and preparedness department	Woman's group representative
11	Information and formation department	Aldeia Queleborouai Chief
12	Information and formation department	Health worker volunteer
13	Mobilization department	Aldeia Uaitunau Chief
14	Mobilization department	Youth representative
15	Community-based organization (UNIDADE BERCOLI)	Aldeia Uaite Chief

that were drawn up by both male and female community members. Male and female groups then presented their maps to each other in order to establish and agree upon any differences between the maps as well as to point out the differences in hazard impact upon men and women. To explore the hazard information identified on the map in more detail groups of men and women in both Sukos also developed historical timelines. The timelines were used to discuss the hazards experienced within the community over time and their subsequent impact upon life and livelihood.

In both Suko's, groups of men and women identified hazards including animal diseases, locust attacks on crops, fires, high winds, diarrhoea, malaria, floods, and landslides. The practice of slash and burn was the subject of much debate within each Suko. This too was also identified as a hazard due to the resulting impacts upon their environment but also due to its contribution to fire as a hazard as a result of "controlled" burning becoming uncontrollable and therefore posing further threat to life and livelihood. Once all the hazards impacting upon Uma Ina Ico and Uma Ana Ulu were identified, the PDRA team then asked each Suko to prioritize identified hazards using pairwise ranking. This involved comparing each hazard against others to identify which ones Suko members felt were impacting upon them most and therefore the highest priority in terms of identifying strategies to address their impacts. The final results in terms of hazard ranking are outlined in Table 3 for Suko Uma Ana Ico. Upon presentation of the final scoring results, there was an opportunity for community members to discuss and make changes if they felt that use of the pairwise ranking process did not reflect the Suko reality. For both Suko's, no changes were made and community members were satisfied with the results.

After prioritization of the hazards, community members decided to focus upon top priority hazards identified as having the most impact in terms of destruction to life and livelihoods. In the case of Uma Ana Ico, the priority hazard identified was high winds, whereas for Uma Ana Ulu, the priority hazard was fire. In Uma Ana Ico Suko, members felt the impacts of high winds were related to the practice of slash and burn agriculture within their Suko. To explore this in more detail, the PDRA team facilitated discussions with the community around an analysis of their livelihoods and seasonal calendars. This was to explore any issues and identify any links in terms of seasonal fluctuations (climate variability and climate change), land use practices, and hazard impact. For example, the community had identified that they felt the cutting down of vegetation in their area was contributing to an increased impact of high winds. However, they also felt that seasons were changing and that more high winds were being experienced than in the past.

Table 3. Hazard Ranking for Suko Uma Ana Ico.

Hazards	Animal disease (A)	Locust (B)	Fire (C)	High wind (D)	Diarrhea (E)	Malaria (F)	Floods (G)	Landslides (H)	Slash and burn (I)	Total	Priority
Animal disease (A)		A	C	D	E	F	A	H	I	2	6
Locust (B)			C	D	E	B	B	H	B	3	5
Fire (C)				D	E	F	C	C	I	4	4
High wind (D)					D	D	D	D	D	8	1
Diarrhea (E)						E	E	E	E	7	2
Malaria (F)							F	F	I	4	4
Floods (G)								H	I	0	7
Landslides (H)									I	3	5
Slash and burn (I)										5	3

Developing upon these discussions, the PDRA team utilized the livelihoods framework (for more information, see DFID, 1999) and reviewed the five capital assets with community members including human, physical, social, financial, and natural. In addition, two more capital assets were also discussed – that of political and cultural assets. Community members in each Suko were again divided up into male and female groups to ensure each gender had a voice in the process and to identify different vulnerabilities experienced by men and women. In Suko Uma Ana Ico, groups of male and female community members were asked to produce a problem tree analysis (for more information on PRA techniques, see Kumar, 2002) outlining their vulnerability to high winds under each of the assets within the livelihoods framework. Women specifically identified slash and burn practices, lack of education, dependence on agriculture, not following traditional resource management practices, poor construction, lack of wind breaks, and lack of trees as factors contributing to their vulnerability to high winds. In this case, men identified similar vulnerability issues but also identified a lack of access to better building materials, no support from the government and lack of knowledge of different and/or more appropriate farming techniques. Both groups also felt that conflict was a potentially contributing factor given high rates of unemployment and youth within the community. However, mobilization of youth in different development programs to support the community was contributing to a reduction in this risk.

After this process, each group presented their problem tree analyses to each other and discussed the differing vulnerabilities to high winds between men and women. This enabled both genders to understand the differing perspective and different vulnerabilities experienced by men and women. A focus group discussion was then initiated by the PDRA team with the community to identify those most vulnerable to the impacts of high winds. Uma Ana Ico community members felt that those living in upland areas or areas where the most trees had been cleared were the most vulnerable households to the impacts of high winds. Upon completion of the hazard and vulnerability analysis, community members then concluded by reviewing the existing capacities within their community to cope with the hazard of high winds. Capacities, as with vulnerabilities, were discussed in groups of men and women using the identified assets of the livelihoods framework (in addition to political and cultural assets) and an analysis of existing support networks available to the community. Capacities identified by men included the use of the existing social network among neighboring communities, a community early warning system of shouting and drumming and diversifying income sources in anticipation of hunger seasons. While capacities identified by women included the diversification of livelihood strategies through the production and sale of handicrafts, planting of candlenuts for long-term investment and growing vegetables for consumption and markets. To help identify capacities existing within a community, a Venn diagram was used to determine access and support from various stakeholders at the Suko level. An example of a Venn diagram is provided in Fig. 2 for Suko Uma Ana Ico. This was then analyzed further through focus group discussions with the community to determine the contribution of each of these actors to community development and what form of contribution may occur in the future.

After the completion of the HVCA, the SDMC then presented the information back at Aldeia level. Suko Uma Ana Ico and Uma Ana Ulu consisted of four Aldeias each and so two large meetings were held to corroborate and validate the information gained at a Suko level with those at the Aldeia level who were unable to attend the initial process. Information was then revised and developed accordingly before the development of CBDRR action plans for Suko's Uma Ana Ico and Uma Ana Ulu.

CBDRR Action Plan in Suko's Uma Ana Ico and Uma Ana Ulu

Suko Uma Ana Ico and Uma Ana Ulu then developed CBDRR action plans to reduce their underlying vulnerabilities and increase their capacities to the hazards identified. This was firstly initiated by the development of a vision map by each Suko. The vision map helped community members to visualize what they hoped their community to look like in 5–10 years time. Scientific projections in terms of climate change impacts for Timor-Leste were also discussed and taken into account at this stage (Barnett, Dessai, & Jones, 2007; Kirono, 2010). The DDMC, SDDMC, and SDMC's also felt it was important that identified CBDRR action plans were integrated and developed in partnership with neighboring communities and in line with existing development plans for Baucau district. This was given special consideration in order to ensure all stakeholders agreed with and were behind the plans proposed as well as to ensure that any activity undertaken in one Suko would not have an adverse effect in neighboring Suko's.

Upon completion of the CBDRR action plan (see Table 4 for an example of the initial CBDRR action plan developed for Uma Ana Ico), each Suko then identified how the actions proposed would be implemented in both the

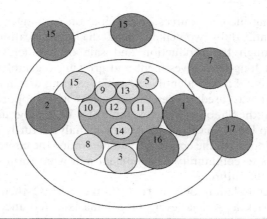

No.	Name of Institution	Type of intervention for addressing the community vulnerabilities
1	Catholic Relief Services (CRS)	Supports the development of candlenut industry and works with communities to improve the candlenut quality. Capacity building on DRM and support in the implementation of action plans.
2	Timor Global	Support growing and selling of peanuts.
3	Caritas Baucau	Facilitates PDRA and provides capacity building for SDMCs.
4	Education Development Center (EDC)	Dissemination of information on peace education.
5	Centro Informasaun Education Sivica Timor Leste (CIESTL)	Provides civic education.
6	German Company for International Cooperation (GIZ)	Provides seeds for communities rice, agricultural advice etc.
7	Food and Agricultural organization (FAO)	Livestock and poultry.
8	Micro Finance Group	Provides cash credit for communities.
9	Suko Council	Leads the communities in terms of development activities and community representation.
10	Church	Conducts moral and spiritual activities.
11	Agriculture Group	Supports the growth of candlenuts, vegetables and other cash crops.
12	Youth Group	Supports peace and community wellbeing.
13	Rede feto (Women's organization)	Leads woman's activities e.g. handicrafts and other income generation activities for women.
14	SDMC	Develops action plans and facilitates the CBDRR activities and provides monitoring and evaluation.
15	Futuro sosiedade Propero (FSP)	Improves candlenut quality through the CRS partnership.
16	National Police of East Timor (PNTL)	Promotes the rules of law and provides protection for the communities.
17	World Food Programme (WFP)	Food for work activities.

Fig. 2.   Venn Diagram Identifying Institutions Involved with Suko Uma Ana Ico.

Table 4. Initial CBDRR Action Plan Developed by Uma Ana Ico.

Disaster Scenarios	Activities	Location	Responsibilities	Resources		Time frame		Indicator
				Available	Need	Start	End	
Looking beyond 2010 at expected seasonal changes approximately 200 households are considered at risk from high winds and other annually occurring hazards. Those most vulnerable do not have access to shelters	Attend proposal and budget training for submission to NDMD	Baucau district	CRS and DDMC	Wood Stone	Cement, iron, nails, etc.	August 27, 2009	November 5, 2010	Three SDMC members attended proposal writing and budget development training
	Write proposal and develop budgets for activity implementation to submit to stakeholders	Uma Ana Ulu	SDMC	Tradesman				No's of proposals developed after training
	Construction of adequate shelter	Uma Ana Ulu Center	SDMC					Community able to access temporary shelter from 2010
Environment degradation, erosion, landslide, high winds, etc., are all exacerbated by existing agricultural practices of slash and burn	SDMC disseminate information at Aldeia level on sustainable land use management and alternative practices	Uma Ana Ulu	SDMC		Seedlings	November 2009	April 2010	Numbers of proposal submitted to different stakeholders and acted upon
	SDMC facilitate reforestation activities with communities	All four aldeias						

Table 4. (Continued)

Disaster Scenarios	Activities	Location	Responsibilities	Resources		Time frame		Indicator
				Available	Need	Start	End	
Approximately 31 hectares of rice field in Uaicasa and Uaidere were abandoned due to hazard impact contributing to food insecurity, low income, and malnutrition, which will especially affect 70 vulnerable households if irrigation channels are not established during drought seasons	Conduct needs assessment	Uaiderean and Uaidasu	SDMC	Stones	Transport for sale of goods	September 2009	December 2010	Numbers of proposal submitted to different stakeholders and funded
	Present the needs assessment and present the proposal to relevant stakeholders and government	Central Uma Ana Ulu						
495 children lack access to education contributing to increases in adult illiteracy rates. Social conflict will increase as a result	Write proposal and develop budget planning to district and national government							
	Uma Ana Ulu		SDMC	Engineering		December 2010	December 2011	Communities can access solar panels or electricity in evenings so children can study

The road conditions will be the main community challenge. 270 households will be affected by landslides if there is no drainage construction and road rehabilitation	Write proposal and develop budget planning on food for work program to World Food Program	Uma Ana Ulu	SDMC	Food for work	December 2010	March 2011	Community can access transport network during the rainy season
Beyond 2010, farming in upland areas will be affected by high winds. If there is no crop diversification, food insecurity will increase as the staple crop maize is often badly affected	Introduce crops resistant to high winds for farmers in upland areas	Upland area (Venilale and Nunudocu)	SDMC		March 2011	March 2012	Community can access different varieties of crops, which are hazard resistant
Beyond 2010, drought will affect 470 vulnerable households in terms of their access to clean water and ability to farm if there is no piped water supply	Write proposal and develop budget planning to water stakeholders and government for clean water and pipelines	Ossoggi, Cai Hula, Venilale, and Nunudocu	SDMC		June 2012	June 2015	Communities have access to a regular clean water supply

short term and the long term with associated stakeholders. In partnership with all stakeholders, community members identified activities they could implement immediately with their own resources, those that the SDMC, SDDMC, and DDMC could assist with and those that would need close liaison and support from the NDMD at the national level. In order to support the process and start the implementation of the CBDRR action plan, CRS and Caritas Baucau established a small grants scheme administered by each SDMC. In addition, SDMC's were also given training and support for institutional capacity building in terms of proposal writing and budget planning. For example, both Uma Ana Ulu and Uma Ana Ico used the small grants scheme to establish a community shelter for use during high winds or when people's houses were destroyed as a result of a hazard. When not in use as a shelter, the building is used as a community meeting house – SDMC meetings are held here regularly.

In Suko Uma Ana Ulu, fire was identified as a priority hazard. This is especially a problem in Timor-Leste given the practice of slash and burn agriculture and construction materials being highly flammable. Here, the SDMC utilized the small grants scheme to develop evacuation plans and emergency drills in the event of a fire hazard. The SDMC prepared and developed the evacuation drill process, identifying those most vulnerable, for example, elderly, disabled, women, and children and whose responsibility it was within the community to ensure the safety of these people. First aid training was provided for identified community first aid volunteers with a plan to regularly keep this training up to date. The SDMC also developed an assessment form to determine damage to property as a result of the hazard along with procedures in place to compensate for this within the Suko. Regular practice drills take place to ensure community members are aware of what to do and what will happen if a fire occurs. This has not only ensured community members are aware of what to do in an event of a fire hazard but has also increased awareness of the various roles of the actors involved including the DDMC, SDDMC, and SDMC. A short video clip has also been produced by Uma Ana Ulu and Caritas Baucau to help inform other communities of good practice in Baucau district and how to address fire as a hazard.

Working with District, Subdistrict, and Suko Disaster Management Committees

In Timor-Leste, CBDRR would not be sustainable if not implemented in partnership with the local government and established district, subdistrict, and Suko DMC's. The DDMC's, SDDMC's, and SDMC's provide clarity on the operational implementation of coordination mechanisms between themselves and the NDMD so that community members are clearly aware of the chain of command and who to go to for support in terms of both risk reduction and emergency response. As with the NDMD, DDMC's have a remit for disaster prevention, preparedness, mitigation, response, and recovery, and therefore, it is essential that SDDMC's and SDMC's are linked with this body to provide an integrated response to DRM in a particular district. In Baucau, SDDMCs and SDMCs have been heavily involved in the development of CBDRR action plans, supporting both their development and their implementation, often with limited resources. Integration of CBDRR action plans into general development plans at the district level has been seen as a significant step forward in ensuring risk reduction is integrated across the various sectoral needs of a community. The process of institutionalizing CBDRR action plans has been greatly facilitated through the involvement of SDMCs, SDDMCs, and DDMC at all stages of the CBDRR process. In addition, this process is also supported at the national level through a joint CBDRR working group with the NDMD.

However, the process of institutionalizing CBDRR action plans and working with DDMC's, SDDMC's, and SDMC's is not without its challenges in Timor-Leste. There currently exists a lack of linkages between Timor-Leste's NDRMP and long-term development goals, with the two goals currently operating in isolation and DRM not seen as a priority or cross-cutting issue. This makes it difficult to integrate local-level CBDRR action plans into overall development planning at the district level and restricts the sustainability of any actions implemented as they are not adopted as long-term goals by district-level governments. In addition, there is an inadequate understanding of DRM and the NDRMP at the district, subdistrict, and Suko levels. The NDRMP was developed with little district-level consultation and has not been discussed or developed in detail with DDMCs who in turn have not communicated it to SDDMCs or SDMCs. This has resulted in the continuance of traditional response modes to disaster rather than proactive attempts to reduce risk through prevention, preparedness, and mitigation. CBDRR in many cases is still viewed as emergency response and preparedness. This contributes toward a culture of passivity as opposed to a culture of proactive risk reduction prior to an event occurring.

It is also difficult to engage DDMCs at the Suko and the Aldeia levels as DDMC members consist of government representatives drawn from various government departments. The work of DDMC members is often considered additional to their various positions within Timor-Leste's government and is given second priority to other demands upon their time. In addition, despite the decentralized nature of the DDMCs, decisions are still not made without referral back to the NDMD at the national level. In addition, while the NDRMP provides clear guidelines for DDMCs, it is difficult to implement in practice without being adequately resourced. For example, the NDRMP outlines that each Suko should have emergency stocks of food and nonfood items for at least 30 households, but this has yet to be achieved (NDMD, 2008). There is still an ongoing focus of the NDMD upon emergency and recovery funds due to lack of resources available to build up risk reduction capacity prior to an event. There is also no clear chain of command for reporting and/or monitoring, which results in confusion at district, subdistrict, and Suko levels of who to report to or to request help in terms of risk reduction and response activities.

CHALLENGES AND LESSONS LEARNT IN IMPLEMENTING CBDRR IN TIMOR-LESTE

Engaging community members in an HVCA raised community expectations that concrete help would be provided and/or facilitated as a result. In undertaking such a process, it is necessary to carefully handle community expectations from the outset in order to ensure the sustainability of any action implemented. The following actions are recommended:

1. There needs to be a detailed and thorough community briefing undertaken prior to any form of risk assessment being undertaken. This is in order to clarify the objectives, methodology, and required resources of the risk assessment and associated follow-up activities as well as to level off community expectations regarding the process and its limitations.
2. There needs to be a complaint mechanism process established whereby communities are able to feedback any identified issues. These then need to be addressed throughout the implementation of a CBDRR program and beyond to ensure ownership and sustainability within a community.
3. In order to sustain people's participation in the process, the HVCA needs to be followed up by action that meets at least some of a community's expectations after the initial assessment is conducted.
4. For a PDRA to be successful, enhanced facilitation and analytical skills are necessary. Aside from the usual flip charts and markers, it is

important locally available materials are used to generate discussion and facilitate participation, for example, sticks, stones, and leaves (Chambers, 1994). The facilitator (whether from within or outside a community) must possess not only thorough skills and knowledge of facilitating the process and using the tools but must also know when the quality of information being generated needs to be improved.

5. It is essential the right assessment tool is chosen. Time pressure could compel PDRA teams to rush and collect as much information as possible. This limits dialogue and participation (Chambers, 1994). To make sure PDRA teams collect the right information within the set time frame and without sacrificing the quality of participation, members must first agree on what aspects of the community they need to look into (key areas of inquiry), then select the most appropriate tool to use. It is not necessary to use all PRA tools available. What is important is to match information needs and tools. While each tool generates information that is unique for that tool, it may produce information that may overlap with other tools. However, overlaps in information do provide a way to cross-check and validate information throughout the process.

6. The community-level PDRA can be further enhanced with a macro-level assessment of capacities and vulnerabilities for longer-term multi-sectoral programming. The micro-macro link can provide a deeper analysis and wider perspective on how national and global systems, structures, and processes are directly linked to and could exacerbate vulnerabilities within communities in the future (Mohan, 2001). A study on the national and regional policies can guide in coming-up with an in-depth assessment of local vulnerability and capacity contexts.

7. It is essential community members are listened to and kept informed of expected future vulnerabilities and anticipated change (Kelman, 2010). For example, community members may not be aware of scientific projections for climate change in Timor-Leste. Any identified CBDRR action plan needs to ensure it takes into account both inside and outside knowledge in a culturally, compatible, and sustainable manner (Mercer, Dominey-Howes, Kelman, & Lloyd, 2007). This is in order to identify sustainable strategies addressing existing and future vulnerabilities.

8. All associated stakeholders should be involved from the outset in order to ensure ownership of the process and the institutionalization of CBDRR action plans at both a community level and within local government structures.

CONCLUSION

Timor-Leste as a country a little under a decade old is only just beginning to develop adequate and sustainable DRM processes at local, district, and national levels. While CBDRR is only in its early stages of development in Timor-Leste, in the first year of CBDRR implementation in Baucau district, the two Sukos outlined in this chapter have been able to identify with and understand their disaster situation and develop suitable Action Plans in response to this. The PDRA team in each Suko created a space in which all relevant stakeholders were able to come together and led by a community analyze a community's situation, identify needs, and come up with solutions to address those needs. Primary importance was given to the participation of vulnerable groups in the process.

While there has been some success in the implementation of CBDRR in Timor-Leste, there needs to be greater coordination and linkages in terms of bottom-up planning and top-down decision making (Lavell, Gaillard, Wisner, Saunders, & van Niekerk, 2011). The development of CBDRR action plans for communities in Timor-Leste goes some way toward meeting the goals of the NDRMP in terms of risk analyses and awareness raising. However, the process needs to be adequately resourced at the local level in order for underlying vulnerabilities to be adequately addressed. In both Suko Uma Ana Ico and Uma Ana Ulu, community members expressed major concerns affecting their lives other than those brought about by environmental hazards. CBDRR action plans included activities not only to prepare for, mitigate against, and prevent hazards such as high winds, but also to address sustainable livelihoods and food security, health and nutrition, and environmental management issues. This outlines a need to address wider development problems in Timor-Leste in order to reduce vulnerability to existing and future hazards, both natural and man-made (Wisner, Blaikie, Cannon, & Davis, 2004). As a result of the lessons learnt from this initial pilot stage of implementing CBDRR in Timor-Leste, CRS and Caritas Baucau will continue to strengthen the nascent DDMC structure in Baucau district. In addition, work will continue to establish SDDMCs and SDMCs in further sub-districts of Baucau, while building community-level DRM capacity at Suko and Aldeia levels to develop an integrated response to DRM embedded within local development planning.

Community management of implementing, monitoring, and reviewing CBDRR action plans is an essential aspect of ensuring the sustainability of any CBDRR process (Delica-Willison & Gaillard, 2011). However, it is important that this is linked with existing local government processes and development plans to ensure long-term sustainability of the process and to generate impact in improving people's lives and livelihoods. Timor-Leste as a country fairly new to developing DRM processes would benefit from learning lessons from neighboring Pacific SIDS who experience similar geographical and development challenges.

ACKNOWLEDGMENTS

We gratefully acknowledge funding support from the International Organization for Migration (IOM) and the Australian Government's Overseas Aid Program (AusAID) under which this work has been funded.

REFERENCES

Barnett, J., Dessai, S., & Jones, R. N. (2007). Vulnerability to climate variability and change in east Timor. *Ambio, 36*(5), 372–378.

Chambers, R. (1994). Participatory rural appraisal (PRA): Analysis of experience. *World Development, 22*(9), 1253–1268.

Delica-Willison, Z., & Gaillard, J. C. (2011). Community action and disaster. In B. Wisner, J. C. Gaillard & I. Kelman (Eds.), *Handbook of hazards, disaster risk reduction and management* (Chapter 59). London: Routledge.

DFID. (1999). Sustainable livelihoods guidance sheet 2.1. Retrieved from http://www.eldis.org/vfile/upload/1/document/0901/section2.pdf. Accessed on 25/04/2011.

Government of Timor-Leste. (2010). 2010 Census results. Retrieved from http://timor-leste.gov.tl/?p=4144&n=1&lang=en. Accessed on 25/04/2011.

Hill, H. (2001). Tiny, poor and war-torn: Development policy challenges for East Timor. *World Development, 29*(7), 1137–1156.

Kelman, I. (2010). Hearing local voices from small island developing states for climate change. *Local Environment, 15*(7), 605–619.

Kirono, D. (2010). *Climate change in Timor-Leste – A brief overview on future climate projections.* Australia: CSIRO.

Kumar, S. (2002). *Methods for community participation: A complete guide for practitioners ITDG.* Warwickshire: ITDG Publishing.

Lavell, A., Gaillard, J. C., Wisner, B., Saunders, W., & van Niekerk, D. (2011). National planning and disaster. In B. Wisner, J. C. Gaillard & I. Kelman (Eds.), *Handbook of hazards, disaster risk reduction and management* (Chapter 51). London: Routledge.

Mercer, J., Dominey-Howes, D., Kelman, I., & Lloyd, K. (2007). The potential for combining indigenous and western knowledge in reducing vulnerability to environmental hazards in small island developing states. *Environmental Hazards, 7*(4), 245–256.

Mohan, G. (2001). Beyond participation: Strategies for deeper empowerment'. In B. Cooke & U. Kothari (Eds.), *Participation: The new tyranny?* (pp. 153–167). London: Zed Books.

National Disaster Management Directorate (NDMD). (2008). *National disaster risk management policy*. Timor-Leste: Ministry of Social Solidarity.

Sandlund, O., Bryceson, I., Carvalho, D., Rio, N., Silva, J., & Silva, M. (2001). *Assessing environmental needs and priorities in east Timor: Issues and priorities*. Norway: UNDP and Norwegian Institute for Nature Research.

UNMIT. (2007). Timor-Leste administrative boundaries Map No. 005, Edition 1, 8 December 2007, UNMIT GIS Unit, Timor-Leste.

Wisner, B., Blaikie, P., Cannon, T., & Davis, I. (2004). *At risk: Natural hazards, people's vulnerability and disasters* (2nd ed.). London: Routledge.

CHAPTER 13

COMMUNITY-BASED DISASTER RISK REDUCTION IN VIETNAM

Tong Thi My Thi, Huy Nguyen, Rajib Shaw and Phong Tran

INTRODUCTION

Community-based disaster risk management (CBDRM) has been recognized since the mid-1990s. However, in the changing environment of the new millennium and the move toward disaster risk reduction (DRR), the community-based disaster risk reduction (CBDRR) has been evolving in recent years. In Vietnam, many projects and programs in CBDRR have been carried out since the year 2000, and these programs tried to increase the resilience of the most vulnerable villages and communes. These projects aim to strengthen the capacity of the communities to become more aware and responsive to their short-and long-term needs through participatory risk assessment and identification, prioritization, and implementation of risk reduction measures.

Evidence from assessments on natural disaster impacts showed that local communities are directly affected and most susceptible to disasters, particularly people in the rural areas. In order to reduce the impact of disasters, it is critical to enhance livelihood security. Local communities themselves have a huge hidden capacity that needs to be utilized. As a large number of people, they have their own traditional knowledge and close

Community-Based Disaster Risk Reduction
Community, Environment and Disaster Risk Management, Volume 10, 255–273
Copyright © 2012 by Emerald Group Publishing Limited
All rights of reproduction in any form reserved
ISSN: 2040-7262/doi:10.1108/S2040-7262(2012)0000010019

connection among each other in their social lives, which will set up a strong social capital for disaster management.

Many studies of disaster management show that a top-down approach did not work in CBDRR because it failed to meet the actual needs of the vulnerable people, ignored the potential of local resources, and may even have increased communities' vulnerability (Van Staden et al., 2006). Affected communities themselves must be at the heart of decision making when it comes to planning and implementation of DRR measures. Therefore, it is necessary to increase the role of local community toward DRR. Community-based approaches to development are becoming more commonplace as the development community come to realize the bene!ts of this approach (Uitto & Shaw, 2006).

In 2005, the Natural Disaster Risk Management Project (NDRMP) funded by the World Bank adopted an innovative approach to DRR in Vietnam and it provides support for disaster prevention and mitigation measures at all levels, especially at the local community level where vulnerability is most significant. The NDRMP aims to reduce the impacts of natural hazards on development process, and CBDRR is one among four main components of this project in Vietnam (World Bank, 2005).

Regarding the development of CBDRR in Vietnam, this chapter aims to provide the status of existing CBDRR activities and case studies from CBDRR in Thanh Hoa, Thua Thien Hue, and Quang Nam Province will be discussed. From that, the authors try to point out the shortcomings of CBDRR projects and propose the potential measures that can be applied to upscale the implementation of CBDRR in Vietnam.

IMPACTS OF NATURAL DISASTERS IN VIETNAM

Located in Southeastern Asia, along the Indochinese peninsula, Vietnam's mainland stretches from 23°23' to 08°02' North latitude and widens from 102°08' to 109°28' East longitude. Length measured in a straight line from North to South stays at about 1650 km. The entire territory of Vietnam includes 331,112 km^2 of mainland and 1 million square kilometers of territorial sea (GoV, 2005). Vietnam's climate is generally hot and humid. In Central and Southern Vietnam, seasonal variations are slight and marked only by a dry and a wet period. Along the central coast, temperatures range from 18°C to 28°C in January and from 24°C to 37°C in July.

The location and topography of Vietnam make it one of the most disaster-prone countries in the world. Estimation from the Global Facility for Disaster Reduction and Recovery (GFDRR) shows that 59% of Vietnam's total land area and 71% of its population are vulnerable to cyclones and floods (GFDRR, 2011). The diversity of Vietnam's land and water areas makes it vulnerable to natural disasters such as typhoons, tropical storms, floods, inundation, drought, desertification, salt penetration, landslides, and earthquakes. Floods and storms are the two main natural disasters, as they occur frequently and cause severe damage to lives and properties. Over the past 20 years, natural disasters have resulted in the loss of over 13,000 lives (GFDRR, 2011). In 2010, according to the report from the Statistics General Department, natural disasters left 173 dead or missing and injured 168 others in October 2010 alone (GSO Vietnam, 2010). Damages were estimated at over 8.5 trillion VND, of which the central province of Ha Tinh alone suffered 5.2 trillion VND in losses from typhoon Megi. The other two hard-hit central provinces of Quang Binh and Nghe An were reported as suffering damages worth some 1.9 trillion VND and 1.2 trillion VND, respectively (GSO Vietnam, 2010). Besides, a prolonged drought caused serious electric power cuts during the hot summer (May–July) that strongly affected economic activities (CCFSC, 2010). In 2009, Storm No. 9 (Typhoon Ketsana) seriously affected 15 provinces in the Central and Central Highlands regions of Vietnam, killing 174 people and causing damage of over 14,000 billion VND (CCFSC, 2009).

In recent years, Vietnam experienced an upsurge in both frequency and intensity of natural disasters. The country has suffered from vast loss of lives, and economic and infrastructure devastation caused by onslaughts of floods, typhoons, and droughts, among others. It was recorded that from 1995 to 2006, the total estimated loss from storms, floods, and droughts was at 61,479 billion VND (around 32 million USD), not to mention massive loss of lives, infrastructures, and livelihoods (MARD Vietnam, 2009).

The spreading of economic activities into marginal areas such as floodplains, coastal swamps, drainage channels, and other natural buffers is increasing and posing dangers to the local communities. Around 18 million people now live in low-lying river basins and coastal areas, and they are exposed to risks from multiple natural hazards. During the period from 1989 to 2009, natural disasters including typhoons, floods, and droughts left more than 10,000 missing and dead, and economic loss of about 8,000 million USD (CCFSC, 2010) (Figs. 1 and 2).

According to a report of GFDRR (2011), Vietnam lost at least 1% of GDP per annum from 1989 to 2008 due to natural disasters. The report stated that the post-disaster damage assessment and reporting system tended to underreport the economic value of damages. In addition, Vietnam could experience even higher losses in the future due to an increase in the concentration of assets at risk, and possibly an increase in the frequency and intensity of major events linked to climate change (GFDRR, 2011).

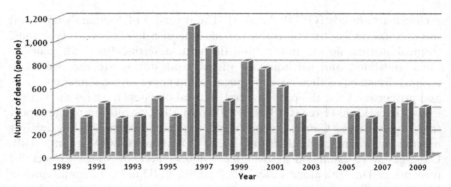

Fig. 1. Number of Deaths from 1989 to 2009 Caused by Natural Disasters in Vietnam (CCFSC, 2010).

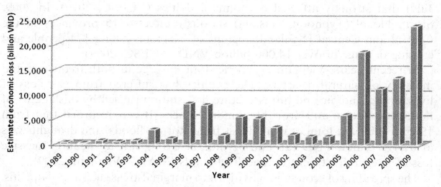

Fig. 2. Estimated Total Losses (Billion VND) from 1989 to 2009 Caused by Natural Disasters in Vietnam (CCFSC, 2010).

DEVELOPMENT OF COMMUNITY-BASED DISASTER RISK REDUCTION IN VIETNAM

Institutional Basis of CBDRR in Vietnam

Vietnam has consolidated the legislative systems to create a legal corridor for natural disaster prevention, response, and mitigation. The government have developed the Dyke Management Law, the Water Resources Law, the

Law on Protection and Afforestation, the Law on Environment Protection, the Law on Land Use, the Law on Natural Resources and Minerals, the Law on Aquaculture Products, etc., the Ordinance on Flood and Storm Control, the Ordinance on Exploitation and Protection of Water Resources Works, the Ordinance of Protection of Hydro-Meteorology Works, and so on together with Resolutions to direct the implementation of these Laws. The official development assistance (ODA) Master Plan 2006–2010 gives priority to reduce losses and damages caused by natural disasters. In particular, on November 16, 2007, the Prime Minister approved the National Strategy on Disaster Prevention, Response and Mitigation to 2020 (GoV, 2007a). Only one year after that, on December 2, 2008, the Decision No. 158/2008/QD-TTg on "National Target Program on response to climate change" was approved (GoV, 2008). This emphasizes that the guiding principle in disaster preparedness and response is "4 on-site motto – leadership, human resources, materials and logistics" (GoV, 2007b). It also points out an important task of "Socialization of disaster preparedness and response," which includes (1) creating favorable conditions for people to participate in the development of legal documents, planning, management, and monitoring the implementation of programs and projects in local areas; (2) fostering dissemination activities and community awareness rising, building capacity for self-disaster preparedness, promoting the tradition of mutual support in emergency relief operations, establishing community voluntary groups to participate in search and rescue operation, promoting the role of social organizations in preparedness, response, and recovery, developing the volunteer network to assist in dissemination, mobilization, recovery, and rehabilitation of production, encouraging organizations, individuals inside and outside the country to contribute diverse and effective support for people and localities affected by natural disasters; (3) reinforcing training for human resources to meet the requirement of disaster prevention, response and mitigation, especially for disaster management, advisory, and coordination offices (GoV, 2007b). Both national schemes are crucial milestones setting the courses for ongoing and future endeavors on DRR in Vietnam. They manifest the efforts of Vietnam to boost up disaster prevention, response, and mitigation activities in the coming time.

The role of stakeholders in implementation of CBDRR projects has been clearly defined in the Decree No. 168/HDBT issued by the Council of Ministers. It established and outlined the tasks of the Central Committee of Storm and Flood Control (CCSFC) and committees and sectors at all levels (Table 1). Apart from this, the Steering CSFC also was established at key works and locations to actively respond to flood and storm. Accordingly,

Table 1. The Roles of CCFSC at All Levels.

The Central Committee for Flood and Storm Control (CCFSC)	People's Committees of All Levels establish the CFSC at Each Level	Ministries and Central Sectors Establish Sector CFSC
– To observe and investigate the establishment and implementation of the annual plan on flood and storm preparedness; – To issue mandates on mobilizing labor forces, equipment, etc. to timely respond to emergency situations; – To instruct the local people to overcome consequences; – To organize final workshops to propagate experiences, lessons, and advanced technologies in disaster preparedness and mitigation in the localities and sectors.	– To help the equivalent People's Committee to build and instruct the implementation of flood and storm measures; – To organize dyke protection, flood and storm preparedness and mitigation, and protect local socioeconomic areas; – To help in overcoming flood aftermath.	– To build and implement flood and storm preparedness and mitigation, protect people, physical and technical materials under the sector's management; – To manage contingency materials and equipment in supporting to flood and storm preparedness and mitigation under the sector's management function; – To timely supply materials, equipment, technologies, etc. to affected areas in emergency situations and support flood and storm aftermath overcoming, following the mobilizing mandates of the CCFSC; – To draw out experiences in flood, inundation, and storm preparedness and mitigation and propagate them to localities and sector.

the organization of disaster preparedness and mitigation was strongly strengthened. Flood and storm preparedness and mitigation implemented in three stages: response preparation, response, and overcoming the aftermath. It helps to mitigate damage and losses and quickly stabilizes people's lives and restores production.

In this view, there have been both "top-down" and "bottom-up" approaches, but at different levels. Some cases are still based on top-down approach as a result of the centralized planning mechanism in the past years. Therefore, it needs more time to fully apply the CBDRR approach for the whole country. Besides, those principles and mottos have strengthened responsibility of the relevant stakeholders. They also mobilized traditional experiences and ensured the sustainability and effectiveness of disaster management activities.

Recent CBDRR projects and policies indicated that there has been a combination of multipurposes in some disaster mitigation activities and socioeconomic development. Some typical examples are: improving the surface of river and sea dykes as road; constructing drainage for irrigation combined with aquaculture production; evacuating to new residential areas linking the promotion of livelihood and flash flood safety; safe harbors for boats, and so forth.

The Vietnamese government also focuses on strengthening international cooperation through wide and effective participation in regional and international disaster management mechanisms such as Hyogo Framework for Action (HFA) to 2015, Asian Disaster Reduction Center (ADRC), Asian Disaster Preparedness Center (ADPC), ASEAN Committee for Disaster Management (ACDM), World Meteorology Organization (WMO), Typhoon Committee (TC), Natural Disaster Mitigation Partnership (NDM-P), and United Nation International Strategy for Disaster Reduction (UN/ISDR). Furthermore, the government has created favorable conditions and actively cooperates with international organizations and nongovernmental organizations working in disaster risk management in Vietnam such as United Nations Development Program (UNDP), United Nations Economic and Social Commission for Asia and the Pacific (UN ESCAP), World Bank (WB), Asian Development Bank (ADB), and others.

Most CBDRR projects in Vietnam are funded by international donors and are implemented through local nongovernment organizations, while local authorities serve as cooperating agencies. These projects have combined nonstructural and structural measure (small structures) in order to enhance the projects' sustainability. In contrast, projects funded by the government are structural projects that mainly focus on flood mitigation. The budget for capacity building component accounts for 70% of project budget, and 30% for structural measures. The average budget for CBDRR projects is around 200,000–300,000 USD. Other CBDRR projects have an implementation budget of about 800,000 USD. A part of this budget is directly transferred to local authorities for management and monitoring (ADPC, 2008).

CBDRR Implementation in Vietnam

Following the change toward DRR, CBDRR activities have been paid more attention in recent years. There is a shift from response and recovery attention to raising awareness and preparedness. Most CBDRR projects have focused on enhancing the capacity of the communities and building safer villages through participatory risk assessment and implementation of risk reduction measures. These projects intend to help communities deal with disasters through capacity development in participatory planning and management. Furthermore, many projects for safer villages and communes are planned to be developed, focusing on long-term intervention and preparedness measures.

One of the CBDRR initiatives was carried out in Thua Thien Hue and Quang Tri provinces since 2001 by the Center for International Studies and Cooperation (CECI) and World Vision. Since then, community capacity building for better disaster preparedness has attracted the attention of NGOs (ADPC, 2008). In 2003, a total of nine provinces had their CBDRR activities. These were Nghe An, Ha Tinh, Quang Binh, Quang Tri, Danang, Quang Ngai, Binh Dinh, Ninh Thuan, and Binh Thuan. Until 2007, there were 23 out of 64 provinces/cities that have some levels of CBDRR activities. These included Thanh Hoa, Yen Bai, Nghe An, Ha Tinh, Quang Binh, Ninh Thuan, Binh Thuan, Son La, Ha Giang, Thua Thien Hue, Lao Cai, Kon Tum, Da Nang, Binh Dinh, Quang Ninh, Hai Phong, Thai Binh, Nam Dinh, Ninh Binh, Tien Giang, Quang Ngai, and Ben Tre.

A total of 17 international and local nongovernment organizations have implemented or are currently implementing CBDRR projects in 23 provinces. These are World Vision, Netherlands Red Cross, Spanish Red Cross, Development Workshop France, Care International in Vietnam, Center for International Studies and Cooperation (CECI), Save the Children Alliance, International Federation of Red Cross and Red Crescent Societies (IFRC), Church World Services, Australian Aid (AusAid), United Nations Development Program (UNDP), World Bank, Deutche Ges-selschaft fur Technische Zusammeinarbeit (GTZ), ActionAid, Asian Disaster Preparedness Center (ADPC), Oxfam, Japan International Cooperation Agency (JICA), and Kyoto University (collaborated with Hue University).

Many CBDRR projects focus on water-induced disasters while few focus on flash floods and droughts. Most of them are implemented in the Northern, Central, and Southern provinces. Among them, only two projects have been implemented in the Central Highlands provinces. These projects aim to build resilience to disasters for the communities in the upland areas of Vietnam.

The participation of local authorities in CBDRR most visible at Steering Committees for Flood and Storm Control (CFSC) from the central to the local levels, People's Committees at all levels, Education Department, Women's Association, and in the Red Cross Society System. With assistance from local authorities, many CBDRR activities have been successfully implemented. As chief representative and administrative agency of the community, the local authorities of disaster-prone are as often act as links between the programs and the vulnerable groups. They are considered as a determinant of the project's sustainability due to their unique responsibility for the project's maintenance and improvement. Hesitation and failure of local authorities to work with the projects may render the project ineffective and unstable.

CASE STUDIES OF CBDRR IN VIETNAM

Vietnam has learned many valuable lessons from practical experiences in raising awareness on DRR and disaster preparedness and response. The CBDRR activities in Vietnam have contributed to effective DRR and focusing on the major work such as raising awareness, planning village safety for local people to response by their own, providing effective measures in order to reduce losses of life and property. The special new characteristic of CBDRR programs is that local people themselves plan and give out solutions and thus unify the authorities from the central to the local levels in the works of DRR. The key principle for risk reduction activities has been highlighted by the government is the participation of local people from the beginning to the end. One of the most success of CBDRR activities is the implementation of the "four on-the-spot motto," which includes Leadership on the spot, Human resources on the spot, Materials on the spot, and Logistics on the spot. It took effect in helping local people to overcome many extreme events such as the storm No. 7 in Thanh Hoa Province, the historic floods in 1999 in Thua Thien Hue Province, and the typhoon Ketsana in Quang Nam Province in 2009. The following are some practices of CBDRR in Thanh Hoa, Thua Thien Hue, and Quang Nam Province (Fig. 3).

Practices in Thanh Hoa Province

In September 2005, typhoon Damrey (storm No. 7) hit the east coast of Vietnam, causing a total damage of 220 million USD. A number of 59 casualties (5 in coastal area, 54 on inland), 16 missing, 28 injured, and

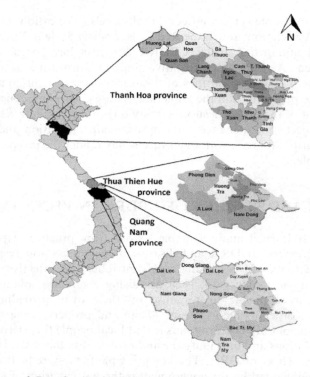

Fig. 3. Maps of Case Studies in Thanh Hoa Province, Thua Thien Hue Province, and Quang Nam Province of Vietnam.

337,632 evacuated was reported. Another 4,746 houses were collapsed or swept away, 113,523 household inundated, and 275 meters of coastal dikes in Nam Dinh and Thanh Hoa collapsed. In the north of Thanh Hoa Province, winds of more than 100 kilometers per hour devastated poor coastal communities, demolishing protective dykes, and destroying houses, water and sanitation facilities, rice fields, and livestock. Only one area in the Province, Hau Loc District, escaped extensive damage. From this, there is a good practical lesson that has been learned about CBDRR by the Steering CFSC of Hau Loc District.

At that time, a part of the coastal dyke was broken, and low-lying areas of the district were inundated, causing a heavy flood. According to the Steering CFSC of Hau Loc District, no deaths were reported, and only four people were injured. Before the storm hit, a preparedness plan to response to the storm was finalized by the leaders of the Steering CFSC at the provincial and district levels. In addition, the District Police Department and Health Center were also directed to reinforce commune public security and to provide first aid support if necessary. The Steering CFSC were directed to strengthen coastal dykes by making earth dams, using sand bags to reinforce the dyke's foot and at the same time beginning to evacuate people. Within three days (from September 24–26, 2005), 29,000 people were evacuated to concrete buildings within the villages and the district. A force of more than 1,500 people, comprising of district youth and rescue teams along with the police and military (1,200 people from the district rescue team and 300 people from the military) were mobilized to help local people evacuate and to provide search and rescue support as well as recovery work afterward. As a result, the impacts from flood have been incredibly reduced, based on the proper evacuation of the local people.

In contrast, there was one case that CBDRR practice was failed to respond to in the 2007 typhoon Lekima, which resulted in devastative damages in Thanh Hoa Province. The main reason of this damage was incomplete implementation of the "four on-the-spot motto" strategy. Although the local authorities and the Steering CFSC had been warned about the typhoon, but they thought the water level would not reach the level of the 1996 historic flood while in fact, it was 0.85 m higher. In Thach Thanh and Vinh Loc districts, the flood came when the local people had harvested their rice and stocked their food and commodities in a safer place. However, because the flood came very quickly at night and the level of water was higher than ever before, the available plan for evacuation and rescue was ineffective at that time. It was reported that a large number of families in the flooded areas lost all their stocked food and basic commodities which resulted in hunger and insecurity during seven flooding days. From this, it is important to highlight the role of raising awareness among the communities on response to the changing climate.

Practices in Thua Thien Hue Province

Thua Thien Hue Province is one of the most disaster-prone areas of Central Vietnam. After the historical flood in 1999, there is increased awareness on DRR among the local authorities and the local people in Thua Thien Hue Province. They have been trying to implement preparedness measures and build safer villages. In particular, they strictly applied the "four on-the-spot motto" strategies at all district and commune levels. The CFSC together with local authorities of Thua Thien Hue Province has developed an annual plan to prepare for floods and storms, which defines preparedness measures for each type of disasters and sets priorities for each vulnerable area, in keeping with the spirit of the "four on-the-spot motto."

The first lesson in the active preparation of on-the-spot materials has been learned by the local authorities in Quang Tho commune. It lies in a low-lying area of Quang Dien district seriously affected by the 1999 flood. Following the "four on-the-spot motto" strategies, the Commune People's Committee has purchased two large boats (with a combined carrying capacity of 35 to 40 people). The Steering CFSC has listed and mobilized 12 engine powered boats owned by residents available to use when needed. Especially, each owner of boats was requested to regularly check their boats and to reserve about 10 liters of gasoline so that they can be proactive in an emergency situation. In addition to that, the commune has reserved 100 liters of diesel and prepared adequate life vests and life buoys for the rescue team. The Steering CFSC in Quang Tho commune also included reserving of food as an essential element of disaster preparedness plan. According to this, the local people were required to reserve food and drinking water for 10 to 15 days, as the commune was often flooded for long periods. As a result, local people living in vulnerable areas have not suffered from lack of food and drink during flood seasons in recent years. From their experiences, local people now reserve drinking water in buoyant nylon bags that are able to float. Additionally, lamp oil, flint, and medicine are indispensable items stockpiled before storms.

Another lesson learned in the development of on-the-spot human resources was recorded in Quang An commune of Quang Dien district in Thua Thien Hue Province. The Steering CFSC of Quang An commune selected and mobilized young people to establish the pioneer teams. There were about 10 to 20 young people belong to each team at village level. At the commune level, each pioneer team included about 32 people and operated under the leadership of the communal chairman and the communal police. Their responsibilities were to assist the communal authority in evacuating all households living near Tam Giang Lagoon or beside the river and to support the search and rescue work during an event. These pioneer teams were provided annual training by the district Red Cross. As a result, the commune and village pioneer teams have effectively evacuated many people from An Xuan village and the Tam Giang lagoon during the typhoon No. 9 (typhoon Ketsana) in 2009.

Practices in Quang Nam Province

Quang Nam Province is a poor agricultural province located in Central Vietnam, which was separated from Da Nang in 1997. Most of 1.4 million of populations are living in rural areas (82.5%) and often involve in low-income practices and unemployment. Floods and storms are among those which occur regularly and rapidly causing serious impacts to the local communities, especially in the coastal areas, the low-lying deltas and the down-streams of river. In the dry season, high temperature and Southwest monsoons also cause droughts in Quang Nam Province.

In 2007, it was reported that nine consecutive floods in Quang Nam Province killed 67 people, injured 339 people, and caused a total damaged cost of 200 billion VND (about 120 million USD). The local authorities cooperated with the military forces had evacuated about 70,000 people from the inundated areas to the public buildings. There were 200,000 people need urgent aids of foods and water. From this experience, the Steering CFSC of Quang Nam Province has made evacuation to be prepared on the spot, including the work of search and rescue. According to this, people living in flooded areas were directed to evacuate to a safer place within the commune (on the spot), which could be a neighbor's house or public facilities nearby. This policy helped minimize loss of people life and property when typhoon Ketsana occurred in Quang Nam Province. At that time, the weather forecast predicted that the storm would land in Thua Thien Hue Province. However, the Steering CFSC of Quang Nam Province was aware and directed the preparedness and response activities. Following the spirit of evacuation on the spot, the Steering CFSC had instructed the Department of Transportation to prepare a list of available cars and to ensure their roadworthiness. The authority also encouraged the communities to prepare their on-the-spot boats to assist in disaster response and evacuations. Regarding to the on-the-spot human resource, a force of about 2,000 people from the provincial and district rescue teams, military forces, and police were mobilized to participate in evacuation process before and during the typhoon occurred. As a result of active evacuation, most local people living in unsafe houses and near the coastal areas were evacuated to higher places by their means of transportation, their neighbors' vehicles, or even by walking. This evacuation on the spot also demonstrated the spirit of mutual support between local people as they could preserve their own properties and those of their neighbors. Besides, it helped in saving both money and resources for the Steering CFSC of Quang Nam Province.

Following the heavy flooding in 1999, the Steering CFSC of Quang Nam Province encouraged people living in low-lying areas to buy boats and build a mezzanine area in their house to store properties. The storing of food was conducted at the commune and village levels instead of at the district level, as was done in the past. In remote mountainous villages, people built small storage containers to reserve rice seed in order to raise their awareness on "self-protection." Under the direction of the local level Steering CFSC, villages and households already reserve sufficient food for 10 to 15 days. During typhoon Ketsana, Tay Giang district was flooded for almost half a month. However, people in the area still had enough food. Furthermore, people in many areas of Quang Nam Province also shared their experience in storing drinking water in big water jars (they only stored two-thirds of the jar's volume so that the jar could float during the flood).

SHORTCOMINGS AND MEASURES IN IMPLEMENTING CBDRR IN VIETNAM

Shortcomings of CBDRR Implementation

As seen in the many case studies above, the implementation level of CBDRR projects in Vietnam has been improved through experience learning. However, besides the good practices, there are still many constrains that limit the complete application of CBDRR. Most CBDRR projects have been implemented under the framework that designed by the donors and the government and then transmitted to local communities. This does not meet the actual needs of vulnerable communities. It may also ignore the potential of local resources and even increase people's vulnerabilities. In addition, there is an unbalanced focus for CBDRR projects. First, floods and storms are considered as the only disasters to be taken into account. Many CBDRR projects made their plan to response to floods and storms only. It is feared that the onslaught of a disaster other than floods and storms leave local authorities without any plan or response preparation, which may result in tremendous losses and damages. Second, there is a big gap between preparation in the coastal areas and mountainous areas. In coastal areas, the authority evacuated residents in advance; army and police patrolled flood-hazard areas, and so on. On the contrary, the death toll in mountainous areas is often high because there is not enough preparation in the mountainous areas.

Human resource constraint is another issue of CBDRR in Vietnam. There is no real volunteer system in the community. Most of the people who participate in the CBDRR projects are the local officers with official duties. Therefore, they could not spend much time on the project's activities. The capacity of local authorities and officers of communities and hamlets are also limited and may not meet the requirements of the projects. Moreover, limited capacity of communities also makes it difficult for CBDRR to take ultimately effective, especially to the poor communities who are strongly impacted by disasters. The losses and damages are even more serious if they cannot secure their livelihood. As a result, the poor communities do not have much time to take part in the projects' activities, which in turn limit their capacity to respond to disasters.

Communication and coordination of efforts between implementing units of the local authorities were also identified to be weak. In some cases, DRR works have been considered as responsibility of the CFSC agencies only. In another cases, it is defined that DRR works belong to the organizations implementing the CBDRR projects. Thus it depends mainly on external resources rather than on the internal capacity of the local communities. In addition, insufficient participation of relevant stakeholders among sectors and levels (central, provincial, district, commune, NGOs, etc.) also make it difficult to disseminate the experiences of CBDRR and restrict its effectiveness in the longer term. In another way, sustainability and replication to widen impacts of the CBDRR projects are recognized important among stakeholders. Most CBDRR projects in Vietnam face the main challenge of sustainability after the completion (Shaw, 2006a). It is because the implementation period is often one to two years, which is not enough for training and practice as well as impact assessment to take into effect. Besides, the lessons learned from the CBDRR projects could not be put well into practice in the overall management system.

Measures to Increase the Implementation of CBDRR in Vietnam

Government agencies from the central to the local levels have recognized and positively assessed CBDRR as an effective approach. However, the institutionalization of CBDRR is a long process which requires time and efforts of relevant stakeholders. This process encompasses the establishment of good institutions, policies, and organizational and managerial activities as well as the local communities' participation in disaster management. In order to strengthen the institutional basis for CBDRR activities, it requires the recognition of necessity and importance of CBDRR by decision-makers (both those developing and enforcing laws) at all localities and in all sectors. Besides, it is important to have the local authorities' support and assistance to ensure institutionalization and prioritization for CBDRR projects. As pointed out in Shaw (2006b), local institutions (both formal and informal) play a critical role in sustaining the efforts in community-based activities. Thus the local authorities should play a crucial role throughout the implementation of the CBDRR activities, from providing support to supervising deployment.

Implementation of both top-down and bottom-up approach is equally important to encourage participants of all relevant stakeholders in all steps of the projects (Fig. 4). A successful CBDRR project cannot be achieved with a mere reliance on the community. It needs effective manpower, high technical support, constant follow-up, as well as strict supervision. In addition, strong involvement and cooperation among sectors and levels (central, provincial, district, commune, NGOs, etc.) will help to disseminate the lessons learnt from CBDRR projects to various practitioners and enhance the joint agreement on a large scale. Not only will they be able to share relevant experiences and lessons learned, organizations implementing CBDRR will also be aware of gaps and future needs (Gero, Méheux, & Dominey-Howes, 2011). However, it is also necessary to strengthen regulating activities among sectors at central and local levels, including the governance system and project administration committees appointed by the government. The responsibility between the local authority and other stakeholders should be balanced to attain consensus and receive adequate support for CBDRR projects.

Regarding capacity building for CBDRR, it is necessary for the organizations implementing CBDRR projects to carry out trainings and practices to the Steering CFSC, the local authorities, and the local people. These trainings should focus more on preparedness rather than on response to help the local communities to prepare themselves better to respond to disasters. Moreover, preparation and updating materials about the good practices to propagate to the general public is also needed. At the same time, they need to address the practical concerns of beneficiaries, and to ensure the livelihood security for the local communities.

The climate is changing, and according to many scenarios for climate change in Vietnam, the impacts of natural disasters will increase in both frequency and intensity, thus it is important for the CBDRR projects

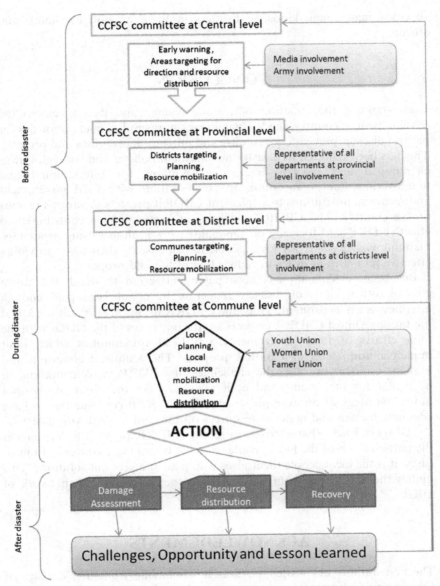

Fig. 4. Conceptual Framework for Development of CBDRR in Vietnam.

to cover many main kinds of disasters in Vietnam, not just floods and storms.

CONCLUSION

Understanding the situation of climate change and its impacts to the development of country, the Vietnamese government has made priorities for natural disaster prevention, response and mitigation programs and projects. This has been reflected in disaster management policies and strategies, thus encouraged and created favorable conditions for international and nongovernmental organizations in collaboration with local government and technical institutions to implement CBDRR projects in various regions of the country. The CBDRR activities in Vietnam have contributed to effective DRR and focusing on the major work such as raising awareness, planning village safety for local people to response by their own, providing effective measures in order to reduce loss of life and property.

But because Vietnam has been paying attention to flood and storm control, other kinds of disaster reduction have not been paid enough attention, such as drought. Thus, the CBDRR in this area is still weak and limitation. Almost CBDRR projects are the initiatives of the NGOs with the joint efforts of local governments and local communities which limit implementation level of CBDRR projects. The economic condition and human resources are also the challenges of CBDRR implementation, in particular for the remote and poor regions. Take the "four on-the-spot motto" strategy as an example. It requests the local communities to have adequate human and material resources on the spot to deal with disasters.

The special new characteristic in recent CBDRR projects in Vietnam is the participation of the local people from the beginning to the end. In most cases, it is the local people themselves who plan and give out solutions. This unifies the authorities from the central to the local levels in the work of DRR.

ACKNOWLEDGMENTS

The first authors acknowledge research scholarship from the Ministry of Education, Culture, Sports, Science and Technology (MEXT) of the Government of Japan and support from the Kyoto University Global COE Program (GCOE-ARS).

REFERENCES

ADPC. (2008). Monitoring and reporting progress on community-based disaster risk management in Viet Nam. Asian Disaster Preparedness Center, Hanoi, Vietnam.

CCFSC. (2009). *Central committee for flood and storm control of Vietnam.* Retrieved from http://www.ccfsc.gov.vn/KW376B3F/Publications.aspx. Accessed on 20 March 2011.

CCFSC. (2010). *Central committee for flood and storm control of Vietnam.* Retrieved from http://www.ccfsc.gov.vn/KW6F2B34/Disaster-Database.aspx. Accessed on 20 March 2011.

Gero, A., Méheux, K., & Dominey-Howes, D. (2011). Integrating community-based disaster risk reduction and climate change adaptation: Examples from the Pacific. *Natutal Hazards and Earth System Sciences, 11*, 101–113. doi:10.5194/nhess-11-101-2011

GFDRR. (2011). *Fiscal impact of natural disasters in Vietnam. Global facility for disaster reduction and recovery.* http://www.aseandrr.net/Portals/0/OK/DRF/Vietnam%20Fiscal%20Impact%20Study_Final.pdf. Accessed on March 20, 2011.

GoV. (2007a). Decision to approve the national strategy for natural disaster prevention. Response and Mitigation to 2020, No: 172/2007/QD-TTg, Government of Vietnam, Hanoi.

GoV. (2008) Decision on approval of the national target programme to respond to climate change decision No: 158/2008/QD-TTg, Government of Vietnam, Hanoi.

GoV. (2005). *National report on disaster reduction in Viet Nam. World Conference on disaster reduction.* Kobe-Hyogo: Government of Viet Nam.

GoV. (2007b). *The national strategy for natural disaster prevention, response and mitigation to 2020.* Hanoi: Government of Vietnam.

MARD Vietnam. (2009). *Disaster impacts in Viet Nam. A summary report at the national forum on DRR and CCA.* Hanoi: Ministry of Agricultural and Rural Development.

Shaw, R. (2006a). Community-based climate change adaptation in Vietnam: Inter-linkages of environment, disaster, and human security. In S. Sonak (Ed.), *Multiple dimension of global environmental changes* (pp 521–547). New Delhi, India: TERI press.

Shaw, R. (2006b). Critical issues of community-based flood mitigation: Examples from Bangladesh and Vietnam. *Journal of Science and Culture, 72*(Special Issue on Flood Disaster Risk Reduction in Asia), 1–2.

Van Staden, D., Rogers, E., Makaudi, I., Winkler, J., White, J., Kangale, M., ... Coetzer, T. (2006). *A transect walk undertaken in itereleng informal settlement to observe community vulnerability.* Pretoria: City of Tshwane Metropolitan Municipality Disaster Risk Management Centre.

Statistic data. (2010). *General statistics office of Vietnam.* Retrieved from http://www.gso.gov.vn/default_en.aspx?tabid=491. Accessed on 20 March 2011.

Uitto, J. I., & Shaw, R. (2006). Adaptation to climate change: Promoting community-based approaches in the developing countries. *Sansai, 1*, 93–108.

World Bank. (2005). The natural disaster risk management project.

PART III
CENTRAL AMERICAN
EXPERIENCES

CHAPTER 14

PROFILE OF COMMUNITY-BASED DISASTER RISK MANAGEMENT IN CENTRAL AMERICA

Tsuneki Hori and Rajib Shaw

INTRODUCTION

Central America is exposed to a variety of natural hazards such as earthquake, volcanic eruption, landslides, and floods. This study considers Central America as a group of six countries: Guatemala, El Salvador, Honduras, Nicaragua, Costa Rica, and Panama, on the basis of their geographical, cultural, historical, and geopolitical backgrounds. The region, located on four conjunct tectonic plates, with 24 active volcanoes, and in the path of hurricanes, has experienced 348 disasters in the last 40 years (from 1980 to 2010), resulting in 29,007 deaths (725 on an average per year) and US$16.5 billion in economic losses (US$400 million per year) (Emergencies Disasters Data Base (EM-DAT), 2009). This amount of US$16.5 billion in economic losses is nearly three times greater than Nicaragua's GDP in 2009 (US$6.14 billion), according to Central Intelligence Agency (CIA) (2010) data. High disaster risk in the region is also demonstrated from the World Bank (2005) indicating that all six Central American countries rank among the top 35 countries in the world at high mortality risk from multiple hazards.

Community-Based Disaster Risk Reduction
Community, Environment and Disaster Risk Management, Volume 10, 277–300
Copyright © 2012 by Emerald Group Publishing Limited
All rights of reproduction in any form reserved
ISSN: 2040-7262/doi:10.1108/S2040-7262(2012)0000010020

The region began an initiative related to Community-Based Disaster Risk Management (CBDRM) nearly 30 years before the present study. The idea of CBDRM was originally proposed during 1980s in the Latin American region (Maskrey, 1988; Wilches-Chaux, 1988). There have been numerous attempts to develop its methodologies between 1997 and 1998 (Zilberth, 1998). However, what focused certain attention on the region's CBDRM needs were after Tropical Storm and Hurricane Mitch in 1998 (Mitch), the region's worst catastrophe of the century according to Duran (1999), affecting 10% of the population, causing 10,000 deaths, and costing US$5 billion in economic losses throughout Central America. The occurrence of disasters is generally assumed to be a window of opportunity for addressing disaster risk management (Christoplos et al., 2010). Mitch provided this opportunity for Central America to open the window to reduce disaster risk, since the Guatemala Declaration II ratified in 1999 by six Central American presidents recognize the region's priority to reduce vulnerability to natural hazard impact.

The objective of this study is to discuss the progress and challenges of CBDRM in Central America from Mitch to date. This study applies Bollin's (2003) CBDRM definition, which is "an application of measures in risk analysis, disaster prevention and mitigation and disaster preparedness by local actors as part of a national disaster risk management system." Indeed, a variety of terminologies and concepts related to CBDRM are found in literature. For example, "community-based disaster preparedness" (CBDP) applied by Allen (2006), van Alast, Terry, and Ian (2008), and Asian Disaster Preparedness Centre (ADPC), (2003); "community disaster reduction" by Na, Okada, and Fang (2009); "community-based preparedness and mitigation" by the World Bank (2007); and "community-based disaster management" by Victoria (2007). Among these, Bollin's (2003) CBDRM definition has been applied in the countries in the region by the Coordination Center for the Prevention of Natural Disasters in Central America (CEPREDENAC), a regional official DRM organization.

The study includes literature review, project data (or project profile) collection and its statistical analysis, and conducted interviews. The chapter is organized in five sections: the second section briefs the profile of the CBDRM in the Central American region. The third section identifies the results, outcomes, and lessons. The fourth section discusses for effective and sustainable CBDRM initiative, and the fifth section briefly concludes with implications for further researches.

PROFILE OF THE CBDRM IN THE REGION

Policy Framework

The mission of the regional official DRM organization, CEPREDENAC, is to promote DRM policy among the member countries. Among the efforts made, CEPREDENAC has promoted, including the above-mentioned Guatemala Declaration II, six DRM policy instruments since Mitch (Table 1). The presidents, or DRM authorities of the CEPREDENAC member countries, have ratified these instruments. All of these instruments have incorporated the consideration of local governments as one of the key actors for disaster risk reduction. However, the context of CBDRM became explicitly incorporated into the regional DRM policy at a later stage, when

Table 1.   List of DRM Policy Instruments in Central America Since Mitch.

Year	Title	Context related to CBDRM
1999	Guatemala Declaration II	Recognizes the needs to reduce vulnerabilities and mitigate future damage caused by disasters in the region.
1999	Strategic Framework for Vulnerability Reduction	It should be formulated and implemented strategies and plans to strengthen the capacity of municipal and local governments in the prevention and mitigation, in coordination among regional level.
2003	Tegucigalpa Declaration	Progress made, especially as regards policies, programs and projects directed at [...] increasing capacities for local level risk management.
2006	Regional Disaster Reduction Plan 2006–2015	Municipal and local governments should assume a role for implementation, monitoring and evaluation of strategic and operational objectives of the Plan.
2009	Mitch + 10 Declaration	Local capacity building for risk reduction and disaster response must be intensified to consolidate the autonomy and resilience of communities and territories.
2010	Central American Policy for Integrated Disaster Risk Management	Vulnerable people and vulnerable communities [...] have the right to have processes, plans, and development programs, considering current conditions of risk and avoiding creation of new risks and vulnerabilities through integrated risk management.

Source: CEPREDENAC (1999a, 1999b, 2003, 2006, 2009, 2010).

the Central American Policy for Integrated Disaster Risk Management (la Política Centroamericana de Gestión Integral de Riesgo de Desastres, PCGIR), was ratified by the Congress of Central America in October 2010.

CBDRM Activities in the Region

One of the reasons to adopt explicitly the context of CBDRM in the PCGIR may be that sufficient experiences on CBDRM have been accumulated in the region. Table 2 shows 60 examples of CBDRM-related projects after Mitch, collected from records of the Executive Secretary of CEPREDENAC (SE-CEPREDENAC) and the DRM authorities of the member countries.

The list of examples may have several limitations. First, the projects in the list are donor-driven or donor-financed activities. The funds for these projects are administrated by the SE-CEPREDENAC or national authorities. Therefore, most of the projects in the list are apparently executed by SE-CEPREDENAC, national governments, or national NGOs. In other words, projects that were financed by local governments, communities, or local NGOs and bypassed coordination with the SE-CEPREDENAC, or national DRM authorities have not been included in the list. Second, the data resources collected from the SE-CEPREDENAC and the DRM national authorities do not clearly show the budget size. This implies that some items in the list might have spent millions of US dollars and others only hundreds of US dollars. Third, the data resources collected here include a variety of territorial intervention sizes for project execution; one includes 333 municipalities as its intervention area, others include only one community. Despite such limitations, the SE-CEPREDENAC and national DRM authorities manage numerous projects with donor agencies or international organizations, so that listed projects do still illustrate the characteristics of CBDRM in the region.

Methodology to Profile the CBDRM in the Region

Based on Bollin's (2003) definition, the methodology to analyze profile of CBDRM in the region focuses primarily on the following two questions: which types of activities (risk analysis, disaster prevention and mitigation, or disaster preparedness) were implemented in the region and what does "local actors" signify in the definition – municipalities or communities? The timing of the CBDRM project implementation is assumed to be another important element for analysis, since 12 years have already elapsed between Mitch (in 1998) – the starting point – and the approval of the PCGIR ratified in

Table 2. List of CBDRM Projects Implemented in Central American Countries.

Year	Project Title	Project Area	Executing Agency
Costa Rica			
1997–1999	Strengthening Local Structure in Disaster Mitigation	Province of Cartago	SE-CEPREDENAC
1997–1999	Comprehensive Strategy for Risk Management in multi-hazard area	Costa Rica	SE-CEPREDENAC
1999–2001	National System against Disasters	Costa Rica	National Government
2000	Vulnerability Reduction, Mitigation and Community Risk Management	Municipality of Tapezco	SE-CEPREDENAC
2001	Strengthening Emergency Communications Network in the Central Chorotega	Municipality of Chorotega	SE-CEPREDENAC
2001	Landslide Early Warning System (EWS)	Costa Rica	SE-CEPREDENAC
2002–2003	Physical vulnerability reduction against Seismic hazards	Municipality of Canas	SE-CEPREDENAC
2004	Local disaster risk management in vulnerable communities	Municipality of San Jose	National Government
2004–2007	Institutional Risk Management Plan in Lloente School	Province of Heredia	National Government
2006	Local educational Committee of disaster risk management	Province of Limon	National Government
2010	Urban risk evaluation	Minucipality of San Jose	National Government
El Salvador			
2000–2001	Vulnerability reduction in San Salvador	Municipality of San Salvador, Berlin, Alegria and Usulután	National Government
2000	MARLAH proyect	Department of Ahuachapan In the Juayua region	National Government
2001–2003	Development of methodology and criteria for relocation		National Government
2002	Preparation of local emergency	El Salvador	National Government
2002	Local Disaster Risk Management Initiative	Municipality of San Salvador	National Government

Table 2. (*Continued*)

Year	Project Title	Project Area	Executing Agency
2002	Disaster mitigation at municipal level	San Vicente, Verapaz, Teoetilan and other 22 municipalities	National NGO
2002–2003	Organization for local emergencies	El Salvador	National Government
2002–2003	Flood and Landslide Risk Analysis	Municipality of San Salvador	SE-CEPREDENAC
2005–2008	Disaster risk management at municipal level	Department of Sonsonate	National NGO
2007–2008	Capacity development for disaster risk management	River basin area in San Salvador	National Government
2007–2008	Improved local capacity for risk management in Metropolitan Area	Municipality of San Salvador and Mejicanos	National NGO
2007–2008	Local management of Risk due to Landslides	Department of Ahuachapan	National Government
2008	Vulnerability reduction at community level	Department of Sonsonate	National NGO
2008–2009	Community and municipal capacity for disaster preparedness	Department of Usulután, Ahuachapán, etc.	National NGO
2010	More safe community	Municipality of Cojutepeque and San Pedro	National NGO
Guatemala			
2000–2002	Local Early Warning System	Guatemala	SE-CEPREDENAC
2000–2002	Training and knowledge dissemination	Guatemala	SE-CEPREDENAC
2001	Disaster Risk Assessment in Metropolitan Area	Municipalities in Metropolitan area in Guatemala	SE-CEPREDENAC
2001	Disaster Risk Reduction in the metropolitan area of Guatemala	Municipality of Guatemala, Chinautla and Villa Nueva.	SE-CEPREDENAC
2002	Institutional strengthening for inter-institutional coordination	Guatemala	SE-CEPREDENAC
2002–2003	Natural Hazard Zoning and Vulnerability analysis	Samala River basin and Reththuleu Community	SE-CEPREDENAC
2007	Disaster risk reduction in the Escolarizado region	333 municipalities of Guatemala	National NGO

Year	Project	Location	Organization
2008–2009	Community capacity development on Disaster risk management	Rio Coyolate, Rio Polochic and other 5 municipalities	Local NGO
Honduras			
2001	Local disaster risk management development	N/A	SE-CEPREDENAC
2001	Community strengthening for radio communication	Municipally of Colón, Atantida, Cortés, and other 6 municipalities	SE-CEPREDENAC
2002–2003	GIS application for hazard and risk identifying	Tegucigalpa municipality	SE-CEPREDENAC
2006–2008	Local strengthening for integrated risk management	10 municipalities in the Province of Colon	National Government
2006–2008	Community education on disaster prevention	Municipality of Aramecina, San Jose and Prespire.	SE-CEPREDENAC
2006–2010	Community living with risk	Cholteca, SanRafael Sentro and other five communities	Local NGO
2007	Local disaster risk management	Municipality of San Esteban Honduras	National NGO
2007–2008	Organization of Municipal committees		Local NGO
2008–2009	Community capacity development on Disaster risk management	Municipalities of Francisco Marazan, and other 4.	SE-CEPREDENAC
Nicaragua			
1998–2008	Local Capacity Strengthening in Disaster Risk reduction	Department of Chinandega, Leon, Masaya etc	SE-CEPREDENAC
2001	Disaster prevention culture	Muy Muy, El Tuma and other 8 municipalities	SE-CEPREDENAC
2001	Comprehensive Risk Management for Local Disaster Reduction,	Ometepe Island	SE-CEPREDENAC
2001–2002	Local support for Analysis of Risk and Natural Hazards	Santo Domingo, La Trinidad and other 8 municipalities	SE-CEPREDENAC
2003–2006	Community development and disaster risk management	Province of Villa Nueva	National Government
2003–2005	Disaster Management and Atention	Municipalities of Raspan, Rio Coco and Puerto Cabezas	International NGO

Table 2. (*Continued*)

Year	Project Title	Project Area	Executing Agency
2002–2004	Establishment of Educational Center for Climate Change and Disaster Preparedness	Municipality of Puerto Cabezas	National NGO
2006	Community sensitization and organization for Early Warning System	Dept. of Managua	National NGO
2004–2009	Enhancing capacities on disaster response at community level	Rama, Bluefields and Kukrahill	National NGO
Panama			
1997–1998	Early Warning System for floods	Eastern Region of the country	SE-CEPREDENAC
2004–2007	Local Disaster risk Management	Province of Bocas del Toro	National Government
2004–2005	Local Disaster Risk management	Province of Darien	National Government
2006	Community Emergency Responce	Province of Chiliqui	National Government
2006	Local Capacity development on Disaster Risk Management	Province of Panama	National Government
2007	Scholl protection	Municipalidad Panama	National NGO
2007	Flood risk reduction	Municipalidad Panama	SE-CEPREDENAC
2009	Mainstreaming climate change adaptation and disaster risk reduction	Communities in Chucanaque and Tabasara	National Government

2010 – a significant milestone. The analysis examines changes of the number of CBDRM projects in the execution during this period.

Types of Activities
For further specification of each category based on Bollin's definition (risk analysis, disaster prevention and mitigation, and disaster preparedness), the present study applies the Inter-American Development Bank (IDB's) (2008) definition of Risk Management Indicators (RMI). The RMIs are consistent with Bollin's definition and have been applied by the governments in Central America. The specification states: risk identification (RI) matching "risk analysis," which signifies identification of hazard type and magnitude, vulnerability, and risk factors; risk reduction (RR) matching "disaster prevention and mitigation," implies the plan and implementation for mitigation and prevention activities; disaster management (DM) matching "disaster preparedness," implies early warning system and disaster preparedness.

Certain items in Table 2 address more than one category. For example, the "Building partnerships across sectors, hazardous assessments and identification of vulnerabilities" project in three municipalities in El Salvador addresses both RI and RR. In such cases, analysis allows a double count for both RI and RR. In contrast, several items lack sufficient data to be categorized. For example, Panama's project "community development on disaster risk management" has no description in the SE-CEPREDENAC's records beyond its title. Such projects count in none of the categories.

Results indicate that 81% of the listed projects (49 out of 60) addressed DM, 13% RR (8 projects), and 17% RI (10 projects). Thus, the majority (81%) of the CBDRM initiatives in the region's response after Mitch addressed disaster preparedness, or DM (Fig. 1).

Considering contents of all 49 projects categorized as DM and dividing into two components: hard components (such as equipment of the early warning systems and/or radio communication system); and soft components (such as community workshop, seminars, or first aid training), results revealed that 39 out of 49 projects (80%) addressed mainly soft components, including the project "Training and knowledge dissemination" in Guatemala (2000–2002), which has disseminated a series of workshops to sensitize residents to flood disaster preparation. Another 10 out of 49 projects (20%) addressed mainly hard components, including the project "Landslide Early Warning System (EWS)" in Costa Rica in 2001, which installed pluviometers and radio communication systems in communities (Fig. 2).

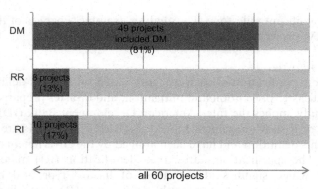

Fig. 1. Type of Activities.

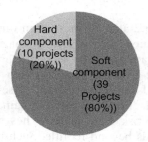

Fig. 2. Three Types of Contents of 49 Projects Categorized as DM.

Local Actors (Projects' Targeted Beneficiaries)

The study categorizes two levels of local actors targeted as project beneficiaries: local governments (municipalities) and communities. Results show that 48% of the listed projects were implemented directly toward communities. For example, the project "Development and installation of early warning and radio communication system" in El Salvador in 2008 has installed the system in 24 communities in the Department of Sonsonate. Another 22% were designed for both communities and local governments, including the project "Local development and flood risk reduction through school education and community sensitization" in Panama in 2007, which developed DRM nonformal education materials for local governments as well as pilot dissemination targeting four communities. The remaining 30%

were only toward local governments. For example, the project "Support Education with a focus on disaster risk reduction and development of curriculum" in Guatemala in 2007 developed a formal DRM education material and disseminated it in 333 municipalities, but the project did not support implementation in communities (Fig. 3).

Results indicate that 70% of the projects in the region have been implemented directly toward community level with or without the participation of local governments, suggesting that the CBDRM "local actors" in the region were primarily communities and secondarily local governments.

Execution Year
It was previously assumed that the number of CBDRM project implementations was higher immediately after Mitch, when the lessons were still fresh. In order to validate that hypothesis, analysis in this study divides the duration since Mitch into five periods (1998–2000, 2001–2003, 2004–2006, 2007–2009, and 2010 to present) and counts the number of executed projects in a period. Results indicate that the CBDRM project was executed nearly continuously across all periods so that the hypothesis is not supported (Fig. 4). This finding indicates that the SE-CEPREDENAC and national DRM authorities continued implementing CBDRM in the region with donor agencies' support. This continuity may be one of the reasons for the PCGIR being approved finally incorporating CBDRM context 12 years after Mitch.

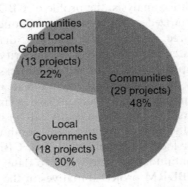

Fig. 3.   Project's Target Beneficiaries.

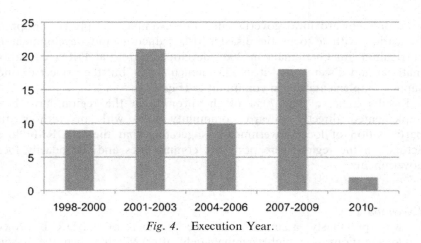

Fig. 4. Execution Year.

Project Duration

The 60 projects are categorized by project duration periods: (i) within one year; (ii) in one or two years; and (iii) in three years or more. The results indicate that 45% of the listed projects were executed within one year, 43% within two years, and only 12% in three or more years (Fig. 5). This finding suggests that the majority of the CBDRM project initiatives in the region (88% of the listed projects) were implemented in a relatively short period (within two years).

Summary of the CBDRM Project Activities

On the basis of the above analysis, the profile of CBDRM project activities in the region is summarized as follows: First, although Bollin's concept of CBDRM includes three elements (risk analysis, disaster prevention and mitigation, and disaster preparedness), the majority (81%) of the listed CBDRM projects implemented in the region addressed disaster preparedness, preponderantly addressing soft component activity improvement (formulation of community disaster committees or emergency drills) rather than hard components. Second, the majority (70%) of the listed CBDRM project activities in the region executed for community as beneficiaries compared to 30% for local governments. Third, CBDRM initiatives have been implemented continuously from Mitch to date. Finally, the majority (88%) of the listed CBDRM project initiatives in the region were executed less than two years, in other words, in a short period.

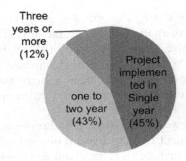

Fig. 5. Project Duration.

Results and outcomes of the CBDRM activities

This section identifies the results, outcomes, and lessons from CBDRM project implementation in the region. In doing so, the following methodology was applied: first, a random sample of 20 projects from the entire list in Table 2 was selected; second, each project's manager in the national government or local government, community leaders, or NGO counterparts were contacted in order to perform interviews (face-to-face or via telephone); and third, of which 10 interviewees of the 20 chosen samples were responded and the interviews have been completed. Interviews were conducted during January to March 2011, covering all six Central American countries. The interview included three questions: (i) the results of the project; (ii) the outcomes of the project; and (iii) the lessons learned from the project implementation. Finally, the results of the interviews are analyzed and systemized as the following way.

Results of the Projects

The interviewees responded with a variety of results from the CBDRM projects implemented in the Central American region, and these can be categorized as three types. The first category is "soft component" which includes (i) execution of community capacity building and sensitization workshops or seminars for disaster preparedness, (ii) establishment or strengthening of the local (or community) committee for disaster prepared-ness, and (iii) facilitate training activity for community first aid drills or evacuation simulations during the period of project execution. These results coincide with the above analysis of the profile of CBDRM project activities in the region, which the 39 projects listed in the Table 2 addressed. These results also coincide with the European Commission (2008) findings on CBDRM in the region: "there has been a demonstrated increase in the capacity of local institutions, mandated with protecting vulnerable population against disasters."

Second, the interviewees other than Honduras and Nicaragua identified the project's improvement in the provision of hard components (equipment and materials). These include (i) formal and nonformal education material used in schools and community workshops, (ii) monitoring equipment (such as rain gauges for floods) for community use, (iii) radio communication equipment for emergency situations in the community, among communities, and between community and local or national institutions, (iv) materials necessary for first aid (small boats and tents) and provisions for emergency shelters (water bottles, food for emergency use, and medicine). Again, these are coinciding with the RM category. The interviewees from Honduras, Panama, and Costa Rica stated that community hazard (or risk) maps had also been developed through community participation during the projects' implementation period.

Third, the interviewee from Costa Rica responded to the construction of small-scale embankments (300 m longitude along the river at project site) provided as one of the components of the project. This small-scale embankment was created from used tires and constructed through community participation. The interviewee stated that community participation in the construction process included woman and children volunteers.

Outcomes of the Projects

The interviewees responded with a variety of outcomes of the CBDRM projects, which fall into three categories. The first category is saving lives, particularly mentioned by the interviewees in Costa Rica and Panama. The interviewee in Costa Rica explained the experience in the municipality of La Masica, northern Honduras (the Costa Rican interviewee had worked for the Honduras project). The project had provided equipment for the community early warning system (the rain gauge for the river and radio communication equipment for flood alerts) in 1997. The involved communities were affected by a flood during Mitch in November 1998. The system worked effectively and community residents were evacuated prior to the flood, with no deaths reported in the community. This successful experience reflects the opinion of Lavell (2001), who called it "a regional and international example of good practice," as well as Duran (1999), who also comments that this successful experience is noteworthy because other communities in the municipality lost 150 to 200 lives each during Mitch, whereas La Masica lost none.

Similar life-saving outcomes were reported by the interviewee from Panama. The project on nonformal education for disaster preparedness, organization of community emergency committees, and developing a flood evacuation route map was provided in the province of Darien, in the eastern Panama in 2007. Each project-involved communities training through five workshops on self-evacuation in flood emergencies. Proof of its effectiveness was thus reported by the interviewee: when one of the project-involved communities, El Salto, was flooded in November 2010, the community residents self-evacuated and were in a public primary school, an assigned shelter. According to the report from the national civil protection (SINAPROC), 96 houses and 261 people in the community were affected by the floods (Sistema Nacional de Proteccion Civil (SINAPROC), 2010). However, no major damage was reported.

The second category is collaboration for community solidarity. The Panamanian interviewee discussed the following experience in the province of Darien, located on the border with Colombia. In recent years, Colombia immigrants in this area have formed their own communities. However, these new-formed immigrant communities are isolated, and do not engage in social exchanges with traditional communities. One of the reasons is that other projects implemented in the region such as rural community agriculture development and community folk-craft development, sometimes cause conflicts between project beneficiary (traditional communities, in most cases) and non-beneficiary communities (the majority of new-formed immigrant communities). In contrast, the CBDRM project directly related to natural phenomena and did not stimulate economic activity for community residents, which ensured that people from traditional and newer communities participate equally in the project, and eventually relieved some of the conflicts among these communities.

The Costa Rican interviewees described the effectiveness of community hazard map development in the primary school curriculum (at the second grade level), an activity engaging students in town observation, sketching community hazardous risks and vulnerabilities, developing neighborhood risk maps, scale modeling, and presentations to the communities. The interviewee stated that the youngsters enjoyed these activities and disseminated their knowledge to their families, so that such activity also strengthens community solidarity led by school children – a habit that may continue into the next generation. This example coincides with the United Nations International Strategy for Disaster Reduction (ISDR) (2007) stating that young people can act as informants through unofficial communication networks that evolve within a community.

The Honduran interviewee believed that it is fundamental human nature for every human being (poor, rich, women, men, young, old, highly educated or not, disabled, migrants, or visitors) to want to support their neighbors. The CBDRM project implemented in the City of Comayagua made it relatively easy for women and children to participate in the disaster risk committee, community sensitization workshops, and the elaboration of evacuation planning and evacuation drill exercises. Women who participated in these activities seemed satisfied with having participated in community development and were eager to disseminate their experience among their neighbors who did not participate.

The third category is the influence of the CBDRM project initiative on reforming the local government's legislative framework. One example comes from the El Salvadoran interviewee. The project on community DRM sensitization workshops was conducted in the City of Santa Tecla in 2004 and 2005. The manager of the department of planning in the municipality participated in the project as a local counterpart and realized that activities for disaster preparedness are significant for community residents. After the project implementation, he requested the San Salvador Metropolitan Mayor Councils (Consejo de Alcaldes del Area Metropolitana de San Salvador [COAMSS], of which the City of Santa Tecla is a member) to incorporate CBDRM content into the Municipality's development planning policy instrument (Strategic Plan for Municipalities of Metropolitan Area). The Council approved the Strategic Plan in December 2008, incorporating DRM as a permanent action for local development in the San Salvador Metropolitan area.

Lessons from the Projects

Interviewees in Honduras, Nicaragua, Panama, and Costa Rica stressed that the lessons they learned were related to the difficulty of continuing activities after the project execution period. The Honduran interviewee stated that the donor agency had visited the municipality at the beginning of the project and discussed the project design, including project result indicators for post-project impact measurements (for example, the number of community emergency committees to be established, emergency plan to be prepared, and emergency drills to be executed). The project's execution period was only one year, and the local project promoter (a contracted local NGO) seemed to be obliged to accomplish only the targeted indicators. Therefore, they urged community residents to volunteer as emergency committee members, copied donor agency's local emergency plan example, and submitted it to the municipality as the proposed municipal emergency plan, and conducted community workshops regardless of the number of community residents who participated. As a result, each target indicator designed at the beginning of the project had been accomplished, but only in theory. In reality, the project's purpose was understood by very few community residents (although many people in the community did participate in the project activities). Therefore, the project achieved no self-continuity by the community residents after the project implementation ended.

The Honduran interviewee also described the ineffectiveness of the "high-technology" digital GIS system provided by the project and installed in the municipality. The objective of this installed system in the municipality was to develop and provide hazard maps to the community residents. Although the quality of the exampled maps were attractive (high-resolution colored hazard maps), few staff members in the municipality had used the GIS system because it was difficult to operate, understand, and maintain, and no data updates had been performed since the initial installation. Thus, the information of the GIS system was outdated, maps in the digital GIS system were different from the city's actual figure and profile. Eventually, the municipality never disseminated hazard maps to the communities.

The Nicaraguan interviewee discussed other lessons learned regarding continuity of the local disaster committee. Many people migrate from the city to find better jobs in Managua, the capital, or major cities in Costa Rica, a neighboring and macro-economically stable country. Members of the local disaster committee had left with no prior notification, and so the committee did not work as originally designed. Ironically, people from other areas or countries come and settle in the city, and the population is growing, causing denser population in the city center. Newcomers also spread toward suburbs, including the river basin area, increasing the magnitude of their vulnerability to flood events.

The Panamanian interviewee described the local government's weak follow up capability to a "seeded" CBDRM activity financed and administrated by the donor agency. A project in Darien was designed, including local government capacity development activities (such as technical seminars for local government workers and installation of emergency aid equipment), so that they would undertake community activities after the project execution. However, these activities were insufficient for local governments; the project executed only a few seminars and installed equipment with insufficient explanation regarding their use for a "real" emergency situation. Another problem was that the local government lacked human resources and budget to follow up, update, and upgrade the CBDRM activities. The lesson, according to the interviewee, includes the need for much more technical support from national authority to local governments. Although, as discussed earlier, one of the communities in Darien has successfully operated a self-managed flood evacuation plan, the interviewee commented that if the community was aware that there was no support from the local government, the residents would no longer prepare for emergency self-management, instead just stay home and blame no support from the local and national governments.

The El Salvador interviewee stated the lessons learned regarding maintenance of equipment provided by the projects. The city of Santa Tecla experienced landslides after a strong earthquake in January and February 2001 resulting in more than 500 deaths. After this catastrophe, a donor organization supported the local government and installed landslide early warning monitoring equipment. The equipment was sophisticated, with a siren that automatically alerts the communities when rain exceeds 35 mm per hour. The system was installed in a local police office and functioned effectively for five years since its installation. However, after this period, the equipment became faulty and ceased to operate. The city government officer tried to repair it, but could not because equipment documentation was lost and the equipment contained many complex large-scale integration (LSI) electronic parts for which there were no experts to repair in the city or even in the entire country. Since then, the system has never been used. The interviewee suggested that the lesson is that any equipment installed in the local area should be simple to maintain so that local people could use it permanently.

Summary of the Interviews on CBDRM Progress in the Region

The results, outcomes, and lessons from the CBDRM activities in the region are summarized in Table 3 in both aspects of short and medium/long term.

Table 3.   Summary of the Interviews on CBDRM Progress.

	Short term	Medium/long term
Results	• Soft components (community capacity building, strengthening of the local committee, first aid drill). • Risk or hazard maps. • Equipment and materials. • Small-scale constructions.	
Outcomes		• Saving-lives activity by community self-management. • Improvement of community solidarity. • Disaster risk management incorporated into local government's legislative and institutional framework.

Lessons		• Continuing to provide activities after the project execution period:
		  ✓ Object of activity understood by very few community residents;
		  ✓ No maintenance of GIS system nor data updating;
		  ✓ Discontinuation of the member of local disaster committee;
		  ✓ Weak follow up capability of local government.

DISCUSSION: HOW TO MAKE THE CBDRM INITIATIVE MORE EFFECTIVE AND SUSTAINABLE

On the basis of the examples demonstrated in the previous Section, a challenge for more effective CBDRM project initiatives in the region seems to focus on project sustainability. It is true that 88% of the projects listed in Table 2 were implemented within two years, but thereafter, communities received little support from the projects. From the community perspective in practice, disaster risk is one of the many risks that communities face in daily life particularly for poor communities in the Central American region, including families of social violence, unemployment, lack of income, malnutrition, or health problems. Disasters due to natural hazards may occur less frequently than other kind of risks faced by the community.

Eventually, the priority of DRM in these communities may have decreased soon after the withdrawal of direct support from the projects.

The following event recently occurred in Costa Rica, as recounted by the interviewee from Costa Rica. In November 2010, the country suffered Tropical Storm Thomas, which spread intense rainfall in a broad area. Among many areas, the community of Escazu in the city of San Jose was the most affected area by rain-triggered landslides. The community is covered by the nation's early warning system and the community has been educated for self-evacuation in case of hazardous events (mostly for floods and intense rains). Indeed, the local emergency committee issued the alert and recommended that the community immediately evacuate to the assigned shelters. However, not many residents reacted to the alert. Hours later, a landslide occurred in this area, destroying several homes and causing 23 deaths. This tragic experience in Costa Rica fundamentally shares the lesson learned in Nakagawa (2010) that even with a sophisticated early warning system in place, a successful evacuation and disaster loss reduction occurs only when people respond appropriately to the early warning information and instructions. Therefore, CBDRM should be permanently established, even after the project implementation period.

Bollin (2003) suggests that local disaster risk management capabilities are organized most effectively when responsibility is borne jointly by the municipal authorities and other representatives of the population. Municipal or local authorities' support for the communities may be the key to the permanent establishment of CBDRM. This also enables local authorities to develop a better understanding of communities' daily problems, risks, and needs, as well as to bridge good relationships between national authorities and communities. Risk identification and risk reduction are elements that should be incorporated in the local development process and development planning (Lavell, Mansilla, & Smith, 2002). Nevertheless, it seems that not all local governments in the region have sufficient capacity to provide efficient and permanent support for that. The region already recognizes this challenge, because 52% of the listed projects in Table 2 have included many components for local governments' capacity development. However, that effort may still not provide sufficient community support initiatives, as indicated by the interview in Honduras and Panama.

In the end, when the project execution period is short (less than two years for 88%) and direct support from the project terminates, given that local authorities' support cannot be much expected, one alternative for a sustainable CBDRM may be self-continuation through community ownership. Fortunately, several interviews demonstrated that certain activities in the region stimulated community ownership of DRM. For example, in Costa Rica, youth develop hazard maps in school and their learning is disseminated among their families. This positive experience implies that the primary school curriculum is one of the key elements of self-continuation for community-owned CBDRM. The case of the City of Comayagua suggests that it is fundamental human nature to help neighbors, and thus, CBDRM activity may involve all residents (including socially vulnerable people such as the poor, the women, the elderly, and children) in collaborating with their neighbors to improve awareness against hazardous risks. The case of the province of Darien suggests that CBDRM activity is a kind of natural phenomenon-based initiative and noneconomical incentives so that every status of people, including traditional communities and new-formed immigrant communities, can participate freely, and this relieves conflict between traditional communities and newer migrant communities.

CONCLUSION

The goal of DRM – including CBDRM – is quite simple in theory: to reduce, minimize, or eliminate damage and loss resulting from hazardous events. Certainly, such a "super goal" is not easy to achieve in practice, because disaster risk is unpredictable and under latent condition depending on the vulnerability of structures and human beings that vary day-to-day and from land-to-land. The study found that one of the outcomes of the CBDRM in the region is related to saving lives. Though it seems to be only a small positive impact in achieving DRM's "super goal," it is also true that CBDRM activity, in this case the specific activities categorized in RM, addressed 81% of the listed CBDRM projects in Table 2, compliments directly such "super goal" of DRM in the region. Moreover, the study found the CBDRM brings opportunity to collaborate community solidarity and influences on reforming local government's legislative framework.

Project sustainability seems to be a major challenge for effective CBDRM in the region, and the result of the interviews includes some lessons leaned for project formulation. These include (i) technology used in the CBDRM should be adapted for community and local government's use, thus its maintenance should be as easy as possible; (ii) project design should focus more on the process of community participation, or community capacity development process rather than on just tangible, or materialized project results; and (iii) a member of community emergency committee and hazard maps should be regularly updated after project initiation to cover a current and accurate profile of the local area.

The study concludes that self-continuation through community owner-ship is a practical and effective way for project sustainability and some implications is also found for that. This includes (i) youth develop hazard maps in school as an effective way for dissemination of their learning among their families and rise communities' disaster risk awareness; (ii) CBDRM activity allows all kind of participants (including socially vulnerable people such as the poor, the women, the elderly, and children) and collaborates to improve community solidarity; and (iii) CBDRM, as noneconomical incentives activity, relieves conflict between traditional communities and newer migrant communities.

Indeed, this study meets several limitations. The projects listed in the Table 2 are only donor-driven or donor-financed activities, and most of these are executed by SE-CEPREDENAC, national government, or national NGOs and thus, projects that were financed by local governments, communities, or local NGOs have not been included in it. It did not interview the people in the beneficiary and non-beneficiary communities to monitor the result of this study. It has been only 12 years from Mitch, thus it is obvious to be followed up to monitor and provide further analysis for more effective CBDEM in the region.

REFERENCES

ADPC (Asian Disaster Preparedness Centre). (2003). Community-based disaster risk reduction in central Sri Lanka e Mitigating landslide and rock-fall damage in urban Nawalapitiya. Safer Cities, Case Study 5. Colombo, Sri Lanka: Intermediate Technology Development Group, ITDG-South Asia. Retrieved from http://www.adpc.net/AUDMP/library/safer_cities/5.pdf. Accessed on January 13, 2011.

van Alast, M. K., Terry, C., & Ian, B. (2008). Community level adaptation to climate change: The potential role of participatory community risk assessment. *Global Environmental Change*, *18*, 165–179.

Allen, K. M. (2006). Community-based disaster preparedness and climate change adaptation: Local capacity-building in the Philippines. *Disaster*, *30*(I), 81–101.

Bollin, C. (2003). *Community-based disaster risk management approach – Experience gained in central America*. Eschborm: GTZ.

CEPREDENAC (Coordination Center for the Prevention of Natural Disasters in Central America). (1999a). *Guatemala Declaration II*. Guatemala City, Guatemala.

CEPREDENAC (Coordination Center for the Prevention of Natural Disasters in Central America). (1999b). *Marco Estrategico para la reduccion de vulnerabilidades y desastres naturales in centroamerica* [*Strategic Framework for Vulnerability Reduction.*] Guatemala City, Guatemala.

CEPREDENAC (Coordination Center for the Prevention of Natural Disasters in Central America). (2003). *Tegucigalpa Declaration*. Tegucigalpa, Honduras.

CEPREDENAC (Coordination Center for the Prevention of Natural Disasters in Central America). (2006). *Plan Regional de Reduccion de Desastres 2006-2015 [Regional Disaster Reduction Plan 2006-2015.]* Guatemala City, Guatemala.

CEPREDENAC (Coordination Center for the Prevention of Natural Disasters in Central America). (2009). The Mitch + 10 Declaration. Guatemala City, Guatemala.

CEPREDENAC (Coordination Center for the Prevention of Natural Disasters in Central America). (2010). *La Política Centroamericana de Gestión Integral de Riesgo de Desastres [PCGIR Central American Policy for Integrated Disaster Risk Management.]*. Guatemala City, Guatemala.

Christoplos, I., Rodríguez, T., Schipper, L., Narvaes, E. A., Bayres, M., Karla, M., ... Pérez, F. J. (2010). Learning from recovery after hurricane Mitch. *Disasters, 34*(S2).

CIA (Central Intelligence Agency). (2010). *The world factbook 2010*. New York, NY: Skyhouse Publishing.

Duran Vargas Luis Rolando. (1999). *Centroamerica despues del hucaran Mitch: Gestion del riesgo y preparativos para desastres, una tarea pendiente [Central America after Hurricane Mitch: Risk management and preparedness for disaster, a pending task]*. Panama City: CEPREDENAC.

EM-DAT (Emergencies Disasters Data Base). (2009). *The international disaster database*. Center for Research on the Epidemiology of Disasters (CRED), Ecole de Santé Publique, Université Catholique de Louvain, Brussels. Retrieved from http://www.em-dat.net/index.htm. Accessed on January 11, 2011.

Europian Comission. (2008). *Evaluation of DIPECHO action plans in central America (1997–2007)*. Nicaragua: Managa.

IDB (Inter-American Development Bank). (2008). *Indicators of disaster risk and risk management*. Summary Report. Washington, DC: IDB.

ISDR, (United Nations International Strategy for Disaster Reduction). (2007). Global network of NGOs for disaster risk reduction (2007) building disaster-resilient communities – Good practices and lessons learned. Geneva.

Lavell, A. (2001). *Initiativas de Reduccion de Riesgo a Desastres en Centroamerica y Republica Dominicana: Una Revision de Recientes Desarrollos, 1997–2001 [Initiatives of Disaster Risk Reduction in Central America and Dominican Republic: A review of Recent Development, 1997–2001.]* CEPREDENAC: Panama City.

Lavell, A., Mansilla, E., & Smith, D. (2002). *Local risk management – Ideas and notions relating to concept and practice*. Panama City: CEPREDENAC.

Maskrey, A. (1988). *Community based approaches to disaster mitigation*. Oxford: OXFAM.

Na, J. I., Okada, N., & Fang, L. (2009). *Collaborative action development for community disaster reduction by utilizing the Yonmenkaigi system method*. Conference Paper, IEEE International Conference on Systems, Man, and Cybernetics San Antonio, TX. October 2009. Retrieved from http://hdl.handle.net/2433/109798

Nakagawa, Y. (2010). Community-based disaster management and social capital. In S. Rajib & R. Krishnamurthy (Eds.), *Disaster management: Global challenges and local solutions* (pp. 345–383). Chennai: Universities Press India Limited.

SINAPROC (Sistema Nacional de Proteccion Civil). (2010). *Centro de Operacones de Emergencias – Informe de Novedades a Nivel Nacional*. Panama City, Panama.

Victoria L. P. (2007). *Community based disaster management in the Philippines: Making a difference in people's lives*. Retrieved from http://unpan1.un.org/intradoc/groups/public/documents/APCITY/UNPAN025912.pdf. Accessed on January 8, 2011.

Wilches-Chaux, G. (1988). *La Vulnerabilidad Global [Global Vulnerability.]*. In Maskrey, A. (Ed.), Los desastres no son Naturales. LA RED. Tercer Mundo Editores.

World Bank. (2005). *Natural disaster hotspots*. Washington DC: World Bank.

World Bank. (2007). *Community based disaster risk management*. Environmental planning Collaborative, Ahmedabad, India and the World Bank Institute. On-line course.

Zilberth, L. (1998). *Modulos de Capacitación para la Gestión Local de Riesgo [Modules for Capacity development for Local Risk Management.]* LA RED- ITDG, Peru.

CHAPTER 15

COMMUNITY-BASED DISASTER RISK REDUCTION IN GUATEMALA

Gaby Breton

INTRODUCTION

In creating a response to tropical storms Stan (October, 2005) and Dolly (May, 2008), the Center for International Studies and Cooperation (CECI) began encouraging the Guatemalan residents to get involved with disaster planning. Other international organizations are, also, beginning to finance projects to train the poorest communities in disaster planning but, funding is difficult because, sadly, avoidance does not "sell" as well as post-disaster relief and reconstruction projects.

CECI's model emphasizes investment in disaster prevention and preparedness as part of their program to mitigate the effects of climate change. Evacuation planning alone is insufficient to address the spectrum of human suffering. There are many decisions that need to be taken to protect people and land from expected catastrophe. Inefficient and inadequate preparation endangers communities, and this is compounded when people have no idea what to do for themselves. Chaos increases with population growth, and therefore a prudent policy is required to organize communities in advance.

This chapter abstracts the lessons learned in Guatemala from *The Program of Risk Reduction in the Reconstruction Process of the Communities' Pro-Habitat Project* sponsored by the United Nations Development

Community-Based Disaster Risk Reduction
Community, Environment and Disaster Risk Management, Volume 10, 301–311
Copyright © 2012 by Emerald Group Publishing Limited
All rights of reproduction in any form reserved
ISSN: 2040-7262/doi:10.1108/S2040-7262(2012)0000010021

Programme (UNDP) through funds of the Swedish International Development ment Cooperation Agency (SIDA) and of the United States Agency for International Development (USAID) (Table 1).

The rough topography of Central America has been created by volcanic eruptions and this region is still geologically active. Guatemala is routinely exposed to mudslides, earthquakes, and volcanic eruptions. More than 60% of the population is indigenous Maya. During the Guatemalan civil war (1960–1996), these indigenous people fled to remote areas that had limited public infrastructure and few social services. Today, they remain the poorest and the most vulnerable population in Guatemala. The Department of Sololá has about 85% Maya population. In this area, people speak three dialects Quiche, Kachiquel, and Tzutuil, and 90% of them are illiterate. To a great degree, the people still maintain the ancestral way of living. They are excluded from the mainstream economy – living as farmers and artisans. If their disadvantaged position does not favor them, then obviously disasters can be expected to hit them harder. Politically, Guatemala is divided into 22 states or departments and CECI's reconstruction intervention, under the UNDP program, was implemented in five of the highland departments: Sololá, Chimaltenango, San Marcos, Zacapa, and Escuintla (CECI, 2010).

Central America has a very high crime rate, which has many root causes, but the problems are mainly due to lack of access to public resources such as easy credit and affordable schools. The C5 countries have one of the highest

Table 1. CECI's Intervention Areas in the UNDP PRO HABITAT Program.

No.	Place	Date of Intervention	Number of Beneficiaries
1.	Nueva Esperanza, San Andrés Semetabaj, Sololá	June 2007	115
2.	Xecotoj, San Andrés Semetabaj, Sololá	June 2007	45
3.	Sibinal, San Marcos	July 2008	65
4.	Patzún, Chimaltenango	December 2008	37
5.	La Esperanza, Bárcenas Villa Nueva, Guatemala	June 2009	65
6.	Los Pinos II, Palín, Escuintla	June 2009	93
7.	La Unión, Zacapa	September 2009	282

unemployment rates in the world; this combined with a staggering gap between the poor and the rich acts to fully marginalize the Maya population. Despite years of "land reform," the indigenous people do not participate as property owners, nor do they have share in controlling the resources of the country.

This chapter focuses on the part of the UNDP program that was executed by CECI, an NGO that has been active in Central America since the 1990s and is currently operating in Guatemala and El Salvador. Unlike the standard humanitarian models, CECI specializes in "development projects." This means that although it can and does dispense medical supplies and food, under certain circumstances, CECI does not position itself as a deliverer of relief per se. Instead, CECI concentrates on emergency preparedness training in communities. It is this participatory, community-based approach that has resulted in CECI's gold standard for intervention *before* important catastrophes.

In the aftermath of the storms Stan and Dolly, Guatemala routinely has had to recover from massive damages. This case study is a comprehensive analysis of an extended disaster and reconstruction effort that covered both storms. CECI sought to include much more than the traditional disaster services. The NGO studied, identified, and assessed new economic potentials and suggested productive alternatives. CECI engaged local families in planning and reconstructing their community using the Habitat for Humanity model.

CECI relocated a group to a "safe" place and, then, provided disaster preparedness training along with small business development advice. With this support, the displaced families could begin to regenerate resources.

CECI's objectives were:

1. To work with the government to develop strategies;
2. To mitigate threats at the local level;
3. To develop suitable economic solutions for people, who had lost everything; and
4. To enforce better methods of reconstruction.

CECI believes that the use of the community-based disaster risk management (CBDRM) approach completes a reconstruction project by preventing fresh impacts and avoiding future losses, especially, in areas that have been newly settled. CECI seeks to integrate economic recuperation activities as part of their assistance package. The first part of this chapter evaluates the ability of this methodology to promote people's security while actively involving the affected population in identifying risks and in prioritizing the measures to be taken.

OVERVIEW OF INTERVENTION OF RECONSTRUCTION PROGRAM

Factors such as geographic remoteness and the rapid onset of disasters require that risk reduction measures be specifically tailored to each area and, to be worthwhile anything, be done in advance. Roads can collapse and people can be stranded for days without relief. In Guatemala coastal and mountainous areas are increasingly bearing the negative impacts of climate changes. And, as we have seen in New Orleans (2005), efforts of a rich "First World" country to implement policies and programs failed utterly and were absolutely insufficient in avoiding that disaster. Worldwide, negative impacts from natural phenomena and from human activity (such as clearcutting forests) are exposing people to more risks.

CECI's mission is to salvage the daily lives of people, who are barely managing on a subsistence economy. Typically, it is the poorest people (like Guatemala's indigenous groups) who suffer the most harm. Traditional coping mechanisms are easily overwhelmed. The financial impact of disasters weighs heavily on rural populations. And, just because the net loss is comparatively small, it does not mean it is any less devastating.

The CECI team began working with the UNDP between May 2007 and February 2010 in the above communities. A total of 671 families benefited from the project. CECI relocated people so that they could benefit from more plentiful basic services and be housed in a relatively safer environment. Some of those families were also assisted in finding employment near their new homes.

Fiscally, the country is unable to fund either preventative measures or massive reconstruction. These two storms killed many thousands, damaged fields, and ruined the infrastructure. The post-disaster events obviated the lack of planning and pointed to the need for appropriate social organization to handle shared threats. Efforts are often thwarted by corruption and hidden agendas. For example, during an emergency, it is possible to bypass the bidding process and this opens the door for insider contracting. Worse, there is little that can be done to get around this systemic corruption. Nonetheless, community organizations were mobilized and trained with the aim of promoting sustainability. CECI invested in a wide training program that incorporated several components for economic development.

It is important to note that *The Program of Risk Reduction in the Reconstruction Process of the Communities' Pro-Habitat Project* was based on a successful reconstruction project that also included a component on youth-at-risk prevention. It was the at-risk component that earned CECI the post-Stan contract. CECI ran a prior project without the at-risk youth: *Recuperation of the Production Capacity and a Nutritional Food Security Program*. After that, CECI's reconstruction projects were designed to include an analysis of job availability, the equitability of procurement, and, recently (2007), the provision of microloans to restore former workplaces. The combination of the nutritional, economic, preparedness, and at-risk mitigation elements all work together to recreate and sustain a safe habitat for the afflicted families of Atitlán.

CECI advocated for their Mayan beneficiaries, providing financial assistance and other resources in a vain attempt to fill the gap between the demand for rehabilitation/reconstruction and official government land grants and inadequate housing subsidies.

The complete project consisted of six components (Fig. 1):

1. **Microlocalization** – resettle the people
2. **Urbanization** – model of the village to fit custom
3. **Housing construction** – prepare cost-effective and appropriate design
4. **Economic activities** – reestablish basic services and markets

Fig. 1. Intervention Process of PRO HABITAT.

5. **Risk management activities** – work toward an effective program
6. **Organizational assistance** – conduct elections and assigning the administrative tasks

STRATEGY FOR INTERVENTIONS

The organizational strategy implemented by CECI for the PRO HABITAT project was, at heart, an institutional capacity building program for the communities. To accomplish this, CECI recruited local, allied NGOs and other institutions to execute some components of the project. These partnerships both sped up implementation and diminished costs.

CECI contracted three local NGOs: COPADES, *Kiej de los Bosques*, and *Vivamos Mejor*. COPADES developed community-based approaches for risk management and strengthened social organization. *Kiej de los Bosques* researched and trained the people on "productive chains" that yielded new products. One was gourmet mushroom "farms" that employ people who can no longer go to the fields. They conducted market studies identifying outlets for the community's new services and products. *Vivamos Mejor* advised CECI on housing construction.

The project was a people-centered development versus a "cooperative" effort that focused on, say, a member-owned and controlled organization. Rather,

Table 2.   Some Results Achieved by the CECI Intervention in the PRO
HABITAT Program.

- Total of 958 families are listed and characterized
- The 650 families that were affected by the storm Stan reseated with low levels of risk have a house with basic municipal services (water and sanitation)
- At least 525 of the rebased families have been trained on different vocational programs, and have a minimal condition of employment and income
- The incorporation of the members of the community into the risk management commission of the national system, and the transfer of capacities of planning and risk management toward the local levels that contribute to diminish the vulnerability in the municipalities of the project intervention
- All communities had roads and educational infrastructure for the children
- Trained and organized in commissions of risk management
- All communities have a local contingency plan for risk management, which allows them to be organized to face future natural disasters
- All communities have a territorial plan and an urban development plan that serve as a tool to improve their development

---

CECI's development process was intended to be equitable; in fact, it delivered a fully democratic context for the community members to participate.

The following section discusses few problems CECI encountered and some of the lessons learnt from the six components. Here, the special emphasis is on the economic component – support of the production of goods and services (Table 2).

COMPONENTS OF INTERVENTIONS

This section describes the CECI's intervention in the PRO HABITAT program.

Microlocalization

CECI assessed how land was certified as "safe to occupy" by the National Network for Risk Evaluation (CONRED). The same agency was also charged with risk assessment for the lands scheduled for victim relocation. And, it also specified infrastructure improvements and which services would be proper for the incoming population. One of the problems CECI discovered was that this appeared as a "conflict of interest." The agency was responsible for both land certification and selection of the families eligible for relocation. Beneficiaries were selected based on degrees of poverty. But that "changed." Some suspect that local authorities were moved to alter the list of beneficiaries in order to secure votes for the next election.

Another problem was that the designated lands suddenly "appreciated" in value. This spike was due to the opportunistic demand – a cynical response to the situation. This was an unanticipated abuse. The budget of the project could not possibly have made up for this "inflation." Additionally, title search procedures required for land transfer were complicated and delays were created, which slowed down the disbursement of subsidies – by the time the property was cleared, the government had withdrawn access to the funds.

Urbanization

It is important to mention that some land identified for the relocation was quite distant from existing communities and had to be developed de novo. Urban planning costs money and, so, it is often not included in the budget.

Urban planning is crucial to assuring that the infrastructure has sufficient capacity to carry a given population. In the absence of planning, development proceeds in a haphazard fashion, increasing the dangers of informal construction and excess population. CECI managed to ensure an efficient collaboration with the key partners to achieve the following:

o Secretaría de Asuntos Agrarios (SAA) – selected and bought the land
o Secretaría Ejecutiva de la Coordinadora Nacional (SE CONRED) – produced a risk management plan
o Secretaría de Coordinación Ejecutiva de la Presidencia (SCEP), Fondo Nacional para la Paz (FONAPAZ), and Unidad de Construcción de Edificios del Estado (UCEE) – produced a budget for infrastructure
o Oficinas Municipal de Planificación (OMP) – informed about the municipal development process

Agreements made by one ruling party are voided by the incoming ruling party. This kind of shake up is common in Central America. The victory of a political party drives changes for all the state employees.

Another characteristic of the country is the privatization of the urban services. Poor families that were relocated, as an extension of an existing community, were reported to have been cut from basic services. Investigations revealed that these cuts were due to the inability of the incoming Mayan families's to pay the high costs of these basic services.

Once the new urban zone was established, a water sanitation committee was appointed and then trained to calculate the rates for each family and to operate, manage, and maintain the infrastructure.

Housing construction

Housing construction was financed by two subsidies assigned to each family. The first subsidy was provided and administered by the national government (the Guatemalan National Fund for Housing – FOGUAVI) and the second was funded by the PRO HABITAT project and administered by CECI.

The first step was to define the design of the housing based on sustainability and other criteria such as quality, economy, and availability of supplies near the area of intervention. Floor plans were adapted to familiar patterns. Three house models were designated as "disaster resistant." Clearly, infrastructure must be completed before the houses are built. The construction companies were selected through the usual call for proposals. Some contractors were unable to complete their work due to cash flow difficulties. So, going forward, CECI will ensure their contractors against delays and interrupted contracts.

Support to the production of goods and services

This component is the most important in restoring the economic viability of the beneficiary's family. This intervention will allow them to generate income. Vocational (re)training supports the beneficiary in accessing the same or other kinds work.

The first step of this component offers immediate sources of revenue for required activities such as contracting specialized or unspecialized workers for construction of the house, making provisions of basic services, and performing some specific tasks for risk mitigation – a subproject financed by the project. The second step consists of implementing a technical training program at the local level to get stable employment.

The main subjects covered under the project were community organization, administration and management of cooperatives, agricultural practices, and learning on new trades. The project also had a fund for incubating small enterprises that had been identified by a local NGO. It is also important to create partnerships with local organizations in order to support the new enterprise's access to capital, to market, and to technical assistance. Sustainability of the new small enterprises can be assured to live on after the project. The development of human capital through training is CECI's key strategy for the reintegration of the population back to post-traumatic life. The diagnostics acted to identify the interests of the population regarding future production activities and the best training programs that could be implemented to bring about change. The acquisition of knowledge through capacity building and training programs spanned agricultural production, including nutrition, food security, and income generation; marketing and trading of products; quotidian administration; management; and organizational processes. The technical assistance from partners guaranteed quality standards and that the market requirements would be accurate.

The lesson learned from this component was that when the beneficiaries were involved in the construction of their new houses, they were very distracted. Their attention and time were too stretched, and so it was just too difficult for them to be in a long process of intensive training at the same time they were involved in capacity building. It is important for the local organization to be flexible and adapt itself to the limitations of the beneficiaries. A small fund was allocated for the training program for an experimental initiative – a pilot plot was dedicated to increase experimental production of flowers and new produce.

CECI learned that a lack of commitment on the part of the communities resulted in some of them selling the dedicated land to a third party and pocketing the profit. That is why it is also crucial to create a sense of solidarity and trust among the people. Inevitably, newcomers will make it more difficult to continue to organize a collective experience.

Risk management

Some of the members of the communities trained on CBDRM have created a commission that was incorporated to the CONRED to be further accredited by a departmental risk reduction commission. Presentations were very helpful in getting them to visualize the risk management and planning processes.

The identification of risks and prioritized measures for risk mitigation were implemented to ensure the best development for the relocated communities. Scarce national resources make it difficult to maintain the national network on disaster preparedness without regular training. CECI learned that it is important to budget for a refresher training every year. The project supported a radio campaign on awareness, but the funding for this program has not been ensured for the future. All the communities were left with some plans to reduce their vulnerabilities.

Organizational assistance

This component was necessary for the resettled communities to embody their own social organization and to transition the families into their new territory. Developing a community's spirit is beyond the scope of CECI's work. In the beginning, community leaders had a feint sense of their organizational and administrative needs. It was necessary for the community leaders to be integrated into an extant municipality's offices and institutions. CECI has developed a manual and tools to support political integration.

CONCLUSION

The real key to CECI's success is involving local communities in every step of the project. And, CECI has demonstrated that it is a good practice to incorporate risk mitigation into economic development projects and it is likewise important to include an economic component in any reconstruction project. Based on CECI's experience in Guatemala, we recommend that every investment by an international agency contain a risk mitigation component. Such a step protects investments from both malfeasance and mistakes. A good reconstruction project is one that includes an economic development component and helps communities to escape from cycle of poverty.

REFERENCE

CECI (Center for International Studies and Cooperation). (2010). *Informe de sistematización, 2010* (88 pp.). Guatemala City, Guatemala: CECI.

CHAPTER 16

ELEMENTS FOR A SUSTAINABLE COMMUNITY EARLY WARNING SYSTEM IN CARTAGO CITY, COSTA RICA

Tsuneki Hori and Rajib Shaw

INTRODUCTION

Cartago City is located in the central valley of Costa Rica. Situated at the southern foot of the Irazu volcano and characterized by rugged mountainous topography, the city in general is exposed to multiple natural hazards including floods, volcanic eruption, and pyroclastic flows. Indeed, the city has experienced catastrophes in 1724, 1861, 1891, 1928, and 1951. The most recent one was a combination of pyroclastic flows and several floods in 1963–1964. This catastrophe caused US$3.5 million of economic damage as well as 20 deaths (ICE, 1966).

The project titled "Strengthening Local Structures and Early Warning Systems (Reforzamientos de Estructuras Locales y Sistemas de Alerta Temprana: RELSAT)" was implemented in Cartago City during 1999–2001. The objective of this project was to establish efficient community early warning systems and increase the community's capability to reduce local flood risk. The target beneficiary of this project was one of the poorest areas

Community-Based Disaster Risk Reduction
Community, Environment and Disaster Risk Management, Volume 10, 313–330
Copyright © 2012 by Emerald Group Publishing Limited
All rights of reproduction in any form reserved
ISSN: 2040-7262/doi:10.1108/S2040-7262(2012)0000010022

of the nation, Dique de Taras (the Dique area), where residence is prohibited by national law. Nonetheless, there are four illegal communities (50–100 families in each) in this area, where most houses are self-constructed, look humble, and have limited access to basic human needs.

RELSAT is a type of project related to Community Early Warning System (CEWS) operation, or community-based disaster preparedness actions. CEWS is defined by the United Nations International Strategy for Disaster Reduction (UN/ISDR) as: "to empower individuals and communities threatened by hazards to act in sufficient time and in an appropriate manner to reduce the possibility of personal injury, loss of life and damage to property and the environment" (UN/ISDR, 2006). This community participative approach for early warning is inexpensive and requires little technical expertise (Dangles et al., 2010; OAS, 2010). As the UN/ISDR (2010) reported, CEWS has been implemented in many countries around the world, especially for poor rural communities in developing countries.

Sustainability is an important key element and challenge for establishing early warning systems (Sagala & Okada, 2007). However, in general, there is very little knowledge regarding the long-term outcomes of these community-based disaster preparedness activities (Allen, 2006). Against these challenges, the communities in Cartago City have effectively used the CEWS provided by RELSAT, even 10 years after the project implementation.

The objective of this study is to identify elements for sustainable CEWS operations through community ownership in Cartago City. In doing so, the study has conducted literature reviews, interviews with community people participating in RELSAT, and discussions with the local Red Cross and the national authority on disaster risk management (DRM) in Costa Rica. Field interviews and discussions were conducted three times: August 25–31, 2010; November 10–15, 2010; and February 15–19, 2011.

The chapter is organized into five sections. The second section describes the profile of RELSAT and its results at the moment of project implementation. The third section reviews the status of the CEWS operation 10 years after RELSAT implementation and identifies factors affecting the maintenance of CEWS. The fourth section discusses the probable elements for sustainable CEWS through community ownership, and the fifth section briefly concludes with implications for project designers or planners at the national and local government, NGOs, and donor agencies toward sustainable community-based disaster risk preparedness.

PROFILE OF THE PROJECT RELSAT

General Background of the Dique Area

Following the 1963–1964 catastrophic event in Cartago, the ministry of public works built a 12 km dike along the Reventado River in 1965 in order to mitigate the city's flood risk. The same ministry approved Law No. 3459 in 1964: Creation of the National Reserve area of Reventado River (Creación de la Reserva Nacional del Río Reventado, in Spanish language). Articles 3 and 4 of this law state that any construction for residence, commercial, and industrial use upon and inside the dike is prohibited. The area is now called the Dique area.

Nonetheless, poor families gradually entered this area and built their homes illegally in the 1970s. The first illegal community built in this area was called Maria Auxiliadora. In the 1980s and 1990s three other communities, Linda Vista, Barrio Nuevo, and Miraflores, also settled (Fig. 1). Chinchilla (2003) reports that residents in this area primarily include illegal immigrants from neighboring countries.

Project Inception

Project RELSAT was financed by the Deutsche Gesellschaft fur Technische Zusammenarbeit (GTZ), implemented in six Central American countries

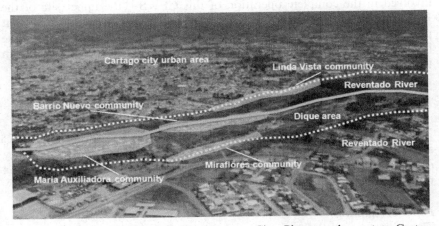

Fig. 1. Image of the Dique Area and Cartago City. Photograph courtesy Cartago Municipality.

including Costa Rica. Regional coordination was performed by the Coordination Center for the Prevention of Natural Disasters in Central America (CEPREDENAC), a regional official DRM organization. The National Risk Prevention and Emergency Management Commission (Comisió Nacional de Emergencias, CNE) took responsibility for the project execution in Cartago.

The CNE began to design this project in 1997. Prior to project area selection, the CNE conducted a preliminary study of local hazard and vulnerability conditions for the entire country. After the study, it identified the Dique area as one of the areas with the highest disaster risk, because of multiple hazardous conditions as well as physical and social vulnerability related to illegalities. It conducted the first community workshop in the Dique area in 1998 with 20 local participants. It explained the purpose of RELSAT and the participants finally agreed upon flood risk reduction as a project target, despite the fact that their primary requirement was poverty reduction.

Project Design

Fig. 2A displays the overall design of the CEWS operation. RELSAT served as a pilot CEWS project for future implementation in other areas by the CNE or other national and local public entities. Therefore, community involvement of RELSAT was limited to only two beneficiary communities, Miraflores and Barrio Nuevo, in the Dique area. The other two areas are involved in the complete operation of this CEWS – the upper site of the Reventado River, which covers Tierra Blanca and Piedra Grande areas that perform flood monitoring and provide the flood alert information to the lower site. The Dique area, a beneficiary site, receives alert information from the upper site and organizes self-preparation for eventual flood events.

Project Activity and Result

RELSAT includes three functions: flood hazard monitoring at the upper site; alert communication between the upper and lower sites; and community organization for eventual flood events at the lower site. This section reviews results of the project from the time it was implemented.

Flood Monitoring

The project installed a transparent plastic pluviometer (Fig. 3A) at two sites of the upper river basin, Tierra Blanca and Piedra Grande. This equipment

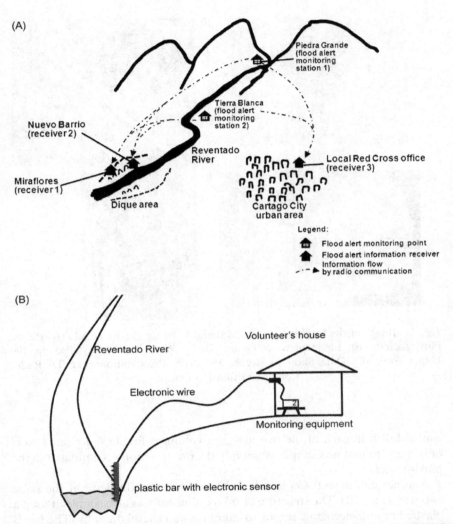

Fig. 2. Image of the RELSAT Functions: (A) Overall Designs for the CEWS Operation and (B) Function to Gauge Real-Time River Water Level at the Upper Site.

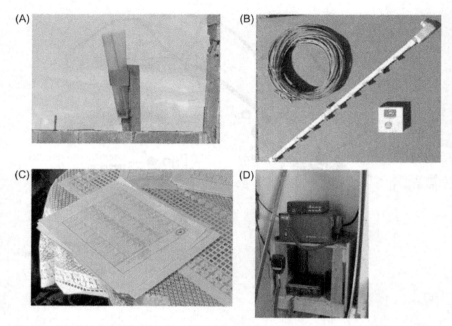

Fig. 3. Image of the Equipments and Material Used for the RELSAT: (A) Plastic Pluviometer; (B) Equipment to Gauge River Water Level Installed in the Upper Area; (C) Data Sheet to Record the Daily Precipitation; and (D) Radio Communication Equipment.

was installed in each of the two assigned volunteer families' houses. Usage of this equipment was simple: observing the precipitation accumulated in the pluviometer.

Another equipment was installed to gauge river water level at the same two sites (Fig. 3B). The structure of this equipment was also simple: it used a plastic bar and electronic sensor to calibrate water level digitally. The bar is installed in the river and connected with electronic wires to each volunteer family's premises (Fig. 2B). These families perform real-time water-level monitoring from 0 (low) to 8 (high). Each level on the bar marks 20 cm height. For example, level 1 implies the river water level is 20 cm higher than the normal level, and level 4 indicates 80 cm higher.

The two volunteer families accepted the responsibility for flood hazard monitoring at the first workshop. After that, the CNE organized a one-day seminar on the use of the equipment. The two volunteer families learned to use this equipment and agreed to monitor (i) river water level every day at 6 am and during intense rainfall, and (ii) precipitation accumulation in the pluviometer three times every day (6 am, 12 pm, and 6 pm). The CNE formatted a data sheet to record the daily precipitation accumulation data (Fig. 3C).

Flood Alert
The project provided radio communication equipment for flood alerts from the upper to the lower sites (Fig. 3D). This equipment was installed at five nodes: at the residence of one family each in Tierra Blanca and Piedra Grande at the upper site (the same two volunteer families responsible for flood hazard monitoring); at the residence of one family each in Miraflores and Barrio Nuevo at the lower site (the Dique area); and at the local Red Cross office in Cartago. The radio communication equipment works by both electric power and batteries. Since the Dique area has limited electric power supply, the project also provided batteries for their emergency use.

The two families responsible for the use of radio communication equipment at the lower site also volunteered at the first workshop. The CNE organized a one-day seminar at the local Red Cross office in March 1999 to provide instructions regarding its usage. The four families responsible for flood alert communication and a member of the local Red Cross participated in the seminar and learned the basic protocol for flood alert communication. The protocol is as follows. During intense rainfall, when at least one of the two families at the upper site observes precipitation greater than 30 mm within 30 minutes, or when a gauge shows a level of 5 (1.0 m higher than normal) or higher, they use the radio communication equipment to send a flood alert to the two assigned families at the lower site and to the local Red Cross office.

Community Organization
The CNE organized a total of 12 workshops to (i) sensitize community for proactive response in flood hazard events, (ii) create community organizations for flood preparedness, and (iii) develop a community contingency plan to draw evacuation routes to assigned shelters (primary schools in neighboring communities). The CNE also conducted two drills for self-organized evacuation in flood events in each lower site community, Miraflores and Barrio Nuevo. The local Red Cross and the municipality of Cartago also observed these activities. Previously, the two beneficiary communities in Dique area had no form of community organization.

Thus, the families in Miraflores and Barrio Nuevo who were assigned to be flood radio alert receivers subsequently became community leaders.

Follow-up after Project Implementation

The RELSAT project began its implementation in January 1999 and ended in December 2001. Since then, neither the CNE nor other institutions have provided any official follow-up or maintenance activities. The CNE periodically (every six months) visits the two families at the upper site to collect datasheets recording the daily precipitation observed. Additionally, the CNE occasionally meets (every two or three years, usually on weekends) on a voluntary basis with community leaders in Miraflores and Barrio Nuevo to check if the CEWS installed in this area functions effectively.

FUNCTIONING OF THE CEWS AFTER 10 YEARS

This section reviews the status of CEWS maintenance (both hard and soft components) 10 years after the project implementation and identifies outcomes and lessons.

Status of Project Legacy

The complete status of the project's legacy (hardware and soft component) is summarized in Table 1. A man in the family at Tierra Blanca has faithfully continued his assigned daily flood monitoring duty even after the project's completion. He has observed the precipitation accumulation in the pluviometer three times a day at the assigned hours and the river water level at 6 am every day since March 1999. The other family in Piedra Grande, however, discontinued their duty in late 2006. The equipment of the river water level gauge and radio communication became faulty and ceased to operate and they discontinued their use, thus subsequently discontinuing their flood-monitoring duties. The family at Barrio Nuevo also discontinued its usage in 2008. The radio communication equipment installed in the family at Tierra Blanca, Miraflores, and local Red Cross office has been maintained effectively; thus, flood alert communications are also effective only among these three nodes.

Table 1. Status of the Project Legacy after 10 Years.

	Piedra Grande	Tierra Blanca	Miraflores	Barrio Nuevo	Local Red Cross
Flood monitoring	Discontinued	Ineffective	–	–	–
Maintenance of radio communication equipment	Discontinued	Ineffective	Ineffective	Discontinued	Ineffective
Community organization for flood preparedness	–	–	Ineffective	Discontinued	–

The Miraflores community organization is effective. When the community leader in Miraflores receives alert information from Tierra Blanca, she informs the approximately 50 other families in the community, recommends evacuation, and requests support from the local Red Cross office. She cannot contact all 50 families in the community alone, and therefore asks neighbors to spread the word.

Outcomes

This study identifies three types of outcomes 10 years after the project's implementation. The first is the improvement in proactive disaster preparedness in this area. Indeed, no major floods, mudflows, or avalanches have occurred in the study area since the commencement of RELSAT. Nevertheless, successful partial use of CEWS has been observed. For example, in October 2006, the man in the volunteer family at Tierra Blanca observed the river water reaching level 7, and informed Miraflores and Barrio Nuevo as well as the local Red Cross. Two leaders have responded, informed neighbors, organized and collaborated with each other to close a bridge across the Reventado River on a road in the Dique area (this action is not considered an original project design). Both leaders guided families in their communities to evacuate, and requested from the local Red Cross by radio for further support of evacuation. Hours later, Red Cross officials arrived and closed the bridge, guided vehicles to the detour, and provided support for refugees from the Dique area. This is just an experience of CEWS function, and indeed the man in Tierra Blanca reports flood alert to the Dique area and local Red Cross, including the above experience, one to three times a year.

The second is collaborating to establish community solidarity. The Miraflores community leader uses radio communication equipment in a variety of ways, including requesting local Red Cross support for other than flood disaster preparedness. For example, in May 2010, her neighbor came and said that the floor of his house was cracked and he feared ground erosion. She radioed for support from the local Red Cross. A few days later, the local Red Cross staff visited his residence and made a temporary repair. Another example occurred in October 2010, when an elderly woman suddenly fell sick, and the family came to the community leader asking her to call an ambulance. The community leader radioed the local Red Cross, and the ambulance arrived an hour later. The local Red Cross stated that they receive such requests from Linda Vista three to five times a year. The Miraflores community leader said that direct communication with the local Red Cross makes the entire community feel safer. Miraflores is located in the illegal Dique area and so receives little social benefit or support from the local and national government. The community leader of Miraflores stated that people in this community feel abandoned by the city, but the community connects directly to the local Red Cross by radio, and its responses are so prompt that people believe they can rely on both the radio communication facility and the local Red Cross. According to the community leaders, such integrative force has established more community solidarity over time.

The third is regarding collaboration for raising residents' awareness of natural phenomena, which is specifically seen in Tierra Blanca. In general, community leaders and city planners tend to underestimate or deny risk (Nathan, 2008). This problem is caused often a lack of local risk based on experience (Burningham et al., 2008). Despite these reports in general, the man in the family at Tierra Blanca has continued the precipitation observation and data recording three times a day since March 1999. This continuous work makes him more sensitive to climate variability or change. He said that he has noticed signs of climate variability or climate change since 2005. Although the accrued data indicates that the annual average precipitation has been nearly the same since 1999, he has noticed certain changes from the details of the data: since 2005, the frequency of intense rainfall in a short duration (less than one hour) has been increasing during the rainy season, and the duration of the dry season is increasing. He owns a small farm and produces potatoes and onions. Based on what he has learned from his daily precipitation observation, he is now planning to upgrade to other species of potato breed for adaptation to frequent intense rainfall.

Lessons

The volunteer families at Piedra Grande and Barrio Nuevo had discarded their CEWS duty five to seven years after the project implementation. This experience offers lessons related to the difficulty of continuing each actor's assigned CEWS responsibility at voluntary base for a longer period. The elderly woman in Piedra Grande who discontinued flood monitoring duty since late 2006 said that she wanted to continue helping others in the city through her assigned duty. However, because the river water level gauge broke, as did the radio communication equipment, she could not continue. She said that she continues to hope that the CNE people will visit her house and repair both pieces of equipment, and that she feels honored to communicate directly with representatives of the national authority and to collaborate in the CEWS initiative, a "big national" project for her. She also said that radio communication helped her to know and communicate with people in other communities at the lower site, because Piedra Grande is located far from there and both sites' residents have no other means of knowing each other.

The woman of the family in Barrio Nuevo also stated that a technical problem forced her to discontinue using the radio communication equipment. She said that she wants to continue using it and collaborate in the CEWS initiative, and that the radio communication equipment was helpful in communicating with other people in Miraflores or the volunteer family in Tierra Blanca, not only for flood alerts but also for casual chats. Her child also liked to communicate via the radio. She feels a sense of worth or "power" from representing the community for requesting local Red Cross support and possessing the radio communication equipment, because neighbors rely on her and come to discuss their daily problems. She explained that the problem with the radio communication equipment seems to be just the battery or power source, so she is waiting for the CNE staff to repair it. According to her, the community would feel abandoned if the CNE does not visit periodically.

These two examples offer the following lessons for sustainable community managed CEWS: (i) equipment failure is the primary reason that volunteers discontinue their CEWS responsibilities; (ii) volunteers find CEWS involvement fulfilling – both families who discontinued their CEWS activity remain interested in continuing their CEWS responsibilities if the equipment is repaired; (iii) the radio communication equipment serves additional purposes, such as general communication with other communities, or calling for local Red Cross support; and (iv) the CNE represents an important presence for these communities, in that people feel honored to participate in the CEWS initiative and eagerly anticipate CNE visits (Fig. 4).

DISCUSSION: ELEMENTS FOR SUSTAINABLE CEWS

Residing in the Dique area is illegal. The people in the area suffer from poverty and lack basic services including lifelines and other social services. This social vulnerability is one of the reasons that CNE selected this area as a RELSAT beneficiary.

The CEWS projects involve complex tasks to implement an end-to-end, people-centered early warning system (Spahn, Hoppe, Vidiarina, & Usdianto, 2010). The primary weakness of community-based approaches lies in the relative lack of resources and decision-making authority such as legislative and regulatory power among the local participants (Lavell, 1994). Adrian et al. (2010) state that the success of local initiatives requires a political climate that understands and supports community participation.

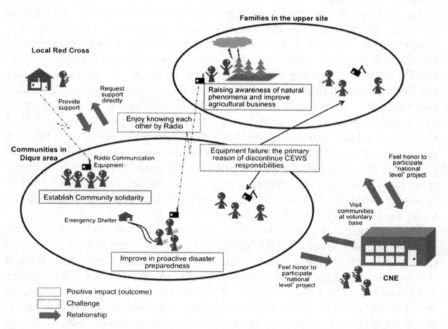

Fig. 4. Outcomes and Lessons for Sustainable Community Managed CEWS.

Project duration is another consideration. The RELSAT execution period in this study area was short (two years), and no major follow-up activity has been performed after the project completion, other than the occasional CNE visits to the area on a voluntary basis just to monitor the CEWS operations.

Despite the local insufficient resources, and the absence of any regulatory power and nonsupportive political climate because of the area's illegality and poverty, the CEWS function here remains operational insofar as technologically possible, although it is not as originally designed. The volunteer family in Tierra Blanca has continued to perform daily flood observation for more than 10 years; the family in Miraflores still receives alert information and organizes flood preparedness, and the local Red Cross supports these activities.

Why have the people in this poverty area continued supporting the CEWS initiative for more than 10 years? What are the elements for sustainable community-based disaster preparedness? This section discusses four probable elements to respond to these questions.

Usage of CEWS Equipments in the Community's Daily Life

The first element for sustainable CEWS may be the use of CEWS equipments by communities in their daily life. This is seen in the use of the radio communication equipment for purposes other than emergency situations: although the equipment was originally intended for flood alerts, the community uses it for other purposes as well. The Miraflores community leader uses it to request a support from the local Red Cross for other than flood alerts too. She stated that radio communication is more useful than telephones (she has a prepaid mobile phone) for emergency use, because of direct calls made to the local Red Cross office free of charge. She feels privileged to be able to help community members through radio communication. This radio communication's capability has opened the door to establishing community solidarity in Miraflores. The Barrio Nuevo community leader also feels a sense of "power" in possessing the radio equipment because neighbors rely on her. She regrets having to discontinue its usage because of its failure.

As the OAS (2010) states in general, radio communication equipment for CEWS can serve a variety of purposes, such as health emergencies, announcing important municipal meetings, and transmitting other important community-related messages. This concept corresponds with the experience in this case study, and explains the volunteers' sense of benefits and privilege in possessing the equipment. This feeling may be one of the major factors in their continued use of it for more than 10 years.

The man in the Tierra Blanca family provides another good example of an auxiliary use of the CEWS equipment. He uses precipitation observation including for his own agriculture business. Although observing precipitation alone is quite simple – just watching and recording the water level in the pluviometer – it takes real dedication to perform this daily duty for more than 12 years. Originally, he began this observation as a volunteer only for flood monitoring and alerts, but, after about five years, he became aware of climate change and its signs. He owns a small farm and is now planning to upgrade to species of potato breed for adaptability to climate change. This link between precipitation observations, originally for flood alert monitoring, and his business benefit of crop production improvement may be another reason for his faithful fulfillment of his CEWS duty in a sustainable manner.

Feelings of Gratitude and Loyalty

The study demonstrates that all four direct participants in CEWS operations (the man in Tierra Blanca, the elderly woman in Piedra Grande, and community leaders in Miraflores and Barrio Nuevo) have a general sense of honor in participating national authorities' initiative. For example, the elderly woman in Piedra Grande said that she feels honored to participate in the CNE's national "big project." The man in Tierra Blanca said that it is an honor for him to participate in the CNE project implemented directly by national authority. Such specific element of people's feelings of loyalty to the project motivated their "volunteer spirit" for a long period, and enabled continued CEWS activity for more than 10 years.

The CNE implemented directly all RELSAT activities in Cartago City with no third-party involvement, such as local consultants, NGOs, or community organizations. After RELSAT's implementation, the CNE staff occasionally visits the project area on a voluntary basis to monitor CEWS operations, but not to further support it. However, from the community's perspective, these visits provide good opportunities to discuss their daily problems. The woman in Miraflores said she always looks forward to meet the CNE people, not only to talk about CEWS but also to discuss all kinds of problems in the community. The woman in Barrio Nuevo said that she feels abandoned if the CNE does not come for a while. Both the elderly woman in Piedra Grande and the community leader in Barrio Nuevo said that they are waiting for the CNE to repair the equipment. Over time, the

CNE's direct project engagement and their ongoing voluntary visits to the project area may have made community residents trustful and respectful of this national authority, and that feeling may continue to positively influence the volunteers' sense of honor from their participation in CEWS activity.

The woman in Miraflores said that not much support from the government is received or expected because of the community's illegal status. The community was established in the 1970s and the number of inhabitants has grown, with new groups never disintegrated for social development despite problems such as increased drug trafficking, alcoholism, and domestic violence. Despite this difficult social environment, the CNE has supported the community through RELSAT project. This history stimulates additional feelings of gratitude and faithfulness in performing their CEWS responsibilities. Eventually, these feelings of trust, respect, honor, gratitude, and faithfulness toward the project initiator may engender the loyalty necessary for participating in CEWS for a long period.

Equipment Durability and User-friendliness

Equipment durability is clearly another key element for a sustainable CEWS. When communities can take advantage of CEWS resources in their daily life and develop a feeling of gratitude and faithfulness toward participating in the national authority's initiative, once the equipment fails to operate, they cannot continue the CEWS initiative. Indeed, those who have ceased performing their CEWS responsibilities at Piedra Grande and Barrio Nuevo have directly attributed their behavior to equipment failure, and both would prefer to continue collaborating with CEWS.

The user-friendliness of equipment operation may be another key element for sustainable CEWS activity. Those involved in radio communication were given training at only a one-day seminar at the beginning of the project, which was sufficient for its operation. Even a child of the family in Barrio Nuevo could operate the radio. This indicates that such simple and user-friendly equipment is best for CEWS projects as long as it can be maintained in working order.

Climate Variability and Change

The final element identified here for sustaining CEWS may be the participants' awareness of climate variability and change for their own purposes. This is observed in the example of the man in Tierra Blanca, who developed a fine sense of climate variability and change through his daily precipitation observation duty. Climate change is only one of the many underlying vulnerability factors (Glantz, 1994; Mercer, 2010), but it is a significant factor for agriculturists. Farmers use many specific coping and adaptation strategies to respond to climate change (Thomas, Twyman, Osbahr, & Hewitson, 2007), so his personal use of the detailed CEWS data from his observations to upgrade the species of potatoes he grows to one that was more adaptable to increased intense rainfall probability. This may have increased his motivation to continue his CEWS duties for more than 10 years.

CONCLUSION

An overriding goal of community-based disaster preparedness is to "empower" local people by supporting them in becoming increasingly self-reliant (Christie & Hanlon, 2000; Uphoff, 1991). The outcomes identified in this study area coincide with this concept, and support the conclusion that CEWS empower illegal immigrant communities in (i) improving on proactive disaster preparedness, (ii) establishing community solidarity, and (iii) raising awareness of natural phenomena. In addition to these findings, the study identifies four elements for sustainable CEWS operations through community ownership. These include the following implications of the roles of stakeholders or project planners for sustainable community-based disaster risk preparedness: (i) provide components of CEWS not only for flood preparedness but also to bring additional advantages to communities in their daily life. This seems key to raising communities' sense of ownership for sustainable CEWS. Radio communication equipment and precipitation observation gauges for agriculturalists are good examples of such multipurpose items; (ii) establish direct trust and respect between the project-executing organization and the beneficiary community. This seems to be the foundation of community participants' growing feelings of gratitude and loyalty toward that authority so that this motivates their activities under their own initiative for sustainable CEWS; (iii) select durable and user-friendly equipment. This directly affects the community's ability to continue their duties. Ongoing support for equipment maintenance would also be effective; and (iv) provide processes for increasing awareness of climate variability and change. The man in Tierra Blanca who continues to observe daily precipitation exemplifies this principle. Awareness of climate variability and change may motivate volunteers to continue to monitor climate phenomena and related risks, and to adapt the project's resources for agricultural applications for a long period. This action of the man in Tierra Blanca seems to be a good case of what Prabhakar, Srinivasan, & Shaw (2009) states, that there is a need to move from the attitude of considering local level players as "implementers" to "innovators."

The study has several limitations and implications for further research. It did not interview the people who did not participate actively in RELSAT, such as community members in Maria Auxiliadora and Linda Vista, the municipality of Cartago, or other local institutions and organizations. This omission limited the ability to verify the results of the study with the comments of external parties. Although the study identified four elements for sustainable CEWS, this case study covers only 10 years from the project's implementation; thus, a follow-up is needed to monitor CEWS's operation for a longer period. Regarding climate change adaptation in general, the project's initial approach to adaptation was dominated by top-down thinking (van Aalst, Terry Cannon, & Burton, 2008), and traditional top-down decision-making process become inadequate (Rojas Blanco, 2006). The case of the man in Tierra Blanca, who continued daily precipitation observation for more than 12 years and his adapting its data for his own agricultural production strategy seems to merit further analysis in the context of the integration of community-based disaster risk management and bottom-up climate change adaptation.

ACKNOWLEDGMENTS

We are grateful to Mr. Douglas Salgado, the director of the Department of Information Management, CNE, and Professor David Smith, director of the Disaster Risk Reduction Program at the National University in Costa Rica, who provided helpful technical and logistical support for the field interviews, and worthy comments that enabled to improve the study.

REFERENCES

Adrian, A., et al. (2010). Evaluation of Golestan province's early warning system for flash floods, Iran, 2006–7. *International Journal of Biometeorology, 53*, 247–254.

Allen, K. M. (2006). Community-based disaster preparedness and climate adaptation: Local capacity building in the Philippines. *Disasters, 30*(I), 81–101.

Burningham, K., et al. (2008). 'It'll never happen to me': Understanding public awareness of local flood risk. *Disasters, 32*(2), 216–238.

Chinchilla, R. M. (2003). *Estudio de Caso los Diques Tara, Cartago [Case study on the dykes in Tara, Cartago]*. San Jose, Costa Rica: University of Costa Rica.

Christie, F., & Hanlon, J. (2000). *African issues: Mozanbique and the Great Flood of 2000*. Bloomington, IN: The African International Institute in association with James Currey, Oxford, and Indiana University Press.

Dangles, O., Carpio, F. C., Villares, M., Yumisaca, F., Liger, B., Rebaudo, F., & Silvain, J. F. (2010). Community-based participatory research helps farmers and scientists to manage invasive pests in the Ecuadorian Andes. *AMBIO, 39*, 325–335.

Glantz, M. H. (1994). Creeping environmental problems. *The World & I, 6*, 218–225.

ICE (Instituto Costarricense de Electricidad). (1966). *Estudio evaluacion del dano por el desastre ocurrido en la provincia de Cartago en 1994 [Disaster damage assessment occurred in the province of Cartago 1994]*. San Jose, Costa Rica.

Lavell, A. (1994). Prevention and mitigation of disasters in Central America: Vulnerability to disasters at the local level. In A. Varley (Ed.), *Disasters, development and environment* (pp. 49–63). Chichester: Wiley.

Mercer, J. (2010). Disaster risk reduction or climate change adaptation: Are we reinventing the wheel? *Journal of International Development, 22*, 247–264.

Nathan, F. (2008). Risk perception, risk management and vulnerability to landslides in the hill slopes in the city of La Paz, Bolivia. A preliminary statement. *Disasters, 32*(3), 337–357.

OAS (Organization of American States). (2010). *Community-centered flood early warning systems in the Central American Isthmus and the Dominican Republic*. Washington, DC: OAS.

Prabhakar, S. V. R. K., Srinivasan, A., & Shaw, R. (2009). Climate change and local level disaster risk reduction planning: Need, opportunities and challenges. *Mitigation and Adaptation Strategies for Global Change, 14*, 7–33.

Rojas Blanco, A. (2006). Local initiatives and adaptation to climate change. *Disasters, 30*(1), 140–147.

Sagala, S., & Okada, N. (2007). Managing early warning systems for tsunami prone communites: Preliminary analysis of the needs for participatory approach (PRA). *Annuals of Disaster Prevention Research Institute*, Kyoto University, No. 50B, pp. 195–203.

Spahn, H., Hoppe, M., Vidiarina, H. D., & Usdianto, B. (2010). Experience from three years of local capacity development for tsunami early warning in Indonesia: Challenges, lessons and the way ahead. *Natural Hazards and Earth System Sciences, 10*, 1411–1429.

Thomas, D. S. G., Twyman, C., Osbahr, H., & Hewitson, B. (2007). Adaptation to climate change and variability: Farmer responses to intra-seasonal precipitation trends in South Africa. *Climatic Change, 83*(3), 301–321.

UN/ISDR (United Nations International Strategy for Disaster Reduction). (2006). Developing early warning systems: A checklist. Paper presented at the Third Early Warning Conference, 27–29. March, 2006, Bonn, Germany.

UN/ISDR. (2010). *Early warning practices can save many lives: Good practices and lessons learned* (67 pp.). Bonn, Germany: United Nations Secretariat of the International Strategy for Disaster Reduction (UN/ISDR).

Uphoff, N. (1991). Fitting projects to people. In M. Cernea (Ed.), *Putting people first: Sociological variables in rural development* (pp. 359–395). Oxford: Oxford University Press.

van Aalst, M. K., Terry Cannon, T., & Burton, I. (2008). Community level adaptation to climate change: The potential role of participatory community risk assessment. *Global Environmental Change, 18*, 165–179.

PART IV
AFRICAN EXPERIENCES

CHAPTER 17

AFRICAN EXPERIENCES IN COMMUNITY-BASED DISASTER RISK REDUCTION

Dewald van Niekerk and Christo Coetzee

INTRODUCTION

Stories of disasters in Africa conjure up images of the helpless hordes, in peril and in need of outside assistance. Most of the major disasters in Africa since the 1970s have a significant food crisis and famine component. These could be linked to failed states and complex emergencies such as inter-, intra-state conflict, and civil unrest. However, the domain of disaster risk reduction (DRR) in Africa has progressed significantly in the last decade. Moreover, we find that African states are celebrating democracy through third and fourth rounds of democratic elections. With the exception of a few, the "old men" of Africa are stepping down after years of Presidency and allowing the democratic wheel to turn. DRR in Africa has not been immune to these changes. Moreover, one finds exceptional examples of political will toward DRR and multi-sectoral approaches toward solving DRR problematic. One such approach that has enjoyed heightened attention is community-based actions and involvement.

This chapter will aim to provide the reader with insight into the current application of community-based disaster risk reduction (CBDRR) projects in a number of African countries. Various cultures and ethnic affiliations on

Community-Based Disaster Risk Reduction
Community, Environment and Disaster Risk Management, Volume 10, 333–349
Copyright © 2012 by Emerald Group Publishing Limited
ISSN: 2040-7262/doi:10.1108/S2040-7262(2012)0000010023

the continent have diverse views on "disasters" and the reasons for their occurrence. It therefore stands to reason that the application of CBDRR would also vary significantly. For the purpose of analysis, diverse case studies from various African countries were selected. Some of the communalities of these projects will be highlighted and some unique features will be discussed. Through this assessment, we hope that the reader will gain insight into CBDRR in Africa. This chapter will also emphasize the challenges in implementing and sustaining CBDRR projects. Attention will be given to the various role-players in CBDRR on the continent and their interactions will be discussed. We will also try to provide possible solution to some of the challenges identified by the research. Firstly, it is important to provide a broad sketch of CBDRR in Africa.

COMMUNITY-BASED DISASTER RISK REDUCTION: THE AFRICAN CONTEXT

The Hyogo Framework for Action (HFA) 2005–2015 (a global agreement emanating from the Kobe/Hyogo World Conference on Disaster Reduction in January 2005, and signed by over 180 countries) promotes the notion of engaging more meticulously with disaster risk and related processes by affirming: "Both communities and local authorities should be empowered to manage and reduce disaster risk by having access to the necessary information, resources and authority to implement actions for disaster risk reduction" (Pelling, 2007b, p. 374). The viewpoint of the HFA is that the communities should benefit from the decisions taken at a strategic level. It defies the point of disaster reduction, if good policy, legislation, and strategies regarding disaster risk are promulgated, yet it is not implemented with the aim of reducing communities' vulnerabilities. A strong community-based approach toward vulnerability reduction with local ownership of the risk assessment process is therefore necessary.

Moreover, African governments find themselves in a position where resources are becoming increasingly scarce, skills and technical abilities at local level are lacking, and budgetary constraints hinder development initiatives. The effect that such a situation has on the ability of a government to address issues of disaster risk is quite evident. Since the signing of the Yokohama Declaration at the turn of the 1980s, its mid-term review in 1995, as well as the HFA of 2005, governments, nongovernmental actors, and communities have come to realize the importance of locally based solution to natural and anthropogenic hazards and the vulnerabilities to them. Two global research projects undertaken by the Global Network of Civil Society Organisations for Disaster Reduction in 2009 and again in 2011 confirms and supports the above notion (Global Network of Civil Society

Table 1. Selected CBDRR Case Studies for Analysis.

Project Description	Community(ies)	Country
Drought cycle management	Samburu, Marsabit, and Moyale districts	Kenya
Multi-stakeholder flood management	Chikwawa district (5 villages)	Malawi
Local level monitoring of desertification	Originally 9 villages in Oshikoto region, than nationwide role out	Namibia
Institutionalizing disaster risk reduction in schools	Praia and Santo Domingos	Cape Verde
Introducing DRR into classrooms before mainstreaming it into school curricula	9 regions in Mali	Mali
Training teachers to help mainstream disaster risk reduction into school curricula	Sofala and Nampula provinces and Maputo City	Mozambique
Preparing state bodies and the public for inclusion of disaster risk reduction in school curricula	Freetown	Sierra Leone
Provinces and municipalities school contest on disaster risk reduction knowledge	Chris Hani District Municipality	South Africa
Disaster preparedness to reduce poverty in a drought-prone area	Kitui district	Kenya
Reducing flood risk through job creation	Sinoe, Grand Gedeh, Grand Bassa, Margibi, and Montserrado counties Buchanan and Kakata cities	Liberia
Drought mitigation	Phalombe district	Malawi
Women improving community livelihoods and resilience	Chididi village	Malawi
Protecting livelihoods with local warning and response systems	Nampula, Cabo Delgado, and Niassa province (Moma, Mecufi, Nacala, Lago, Aldeia Sassalane, and Metanculo districts)	Mozambique
Developing and managing water resources	Hermanus	South Africa
Urban flood mitigation	Lusaka	Zambia
Mangrove conservation	North-eastern coastal region	Madagascar
Adapting to climate change: Increases community resilience to drought	Sakai	Kenya

Organisations For Disaster Reduction [GNDR], 2009, 2011). Communities can no longer be seen as the helpless victims of disasters but should rather be regarded as local resources capable of determining their own development path. Such a development path must be rooted in disaster reduction if they wish to safeguard their future. It is thus a dual development/DRR focus, which should form the foundation of local action.

However, communities do not drive the current state of affairs relating to DRR in the first instance. As will be discussed later on, they are still "recipients" of help and not initiators of change. Within the African context of CBDRR, six actors can be identified: the government, nongovernmental or faith-based organizations, research and institutions of higher learning, international organizations, the private sector, and of course, communities. Each of these actors currently plays a role in the design, development, implementation, and sustainability of CBDRR projects. However, the interaction of these role-players is not always clear in all instances. The sections to follow will focus on the role of the mentioned actors in relation to CBDRR in Africa. Seventeen case studies relating to CBDRR were used (Table 1). The case studies were analyzed according to the role and activities of the various actors described above. Through this analysis, certain challenges and success were identified, and these will form the framework discussion of this chapter.

CHALLENGES IN IMPLEMENTING CBDRR IN AFRICA

A perusal of any of the current DRR strategies or policies present on the continent make the need for disaster risk governance and institutional frameworks abundantly clear (South Africa, 2005; United Nations International Strategy for Disaster Reduction [UN/ISDR], 2005; AU, 2004; Wisner et al., 2011). It is assumed, for DRR to be effective, one firstly needs some form of national organization and policy or legislative commitment, which will escalade disaster risk management to the various local sectors. These frameworks also put the onus on governments to ensure DRR but emphasize the strong need for community engagement and involvement. However, one only but wonders how such a top-down approach can be meaningful and successful in the light of the failure of so many other top-down approaches (see modernization theory, neoliberalism, and dependency theory to name but a few) to deliver on their promises. Linked to the above is the huge financial and human resources constrains

Table 2. Emerging Issue in CBDRR in Africa.

Emerging issues in community-based DRR: The African perspective
Lacking governance structures and institutional frameworks to implement community-based disaster risk reduction programs
Top-down approach to disaster risk reduction followed by many governments
Lack of political will for the disaster risk reduction activity
Lack of financial and human resources to carry out effective community-based DRR projects
Training and skill deficiencies of disaster management officials
Multiple-stakeholder involvement in community-based disaster risk reduction is lacking in some regions/countries

that African governments need to contend with. These are some of the challenges that will enjoy attention (also see Table 2 for a summary of key emerging issues with regard to community-based DRR in Africa).

Governance and Institutional Frameworks

According to priority area one of the HFA, governments and other stakeholders should ensure that DRR is a national and local priority with a strong institutional basis for implementation (UN/ISDR, 2005, p. 6; Wisner, 2003, p. 3). Although much has been achieved in the past decade, individual countries and respective regions in Africa are still struggling to put the required governance and institutional arrangements in place to facilitate an empowering environment for risk reduction at community level (AU/NEPAD, 2004, p. 9; Bräutigam & Knack, 2004, p. 259; Holloway, 2003, pp. 30–31; GNDR, 2009, p. 41; White et al., 2004, p. 52). A 2003 baseline study, commissioned by NEPAD (New Partnership For Africa's Development), to assess the status of DRR in Africa established that although countries were working toward developing policies, plans, and agencies for disaster risk management, these processes were being hampered by limited resources, skills, and capacities (Abebe, 2010, p. 239; AU/NEPAD, 2004, p. 5; Botha et al., 2011; Kim & Lee, 1998; Marianovic & Nimpuno, 2003, p. 198; GNDR, 2009, p. 20; 36). As a consequence of the limitations mentioned, the national DRR policies and institutional mechanisms of many African countries are not completely implemented or wholly ineffective (Ahrens & Rudolph, 2006, p. 209; AU/ NEPAD, 2004, p. 9). Findings from the internationally conducted "Views From the Frontline" study confirms this by indicating that Africa has made the least progress in achieving the outcomes of the HFA (GNDR, 2009, p. 14).

It should, however, be highlighted that significant progress has been made by African governments in establishing multi-stakeholder national DRR platforms. Although one must be realistic in terms of their effectiveness, it cannot be denied that many African governments are trying their best to adhere to the ideals of the HFA. It thus remains to be asked that despite the efforts put forth by government institutions, why are DRR efforts at local level still lacking? A possible answer is that the existing policies and institutional mechanisms do not create a facilitating environment for community or multi-stakeholder involvement in risk reduction projects (AU/NEPAD, 2004, p. 9; Meshack et al., 2007, p. 12; Pelling, 2007a, p. 6; GNDR, 2009, p. 41). Instead, they perpetuate a top-down approach to DRR. This prevailing approach to DRR is the next challenge to CBDRR in Africa.

The Exclusion of Communities: The Prevalence of a Top-Down Approach to DRR by African Governments

Disasters are complex situations that need the inputs from multiple role-players, to be addressed effectively (Abebe, 2010, p. 239; AU/NEPAD, 2004, p. 7; Pelling & Holloway, 2006, p. 4; GNDR, 2009, p. 21;). According to Ahrens and Rudolph (2006, p. 215), less-developed countries still emphasize a top-down approach to DRR. This statement is particularly true in the African context where communities remain passive recipients of disaster risk management activity outputs (AU/NEPAD, 2004, p. 7). At the root of this problem is the orientation by governments that they are the only entity that poses the necessary skills, technologies, and expertise to address the impact of disasters (Ahrens & Rudolph, 2006, p. 215; AU/NEPAD, 2004, p. 7). Contradictory, government institutions are rarely the custodians of entry to communities. This role is much more taken up by nongovernmental organizations (NGOs) or community leaders. The negative impact of this orientation has been that traditional coping strategies and the preservation of traditional knowledge and experience on disasters have not been incorporated into DRR plans (AU/NEPAD, 2004, p. 6). This lack of recognition in national risk reduction plans of traditional knowledge, skills, competencies, and resources on DRR issues not only hampers the implementation of CBDRR but also impacts on the quality of the overall disaster (risk) management plans (Ahrens & Rudolph, 2006, p. 210; Mercer, Kelman, Taranis, & Suchet-Pearson, 2010, p. 234; Pelling, 2007a).

The authors recognize the fact that in some instances, one would need a top-down approach as a catalyst for DRR action. Nonetheless, top-down implementation must be backed by direct community involvement. In Madagascar, CARE (an international humanitarian/development organization) has been working tirelessly with communities in implementing DRR projects. Many of these projects (such as mangrove conservation, cyclone-resistant seed granaries management, local materials cyclone-resistant house building, and water catchments infrastructure in dry areas) needed some form of top-down planning. Yet, their success is rooted in community involvement and ownership of the projects (Young, 2011). To this end, Young (2011) indicates that the CBDRR activities of CARE should be seen as two-fold: structural (creation, equipment, training, early warning, and simulations) and mitigation. The former needs a much more top-down approach, whereas the latter is purely community-based. Young (2011) is of the opinion that a good CBDRR intervention should combine both. "Without a strong structure, composed of local people who really understand what to do and why it is important *(initiated through a top-down approach)*; as soon as you (as an outsider) leave the village everything will be forgotten quickly. Mitigation activities are what you need to motivate the whole community around a small project, like a dam, a shelter, a granary, a new rice variety, or new techniques and must be identified and prioritised by the community itself." In the case of Madagascar, the numbers of DRR role-players are severely limited. One would rarely find local NGOs, and thus, direct government involvement sometimes becomes the only existing change agent. In contrary, an urban flood management project in the capital Lusaka in Zambia is a good example where local interests were mobilized to implement a CBDRR project. The community in partnership with a number of local and international NGOs lobbied the government to bring about change. In this instance, the community became the drivers of the process with significant support from government and the NGO sector. The multimillion dollar solution to the urban flood risk problems was made possible through the direct intervention of the Disaster Management and Mitigation Unit in the Office of the Vice-President. This example further underlines Young's (2011) perception of support to CBDRR projects as indicated above. One element identified in both of examples from Madagascar and Zambia is the need for adequate budget and skilled individuals to ensure the projects are brought to fruition.

Finances and Human Resources

Many African countries often lack the administrative, organizational, financial, and political capacity needed for effective DRR in the most vulnerable communities (Ahrens & Rudolph, 2006, p. 208; McLennan & Ngoma, 2004, p. 285; White et al., 2004, pp. 8–9, 23). Lacking human and financial resources affect all role-players currently involved in CBDDR in Africa. Due to this limitation in resources and capacities, governments have been struggling to implement the institutional frameworks (as mentioned above) that would facilitate CBDRR (AU/NEPAD, 2004, p. 5; Inter-governmental Authority on Development [IGAD], 2002, p. 12; GNDR, 2009, p. 20, 36; White et al., 2004, pp. 8–9). Some of the greatest reasons behind financial and subsequent human resources shortages at government level relates to the fact that African countries do not adequately budget for DRR initiatives (AU/NEPAD, 2004, p. 6; Holloway, 2003, pp. 30–31; IGAD, 2002, p. 14) and many remain overly reliant of outside aid (Gerhardt, 2010). This can be ascribed to the low priority accorded to DRR in national budget and the lack of proper and decentralized disaster reduction funding mechanisms (AU/NEPAD, 2004, p. 6; IGAD, 2002, p. 14; Visser & Van Niekerk, 2009). Although it is worth noting that the lack of resources is not limited to governments. Local and international NGOs working in Africa face endemic human and financial resource shortages, which adversely affect their ability to initiate CBDRR projects (UN/ISDR, 2007a, pp. 32, 37–39, 42; Young, 2011). Without the necessary skills, knowledge, and financial resources, role-players in Africa will continue to struggle to successfully implement CBDRR interventions (IGAD, 2002, p. 14; La Trobe & Davies, 2005, p. 6).

A perusal of the available literature indicates that in 2008, the global development aid budget were in the region of US$129 billion (United Nations office of the Special Adviser on Africa [OSSA], 2010). Over the past four decades, aid to Africa has quadrupled from around US$11 billion to US$44 billion (in 2010), with a net increase of almost US$10 billion during the period 2005–2008 alone. In 2010, the global development aid budget fell to US$119 billion (OSSA, 2010). The portion allocated to Africa was approximately 36% of the total development aid budget. Gerhardt (2010) argues that this development aid is a blessing for all of those directly involved – both those on the giving and those on the receiving end. He says that overseas functionaries on the donor side earn good money, and those on the receiving side are organized in such a way that their personal interests does not get "short shrift" (Gerhardt, 2010). It is therefore not surprising, and a well-known fact, that very little development aid actually reaches those it is intended to benefit most. Almost all of the authors writing on CBDRR emphasize the strong developmental focus that CBDRR projects should have. It can therefore be argued that immediate development needs enjoy priority. Development projects is not per se seen as direct CBDRR projects, or governments and development agencies struggle to link development initiatives and their direct contribution to DRR in general. The overreliance on development aid in Africa is another culprit in this scenario. Those providing development aid dictates the terms, and those receiving lack initiative (Gerhardt, 2010).

ADDRESSING CHALLENGES OF CBDRR IMPLEMENTATION AND SUSTAINABILITY

The following section will consider how the key stakeholder groups of governments and international and local NGOs integrate their activities to facilitate CBDRR. The input from each of these groups will be highlighted through a selection of best practice case studies in DRR. These case studies do not only indicate how these three groups work together but they also indicate where more participation is needed from specific stakeholders.

Advantages of a Conducive Risk Reduction Environment

Governments play a crucial role in the creation of governance and administrative structures that encourage communities and other role-players to participate and own disaster risk management projects (Ahrens & Rudolph, 2006; Comfort et al., 1999, p. 42; Fernandez, Bendimerad, Mattingly, & Buika, 2006, p. 4; Wisner, 2003, p. 3). Good practice in this regard was observed in a multi-stakeholder flood management project undertaken by Tearfund in the Chikwawa district of Southern Malawi. The project was a flood mitigation project aimed at controlling river flows during rainy seasons (Tearfund, 2006, p. 1; UN/ISDR, 2007a, p. 37). Through community-based risk assessment and training of communities, they have learned how to initiate their own mitigation projects. Importantly, local government played a crucial role in the ongoing success of the project by establishing or providing access for the community to the district executive committee, district civil protection committee, and a district assembly (Tearfund, 2006, p. 2; UN/ISDR, 2007a, p. 37). With access to these decision-making bodies, community representatives could inform government officials of their DRR activities and needs. Subsequently, local government responded by endorsing the project and also providing support in the form of resources and training (Tearfund, 2006, p. 2; UN/ISDR,

2007a, p. 38). Appropriate government policy and structures are also crucial to the success of the DRR activities initiated by the NGOs involved in the project (Benson, Twigg, & Myers, 2001, p. 211).

As consequence of appropriate government buy-in in the project, the responsibilities of international and local NGOs working on the project was made much easier in the sense that they could focus on their specific role in the implementation of the project. In this regard, the international NGO, Tearfund, could provide the original idea and funding for the project while the local NGO, Eagles Relief and Development Program, could focus on implementation of the project (Tearfund, 2006, pp. 1–4; UN/ISDR, 2007a, p. 37). The involvement of the local NGO provided a conduit whereby Tearfund could introduce their Participatory Assessment for Disaster Risk methodology (a type of vulnerability and capacity assessment) and whereby community involvement in decision-making bodies could be encouraged (Tearfund, 2006, p. 3; UN/ISDR, 2007a, p. 38). Specifically, NGO Eagles mobilized key role-players such as community elders and community members to become involved in not only understanding and formulating plans to address the identified risks but also to participate in those structures provided by the local government to foster CBDRR (Tearfund, 2006, p. 3; UN/ISDR, 2007a, p. 38).

Importantly even though the proposed flood mitigation structure have been completed the "Eagles," Tearfund and local government relationship with the communities and villages are still ongoing (Tearfund, 2006, p. 1; UN/ISDR, 2007a, p. 37). This continued involvement by the various role-players ensures continued buy-in from communities to maintain the existing flood mitigation structures. By allowing the community to participate in decision-making structures, local government in the Chikwawa district has created an environment that fosters collective discussion, agreement, and action between all role-players (Tearfund, 2006, pp. 1–4; UN/ISDR, 2007a, p. 38).

Referring back to the case study of urban flood management in Luska, Zambia, it is worthy to note that although the project strictly speaking was approached from a top-down perspective, the role-players involved succeeded in ensuring participation from the community, government, and NGOs (in the case CARE Zambia) working in the area. Such interaction allowed both the community and the CARE Zambia to address other issues relating to the flooding such as health and sanitation. The creation of a conducive environment, in which CBDRR can flourish, remains imperative. Yet, efforts toward inclusion of role-players can be stifled if a critical mass of appropriate skills and technical advice is not readily available.

Increasing Capacity and Technical Expertise for Improved CBDRR

As early as 1983, Cuny (1983, p. 121) emphasized the important role NGOs (called "voluntary organizations") play in DRR activities such as disaster preparedness and response. The active involvement of NGOs and governments in improving community disaster preparedness becomes crucial in areas such as Africa where there is a general lack of technical skills and capacity to adequately involve communities in DRR activities (AU/NEPAD, 2004, pp. 5–12; La Trobe & Davies, 2005, p. 6; Marianovic & Nimpuno, 2003, p. 198; Wisner et al., 2011, p. 11). Van Riet and Van Niekerk (2011) in their assessment of a community-based disaster risk assessment project in South Africa emphasize the need for appropriate skills transfer and capacity development of the communities involved.

To determine the current level of involvement of NGOs, governments, and communities in CBDRR in Africa, analysis of the 17 case studies as mentioned above identified a trend where international NGOs emerge as the main contributors of technical expertise and capacity during CBDRR projects, while governments and local NGOs only fulfill supporting roles (Musakuzi, 2011; UN/ISDR, 2007a, 2007b, p. 10, 24, 2008, p. 33,52; Young, 2011). Even though international NGOs do take the leading role in contributing skills and capacities to CBDRR projects in Africa, this does not diminish the input from governments and local NGOs. Often, governments and NGOs (international and local) are found to cooperate in a close symbiotic relationship where the one group provides inputs and expertise on aspects of a specific CBDRR project, where the other group might not have the required expertise. An instance of this has been identified in a "Building Disaster Resilient Communities" project run by Christian Aid and implemented by the Evangelical Lutheran Development Service (ELDS) in Malawi (Christian Aid, 2009, p. 36; Moss, 2008, pp. 1–2; UN/ISDR, 2008, pp. 40–43). During this project, both the local government of the Phalombe District and the implementing agency, ELDS, provided technical skills and capacities toward the successful implementation of the project (Moss, 2008, pp. 1–2). While ELDS provided materials and information on building water pipelines, local government gave technical input on drought mitigation, while still conforming to the participatory, community-based nature of the project (Moss, 2008, pp. 1–2; UN/ISDR, 2008, pp. 40–43).

It is important to note that the transfer of skills and capacity is also directed at communities themselves (Van Riet & Van Niekerk, 2011). The latter is especially evident in education projects focusing on DRR. A good practice in this regard was a project undertaken in Mozambique by the

Mozambique Red Cross Society focusing on training teachers to help mainstream DRR into school curricula (Cheal, 2008, p. 80; UN/ISDR, 2007b, pp. 23–26). During the project, the Mozambique Red Cross trained 99 teachers from 76 schools on the disaster risk they face as well as the importance of DRR and awareness (Komac, 2010, p. 21; UN/ISDR, 2007b, p. 25). Subsequently, the Red Cross also assisted the teachers in setting up seven school nuclei to coordinate extracurricular DRR activities within their school districts. Through these school nuclei, some teachers chose to form drama groups as a way to raise awareness on disaster risk issues in their school (UN/ISDR, 2007b, p. 25). Through these drama groups, greater parts of the communities became involved in and aware of the importance of disaster prevention and risk reduction.

Bridging Financial Constraints of CBDRR Projects

The analysis of the 17 case studies also revealed that international NGOs and intergovernmental organizations working in Africa provide the bulk of financial resources required for DRR initiatives, although this funding also sometimes prove inadequate to finance risk reduction projects in their entirety (AU/NEPAD, 2004, p. 6; Young, 2011). International NGOs acting as main funding partner for CBDRR projects can be seen in many instances within the African continent (UN/ISDR, 2007a, p. 29). Of the 17 case studies, 71% (12) of cases, international NGOs or intergovernmental organizations (i.e., UNISDR, UNDP, DFID, ECHO, and World Bank), emerge as the main funding partners in disaster risk initiatives at community level with governments providing no or only limited financial resource support. Importantly, some governments have started to make attempts to bridge the financial constraints they face in funding DRR projects by integrating them into existing development budgets. An example of this can be seen in South Africa where disaster management legislation calls for DRR projects to be integrated into the IDP (integrated development plan) of each local municipality in the country (Botha et al., 2011, p. 4; South Africa, 2003, 2005). Integrating DRR into existing development planning is seen as a way to get multiple stakeholders involved in the funding and implementation of DRR projects (Botha et al., 2011, p. 4, 17). NGOs also face specific problems when it comes to funding CBDRR projects in Africa.

Due to the limited funds that one single NGO can contribute to a specific project, many international NGOs work in partnership with intergovernmental organizations to acquire sufficient funding to establish and administrate projects (Benson et al., 2001, p. 202; UN/ISDR, 2007a, p. 29, 32, 2008, p. 37, 41, 46). The need for co-funded projects emerges especially in projects focusing on long-term DRR (UN/ISDR, 2007a, p. 32). A good example of this was identified in a community-managed DRR project focusing on drought cycle management in Kenya where the two principle funding partners in the project, CORDAID (Catholic Organization for Relief and Development Aid) and ECHO (European Commission Humanitarian aid Office), had to cooperate in funding longer-term drought cycle program (UN/ISDR, 2007a, p. 32). The need for the cooperation between two or more organizations becomes increasingly necessary as the shift continues from disaster response toward preparedness and prevention (UN/ISDR, 2007a, p. 32).

International NGOs play a crucial role in funding CBDRR projects in Africa. Without the funding provided by international NGOs and intergovernmental organizations, CBDRR projects would seize to exist due to the lack of funds currently being allocated by African governments. In none of the case studies could the direct role of the private sector explicitly be determined. Disaster risk remains a societal commons. The general lack of direct involvement of the private sector in CBDRR is worrisome. Government and communities in Africa would do well to partner with the private sector and through access to their corporate social responsibility/investment funds (Blowfield & Murry, 2008, pp. 24–26) initiative CBDRR projects.

From the above discussion on solving challenges faced by CBDRR projects in Africa, it becomes clear that governments, international and local NGOs, and intergovernmental organizations are all cooperating in some degree to the successful implementation of CBDRR projects. Yet, although the cooperation positively contributes to CBDRR projects, there is a great dependency by governments and local NGOs on international NGOs to provide ideas, resources, and expertise needed for successful project implementation (Holloway, 2003, p. 31; Van Niekerk, 2008, p. 365). Governments, local NGOs, as well as the private sector should change this prevailing situation and become more involved in CBDRR projects. Knowledge transfer and capacity building in communities on DRR issues in this regard becomes increasingly important (Van Riet & Van Niekerk, 2011).

CONCLUSION

This chapter aimed to provide the reader with an overview of CBDRR within the African context. By analyzing 17 case studies of CBDRR in Africa, the authors identified certain trends and challenges that seem to be common in all instances. The first part of the chapter focused on the current context in which CBDRR is applied. It was found that a number of actors, such as government, NGOs, international organizations, institutions of higher learning, the private sector, and of course communities, implement CBDRR projects. The analysis showed that there are a number of challenges with CBDRR in Africa, which include aspects such as governance and institutional frameworks linked to financial, human resource, skills, and competencies constraints. This chapter suggests that in order for CBDRR to become more common in Africa and more relevant, it is necessary for the role-players to interact and find common grounds for CBDRR. In such a way, a conducive environment for application of CBDRR is created. Attention must be given to increased capacities to initiate CBDRR project, and the need for certain technical skills were also highlighted. As with so many development and DRR initiatives, funding remains a major stumbling block. CBDRR projects are not outright funded and in many instances find their application within the development domain. CBDRR in Africa should thus be structured along a developmental focus, which will not only address a direct DRR need but also contribute toward development.

In conclusion, one needs to realistically consider the DRR landscape in Africa in trying to understand the application of CBDRR. This chapter emphasized a number of challenges in CBDRR, which currently compete with more pressing development and service delivery issues. Yet, where robust partnerships emerged, CBDRR is made a priority and becomes fairly sustainable. Thus CBDRR should be viewed as a tool to not only addressing the possibilities of hazards becoming disasters but also as a development intervention that can create an environmental for long-term DRR and sustainable development.

REFERENCES

AU/NEPAD. (2004). Africa regional strategy for disaster risk reduction. July, AU/NEPAD, 16pp.
Abebe, M. (2010). Disaster management in Ethiopia: A review of its checkered history, its transformation and some implications for a vibrant disaster management system, 1975–2008. *Journal of Sustainable Development in Africa, 12*(4), 237–254.
Ahrens, J., & Rudolph, P. M. (2006). The importance of governance in risk reduction and disaster risk reduction. *Journal of Contingencies and Crisis Management, 14*(4), 207–220.

Benson, C., Twigg, J., & Myers, M. (2001). NGO initiatives in risk reduction: An overview. *Disasters, 25*(3), 199–215.

Blowfield, M., & Murry, A. (2008). *Corporate responsibility: A critical introduction* (452pp.). United Kingdom: Oxford University Press.

Botha, D., Van Niekerk, D., Wentink, G., Tshona, T., Maartens, Y., Forbes, K., ... Raju, E. (2011). *Disaster risk management status assessment at municipalities in South Africa.* Pretoria: South African Local Government Association (SALGA).

Bräutigam, D. A., & Knack, S. (2004). Foreign aid, institutions, and governance in sub Saharan Africa. *Economic Development and Cultural Change, 52*(2), 255–285.

Cheal, B. (2008). The role of schools in rebuilding sustainable communities after disasters. Paper presented at international conference on rebuilding sustainable communities for children and their families after disasters. Conference organized by John W. McCormack Graduate School of Policy Studies, University of Massachusetts, Boston, 16–18 November.

Christian Aid. (2009). Christian aid self-assessment review 2009/2010. DFID, 39pp.

Comfort, L., Wisner, B., Cutter, S., Pulwarty, R., Hewitt, K., Oliver-Smith, J., ... Krimgold, F. (1999). Reframing disaster policy: The global evolution of vulnerable communities. *Environmental Hazards, 1*, 39–44.

Cuny, F. C. (1983). *Disasters and development* (278pp.). Oxford: Oxford University Press.

Fernandez, J., Bendimerad, F., Mattingly, S., & Buika, J. (2006). Comparative analysis of disaster risk management practices in seven megacities. 21pp. Paper presented at the 2nd Asia Conference on Earthquacke Engeneering. Manila, Philippines, 10 March 2006.

Gerhardt, K. (2010). Why development for Africa has failed. Spiegel Online. Retrieved from http://www.spiegel.de/international/world/0,1518,712068,00.html. Accessed on 1 April 2011.

Global Network of Civil Society Organisations For Disaster Reduction. (2009). *Clouds but little rain...: Views from the frontline-A local perspective of progress towards implementation of the Hyogo Framework for Action.* Teddington: Global Network of Civil Society Organisations for Disaster Reduction.

Global Network of Civil Society Organisations For Disaster Reduction. (2011). Views from the Frontline 2011. Retrieved from http://www.globalnetwork-dr.org/images/documents/vfl2011_report/VFL2011_Core_Report_en.pdf

Holloway, A. (2003). Disaster risk reduction in Southern Africa: Hot rhetoric, cold reality. *African Security, 12*(1), 29–38.

Intergovernmental Authority on Development. (2002). *Improvement of regional collaboration in disaster risk management.* Volume IV, Project 3, June, 28pp. IGAD, Addis Ababa.

Kim, S. P., & Lee, E. J. (1998). Emergency management in Korea and its future directions. *Journal of Contingencies and Crisis Management, 6*(4), 189–201.

Komac, B. (2010). Risk education and natural hazards. CapHaz-Net, June, 113pp.

La Trobe, S., & Davies, I. (2005). Mainstreaming disaster risk reduction: A tool for development orginisastions. Tearfund, 16pp.

Marianovic, P., & Nimpuno, K. (2003). *Building safer cities: The future of disaster risk.* In A. Kreimer, M. Arnold & A. Carlin (Eds.), Living with risk: Towards effective disaster management training in Africa (Chapter 14, pp. 197–209). Washington, DC: World Bank Publications.

McLennan, A., & Ngoma, W. Y. (2004). Quality governance for sustainable development. *Progress in Development Studies, 4*(4), 279–293.

Mercer, J., Kelman, I., Taranis, L., & Suchet-Pearson, S. (2010). Framework for integrating indigenous knowledge and scientific knowledge for disaster risk reduction. *Disasters*, *34*(1), 214–239.

Meshack, M., Lerise, F., Lupala, J., Kiunsi, R., Mchome, E., Malele, B., & Namangaya, A. (2007). Community initiatives in managing urbanisation and risk accumulation processes: Lessons from Dar es Salaam, Tanzania. In M. Pelling (Ed.), *Investigating urban risk accumulation in six countries in Africa* (13pp.). Cape Town, South Africa: AURAN.

Moss, S. (2008). Local voices, global choices: For successful disaster risk reduction. *ProVention Consortium*, 16pp.

Musakuzi, R. (2011). Disaster risk reduction consultant: Zambia. CBDRR projects in Zambia. E-mail communication with the authors, 13 March 2011.

Pelling, M. (2007a). Making disaster risk reduction work. *ProVention Consortium*, 22pp.

Pelling, M. (2007b). Learning from others: The scope and challenges for participatory disaster risk assessment. *Disasters*, *31*(4), 373–385.

Pelling, M., & Holloway, A. (2006). Legislation for mainstreaming disaster risk reduction. Tearfund, 32pp.

South Africa (Republic). (2003). *Disaster management act, No 57 of 2002*. Pretoria: Government Printers.

South Africa (Republic). (2005). *National disaster management policy framework*. Pretoria: Government Printer.

Tearfund. (2006). Disaster risk reduction multi-stakeholder flood mitigation in Malawi: A case study. Tearfund, 4pp.

United Nations International Strategy for Disaster Reduction. (2005). *Hyogo framework for action: Building the resilient of nations and communities to disaster*. Geneva: UN.

United Nations International Strategy for Disaster Reduction. (2007a). *Building disaster resilient communities: Good practices and lessons learned*. Geneva: UNISDR, 56pp.

United Nations International Strategy for Disaster Reduction. (2007b). *Towards a culture of prevention: Disaster risk reduction begins at school*. Geneva: UNISDR, 143pp.

United Nations International Strategy for Disaster Reduction. (2008). *Linking disaster risk reduction and poverty reduction: Good practices and lessons learned*. Geneva: UNISDR, 75pp.

United Nations Office of the Special Adviser on Africa. (2010). *Aid to Africa*. New York: United Nations, 4pp.

Van Niekerk, D. (2008). From disaster relief to disaster risk reduction: A consideration of the evolving international relief mechanism. *The Journal for Transdisciplinary Research in Southern Africa*, *4*(2), 355–376.

Van Riet, G., & Van Niekerk, D. (2011). Capacity development for participatory disaster risk assessment: The case of the Dr. Kenneth Kaunda District Municipality. (Submitted to: Environmental Hazards: Human and Policy Dimensions.)

Visser, C. B., & Van Niekerk, D. (2009). *Change to: A funding model for the disaster risk management function of municipalities*. ACDS. Potchefstroom: South Africa, 86pp.

White, P., Pelling, M., Sen, K., Seddon, D., Russel, S., & Few, R. (2004). *Disaster risk reduction: A development concern*. United Kingdom: DFID, 65pp.

Wisner, B. (2003). Sustainable suffering? Reflections on development and disaster vulnerability in the post-Johannesburg world. *Regional Development Dialogue*, *24*(1), 135–148.

Wisner, B., Kent, G., Carmalt, J., Cook, B., Gaillard, J.C., Lavell, A., ... Narvaez, L. (2011). Political will for disaster reduction: What incentives build it, and why is it so hard to achieve? A contribution to the review of the draft GAR 2011, Chapters 5, 6 & 7.

Young, D. (2011). Emergency and disaster relief coordinator: CARE Madagascar. CBDRR in Madagascar. E-mail communication with the authors. 9 March 2011 and 28 March 2011.

CHAPTER 18

EXPERIENCE OF COMMUNITY-BASED ADAPTATION IN BURKINA FASO

Aki Kogachi and Rajib Shaw

INTRODUCTION

Burkina Faso is a land-locked country, sharing a border with six other countries, namely Mali, Niger, Benin, Togo, Ghana, and Cote D'Ivoire in the zone of West Africa (Fig. 1). Due to the geographical location of the Sahel region, the country's climate is characterized by rainy and dry seasons. According to the Human Development Report in 2010, the country has a very weak economy with a GDP of 522 USD per habitant, principally based on agriculture (25%), animal production (12%), and forestry/fishery (3%) (MECV & SP/CONEDD, 2006a). The population growth is extremely high at 2.8%, with 46.4% of the population living below the national poverty line and 81.2% living on less than $2 a day (UNDP, 2009). The biomass energy is the largest primary energy source covering 80% of total consumption, thus accelerating soil degradation as well as deforestation.

Community-Based Disaster Risk Reduction
Community, Environment and Disaster Risk Management, Volume 10, 351–371
ISSN: 2040-7262/doi:10.1108/S2040-7262(2012)0000010024

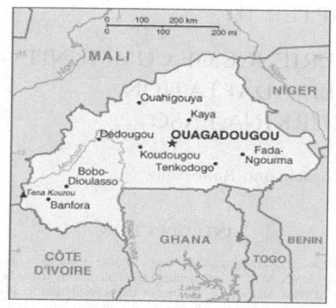

Fig. 1. Location of Burkina Faso in West Africa.

CLIMATE CHANGE IN BURKINA FASO

Trends and Impacts on Key Sectors

Climate projections based on Global Climate Model (GCM) indicate a 3.4% decrease in rainfall and an increase of 0.8°C in temperature by 2025, and a rainfall decrease of 7.3% and an increase of 1.7°C in temperature by 2050. Furthermore, strong interannual and seasonal variability will add to this shortfall of rainfall. The months of July, August, and September will experience 20–30% decrease in rainfall, while the month of November will experience 60–80% increase in rainfall.

In the agriculture sector, the combination of rain pattern variability as well as the increase in temperature may result in significant reduction of agricultural productivity, such as millet in Sahel. In contrast, millet, sorghum, and corn cultivated in subsurface soil in the southern part of the country may have improved productivity due to increased rainfall. However, in the very same area, corn yields are projected to decrease in the surface soil with low water availability in July, August, and September (SP/CONEDD, 2006b).

In the hydrology and water sector, projected rainfall trends will affect water flows in the country's four basin slopes. In forestry and biodiversity, for instance, total biomass is expected to decline from 200 million m^3 in 1999 to a little over 110 million m^3 in 2050. In addition, the impact of climate variability may significantly affect flora and fauna through the extinction of certain species or their migration from the Sahelian to the Sudan zones. Lastly, in the livestock rearing sector, the rise in temperature and drop in rainfall will lead to (i) drastic reduction and degradation of pasturage area for animals, (ii) deficit number of livestock and serious effect on food security of the rural community, and (iii) acute shortage of water for animals. Subsequently, this will result in the shortfall of animal products and decrease in the number of livestock (Ministry of Animal Resource, 2005). The escalation of climate variability and other events (such as drought, locust attack, etc.) could trigger mass extinction of livestock and destruction of livelihoods of agro-pastures, similar to the severe drought of 1972–1973 and 1983–1984 in Sahel (Ministry of Environment and Sustainable Development, 2007).

National Adaptation Programme of Action of Burkina Faso

The National Adaptation Programme of Action (NAPA) provides a process for least developing countries (LDCs) to identify priority activities that respond to their urgent and immediate needs with regard to adaptation to climate change (UNFCCC, 2002). The rationale for NAPA lies in the fact that LDCs have very limited capacity to adapt, and need specific support that will allow them to deal with the adverse effects of climate variability and change. In the case of Burkina Faso, the 2007 NAPA of Burkina Faso identified four sectors, namely water, agriculture, stock-breeding, and forestry, as particularly vulnerable to climate change.

Through a participatory process, 12 urgent and immediate actions (NAPA, BF, 2007) to adapt to climate change were identified by local communities including the most vulnerable groups such as women, youth, and small-scale agricultural producers (Table 1).

COMMUNITY-BASED ADAPTATION ACTIVITIES

The United Nations Development Programme (UNDP) in Burkina Faso, as lead agency and Global Environment Facility (GEF) executing agency, has been assisting the government's effort in implementing adaptation. Following

Table 1. Twelve NAPA Priority Projects Identified in the NAPA.

	Sector	Priority Activities
1	Agriculture	Promotion of climate-resilient agricultural practice in South-East region and West region
2	Agriculture and water	Systemic, institutional, and individual capacity to respond to climate change in the agricultural sector
3		Knowledge management and dissemination of lessons learned and best practices
4		Optimization of the use of irrigation water in the province of Gourma from Nametenga, and Tapoa from Sanmatenga
5	Agriculture and livestock	Demonstration of best practices in climate-resilient agropastoral production for sustainable improvement of food security
6	Agriculture/ forestry	Valorisation of forest product in the East region of Burkina Faso
7	Livestock	Protection of pastoral zone in Sahel and East region
8	Biodiversity	Protection of lake Oursi
9	Food security	Promotion of best practices to protect wild animals in the Mouhoun community
10	Water	Protection of water reserve (ponds, river, lake) from stranding/silting in the national water reserve in Mouhoun, Nakanbe, and Comoe
11		Installation of devices promote the protection of the water resource (lakes, wells, boreholes, etc.) from the pollution in the cotton-producing area in Burkina Faso (Mouhoun, South-West, Comoe, east part of Nakanbe)
12	Energy	Promotion of renewable energy and energy-efficient technique to reduce the utilization of wood in rural community

the adoption of the NAPA in November 2007, the UNDP has supported the government of Burkina Faso in formulating three community-based adaptation projects (Table 2). These three adaptation projects for the period 2009–2012 are administered by UNDP Burkina Faso and executed by the national coordination unit of climate change under the supervision of Permanent Secretariat of Environment and Sustainable Development and Ministry of Environment and Sustainable Development (SP/CONEDD). SP/CONEDD was established in November 2002, placed under administrative technical supervision of the Ministry of Environment. In addition to be in charge of promotion of environmental policy and law, the principal mission of SP/CONEDD is to facilitate effective integration of fundamental principle of environmental management for sustainable development. To maximize the synergy of execution, the projects are implemented as a program where work plans, expert project-steering committees, and pilot sites are shared.

Table 2. NAPA Projects in Burkina Faso.

Project Title	Main Outcome	Site/Duration/Budget
Adapting to climate change in order to increase human security in Burkina Faso	Awareness raising of climate change among key national/ regional/local actors	National component with regional/provincial/ community level intervention (Project site A, B, and C) 2009–2012 DANIDA 835,000 USD UNDP 125,000 USD
Consolidating the national approach to adapting to climate change in Burkina Faso	Burkina Faso to establish dynamic, long-term planning mechanisms to cope with the inherent uncertainties of climate variability and change	National component with regional/provincial/ community level intervention (Project site A, B, and C) 2009–2012 Japan 2.9 million USD
Strengthening adaptation capacities and reducing the vulnerability to climate change in Burkina Faso	Risk of climate-induced impacts on agro-sylvo-pastoral productivities reduced though the testing, understanding, and adoption of best practices through a community-centered approach	Three regions/provinces/ and six villages 2009–2012 GEF least development country funding (LDCF) 2.9 million USD UNDP 500,000 USD

Furthermore, three distinct climate zones are identified where the projects will be piloted to test adaptation practices appropriate to each climate zone as per the Meteorological Department from 1961 to 1990 (Table 3). This chapter examines the activities of the project, "Strengthening Adaptation Capacities and Reducing the Vulnerability to Climate Change in Burkina Faso," in three project sites.

Climate Profile of Project Sites

The villages of Bagawa and Tin Akoff in the province of Ouadlan, Koboure and Safi in the province of Namentenga, and Monkuy and Souri in the province of Boucle de la Mouhun have been selected as project sites representing the Sahelian, North Sudan, and South Sudan climate zones, respectively (Table 4). Based on climate data from 1981 to 2007, daily rainfall and highest and lowest temperatures collected from the nearest weather station in the pilot sites are discussed in the following.

Table 3.   Description of Climate Zones in Burkina Faso.

Characteristic of the Climate Zone	Climate Zone		
	Sahelian	North Sudan	South Sudan
Annual rainfall	300–600 mm	600–900 mm	900–1,200 mm
Duration: rainy season	110 days	150 days	180–200 days
Number of rainy days	<45 days	50–70 days	85–100 days
Annual average temperature	29°C	28°C	27°C
Seasonal amplitude	11°C	8°C	5°C
Average moisture:			
Dry season	25%	25%	25%
Wet season	70%	75%	85%
Annual evaporation	3,200–3,500 mm	2,600–2,900 mm	1,800–2,000 mm

Table 4.   Description of Project Sites.

Climate Zone	Project Site	Pilot Village	Longitude	Latitude
Sahel/North	Sahel region	Tin-Akoff	00° 09′ 52″ –W	14° 57′ 54″ –N
	Province of Ouadlan	Bagawa	00° 15′ 10″ –W	14° 48′ 24″ –N
North-Soudan	Central-North region	Kouboure	00° 31′ 12″ –W	13° 38′ 24″ –N
	Province of Namentenga	Safi	00° 44′ 53″ –W	12° 52′ 36″ –N
North-Soudan	Region of Boucle and Mouhoun	Monkuy	03° 44′ 47″ –W	12°13′ 00″ –N
South-Soudan	Province of Boucle de la Mouhon	Souri	03° 31′ 08″ –W	12°25′ 43″ –N

Rainfall

In all three climate zones, interannual variability is observed (Fig. 2). In the case of Fada, the rainfall trends indicate significant monthly variations. Based on total amount of rainfall, August remains as the month with highest rainfall followed by July and September. However, there is a decrease in rainfall in June and July, while there is a slight increase in rainfall in October. Furthermore, there is a significant increase in annual total wet-day rainfall in the three weather stations as it figures with the increase of extreme rainfall (SDII, R95P, R99P, R10mm and R20mm) (Table 5). While the three zones benefit from the increase in extreme rainfall, they also experience an increase in the number of consecutive dry nights/days (Fig. 3).

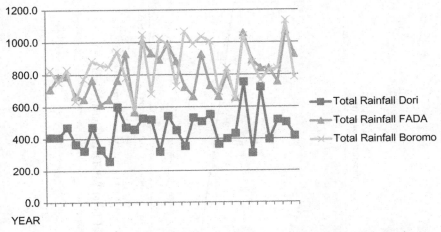

Fig. 2. Annual Rainfall from the Boromo, Fada, and Dori Weather Stations.

Table 5. Rainfall Tendency by Decade for the Period of 1981–2007.

Index	Unit	Tendency by Decade In Dori	Tendency by Decade in Fada	Tendency by Decade in Boromo
PRCPTOT: Annual total wet-day rainfall	mm	37.6	62	35.9
SDII: Simple daily intensity index	mm	−0.1	0.6	0.3
R95p: Very wet day	mm	11.5	25.2	–
R99p: Extremely wet day	mm	−0.9	12.8	–
RX1day: Max 1 day rainfall amount	mm	90.4	0.3	4.6
RX5day: Max 5 day rainfall amount	mm	−1.2	−0.09	11.5
R10 mm: Number of heavy rainfall days	Days	1.4	0.6	2.2
R20 mm: Number of heavy rainfall days	Days	0.3	2	0.9
CDD: Consecutive dry days	Days	−5	13.6	3.9
CWD : Consecutive wet days	Days	0.3	−0.06	0.4

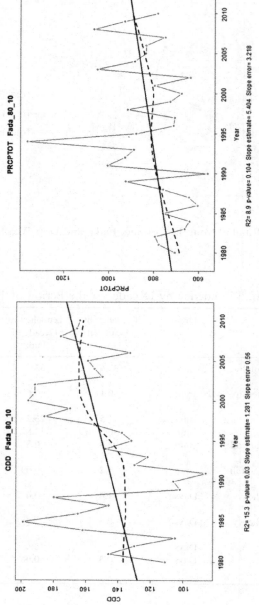

Fig. 3. CDD: Consecutive Dry Days (Fada); PRCPTOT: Annual Total Wet-Day Rainfall (Fada).

Table 6. Temperature Tendency by Decade for the Period of 1981–2007.

Index	Unit	Tendency by Decade In Dori	Tendency by Decade in Fada	Tendency by Decade in Boromo
TXx: Monthly maximum value of daily maximum temp.	°C	−0.1	0.2	0.04
TNx: Monthly maximum value of daily minimum temp.	°C	0.06	0.3	−0.07
TXn : Monthly minimum value of daily maximum temp.	°C	0.4	0.3	0.06
TNn: Monthly minimum value of daily minimum temp.	°C	0.8	0.9	0.8
DTR: Daily temperature range	°C	−0.4	−2.9	−0.06
TN10p: Cool nights	% of days	−2.5	−0.4	−0.3
TX10p: Cool days	% of days	−0.6	−0.8	−0.3
TN90p: Warm nights	% of days	3	0.5	0.4
TX90p: Warm days	% of days	−0.9	1.3	0.3

Temperature

According to the result of the indices of RClimdex (Table 6), temperature indices (TXx, TNx, TXn, and TNn) of two weather stations situated in North (Dori) in the Sahel zone and in East (Fada) Soudan-Sahel zone indicate an increase in extreme temperature. In Dori, for example, monthly maximum value of minimum temperature varies from 0.06 to 0.8 and 0.3 to 0.9 in Fada. However, the weather station in Boromo, situated in Southern part of country, shows less variability due to its geographical location. In the three zones, it is commonly observed that there is a significant decrease in the number of cool nights, in particular in Dori (−2.5) on one hand, and an increase in warm days (+3) in Dori and (+13) in Fada on the other hand (Fig. 4).

Project Activities 2009–2010

The NAPA program implementation began with activities in raising awareness of climate change among central, provincial, and local

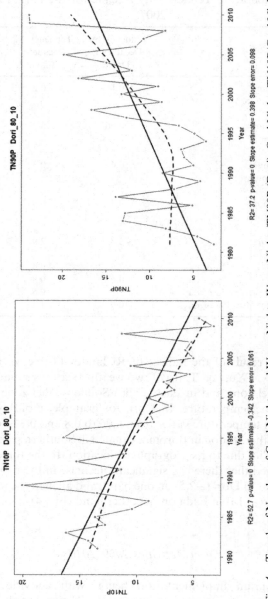

Fig. 4.   Trends of Number of Cool Nights and Warm Nights. Warm Nights/TN90P (Dori). Cool Nights TN10P/Cool Nights (Dori).

decision-makers. Further to national validation of NAPA, the NAPA document was largely disseminated at national level. In parallel, a simplified version of NAPA was elaborated in order to maximize the best understanding of the NAPA and translated into four national languages.

The NAPA as well as its simplified version was distributed during a workshop in the different regions of Burkina Faso. From 2009 to 2010, workshops on sensitizing climate change's effect on key economic sectors were organized in 13 regions. These regional workshops mobilized representatives of approximately 900 people from local government and decentralized actors as well as technical services from the agriculture, livestock, and environment provincial department. With support from a media group named, "Climate Change Journalists," information related to these sensitization workshops were communicated to the public via radio and daily journals, among others. Furthermore, trainings of trainer on climate change were organized among senior officials of the Ministry of Environment, regional directors, and mayors of the 13 regions.

At the community level, the community of Ouarkoye, one of the pilot sites, was selected as the first community to benefit from the workshop. The theme selected for the workshop was "Climate Change and Effect on Inhabitants of Each Community." Specifically, the risk of violent winds and flooding as major hazards related to climate change, climate-resilient materials, zone with least risk, and model of construction were discussed in the workshop. Around 60 resource persons participated, consisting of community advisors, leaders of association, traditional authorities, and local environment department officials (Athanasem, 2010). Similarly, in NAPA DANIDA, mainstreaming of environmental education as well as integrating climate change into national educational program are principal activities. The project finances activities such as sensitization among children and youth, raising awareness of the educational department and teachers, and elaboration of the tool for mainstreaming climate change into educational programs. A number of trainings were organized on the focal points of environmental education by the experts from the ministry of environment and sustainable development and ministry of education (primary and secondary).

Agro-sylvo-pastoral Activities in Two Pilot Villages in Province of Oudalan in Sahel Region

The total area of the province of Oudalan is 9,931 km². The province is known for long dry season with limited duration of rainy season for three months with the total rainfall of 405–462 mm. The weather condition is characterized by a long dry season from October to July and a very short rainy season from July to September. As it is described in the section "Climate Profile of Project Sites," climate trends indicate the variability of rain pattern (increase of annual rainfall meanwhile decrease of daily rainfall added by increase of consecutive dry day). The analysis of migration rate during the period of 1985–1996 shows that the province of Ouadlan records the number of persons leaving the region as 7,667 in 1985 that increased up to 22,862 in 1996 (DRED/Sahel, 2004).

The region suffers more frequently from severe drought; in particular the drought of 1973–1974 resulted in diversifying people's income-generating activities to agriculture in order to increase food security (Kabore & Ouedraogo, 2006). Prior to that, Sahel has always been known as the pastoral zone due to weather condition, which does not opt for agriculture. (Claude et al., 1991; Grouzis, 1988 cited from Ouadba, Hamade, & Harouna, 2008). In fact, animal husbandry represents 16.6% of the revenue of a household (CONEDD, 2008a).

In the village of Bagawa, situated within 28 km of the administrative center (Dori) of the province of Oudalan, the principal activity of about 616 villagers is animal husbandry. The population suffers from the effects of soil degradation, drying up of the pond, lack of water point for livestock, shortage of pasture land, silting up of pond, shortfall of ground water, less productivity of livestock, strong pressure on water resource, and shortage of fodder production (CONEDD, 2008).

On the other hand, the village of Tin-Akoff is situated extremely north of Burkina Faso. The average annual rainfall is 419.3 mm in 23 days for the period 1999–2003 (BBEA, 2002). The principal economic activities of the 1,551 villagers are subsistence agriculture and rearing livestock. The agriculture production is dominated by cereal, millet, and sorghum, among others. Given the use of primitive materials and weak productivity per hectare, agricultural productivity can fluctuate from year to year (CONEDD, 2008a). The effect of climate change is manifested as the interannual variation of rainfall, variability and decrease of number of days of rains, extreme temperatures frequently reaching to 44°C, and increased frequency of violent winds and dust seriously affecting the villagers. The Community Based Adaptation (CBA) practice in these two villages therefore emphasizes on activities related to improvement of animal husbandry technique, sylvo-pastoral activities, and food security (Table 7).

Table 7. Project Activities in Bagawa and Tin Akoff (Dieudonné, 2010).

Village of Bagawa	Village of Tin Akoff
Activity related to livestock: • Development of closure around fodder production area • Support on cattle fattening • Construction of fodder storage • Support on creation of fodder conservation equipment • Diagnosis and sanitary protection from climate-related diseases of cattle	Activity related to livestock: • Cattle fattening for men (support to facilitate microfinance, training, sheep barn and equipment) 20 cattle disinfested and vaccinated, 20 watering place, 20 mangers being set up • Support on fodder production materials and conservation practice • Cattle fattening technique • Support on fodder production materials and conservation for women • Development of closure around fodder production area • Diagnosis and sanitary protection from climate-related diseases of cattle
Activity related to forestry: • Soil fertilization by sylvo-pastoral (50 h), by plantation of 20,000 trees	Capacity development training etc.: • Capacity building and training on agricultural technique in order to adapt to climate change • Capacity development training on agro-sylvo-pastoral adaptation practice • Capacity development training on fodder production • Capacity development training on climate change and fodder production and divers techniques adapted to CC • Training on good adaptation practice to CC
Activity related to water resource: • Creation of 100 m of water bank around Gorol pond Activity related to food security: • Improvement of food bank capacity Capacity development training etc.: • Raising awareness and research of accession in community and partners • Organization of raising awareness on climate change information and training • Training on good adaptation practice	

Table 7. (*Continued*)

Village of Bagawa	Village of Tin Akoff
• Capacity building and training on agricultural adaptation technique to climate change • Capacity development training on agro-sylvo-pastoral adaptation practice • Capacity development training on natural grazing and flow of migrants • Capacity development training on climate change and fodder production adapted to CC • Training on fodder management and conservation	

Agro-sylvo-pastoral Activities in Two Pilot Villages in Province of Namentenga in the Central North Region

The province of Namentenga is located in the central north region. The province has a total area of 6,400 km², characterized by a climate of type Sahel marked by a serious shortage of rainfall and interannual variability. The main economic activity of the province is agriculture. Major agricultural products include sorghum and grain, which constitute 93% of production. The south zone, which consists of Boulsa, Dargo, and Boala, is characterized by a climate of Soudan-Sahel type with rainfall between 500 and 700 mm (CONEDD, 2008b).

In both pilot villages, Safi and Koubre, agriculture is the principal economic activity of 2,150 villagers followed by forestry and livestock rearing. Safi is known as a forest zone; however, this area is increasingly deteriorating due to extensive use by the inhabitants of Safi and surrounding neighboring villages. With regard to livestock management, seasonal migration of livestock (e.g., bovine, sheep, goat, pig, etc.) takes place twice a year, from February until May and from June until September. The effect of climate change is manifested in the variability in rainfall pattern. For instance in 2002, 489.9 mm of rainwater was observed in 41 days against 777.9 mm of water in 40 days in 2003.

Furthermore, the frequency of flooding, silting of lake, and high evaporation rate of surface water would result in deficiency of water availability for livestock and also for agriculture (NAPA, BF, 2007).

Table 8. Project Activities in Safi and Koubre (Jean, 2010).

Village of Safi	Village of Koubre
Activity related to agriculture: • Application of adaptation practice called "Zai" (means "anticipate" in local language) technique to increase soil fertility; action carried out in 10 ha (Fig. 5) • Technical assistance provided to set up compost pit of organic manure (10 compost pits) (Fig. 6)	Activity related to fodder production: • Promotion of fodder production (3 ha) • Cattle fattening (using the familial production model)
Activity related to food security: • Follow–up operation to improve food bank system	Activity related to food security: • Follow-up action on construction of large diameter well • Rehabilitation of 5 diameter wells • Construction of 1 diameter well
Activity related to water resource: • Construction of 5 large diameter wells • Follow-up action for large diameter well as well as water point • Creation of 100 m of water bank	Capacity development training etc.: • Follow-up action on village level ad-hoc committee on prevention of bushfire • Organisation of 2 village-level consultations • Organization of raising awareness on climate change information (1 workshop with 30 people) and farmers' training (Fig. 7)
Capacity development training etc.: • Organization of training on climate change adaptation measures • Follow-up action on village level ad-hoc committee on prevention of bushfire • Set up special committee to manage water bank • Organization of raising awareness on climate change information and training • Capacity development training on agro-sylvo-pastoral adaptation practice	

Those are significantly affecting people's livelihood; the CBA activity in these villages therefore put high priority on water resource management (Table 8).

Agro-sylvo-pastoral Activities in Two Pilot Villages in the Province of Mouhoun in the Region of Boucle de Mouhoun
The Boucle of Mouhoun region is situated in South Soudan climate zone with superficies of 33,700 km^2, which represents 12.3% of national territory. With annual rainfall of 700–900 mm in the northern part and 1,000–1,100 in

Fig. 5.   Practice of Zai in the Village of Safi. (Photograph Taken by NAPA BF Coordination Unit).

Fig. 6.   Large Compost Pit in Safi. (Photograph Taken by NAPA BF Coordination Unit).

Fig. 7.   Farmers' Training in Koboure. (Photograph Taken by NAPA BF Coordination Unit).

the southern part, the region owns a rich natural resource that became the zone of resettlement of people from the north, in particular Sahel region (Ouadba, 2010). The increase of cultivated superficies to 126% in the past 20 years (1984–2002) illustrates this phenomenon of the flow of migrants.

The principal economic activity of the population is agriculture, especially cereal (e.g., corn, sorghum, millet, rice), cotton, leguminous plants (e.g., Niebe and Voandzon), small irrigation agriculture (e.g., onion, tomato, cabbage, water melon), and fruits. Animal husbandry (e.g., apiculture, cattle goat, sheep, pig, etc.) and forestry production (e.g., hunting, charcoal production, and medicine) follows agriculture.

As it is shown in climate trend, there is an increase of annual rainfall accompanied by heavy rainfall while the same region suffers from the consecutive dry days. Effects of climate change manifested as intensified frequency of drought, silting of lake and river, erosion of river bank, and decrease of surface water resulted in lowering water level of Mouhoun River (CONEDD, 2008c). Table 9 describes the activities implemented in two pilot villages, Monkuy and Souri.

Summary CBA Response Adapted to Local Context
Agro-sylvo-pastoral is the principal activity for majority of the population in Burkina Faso, particularly in rural area. Meantime this is the sector most vulnerable to climate change. With NAPA follow-up project approved by GEF, Burkina Faso is currently going through the implementation of pilot activities to test the feasibility of adaptation practices in response to climate change including variability.

Demonstration of agro-sylvo-pastoral community-based adaptation activities in six pilot villages illustrates the distinctive local context differentiated from one weather zone to another in reference to climate tendency and variability of climate change. For instance, in the Sahel region, the CBA focuses on animal resource management and soil fertilization by sylvo-pastoral agriculture. In the Central North region, deficiency of water leads to the focus on water conservation technique; finally, in Mouhoun region the CBA emphasized the importance on the balanced use of remaining natural resource among farmers and pastoral communities. Overall, most of the proposed adaptation activities address the CBA to cope with current climate-related stress as well as climate variability in order to reduce the vulnerability not directly related to climate factors influencing the vulnerability of community.

Table 9.   Project Activities in Monkuy and Souri (Anèbakouri, 2010).

Village of Monkuy	Village of Souri
Activity related to agriculture: • Adaptation practice/soil fertilization by "zai" practices • Set up stable compost pit • Test production of improved seeds in 4 hectors and study visit of 150 participants	Activity related to agriculture: • Adaptation practice/soil fertilization by "zai" practices • Set up stable compost pit
Activity related to forestry: • Reforestation and installation of 100 m of bank	Activity related to livestock: • Cattle fattening • Support on fodder production, 5 ha of NIEBE production • Support on natural fodder production and conservation
Activity related to livestock: • Improvement of existing livestock path/course; joint mission has been held by local government representatives and community, provincial service technique • Improvement of village-level aviculture by introducing well-performed cock	Capacity development and training etc: • Improvement of existing livestock path/course, joint mission has been held by local government representatives and community, provincial service technique • Improvement of village level aviculture by introducing well performed cock • Support to set up mechanism of prevention of bushfire, capacity development of committee for management of bushfire • Climate change raising awareness by theater form • Raising awareness, information, and training of CC for opinion leaders at village level • Training and capacity development training of climate change and diverse techniques of fodder production • Capacity development of monitoring and evaluation and self-evaluation
Capacity development and training, etc.: • Feasibility study regarding Mou Faho flooding, site visit, and discussion held with village responsible • Setting up special committees to protect water bank, use of water, and wet land • Climate change raising awareness by theater form • Raising awareness, information, training of CC for opinion leaders at village level • Training and capacity development training of climate change and divers techniques of fodder production	

Role of Government and Community in Adaptation Activities

In NAPA process, local institution were implicated in its elaboration; however, in the NAPA follow-up project only 20 out of the 173 project reports identify local-level institutions as execution partners. Existing national plans to promote adaptation to climate change have been mostly inattentive to the role of local institutions. Better understanding of institutional access and articulation is essential (Arun, 2008). In the case of Burkina Faso, local institutions are considered as the principal implementation partners of NAPA follow-up activities.

This is followed by the current decentralization process that Burkina Faso has been undergoing for almost two decades. In particular, the decentralization process commonly referred to as communalization has been practiced in Burkina Faso since 1990. It began with the adoption of the new constitution on June 2, 1991. In terms of the use of natural resources, it is defined as follows: natural resources belong to the people (Article 14) and protecting, defending and promoting the environment are the duty of all citizens (Article 29). This process of decentralization was progressively advanced and led to the election of April 2006, which was dedicated to put in place 13 regions consisting of 302 rural municipalities and 47 urban municipalities.

The responsibility of local government in the management of natural resource is announced in the law adopted in 2005, 055–2004 General Code of Local Government. The role of local government in the management/ creation of environment conservation area (Article 90) assures the participation of rural community in the protection/management of natural resources such as natural forests, wild animals, and water. Furthermore, the local government is to elaborate and execute their policy and development plans in respect to national policy/orientation (Article 91).

In the implementation of Burkina Faso's NAPA follow-up project, triangular collaboration represented by the NAPA project team, regional director of environment, agriculture and animal resource, and community council was signed on June 17, 2011 in the region of Boucle de Mouhoun, on July 28 in the region of Central North, and on August 5 in the Sahel region (Ministry of Environment and Sustainable Development, 2010a, 2010b, 2010c). This collaboration symbolizes the ownership of rural community in the implementation of the CBA with technical support provided by regional/provincial department of environment, agriculture and animal resource.

CONCLUSION

Based on the CBA activities currently underway through the NAPA follow-up project, the project focuses on the community's urgent and immediate needs to alleviate poverty and also to cope with climate-related stress and its variability. Under the recent decentralization process, Burkina Faso is going through a transition of top-down to bottom-up approach regarding natural resource management.

In order to assure the sustainability of CBA practice at the local community, one of the key elements is mainstreaming of climate change adaptation in the planning process. Currently, the project team is conducting a study to diagnose local development plans and elaborate tools to integrate CCA into planning. Furthermore, an agro weather station would be located on the project site in order to utilize climate data to improve yield and also to incorporate future risk of climate change into the planning process at local level.

REFERENCES

Agrawal, A. (2008). *The role of local institutions in adaptation to climate change*. Washington, DC: The World Bank.

Anèbakouri, E. P. (2010). NAPA Burkina Faso annual report 2010, CONEDD 33–47.

Athanase, P. K. (2010). NAPA Burkina Faso annual report 2010, CONEDD 11–16.

BBEA. (2002). Monographie du de′ partement de Tin-Akoff (province de l'Oudalan). Rapport final. Gorom-Gorom, PDL/UDL.

BBEA. (2002). Monographie du département de Tin-Akoff (province de l'Oudalan). Rapport final. Gorom-Gorom, PDL/UDL 61.

CONEDD. (2008). Rapport sur la province du Mouhoun et les villages pilotes, Rapport sur la province du Namentenga et les villages pilotes, Rapport sur la province du Ouadlan et les villages pilotes.

CONEDD. (2008a). Rapport sur la province du Mouhoun et les villages pilotes, pp. 8–17.

CONEDD. (2008c). Rapport sur la province du Ouadlan et les villages pilotes, pp. 19–24.

CONEDD. (2008b). Rapport sur la province du Namentenga et les villages pilotes, pp. 9–18.

Dieudonné, D. (2010). NAPA Burkina Faso annual report 2010, pp. 22–32.

DRED/Sahel. (2004). Projet de Schéma Provincial d'Aménagement du Territoire de l'Oudalan (SPAT/Oudalan) 2005 – 2025 – Province de l'Oudalan, pp. 10–28.

Jean, P. S. (2010). NAPA Burkina Faso annual report 2010, pp. 15–21.

Kaboré, D., & Ouédraogo H. (2006). Vulnérabilité et changements climatiques dans le Sahel burkinabé, SP/CONEDD, p. 45.

Ministry of Animal Resource. (2005). Initiative: Elevage, Pauvreté et Croissance (IEPC) Proposition pour un document national, p. 157.

Ministry of Environment and Sustainable Development. (2007). Programme d'action national d'adaptation à la variabilité et aux changements climatiques (NAPA), pp. 1–26.

Ministry of Environment and Sustainable Development. (2010a). Protocole d'accord pour le suivi et la supervision de la mise en œuvre des activites du projet de renforcement des capacites pour la reduction de la vulnerabilite et pour l'adaptation aux changements climatiques (pana-bkf-pnud-fem) au Burkina Faso, Mouhoun, pp. 1–11.

Ministry of Environment and Sustainable Development. (2010b). Protocole d'accord pour le suivi et la supervision de la mise en œuvre des activites du projet de renforcement des capacites pour la reduction de la vulnerabilite et pour l'adaptation aux changements climatiques (pana-bkf-pnud-fem) au Burkina Faso, Namentenga, pp. 1–11.

Ministry of Environment and Sustainable Development. (2010c). Protocole d'accord pour le suivi et la supervision de la mise en œuvre des activites du projet de renforcement des capacites pour la reduction de la vulnerabilite et pour l'adaptation aux changements climatiques (pana-bkf-pnud-fem) au Burkina Faso, Sahel, pp. 1–11.

Ouadba, J. M. (2010). Rapport sur la region de la boucle du Mouhoun et les zovics communautaires pilotes, p. 10.

Ouadba, J. M. Hamade, K., & Harouna, K. (2008). Rapport sur la province du Ouadlan et les villages pilotes, p. 22.

SP/CONEDD. (2006). Contribution à l'évaluation de la vulnérabilite et de l'adaptation aux changements climatiques au Burkina Faso : Volet socio-économique, 23p.

SP/CONEDD. (2006). Evaluation de la vulnérabilité et des capacités d'adaptation aux changements climatiques du Burkina Faso, Ouagadougou, 85p.

UNDP. (2009). *Human development report 2009*. Retrieved from http://hdr.undp.org/en/reports/global/hdr2009/

UNFCCC. (2002). Annotated guidelines for the preparation of national adaptation programmes of action, Least Developed Countries Expert Group, p. 5.

CHAPTER 19

MALAWI SOCIAL ACTION FUND AND ITS EFFECTIVENESS IN DROUGHT RISK REDUCTION

Rajib Shaw

INTRODUCTION

Malawi is a nation with a population estimated at 13.1 million (Government of Malawi, 2008). It was ranked at number 166 out of 177 countries in the 2006 Human Development Index of the United Nations Development Program. The population is predominantly rural (83 percent), and the economy is highly dependent on agriculture, mainly smallholder farming and fishing. The per capita gross domestic product in 2006 was $160, down from $210 in 2001, and the annual national budget is approximately $1.3 billion (for 2007/08).

According to the 2007 Welfare Monitoring Survey, 40 percent of Malawians live below the poverty line and 15 percent are ultra-poor. This is an improvement from previous years: according to the 2005 Integrated Household Survey, 52.4 percent lived below the poverty line and 22.5 percent were ultra-poor. Investments in agriculture, education, health, and nutrition, among others, are deemed essential for sustainable poverty reduction. Short-term income transfer schemes can provide off-farm employment and increase incomes for the poor rural communities.

Community-Based Disaster Risk Reduction
Community, Environment and Disaster Risk Management, Volume 10, 373–386
Copyright © 2012 by Emerald Group Publishing Limited
All rights of reproduction in any form reserved
ISSN: 2040-7262/doi:10.1108/S2040-7262(2012)0000010025

   Historically, an over-centralized governance system created severe
problems in managing development programs. Before 1994, it was not easy
for communities, having mobilized their own contributions, to obtain timely
responses from the government with the financial and technical assistance
they required (World Bank, 1998). Increasing the participation of
communities and civil society in the planning and management of
community-level projects and adopting a "bottom-up" approach have been
recognized as essential elements of the development process in the new
democratic dispensation. Community participation in identification, preparation, and implementation – championed by the birth of the Malawi
Social Acton Fund (MASAF) in 1995 – has improved the setting of
priorities and the efficiency with which resources are used.
   This case study aims to present issues that underline risk reduction
strategies for a drought situation within a social protection framework.

THE MASAF PROGRAM, COMPONENTS, AND PROCEDURES

As client consultations and the implementation experience of the first
phase of MASAF showed, communities are capable of and willing to
cofinance development activities and implement them within reasonable
cost, duration, and quality norms. The Poverty Alleviation Program of
the Malawi government provided the conceptual and institutional
framework for addressing poverty in the national development strategy.
To strengthen the design, a review of similar funds in other countries was
also conducted. The MASAF project has been designed to act as a quick
disbursing instrument for support to development activities at the
community level.
   The Malawi Social Action Fund had three phases:

– MASAF-1, in 1995–1998, $56 million: social infrastructure and assistance
  and economic infrastructure.
– MASAF-2, in 1998–2003, $66 million: designed to build on the success of
  the first phase by reinforcing the spirit of self-help and continuing to deal
  with the country's pervasive poverty.
– MASAF-3 APL I, in 2003–2007 (the focus of this case study), $66 million:
  based on the Malawi Growth and Development Strategy (MGDS). The
  objective of the MGDS is to create wealth through sustainable economic

growth and infrastructure development as a means of achieving poverty reduction.

The guiding principles of MASAF-3 were as follows:

- *Autonomy and flexibility* in project management, procurement, and disbursement procedures but operating in harmony with ongoing decentralization activities to ensure sustainability
- *Demand-driven* following a bottom-up planning and decision-making approach
- *Accountability and transparency* in resource management and service delivery at community, district, and national levels
- *Nonpartisan and apolitical*
- *Leveraged use of public resources* in favor of the poor
- *Community empowerment* through direct financing and participatory project management within the District Development Planning System
- *Enhanced capacities* of members of local development structures, facilitators, and service providers (Government of Malawi, 2003).

Under this overall framework and strategy, specific objectives of MASAF-3 were as follows:

- To improve access to and use of socioeconomic services by communities in urban and rural areas
- To transfer cash income to poor households and individuals through creation of community assets
- To improve the quality of life for the most vulnerable persons
- To increase poor communities' access to savings and investment opportunities
- To develop and strengthen capacities of communities, local authorities (LAs), and civil society organizations for improved development management and local governance (World Bank, 2006).

The MASAF-3 project had five components:

- Community Development Projects to finance subprojects aimed at contributing to improving access to social and economic services
- Social Support Projects to cater to the needs of the critically vulnerable
- Community Savings and Investment Promotion (COMSIP) to promote a savings and investment culture among the poor
- Transparency and Accountability Promotion to promote accountability and capacity development for various participants in the project

– Institutional Development to retain a Management Unit (MU) and a
  support framework for communities and LAs in the implementation of
  the project.

The project objectives would be realized through the financing of five
service packages on education, health, water and sanitation, transport, and
food security defined by sector ministries, with the community subproject
cycle as the key tool for delivering subprojects.

The institutional arrangements for MASAF-3 were designed to support
the improved development management and local governance of LAs and
civil society organizations. At the national level, a Board was constituted to
provide overall policy guidance to MASAF. Two subcommittees provided
support to the Board: a National Technical Advisory Committee (NTAC)
and a National Advocacy Committee for Community Empowerment and
Accountability (NACCEA). The Board contained representatives of the
Office of the President, Secretaries of different ministries, the MASAF
executive director, representatives of traditional leadership, and independent members. It ensured that MASAF carries out its activities in
accordance with the operation manual, and the Board was responsible for
the approval of subprojects and annual work plan. NTAC consisted of
representatives of relevant ministries and was responsible for reviewing and
recommending approval of subprojects, advising on sector devolution
action plans, ensuring adherence to sector norms and standards, and
ensuring adequate budgetary provision. NACCEA consisted of relevant
ministries (Economic Planning, Decentralization), U.N. agencies, and donor
representatives (World Bank and the U.K. Department for International
Development (DFID) and reviewed adherence to accountability, bench-
marks, and monitoring and evaluation (M&E) reports, recommending LAs
that can assume full MASAF functions.

MASAF worked with national-level sector departments with respect to
policy direction and the enforcement of norms and standards. At the LA
level, MASAF worked with the District Executive Committee (DEC), which
includes sector representatives. The MASAF MU was responsible for the
day-to-day operation of the Fund, governed by the provisions of the
Operational Manual and other appropriate legal instruments agreed to by
the government and the funding agencies. It had zones and field offices to
provide technical support and management backstopping to the LAs as
requested. The zone office worked directly with the LAs through DEC and
provided technical support, ensured accountability, and linked districts to
the MU on monitoring, evaluation, and reporting.

DISASTER OCCURRENCES IN MALAWI

Drought, floods, and earthquakes are the three major natural disasters in Malawi. The northern part of the country is prone to drought, while the southern part is prone to both drought and flood. Earthquakes occur along the East African Rift Fault system. The drought of April 1992 was the most severe one in recent years, affecting more than 7 million people (out of a population of 10 million at the time). Floods, unlike droughts, have affected fewer people. The most severe flood occurred in January 2001, affecting more than 500,000 people, mostly in the southern districts. An earthquake in March 1989 was the most severe one in recent years, affecting more than 50,000 people. Thus, drought is regarded as the most severe disaster in Malawi, affecting mostly rural areas, and hence the focus of this case study. Any developmental activities in the rural areas therefore need to address drought mitigation.

Profile of the Drought

Agriculture, which is mainly rain-fed, is the most important sector of the economy in Malawi, accounting for about 39 percent of gross domestic product and employing around 85 percent of the workforce. It contributes to more than 90 percent of the country's foreign exchange earnings. The challenges in drought are to provide immediate relief supplies to the affected population and to design long-term recovery strategies to avert similar situations in the future. The promotion of drought-tolerant crops and crop diversification helps mitigate the impacts of droughts.

In 2005, Malawi faced one of its worst food crises in more than a decade, the result of a combination of factors, including drought, floods, consecutive poor harvests, endemic poverty, and the effects of the HIV/AIDS pandemic. More than 4.2 million people, over a third of the population, were unable to meet their food needs, with 2.8 million estimated to be in severe distress, some of whom were likely to resort to extreme coping mechanisms (such as taking children out of school or selling assets such as land). Production of maize, Malawi's most important staple crop, was estimated at nearly 1.3 million tons in 2005, the lowest in a decade and around 26 percent below production in the previous year, which in turn was also a relatively poor harvest. In November 2004, the Ministry of Agriculture indicated a national food balance of 256,781 tons of maize for Malawi and predicted a food gap of 189,886 tons.

While the shortage of food is a seasonal occurrence in the country, the 2004/2005 farming season saw a number of areas severely hit, with the level of food shortages reaching crisis proportions; many households faced the risk of shortfalls in minimum energy requirements (based on 2,100 kilocalories per person). Among the districts severely affected were Chitipa, Karonga, Kasungu, Dowa, Lilongwe, Dedza, Balaka, Machinga, Mulanje, Phalombe, Mwanza, Neno, Mangochi, Chikwawa, and Nsanje, where household food deficits were estimated at 15 percent or more of their yearly requirements. It is also worth noting that while imports of food through the private sector had improved during the same period, most poor households still had no access to food due to low incomes (Malawi Vulnerability Assessment Committee, 2005).

The crucial rainy season in Malawi runs from November to February. In 2005, early and above-average rains raised hopes for a good crop, but the rains failed during the critical period from late January to the end of February, when the maize crop was pollinating and forming cobs. The dry spell also coincided with cassava and sweet potato planting in some areas. In addition, exceptionally heavy rains in December and early January caused flooding and crop losses, especially in the southern and central part of the country. The impacts of the failed harvest were not felt fully until the lean season set in between October and April.

Most of the areas affected by drought or flooding in this year were already facing critical food shortages, and many families lost both their crops in the field and their food stores. These households needed not only food aid but also agricultural inputs, such as seeds and fertilizers for the next planting season, starting in October 2005. Assistance was also needed to help vulnerable households broaden their economic base. The Food and Agriculture Organization promoted crop diversification (to reduce reliance on maize), small livestock production, small-scale irrigation, and income-generating activities.

Interventions such as the promotion of home gardens and nutrition education for HIV/AIDS-affected households and malnourished children were needed to help improve the health and nutritional status of these most vulnerable groups. Other proposed activities included the promotion of drought-tolerant crops, such as cassava and sweet potatoes, forestation in flood-prone areas to improve soil structure, and establishment of fruit tree nurseries and primary school orchards to improve child nutrition.

Immediate Response

In response to the crisis, the government of Malawi and stakeholders put in place programs to give individuals and poor families access to food.

The programs included targeted food distribution (largely through World Food Program and the Nongovernmental Organization Consortium) and Public Works Programs for cash transfers, as well as programs that combined food and cash transfers. Other programs to address cross-cutting problems included supplementary feeding programs for lactating mothers and malnourished children (below five years of age) and school feeding programs.

The January 2005 Malawi Vulnerability Assessment Committee report on Food Security noted the need for the existing major cash transfer operations to be able to adopt a rapid response approach and to have a nationwide reach in order to play an effective role in ameliorating the effects of the drought (USAID, 2005). It was against this background, and within this overall framework, that MASAF supported an emergency drought response public works program (PWP) that specifically targeted able-bodied persons.

International Responses and Coordination

The Regional Office facilitated the preparation of the Inter-Agency Regional Humanitarian Strategic Framework for Southern Africa, launched in April 2005. This framework guided the humanitarian response, identifying actions required to address immediate and longer-term needs. The response to identified emergency needs was also increasingly integrated into longer-term planning and national development plans. The regional office of the U.N. Office for Coordination of Humanitarian Affairs continued to support the Special Envoy for Humanitarian Needs in Southern Africa, who becomes the relief coordinator in case of disasters in Southern African countries. The regional office supported a regional coordinator, with regular missions and the deployment of humanitarian affairs officers to Malawi, Madagascar, and Namibia. In Malawi, the office helped prepare the Flash Appeal and assisted with monitoring and reporting on progress as well as a revision in November 2005.

The interagency contingency planning process brought together key regional stakeholders, ensuring that participants were informed of the status of preparedness in their respective countries, and consolidated a comprehensive picture of the support expected. The regional office also developed a matrix that strengthened linkages between early warning and early action in the region, contributing to an International Association for the Study of the Commons (IASC) Early Warning-Early Action.

The Malawi Vulnerability Assessment Committee estimated that the equivalent of some 270,000 tons of maize was required. The estimates represented the minimum humanitarian need through March 2006. The World Food Program planned to provide assistance to 2 million vulnerable people in seven districts in the Southern Region, as well as nutrition support in all districts. The remaining 2.2 million people were to be assisted through government, other food distribution, and voucher schemes and through cash interventions.

The second track of the Flash Appeal was intended to increase local production, thereby minimizing the prospect of another food crisis the following year. Malawi's impoverished farm households face conditions of pervasive soil nutrient deficiencies and lack access to critical farm inputs. The result is that crop yields are chronically low and highly vulnerable to transitory shortfalls in rains during the growing season. The appeal called for immediate support to ensure that the government's plan to sell seed and fertilizer at subsidized rates was bolstered, with seed and fertilizer made available to over 1 million poor farm households who could not afford it even at subsidized rates. The government was already leading a logistical operation to manage the targeted distribution of the subsidized seed and fertilizer; the same mechanism was used to ensure that seed and fertilizer were made available to poorer farming households. To support this program in time for the next growing season, the United Nations sought pledges from the international community by mid-September 2005.

MASAF PUBLIC WORKS PROGRAM FOR DROUGHT RESPONSE

The national reach of the MASAF Project management framework presented an opportunity to implement a conditional cash transfer (CCT) operation that would quickly cover the whole country and, in the process, transfer a relatively large volume of cash to individuals and households in distress. Moreover, since the LA had been managing public works projects under MASAF over the past 10 years, there was the capacity to handle and deliver this drought response operation. A total of 1,849 projects were implemented throughout the country between September and December 2005. An estimated 590,000 beneficiaries received MK200 each per day for working on a PWP subproject over 10 days. This amount would enable a household to buy a 50-kilogram bag of maize and a 50-kilogram bag of fertilizer. The total amount of funds spent on the MASAF-funded program amounted to $12.1 million.

The objective of the PWP cash transfer program was to support poor able-bodied individuals with cash transfers to get access to food and farm inputs through participation in a public works program for two weeks. In the process of transferring the cash, the program also sought to support the creation of economic assets such as short village access roads with earthworks of a maximum 12 kilometers (rehabilitation), soil and water conservation systems such as contour ridges, land reclamation, manure creation, dam rehabilitation, and food security projects. To ensure that transfers were made quickly and in time to assist the affected communities, all funds to finance activities under the program were released to LA accounts that were managed by the local assemblies.

In a bid to increase transparency and ensure that communities were informed about the MASAF cash transfer covered, among other topics, sensitization on program objectives and outputs, who was eligible to participate, the period of the cash transfer operation (limited to two weeks), the amount of cash per day, expected use of the cash (purchase of food and farm inputs), a comparison with ongoing LA-managed projects, and stakeholder responsibilities – government, MASAF, district commissioners, district agricultural development officers, and so on. This was done largely through radio, posters, and community meetings.

The key features of the program included the following:

- The beneficiaries would be individuals identified locally from vulnerable households through community targeting arrangements. These would either be people working on ongoing LA projects or people who would be recruited for new projects as part of the PWP-CCT program.
- Implementation of the program was to last two weeks (10 days). For new projects, this meant works had to be completed within the two weeks, while for ongoing regular LA-managed projects, once the two weeks was over the regular PWP implementation procedures would apply – that is, a return to the original cash transfer rate of MK47 per task for town and city assemblies and MK43 for rural areas.
- PWP-CCT transferred MK200 per person per day for working eight hours task toward creating economic assets that would be beneficial to communities.
- PWP participants were required to use the grant element of the wage for the purchase of subsidized farm inputs provided by government.

- The total unskilled wage transfer would not be less than 80 percent of the total subproject cost.
- The project budget would include a 2.5 percent allocation for administrative expenses and 17.5 percent for works and other costs.
- Projects would be launched with a briefing on objectives and modalities of the cash transfer mitigation. Beneficiaries would be encouraged to form Community Savings and Investment Groups to ensure that savings were made to facilitate negotiations for better price.

MASAF public works benefits as part of a national social protection instrument are presented in the Quiet Revolution (MASAF, 1995–2005). Specific outcomes from the 2006 MASAF cash transfer are detailed in the MASAF 3 APL 1 Impact Evaluation Report. The results show that the CCT assisted households to gain access to 14 percent of the total quantity of subsidized farm inputs supplied in 2005/06. The staple food produce from the participants totaled 487,000 tons, which is equivalent to 22 percent of the national annual staple food requirement.

POST-DISASTER APPROACHES

MASAF incorporated the lessons from previous public works programs in the design of the of the 2006 drought response. The lessons have also informed the design of public works interventions included as a subcomponent of the Third Malawi Social Action Fund (MASAF 3) APL II (Local Development Fund Mechanism) for 2008–2013. Before 2006, MASAF had conducted several drought mitigation actions through its programs; these included Relief Cash for Work in 2002–2003 and DFID 1 and 2 (both public works projects) and Emergency Drought Recovery Programme of 2003–2004, which combined public works activities and social support interventions.

This section describes two specific subprojects that illustrate different dimensions of drought mitigation that benefited from the 2006 Public Works Cash Transfer project and a localized Bua Dwangwa Drought Mitigation Irrigation project. The presentation includes a demonstration of how the formation of sustainable savings and investment groups or federations has assisted in the expansion of revenue among potentially ultra-poor communities. This has been done through facilitation by the Community Savings and Investment Promotion, a baby of the MASAF.

The Nkhokwe Forestation Project is located in Kasungu district. The project is a combination of PWP and a Community Savings and Investment Program. Through the facilitation by the Village Natural Resource Management Committee, the project targeted raising people's awareness of the need to develop forest as an alternative livelihood and also a way to recharge groundwater. The planted forest will be the community's common asset, and the income from the forest will be used to develop a community credit system, with the help of the COMSIP program. COMSIP provided training to the local communities on mobilization of savings and development of an investment culture. The afforestation project also helped local communities generate fertilizers through compost. In the long term, this will help reduce farmers' dependence on the costly fertilizer, which often becomes too expensive. Thus, the project is helping the local communities develop a sustainable and resilient system through income-generation activities and through enhancing social and economic capital.

The Manthimba Irrigation Project is located in Thyolo District in southern Malawi. Local farmers started an irrigation system in 2001 with the participation of 15 farmers; with the help of MASAF, this gradually grew to 500 beneficiaries (380 male and 120 female farmers). Through the establishment of the community committee for the irrigation project, the local villagers developed several subcommittees and expanded their work into adjoining areas. The communities decided their own rules for water distribution from the irrigation channel to the cultivated land through mutual understanding. Experience from participation of a MASAF-funded project enabled the communities to submit a proposal to their assembly for funding of a school project and a community bridge as a part of the PWP program. Community leaders and members report that the yield per hectare doubled after the irrigation project and that the crop cycles increased from one to three after irrigation. However, there are still some problems – like access to the market and storage of grains – that need to be solved in order for the village to have a sustainable livelihood scheme. This is why the group is now registered as a cooperative affiliated to COMSIP.

The goal of the Community Savings and Investment Program is to cultivate a culture of savings among all communities in Malawi to help them save resources to be invested in the productive sectors of the economy. The main objective is to create a favorable environment and incentives for the communities to save through groups and clubs and obtain access to financial services. The operations and management of the COMSIP are based on the following principles:

- Voluntary formation of groups and mobilization into savings clubs to access financial services
- Democratic participation by members in the decision-making process at group/club level
- Capacity enhancement for groups or clubs to ensure adequate return, security, and timely access to financial services
- Mobilization of savings and investments in favor of the group/club members
- Accountability and transparency in resource management and service delivery at group/club levels

Thus, COMSIP helps develop the collective savings culture of the community, which helps diversify livelihoods and can in essence act as a drought mitigation measure. COMSIP is now registered as a body corporate as COMSIP Cooperative Union Limited under the Cooperative Act 1998.

LESSONS LEARNED AND RECOMMENDATIONS

MASAF was innovative and proactive in its timely response to drought as well as in bringing the response and recovery lessons to risk reduction, especially for drought mitigation. The following lessons have been linked to the successful operation of MASAF based on this case study. The success of the risk reduction PWP affected the availability of excess food immediately after a disaster; the production was equivalent to a natural surplus declared by the government.

Evolution and Characterization of MASAF:

- The autonomy and flexibility of MASAF was used for fast-track project design in times of disaster.
- Community participation and accountability were the core issues of MASAF, which were enhanced by a performance-driven approach and multiple skills. MASAF had a legacy of performance and speed of response.
- To tap local knowledge in project appraisal, MASAF focused on LAs and traditional authorities.

Drought Response:

- Prompt decision-making helped in timely interventions for the drought response, which helped communities buy seeds and fertilizers to secure livelihoods through the public works program.

- Community empowerment was at the core of MASAF operations, even during the emergency situation. This was evident in the response to the cash issue through the public works program, followed by infrastructure and capacity-building.
- Drought interventions require coordinated efforts from various stake-holders: the Ministry of Agriculture provided data on farm produce, the Ministry of Economic Planning provided vulnerability data, MASAF provided the resources, Local Assemblies provided implementation support to communities, and communities themselves identified the participants.
- The information, education, and communications campaign of MASAF targeted specific messages for specific groups and also focused on accountability, which contributed to the success of the programs.

Diversification and Innovation in Project Components:

- The Community Savings Program instilled a cooperative culture and links to international financial institutions. There were no direct credits from MASAF, but social capital development from the regular program of MASAF was used. Usually during drought, assets were commonly sold, but this was stopped through COMSIP by encouraging group lending.
- The public works program brought additional assets to communities. These include upgrading of paths to roads, construction of community bridges, the cleaning of rivers, and the introduction of water and soil management, afforestation, and small-scale irrigation.

Drought Preparedness Measures:

- The success from irrigation projects has reduced dependence on rain-fed agriculture and the planting of early-maturing crops that result in high yields on short rainfall.
- The COMSIP database on its affiliates can be used as a basis for weather insurance and a source of information on behaviors of market forces during drought (fluctuation of price, demand-supply chain).
- The forestation projects developed in a situation where a demand for forest products was already high have become a source of community incomes.

ACKNOWLEDGMENT

The author acknowledges support from The World Bank Social Fund Community Driven Development (SF-CDD) for this study.

REFERENCES

Government of Malawi. (2003). Office of the president and cabinet. *MASAF III/CEDP Operational Manual*, December. Malawi Vulnerability Assessment Committee, 2005, *Food Security Monitoring Report*, January.

Government of Malawi. (2008). National statistics office, Preliminary National Census data November, 2008.

Malawi Vulnerability Assessment Committee. (2005). Malawi National Vulnerability Assessment Report (118 pages), MVAC, Lolongwe, Malawi.

Malawi Welfare Monitoring Survey. (2007). *Statistical Abstract*. March 2007. MASAF (Malawi Social Action Fund). *The Quiet Revolution*.

MASAF. (1995–2005). MASAF 3 APL 1 Impact Evaluation Report. March 2008.

MASAF (Malawi Social Action Fund) and PWP-CCT (Public Works Program–Conditional Cash Transfer). (2006). *Citizen feedback on performance and implementation of the drought response program*. October 2006

World Bank. (1998). *MASAF Project implementation manual*. Washington, DC.

World Bank. (2006). *MASAF Project implementation status*. Washington, DC.

PART V
THE WAY AHEAD

CHAPTER 20

FUTURE PERSPECTIVES OF COMMUNITY-BASED DISASTER RISK REDUCTION

Rajib Shaw

INTRODUCTION

Disasters are often categorized in terms of numbers, that is, the number of casualties, number of injuries, or number of financial or asset losses. However, for the people and community living in a location, loss of even one life is significant to them. A single lost house is crucial to the affected family. Whether a disaster is major or minor, of national or local proportion, it is the people in the community who suffer most its adverse effects. They use coping and survival strategies to face and respond to the situation long before help from the government or NGOs arrives (Victoria, 2009). The following key features that distinguish community-based disaster risk reduction (CBDRR) from the top-down and traditional-aid approaches are based on current practices and experiences (Victoria, 2009):

a. *People's participation*: In CBDRR, the community members are the main actors. They sustain the disaster risk reduction process and pursue disaster risk management activities. They benefit both in the participatory process and from the results of CBDRR and community development.

Community-Based Disaster Risk Reduction
Community, Environment and Disaster Risk Management, Volume 10, 389–402
Copyright © 2012 by Emerald Group Publishing Limited
All rights of reproduction in any form reserved
ISSN: 2040-7262/doi:10.1108/S2040-7262(2012)0000010026

b. *Priority for the most vulnerable groups, families, and people in the community*: While the participation of all sectors in society is needed for disaster risk reduction, priority in CBDRR is given to the most vulnerable groups. In the urban areas, the most vulnerable sectors are generally the urban poor and informal sector, while in the rural areas these are the subsistence farmers, fisher-folk, and indigenous people. Special attention is given to the needs and concerns of children and women (because of their care-giving and social function roles), the elderly, and the disabled people.

c. *Risk reduction measures are community-specific*: The CBDRR takes into consideration the particular context of the community. Appropriate risk reduction measures are identified after an analysis of the community's disaster risk (hazard exposure, vulnerabilities, and capacities). Various participatory tools are used to consider people's varying perceptions of disaster risk and solutions to community problems and risk reduction.

d. *Existing coping mechanisms and capacities are recognized*: The CBDRR builds upon and strengthens existing coping strategies and capacities. Although lacking in material assets, communities can rely on traditional wisdom, local knowledge and resources, social organizations, shared values and coping mechanisms as cooperative endeavor, close family ties, and attitudes of perseverance and being resourceful.

e. *Disaster risk reduction is linked with development*: Simply put, the aim of the CBDRR is to reduce vulnerabilities by strengthening individuals, families, and communities. It seeks to address conditions, factors, processes, and causes of vulnerabilities brought about by poverty, social inequality, and environmental resource depletion and degradation. It subscribes to people-centered development as well as equitable and sustainable development. The goal of the CBDRR is building safer, disaster-resilient, and developed communities.

f. *Outsiders have supporting and facilitating role*: The community being the main actor in the CBDRR, the role of the NGOs is supportive, facilitative, and catalytic. The government's role on the other hand is integral to the institutionalization of the CBDRR process. Partnerships with less vulnerable groups and other communities are forged for disaster risk reduction.

Based on the case study examples described in the book, this chapter focuses on key issues and future perspectives of the CBDRR.

CASE EXAMPLES: KEY OBSERVATIONS

This book contains in total 18 examples, apart from the first and this last chapters. Among the 18 case examples, the first four chapters focus on stakeholder-based analysis, emphasizing the roles of governments, non-government, academic, and corporate sectors. The next 14 chapters describe specific cases of the CBDRR from 14 different countries and regions. Table 1 summarizes the key observations from the case examples.

INNOVATION: THE KEY ISSUE

One of the key aspects of the CBDRR is its innovation to suit the specific context. These innovations can be internal, made by the local communities based on the experiences, or can be injected successfully by the external actors, and then customized by the local communities. As exemplified in the Bangladesh case (Habiba & Shaw, 2012), the floating garden is a classic innovation approach to cope with the long-time flooding. Most parts of Bangladesh, being very flat and rivers bringing lots of sediments, the characteristic of the annual flooding is slow and long-term flooding, and water remains in the vicinity for 2–3 months. People have been historically accustomed to the flooding; however, the key issue is the food security during this long flooding time, and some source of livelihood income. Floating garden helps to solve these two problems: it provides food for the people, as well as when in excess, it can be sold to the neighbors to get some small amount of money to secure livelihood. Since the water level increases gradually, the level of the garden also increases, and there is not that much of damage to the floating garden due to flooding. This innovative practice is indigenous to the local community, and has been generated over years of experience.

Takeuchi and Shaw (2009) described the unique practices of ring dyke existing over the years in the flood plains in Japan. Since in previous days, the dyke system did not exist in most of the Japanese rivers, people living in the flood plains had their houses close to each other, and created a ring dyke to protect the cluster of houses. The key implication of the ring dyke is not just the protection but also a strong sense of community cohesion, which existed among the community people to check and monitor ring dyke during flood time. However, in recent years, after the creation of dyke system along the major rivers, the need of creating a ring dyke is now no more; however,

Table 1. Summary of Key Lessons from Case Examples.

	Case Examples	Observations	Summary
Stakeholders	Governments	Government ownership of CBDRR through traditional community systems	While it is important for the government to take leadership on CBDRR, it should be done in close cooperation with the NGOs, academics, and corporate sectors through multistakeholder cooperation.
	NGOs	National NGOs play crucial roles in CBDRR	
	Academics	Educational linkages is an important aspect for CBDRR	
	Corporate sectors	Corporate community interface is an important for the CBDRR	
Asian examples	Bangladesh	Innovations in rural CBDRR is the key to cope with different types of hazards	Innovation is one of the key issues for the CBDRR in Asia.
	India	Urban CBDRR needs specific approach of linking to daily environmental management	Urban and rural contexts are different, and need to be treated separately.
	Indonesia	CSOs like women, youth, and religious groups play important roles in CBDRR	Based on the socioeconomic and cultural conditions, it is important to identify the right change agent for the CBDRR activities.
	Japan	Linking disaster risk reduction and daily welfare issue is the key to the success of the CBDRR in Japanese society	Youth always play an important role, and needs to be highlighted.
	Myanmar	To reach the unreachable, it is important to link to the existing community practices and system	Linking to government policy is important to institutionalize the efforts.
	Philippines	Traditional DRR approaches need to be linked to the emerging issues, and need to be enhanced through youth participation	
	Vietnam	CBDRR is recognized widely at the government levels; however, the key to the success is the linking to the changing environment, especially with the youth participation	

Example	Country/Region	Description	Key point
	Timor Leste	Participatory disaster risk assessment is an important process of community involvement. This is especially useful for the newly formed state to institutionalize CBDRR	
Central American Example	Central America Region	Regional review shows that the CBDRR has increased in terms of projects and partnership among different agencies. Long-term emphasis is required to sustain the efforts	The key point is the government interventions, and linking external and internal CBDRR practices.
	Guatemala	In postdisaster reconstruction program, it is important to link the economic activities and basic services to enhance community participation and ensure sustainability	Postdisaster reconstruction is an important process to mobilize community for long-term DRR activities.
	Costa Rica	Need-based solutions (especially for the frequent disasters like hurricane or flood, it is possible to sustain the community-based early warning system)	Need-based approach is important to sustain CBDRR activities.
African example	Africa Region	Regional review shows that the key of CBDRR in Africa is the institutionalize efforts and recognition by the government entities	Livelihood security is the key to the CBDRR activities.
	Burkina Faso	Climate change impacts and livelihood security is the key to the CBDRR activities	
	Malawi	Social fund leads to community-based interventions to sustain livelihood with the argument that it helps in the DRR activities at the community levels	

Note: Some of these key issues and observations would be discussed in the next part of the chapter.

the basic principles practiced in the old days (in terms of community cohesion and community-based flood monitoring) is still applicable, and people practice collective watching during times of flooding. This is a classic example of how the old community practices can still be used in the modern days based on certain modifications to cope with the changes.

In the case of Myanmar example (Shikada, Myint, Gyi, Nakagawa, & Shaw, 2012), the innovation in the concept is introduced by the external agency (nongovernmental organization, in this case). It is a common practice to develop resource centers as a part of the postdisaster recovery process. However, in most cases if the resource centers are not properly linked to the existing education system, it is difficult to continue after certain years. The reason for frequent failures is lack of visitors in the resource center, and Myanmar is no exception to this. To overcome this challenge, the mobile knowledge center concept has been coined, and the target is to reach the unreachable by using truck (to the areas that are accessible by road) and ship (areas not accessible by road, but only through river channels).

In summary, there exist different examples of innovations. It is important to identify them, analyze them, and bring out the lessons or principles behind these innovations. The success of the CBDRR often depends on the nature of the innovative practices by the local communities.

OWNERSHIP: THE DRIVING FORCE

Traditionally, the CBDRR has been practiced by nongovernmental organizations (NGOs), civil society organizations (CSOs), or community-based organizations (CBOs). Since these organizations have their presence at grassroot levels, and have proximity to the communities, they are well equipped and better positioned to conduct the CBDRR activities. International organizations (like United Nations or INGO (international NGOs)) usually partner with the local NGOs, CSOs, or CBOs when conducting the CBDRR activities. However, all these activities have resource limitations, and most of them cease to exist after the completion of the project. Here comes the state ownership of the CBDRR. Although the actual implementation needs to be done at the local level, the national and/or local governments should take the leadership and ownership in the CBDRR. Shaw and Okazaki (2003) in the User Manual, have pointed out the need and justification of state ownership of the CBDRR. Japan is a classic example of this. As shown in Matsuoka, Joerin, Shaw, and Takeuchi (2012), the Kobe city government has promoted the concept of CBDRR through establishing the "Bokomi" ("Bousai fukushi community" in Japanese, meaning disaster prevention and welfare community in English), through funding, providing human resources, and linking them to different activities within and outside the city. The city government's support and extending the platform for community activities has been effective in sustaining the efforts at the community level. The Japan International Cooperation Agency (JICA) has been proactive in implementing and promoting the CBDRR through its bilateral and multilateral donor activities. The key point of JICA's work is to maintain close link with the national governments in counterpart countries. Promotion of CBDRR through this type of bilateral funding enhances the possibility of its sustenance in long term, and in several countries it is found to be included in the national policies and priorities.

China is the other extreme, where 1,000 pilot community formations have been started over the past several years. The national government has formulated criteria of a model community, and different communities can apply based on these criteria to participate in the program. After the evaluation, the national and provincial governments decide on the pilot communities. A trained person is hired to be at the core of the CBDRR activities, who manages the communication within the community as well as outside the community.

After the 1999 Central Vietnam historic flood, the Vietnam government has also started the CBDRR programs at national levels with support from international agencies (like the World Bank, JICA) in house funding (through state budget) and also with support from the INGOs (like Red Cross, etc.). Here also, the sustainability relies on the involvement of the national and provincial government in supporting the CBDRR activities, whereas the actual work is conducted by CBOs like farmer associations, women unions, youth unions, etc.

In case of Bangladesh, the CBDRR has been practiced over time, and major INGOs and national NGOs have been champions for this over the years. However, through the recent national program of Comprehensive Disaster Management Program (CDMP) with the United Nations Development Programme (UNDP), efforts have been made to institutionalize the CBDRR activities in local governments. This is related to the sustainability of efforts, as mentioned earlier. In case of Philippines, the Barangay Calamity Fund (Barangay is the lowest level of administrative unit with development budget) can now be used for disaster risk reduction activities as per the newly approved national law. This has a strong significance in the sense that the local governments can use part of its annual budget to continue the CBDRR activities. In summary, based on the nature of the country, the government or state ownership varies for CBDRR. In one extreme, the national government takes ownership and provides resources to be directly implemented by the local governments. In other cases, the government provides funding for the NGOs or other partners to implement the CBDRR. Both are important forms of ownership, and need to be recognized for the continuation of CBDRR activities.

SOCIAL CAPITAL: BRIDGING AND BONDING

In comparative studies carried out on societal performance, some societies or communities have performed better than others. These relative differences in performance in certain situations, even with the same given capitals and opportunities, have not been fully explained – leading to construction of the concept of "social capital," which became popular since it helped to account for such differences (Nakagawa & Shaw, 2004).

Social capital generally refers to networks, social norms, and trust that attribute to positive or negative results in social or economic performance at individual or group level. The term became popular after Robert Putnam's analysis on regional government performance in Italy (Putnam, Leonardi, & Nanetti, 2003). He claimed that northern Italy showed better government performance than its southern counterpart due to high horizontal networks, which was measured using four indicators (association density, newspaper readership, referenda turnout, and preference voting) in the region. His analysis literally opened up the social capital debate, which continues till now. (It has to be noted that the concept of social capital was used and analyzed by several researchers before Putnam, but current discussions have largely been inspired by his work).

One of the significant features of social capital is to understand it from two perspectives (Nakagawa & Shaw, 2004): "bonding" social capital that literally bonds each member with strong ties in a particular group or society, and "bridging" social capital, which is cross-cutting ties beyond that group. Bonding social capital leads to reciprocity and helping each other, but on the other hand may also create negative results or impacts as a result of exclusion from other groups. Bridging social capital in contrast is "voluntary cross-cutting networks, associations, and related norms based in everyday social interactions that lead to the collective good of citizens." Although both are important aspects of social capital, bridging social capital is said to create synergies for better outcomes. Nakagawa (2009) has mentioned that, in a postdisaster scenario, the response period requires bonding social capital. However, when it comes to recovery and reconstruction, the need for bridging social capital increases to fulfill the necessary preconditions.

A similar observation is made by Mimaki and Shaw (2010) in the postdisaster response recovery and predisaster preparedness experiences of Tosashimizu in Kochi prefecture of Japan. Comparing two communities in the same city, the study shows that the community with a strong leader of both bridging and bonding capacity can enhance the potential of the CBDRR activities in terms of sustainability.

PROCESS AND PRODUCT: THE BALANCED MIX

Another important issue is the process adopted by the local community in CBDRR. This is often ignored or not properly documented. The product becomes more important, and in many cases, the initiatives usually focus on the successful completion of the project. For last several years, the process-based approach has been emphasized, and is considered as a useful technology. Kameda (2009) defines technology as "a set of rational means and knowledge pertinent to realizing specific objectives that have solid logical bases and stability." In a conventional recognition, technology meant just engineering products. But when we consider implementation strategies, technologies should involve not only products but processes as well. This requires innovation of research community to reform from "product-focused research" to "process-oriented research" or to "product–process linked research."

Kameda (2009) classified technology as:

- Implementation-oriented technology (IOT): Products from modern research and development that are practiced under clear implementation strategies
- Process technology (PT): Know-how for implementation and practice, capacity building, and social development for knowledge ownership
- Transferable indigenous knowledge (TIK): Traditional art of disaster reduction that is indigenous to specific region(s) but has the potential to be applied to other regions and has time-tested reliability.

Criteria for process technology (PT) include the following:

- Emphasis on "practical use" of research
- A tested methodology with social, cultural, economic, ecological, and technical feasibilities, developed through an implementation/testing process ensuring results in disaster reduction

- Demonstrated stakeholders' participation and enhanced ownership
  - of the process
  - of results and lessons
- Amenable/adaptable to local context, and with institutionalization potential
- In-depth knowledge and insight gained through experience with disasters and mitigation.

Thus, the CBDRR issues need to be looked at with the above criteria of process technology, where stakeholder participation becomes important. It needs to be recognized that with practical implication of the CBDRR, local adaptable practices and experiences of the local stakeholders are very crucial for the success of the CBDRR.

EDUCATIONAL LINKAGES: ENHANCE PROFESSIONALISM

There have been different training programs of the CBDRR, conducted by different organizations over past several years. These training programs are very important and need to be continued. However, to enhance the professionalism for CBDRR and to generate new and young professionals, it is important to link the CBDRR in the higher education curriculum. By saying that, it is not the purpose to develop separate courses on the CBDRR, rather to incorporate CBDRR in the existing curriculum, and to ensure that the higher education teaching of the CBDRR goes beyond the university boundaries.

To enhance the professionalism in the CBDRR, following can be a few suggestive steps in terms of higher education:

- To link the CBDRR to the existing curriculum in different disciplines (from engineering to architecture, planning to economics to agriculture)
- To ensure that the CBDRR training does not confine to university boundaries only
- To encourage students to perform tasks on the extracurricular activities, and go beyond the schools
- To invite professionals from NGOs or other organizations to provide lectures on the CBDRR.

ENVIRONMENTAL MANAGEMENT: KEY ENTRY POINT

Building up and sustaining urban community institutions beyond certain timeframe is considered very difficult. Success of the CBDRR initiatives heavily rely on such established community-owned institutions (Surjan, Redkar, & Shaw, 2009). In Mumbai, India, Advanced Locality Management (ALM), as a system recognized at ward level, provides people with single window access to most civic services. Today, there are about 783 ALM groups (CDP reports 584 ALM committees) covering a population of about 2 million, functioning in the city. This is an ongoing initiative further adopted in the local government charter in 2006 to scale up as Local Area Citizens Group (LACG) Partnership – 2006.

Until 2005 flood in Mumbai, India, the ALM remained a locally recognized entity that helps in garbage management. Ironically, the city government advocates for the CBDRR but overlooked such citizens' committees' possible role. Interestingly, the ALMs as organized community groups were of tremendous help during the 2005 flood (which was among the heaviest floods in the past 100 years in Mumbai) by directly involving in rescue, relief, and provision of medical aid, food, and water to the affected populations. Had these ALM members oriented beforehand by organizing mock-drills for various disaster scenarios, conducting training and skill development in search and rescue, temporary shelter, mobilizing local resources, and volunteering with other relief agencies, the impact of flood would have been significantly lower. After experiencing disaster, many ALMs voluntarily came forward and searched for capacity-building options in disaster management. The study by Surjan et al. (2009) showed that the active ALMs were well equipped to cope with the flood disasters in 2005. This is significant in the sense that ALMs are mainly built for environmental problem solving, but they enhance people's relationships and community ties for collective actions, which was reflected during the flooding. Thus, there has been a very strong correlation between the environmental management and disaster risk reduction at community levels.

A similar study by Srinivas, Shaw, and Nakagawa (2009) suggested that after the 2004 Typhoon 21 and 23, the city of Toyooka has taken keen initiative to improve its environmental management, and thereby focus on the improvements in disaster risk reduction at community levels. A predisaster environmental planning at the community level helps to enhance the actions in the postdisaster scenario.

Shaw (2009) has described the roles of different local stakeholders in the community-based initiative for disaster risk reduction. The stakeholders may play two roles: (1) whether intentionally or not, they may be contributing to the need of disaster risk in a community, and (2) recognizing that they contribute to disaster risk reduction, they are actively involved in it. Examples from the first category include people who throw garbage into drainage and river systems; NGOs who implement primary health-care projects to reduce morbidity and mortality but ignore the importance of educating women and children on the basics of flood and/or cyclone warning systems in disaster prone areas; local authorities who ignore the existence and movement of informal settlements on dangerous hillsides and river-erosion-prone areas; engineers and artisans who ignore building codes relating to earthquake and other physical risks; and so on.

Naturally, the second category is desirable. For example, a safer community is achieved with school administrators and teachers actively involved in disaster education and school safety programs. Religious groups are promoting awareness of risks and practical measures to reduce them. Local authorities enforce land-use planning and building codes. Local private business groups contribute funds and resources for local risk reduction solutions. There are as many examples that can be highlighted, which essentially suggest that risk reduction is everybody's concern. This is contrary to traditional thinking that disaster management is the exclusive responsibility of emergency services, the IFRC, civil defense groups, and social welfare agencies. The task of implementers of the CBDRR includes facilitating networking and coordination of broad stakeholders' participation, which implies that good governance that encourages constituents' involvement is the basic foundation that contributes to sustainable CBDRR.

Good governance provides a favorable environment for broad stakeholders' participation. Specific roles and responsibilities of a particular stakeholder must be identified based on their own understanding of their own value and abilities. In some cases like in the Philippines and India, these relationships among stakeholders are formal and legislated. But informal relationships also proved to be effective and do not necessarily hinder partnership arrangements at the community level. The choice depends on the political structure in a particular country and the perceived level of governance in the area, although experience shows that formal institutional arrangements among stakeholders improve accountability and transparency, which is important for the sustainability of the CBDRR. Public awareness on disaster reduction is one good practice that may promote easier mobilization of local initiatives and other stakeholders. In this age of speedy media coverage, internet, and advancement of technologies, mobilizing "public" support is greatly enhanced for effective local actions.

ACKNOWLEDGMENTS

This chapter is an output of several years of research on CBDRR in different countries. The experiences and support of the researchers over the years are highly acknowledged.

REFERENCES

Habiba, U., & Shaw, R. (2012). Bangladesh experiences of community-based disaster risk reduction. In R. Shaw (Ed.), *Community-based disaster risk reduction* (pp. 91–111). Bingley, UK: Emerald.

Kameda, H. (2009). Implementation technology for disaster reduction. In R. Shaw & R. Krishnamurthy (Eds.), *Disaster management: Global challenges and local solutions* (pp. 206–219). Hyderabad, India: University Press.

Matsuoka, Y., Joerin, J., Shaw, R., & Takeuchi, Y. (2012). Partnership between city government and community-based disaster prevention organizations in Kobe, Japan. In R. Shaw (Ed.), *Community based disaster risk reduction* (pp. 151–184). Bingley, UK: Emerald.

Mimaki, J., & Shaw, R. (2010). Residents' collective actions for disaster preparedness through community-based organization: A case study of a coastal town in the Kochi prefecture of the Shikoku region. In R. Shaw & R. Krishnamurthy (Eds.), *Communities and coastal zone management* (pp. 201–216). Singapore: Research Publishers.

Nakagawa, Y. (2009). Community based disaster management and social capital. In Shaw, R. & Krishnamurthy R. (Eds.), *Disaster management: Global challenges and local solutions* (pp. 365–383). Hyderabad, India: University Press.

Nakagawa, Y., & Shaw, R. (2004). Social capital: A missing link to disaster recovery. *International Journal of Mass Emergency and Disaster, 22*(1), 5–34.

Putnam, R. D., Leonardi, R., & Nanetti, R. (2003). *Making democracy work: Civic traditions in modern Italy*. Princeton, NJ: Princeton University Press.

Shaw, R. (2009). Role of local actors in community based disaster risk management. In *Perspectives in disaster management* (pp. 123–145). Turkey: METU Press.

Shaw, R., & Okazaki, K. (2003). *Sustainability in grass-roots initiatives: Focus on community based disaster management* (99 pp.). Kobe, Japan: UNCRD Publication.

Shikada, M., Myint, U. T., Gyi, U. K. K., Nakagawa, Y., & Shaw, R. (2012). Reaching the unreachable: Myanmar experiences of community based disaster risk reduction. In R. Shaw (Ed.), *Community-based disaster risk reduction* (pp. 185–203). Bingley, UK: Emerald.

Srinivas, H., Shaw, R., & Nakagawa, Y. (2009). Recovery from typhoon damages. In R. Shaw, H. Srinivas & A. Sharma (Eds.), *Urban risk: An Asian perspective* (pp. 355–373). Bingley, UK: Emerald.

Surjan, A., Redkar, S., & Shaw, R. (2009). Community based urban risk reduction: Case of Mumbai. In R. Shaw, H. Srinivas & A. Sharma (Eds.), *Urban risk: An Asian perspective* (pp. 339–354). Bingley, UK: Emerald.

Takeuchi, Y., & Shaw, R. (2009). Indigenous knowledge for river management and flood control in Japan. In R. Shaw, A. Sharma & Y. Takeuchi (Eds.), *Indigenous knowledge and disaster risk reduction: From practice to policy* (pp. 283–292). New York: Nova Publisher.

Victoria, L. (2009). Community capacity and disaster resilience. In R. Shaw & R. Krishnamurthy (Eds.), *Disaster management: global challenges and local solutions* (pp. 338–351). Hyderabad, India: University Press.

Printed in the United States
By Bookmasters